TRIGGER
SECOND EDITION

TRIGGER

The Lives and Legend of Roy Rogers' Palomino

SECOND EDITION

Leo Pando

Forewords by Corky Randall *and*
Cheryl Rogers-Barnett

McFarland & Company, Inc., Publishers
Jefferson, North Carolina

Photographs are from the author's collection unless otherwise indicated.

Frontispiece: "In a barn on my Double R Bar Ranch in California is a horse named Trigger. He is my pride and joy and to a great extent shares all the success I have had in show business."—Roy Rogers, Preface, *A Pictorial History of Performing Horses* by Charles Phillip Fox (New York: Bramhall House, 1971) (Roy Dillow collection).

LIBRARY OF CONGRESS CATALOGUING-IN-PUBLICATION DATA

Names: Pando, Leo, 1947– author.
Title: Trigger : the lives and legend of Roy Rogers' palomino /
Leo Pando ; forewords by Corky Randall and Cheryl Rogers-Barnett.
Other titles: Illustrated history of Trigger
Description: 2nd ed. | Jefferson, North Carolina : McFarland & Company, Inc.,
Publishers, 2019 | Revison of the author's An illustrated history of Trigger |
Includes bibliographical references and index.
Identifiers: LCCN 2018060120 | ISBN 9781476671635
(paperback : acid free paper) ∞
Subjects: LCSH: Trigger (Horse)
Classification: LCC PN1995.9.A5 P36 2019 | DDC 791.4502/8092 [B] —dc23
LC record available at https://lccn.loc.gov/2018060120

BRITISH LIBRARY CATALOGUING DATA ARE AVAILABLE

ISBN (print) 978-1-4766-7163-5
ISBN (ebook) 978-0-7864-8664-9

Front cover based on a layout design by Jack Tom:
Trigger (Roy Dillow collection)

Printed in the United States of America

*McFarland & Company, Inc., Publishers
Box 611, Jefferson, North Carolina 28640
www.mcfarlandpub.com*

For my father, Leo, who loved horses.

For my mother, Emma, who had a deep appreciation for art.

And to them both for that fall day in 1957 when
they took Eva, Priscilla, and me to the Albuquerque
State Fairgrounds in the old '48 Chevy to see the
King of the Cowboys and his very special palomino.

Table of Contents

Acknowledgments   ix
Foreword by Corky Randall   1
Foreword by Cheryl Rogers-Barnett   2
Preface   3
Introduction: Once Upon a Time on a Horse   13

 1. Remembering Trigger   21
 2. Chasing Trigger   30
 3. Trigger's Tale   42
 4. Dick Weston and the Golden Cloud   57
 5. Trigger's Trail   69
 6. Little Trigger   91
 7. Trigger Jr. and the Roy Rogers Remuda   112
 8. Golden Stallion, Silver Screen   128
 9. Trigger Filmography   176
10. Trigger Television   179
11. Glenn Randall and the Randall Ranch   193
12. The Smartest Horse in the Movies   211
13. Ride 'em, Cowboy   227
14. Trigger Collectibles and Memorabilia   242
15. Trigger Trivia   258
16. Trigger's Peers   269
17. Horse Hero Comic Books   288
18. Golden Slumbers, Empty Saddle   302
19. Golden Sunset, Blue Shadows   314
20. Trigger Timeline   330

Chapter Notes   341
Bibliography   353
Index   357

Acknowledgments

"Be bold and mighty forces with come to your aid."
—Johann Wolfgang von Goethe

Robert W. Phillips' groundbreaking *Roy Rogers* book (McFarland, 1995) was my main inspiration. By meticulously documenting the life and career of Roy Rogers honestly, Phillips celebrated it. He did not fall victim to public relations. Rawhide Bob, as he liked to be called, had the ability to see the big picture, connecting seemingly different aspects of his subject into a coherent whole.

The foundation for this book was laid in the pages of George Coan's newsletter, *The Old Cowboy Picture Show*. As a B-western advocate, collector, and expert, there was not much about the genre he did not know. His posse of saddle pals (including his son Jack) refer to this writer as the Professor of Triggernometry, something I take a great deal of pride in. George passed away in 2009.

Trigger's trainer and caregiver Buford "Corky" Randall was cordial and candid. He was also very generous with information and rare photographs.

This book would not exist without the expertise and generosity of super-fan Roy Dillow, who willingly, and at great expense, shared his considerable photo archive. His enthusiasm for this project never waned. If one picture is truly worth a thousand words, then this book is partially Dillow's. He and Larry "Rocky" Roe are Roy Rogers scholars no matter the topic. Both spent hours viewing Rogers' movies and know them chapter and verse. Roe discovered Trigger in three non–Roy Rogers films.

As a friend to Roy Rogers and Dale Evans, Mike Johnson's insights, knowledge, perspective always amazed. Jerry Dean is a serious student of the life of Roy Rogers. Johnson and Dean are also able to see the big picture and were my primary sounding boards.

Dawn Moore sent a photo of her father, Clayton, with Roy Rogers and Dale Evans. Cheryl Rogers-Barnett not only loaned rare photographs, but was able to clarify a number of things and is quoted throughout. Karla Buhlman vice president of Gene Autry Entertainment, was forthcoming with photographs and fact-checked the section on Champion. Marva Felchlin from the Autry Center deserves a big thank-you for her research.

My sister Eva Radford helped shape this book with great suggestions and much appreciated copy-editing—many thanks. Graphic designer Jack Tom was generous with his time and talent providing great recreations and the cover design. Animation director Henry Anderson spent days enthusiastically researching at the Margaret Herrick Library in Beverly Hills, and his findings were invaluable. Joel "Dutch" Dortch, with ties to the

Rogers family through the Happy Trails Foundation, accessed valuable information and phone numbers including a copy of Trigger's actual bill of sale. The late Bobby J. Copeland, historian/archivist, was very willing to share information. Steve Jensen maintains one of the best sites on the Web devoted to *Clayton Moore/The Lone Ranger*. Jensen fact-checked the section on Silver and put me in contact with Dawn Moore.

Many thanks to: George Mudryj with contact information for Palomino Horse Association president Steven Rebuck; Carolyn Martin for Estes Tarter statue photographs of Trigger; Bart Kooker for research on the Lone Ranger; Alana Coghland for information and photographs of Trigger Street and Trigger Place; Lisabeth West for her expertise on Stuart horses; Malcolm Macfarlane, of the International Club Crosby, for information on Bing Crosby; Faye Thompson, Stacey Behlmer and Louise Hilton at the Margaret Herrick Library, Academy of Motion Picture Arts and Sciences in Beverly Hills; Joseph Rodgers, Chico Public Library, California; Cristina Meisner, research associate II, Harry Ransom Center, University of Texas at Austin (home to the David O. Selznick archive); Petrine Mitchum for rare photographs and important contact information; and Janey Miller for hard-to-find articles and rare photographs. Also many thanks to: Cece Phillips, Margaret and Jim Pananen, Debbie Percival, Tim Lasiuta, Mark Nakamura, Gerard Huerta, Hunter Hampton, Mark Governor, Derwood Harris, Laurence Zwisohn, Bette Orkin Savitt, Don "Jug" Reynolds, Bill Sasser, Bruce Hickey, Billy Holcomb, Jesse Mullins, editor of *American Cowboy* magazine; Boyd Magers of *Western Clippings*, *Lone Ranger* artist, the late, great Tom Gill; and author David Morrell for what is yet to come.

My gratitude to: breed and registry expert Pat Mefferd, who has firsthand knowledge of many of Hollywood's legendary horses; Trigger Jr.'s registration papers compliments of Walter Chism acting executive director, and Rory R. Williams, Executive Director, of the Tennessee Walking Horse Breeders' and Exhibitors' Association; Ann Vincent from the Chatsworth Historical Society for the Harvester-Trigger photos; the Palomino Horse Breeders of America supplied important documents: Dr. Floyd Branson, Carolyn Henderson and Terri Green.

Thanks to Scott Coleman from Edmond, Oklahoma, who discovered the solo cameo by Golden Cloud/Trigger in *Gone with the Wind* (MGM, 1939). A special thanks to James Warren, publisher of *Screen Thrills Illustrated* (Warren, 1963) for his encouragement and referring to my newsletter essay on Trigger as "the greatest thing he'd ever seen on this subject." Robert Barrett has my thanks for information on *Roy Rogers' Trigger* Dell comics and cover artists Harry Pankhurst (aka Harry Parks) and Moe Gollub.

Thank you to Frank Story, from Washington state, for a gift copy of *Trigger Remembered*; Viviane Praz, from Cap d'Agde, France, for articles on Trigger; for an on-air endorsement and DVD I thank "Deadwood Don" Calhoun from the *Marshal Andy Presents: The Riders of the Silver Screen* show broadcast on the PBS affiliate from Knoxville, Tennessee, in 2008; and thank you John Newcomb for the DVD of the *Bob Hope Chevy Hour* rebroadcast of the NBC *Son of Paleface* promo show.

For their love and support, I thank my twin sister Priscilla Marquez and especially Diane Bowen, my wife and shelter from the storm. She made it all possible.

For their inspiration, my affection goes to: gentle Daisy, formidable Beauty, sad Lieutenant, kind-hearted Herman, impressive Pal, precious Mary, angry Annie, reliable Pip, breath-taking Butcher, high-strung Elle, magnificent Zeus, flea-bitten Squeaky, and Navajo, my own beautiful tobiano mare. There was a little bit of Trigger in each when I rode them.

Foreword
by Corky Randall

All I can say about old Trigger is that he was just a lovely, gentle and kind horse. He was a wonder horse in regards to making pictures. For the longest period of time there were no doubles for him. Roy would get off and a stunt man would get on. I don't think that any other picture horse that I know of served their rider the same as old Trigger.

Around strangers and the public or whatever, you had to watch Little Trigger. You know, somebody might reach out and try to touch him or something. If you didn't have your eye on him, he might give them a nip. He would give Roy a nip or two on the stage when Roy was working him.

You can't imagine, I can't imagine the thousands, the millions of people. I don't have a picture but I've seen them where Roy is among a crowd and all these hands reaching out, rubbing and touching that horse. An animal can't tolerate that so much. You can't imagine the thousands of miles that horse traveled. And he traveled by airplane, he traveled by boat, and he traveled by van. And when Roy and my dad started out, why, he traveled in a two-horse trailer behind a station wagon.

Trigger Jr. was the most elegant of the three horses in appearance. He was a nice horse. I showed him in rodeos as Golden Zephyr. Roy only used him for a short period of time. Zephyr came right at the end of Roy's riding career. Zephyr had tricks on him, he had everything on him. When Little Trigger couldn't travel anymore, he took Zephyr and the tricks were there. They just went at it. I don't think people ever noticed the difference, even though none of the three horses looked alike at all.

Of all the western stars that came up a little before Roy and after, there's never been a set of three horses like those Triggers. All at the same time—that's just a phenomenal thing. Three great horses that I had the privilege to ride and care for. I rode all of them; they were in the barn and had to be exercised. Those horses were almost like family. They were the foundation that I stand on today.

Corky Randall began working at Republic Pictures while in high school before taking over Roy Rogers' string of "Triggers" from Randall's father, Glenn, for tours and his weekly television show. Best known for his work on The Black Stallion *(1979), he died in 2009 of cancer at age 80.*

1

Foreword
by Cheryl Rogers-Barnett

It has been a real pleasure to work with Leo on this expansion of his *Trigger* book. I don't know when I have seen anyone who has tried harder to get things right. He has been tireless in tracking down the best sources for the many versions of the Roy Rogers and Trigger stories. Sometimes this has meant just going with the version that made the best sense. But Leo has always consulted enough sources to make sure that what he says does make the most sense.

Leo has found pictures that I didn't know existed (in most cases, I don't think Dad knew of them either). Some of the pictures proved to me that what I had thought I knew was fact, just wasn't so. Trigger did appear in several more movies than any of us realized.

I still consider the original Trigger (Golden Cloud) a king among horses. He was a gentle giant. No other horse photographed better than that beautiful golden palomino.

Little Trigger is still the smartest horse I ever saw. The horse people and trainers I have been around, who were around in the 1940s and '50s, also acknowledged that as fact.

My dad was probably the luckiest performer ever. He had two absolutely incredibly talented horses and he was lucky enough to partner up with Glenn Randall, who was able to bring out the best in both of them.

Thank you, Leo, for allowing me to work with you on this book. You have produced a masterful work.

Roy Rogers' oldest daughter and keeper of the flame, Cheryl Rogers-Barnett, is a tireless promoter of her dad's legacy with a Web page and two published books to her credit: Cowboy Princes *(Taylor Trade, 2003) and* Cowboy Princes Rides Again *(Riverwood Press, 2015). She makes a number of personal appearances yearly; her family anecdotes and recollections are as fascinating as they are entertaining.*

Preface

"...the difference between truth and fiction. Fiction has to make sense."
—Wilhelm Wexler, character in *The International* (2009)

Two concerns inherent in writing a book are the possibilities no one will read it and the fear there are those who actually may. Questions of confidence arise regarding subject, motive, and ability and they require a certain fearlessness. Overly dramatic perhaps, but one comes to understand how nobility lies in the effort. My determination was tempered in the dark: I believed instinctively in the process and accepted the risk. Although at times I found myself running on empty, I remembered what the Johan Spegel character said in Ingmar Bergman's movie *The Magician* (AB Svensk Filmindustri, 1958), "Step by step you go into the dark. The movement itself is the only truth."

This book offers a detailed history of Trigger, the palomino stallion that singing cowboy Roy Rogers rode in movies, on television, and in personal appearances for just over two decades. Trigger was a horse I fell in love with as a little boy. When I thought about him as an adult I became interested in his backstory mostly because what I was reading and seeing didn't add up.

I wrote this book for a number of reasons: the desire to organize Trigger's often intentionally confusing history; as an analysis of how the fantasy of "the Smartest Horse in the Movies" was realized; and as a celebration of talented individuals and animals. It's also very much about image and branding; about controlling a narrative; it is a bit of a cautionary tale, and, as such, not in the least bit anachronistic. I hope my efforts also serve as a way of giving B-westerns another moment of resonance; the genre isn't completely dead—at least not on my watch.

When I saw Roy Rogers movies as a youngster I believed in the fantasy of a singing cowboy hero on a beautiful horse. I accepted the simple stories in which good won over evil. As an adult I still enjoy these movies, but I find myself analyzing how they were made. While I still believe in their spirit and good intentions, I'm more impressed by talent and creativity.

Beyond a great screen persona and the talent to match, what made Roy Rogers special was his proximity to a charismatic animal. Trigger was an equine reflection of his master and as much a star as leading ladies and sidekicks. While I eventually understood the whistles and bells behind the fantasy of a wonder horse, my affection for such a beautiful illusion has never wavered.

Writing this book took me to places I hadn't anticipated. I thought I'd just be writing a straightforward biography of a special horse. I did not expect the process to be so introspective. Our passions define who we are. They can even touch on the spiritual and take us on both an outward and inward journey. They are often unobtainable, and that only adds to their mystique. To fans who prefer I leave the fantasy of Trigger alone, I say, a fresh look at what resonated when we were young can still be as inspiring and there are lessons to be learned by looking behind the curtain.

What kept motivating me to write a book about a horse that's been dead and mounted for more than a half-century? I'll go into more detail later but, simply put, out of fun and curiosity. A thorough, thoughtful book on Trigger was something I'd always wanted to read. Since no one was writing anything of real depth I thought, I'll just do it myself.

I had no first-hand knowledge of the original Trigger. The only times I was around him, or what's left of him, was during two visits to the Roy Rogers and Dale Evans Museum in Victorville, California. I witnessed what the taxidermist did. Although I saw Roy Rogers in person four times, only on one of those occasions was he with a palomino. I've accumulated a great deal of research from books, magazines, the Internet, and feedback from fans whom I consider credible and expert in the B-western genre. I have supplemented my findings with common sense, knowledge gained through observation, and my own experience around horses and the movie-making process (although I could best be described as a film aficionado, I have worked as an assistant film editor and storyboard illustrator).

This book is also an ode to my father.[1] As a child I was fascinated by the stories he told about being raised around horses on a farm in northern New Mexico and using them for transportation before he rode in automobiles. As his health started to fade in the mid–1990s, I renewed my childhood interest in horses and B-westerns. At first not realizing the connection, later I was struck by how, in the shadow of his mortality, I was reconnecting with things that had brought me not only pleasure as a child, but also a sense of security.

Although I didn't know it at the time, I actually started writing this book in 1983 while I was living in New York. The King of the Cowboys was in town for an opening of a Roy Rogers restaurant in Times Square. The night before, he was a guest on *The David Letterman Show* when it was still on NBC. During the course of the interview the conversation got around to Trigger. Letterman asked about the palomino's origins and Rogers replied something to the effect that Olivia de Havilland had ridden him in a picture with Errol Flynn. I almost fell off my chair. I did not have cable or a VCR back then and had to wait a few months until *The Adventures of Robin Hood* (Warner Bros., 1938) was broadcast on television. Forty-five minutes into the film, there he was, Trigger in all his glory. I was stunned. A few months later I happened to be watching *Juarez*, another Warner Bros. film from the same period and there he was yet again. A few years later I found him in *Cowboy from Brooklyn* (Warner Bros., 1938) and *The Rains Came* (20th Century–Fox, 1939). That gorgeous horse obviously had a screen career away from Roy Rogers. I sensed a story, and you know what they say, where there's smoke there's fire.

Second Edition Remarks

History and biography turn on a dime and are never really finished; they do not end in periods but in ellipses. New discoveries change what's known and perspective shifts. Much has surfaced since *An Illustrated History of Trigger* first appeared in 2007. Many first edition readers came forward with all sorts of new information and images. A second edition is a great opportunity to add relevant text, new rare photos, interesting items albeit of a controversial nature, and conclude aspects of Trigger's story that were left partially unresolved.

Sadly, trainer Corky Randall died two years after the first edition. His daughter-in-law, Verla Loomis Randall, invited me to his memorial service in Newhall, California, but regretfully I could not attend. I did write a short note to his widow, Pinky...

> I loved listening to Corky talk about his experiences as a trainer; stories about the countless hours he spent on movie sets, touring anecdotes, and comments about the great people he'd met. In 2008 I finally received an early copy of *An Illustrated History of Trigger* sporting a cover headshot of one of the most beautiful animals who'd ever been in front of a camera. I was especially thrilled and honored by the line "Forward by Corky Randall" ... My deepest sympathies and sincerest best wishes to you Pinky, Corky's family, and friends, the last of which I considered myself to be. Leo

This may be one of the last books having to do with Roy Rogers. Subsequently there's a certain amount of responsibility involved. I honestly cannot tie up the lives of the King of the Cowboys and the Smartest Horse in the Movies with one big happy bow. However, like their films, this book ends on a positive (if bittersweet) note. Roy Rogers and Trigger deserve no less.

For those who knew Trigger, took care of him, worked with and loved him, the glorious palomino was a handsome, gentle, show business professional. For we fans who only saw him on screen he was even more. Trigger goes far beyond what a taxidermist did to his remains. He had a purity no human could touch. He's in our dreams, a thing of beauty, out of reach, magical and, for the seriously devoted, always will be. While I would eventually get over Roy Rogers, I never got over Trigger. May I never get that old.

The K Circle B Show

B-western heroes, especially their horses, meant a great deal to me growing up in Santa Fe, New Mexico, in the 1950s. I have vivid memories that go back to 1952, recollections from my grade school days, watching wrestling matches and local variety shows on a neighbor's television set. By the time my family got our own TV, B-westerns were syndicated on all three Albuquerque channels. I saw only a few on movie screens (Roy Rogers and Trigger in The *Bells of San Angelo* at a local theatre with my dad). I would come home from Alvord Elementary School at 3:30, head straight for our old black and white GE television and watch the films of Kermit Maynard, Bob Steele, and Johnny Mack Brown. These were very early B-westerns, ones without music during the chase sequences. KOB-TV, the NBC affiliate, started an after-school program called the *K Circle B Show*. "Riding' down the trail to Albuquerque. Saddlebags all filled with beans and jerky. Heading for K Circle B, the TV ranch for you and me, K Circle B in Albuquerque!" The host was a local cowboy celebrity, Dick Bills, the uncle of singer Glenn Campbell. On Mondays, Wednesdays, and Fridays, Bills presented the films of Roy Rogers; Tuesdays and Thursdays he'd show Gene Autry movies. They were followed by comedy shorts featuring the Little Rascals.

When I wasn't watching B-westerns on television, I was acting out B-western scenarios, either with the latest Marx toy sets from Sears or in costume with neighborhood pals. We formed a fearsome posse fighting imaginary evildoers in the yard around my home. I still have a stick horse my father carved out of an old piece of pine. With attached leather ears and a lacquer finish, it looked palomino. I named it Goldie.

A rare personal appearance outing for the original Trigger, most likely taken in Southern California in 1947. Roy Rogers started using a flat hat style around the time he appeared in *Apache Rose* in 1947 (Janey Miller collection).

The simplistic world of the B-western where Roy Rogers and his peers thrived gave way to teenaged angst. The genre soon became passé in the wake of rock and roll and the turbulent 1960s. I drifted away from B-westerns by the time I was in junior high. The only connection to them I had in high school was a kid named Roy Autry, believe it or not. Partly out of envy, I used to call him Gene Rogers. In my thirties, however, my interest was renewed unexpectedly in, of all places, Brooklyn, New York. I was working as a freelance illustrator in Manhattan when a friend invited me to go horseback riding. It had been about 12 years since I'd last been in the saddle. Before I knew it we were at Culmit Stables in Prospect Park, Brooklyn. The minute I got on a horse, I was transfixed. I felt as if I'd come home. I asked myself, "Why haven't I done this sooner?" The horse I'd rented that fateful day was a little palomino with a white blaze, named Trigger.

I rediscovered B-western movies about the same time I bought a VCR. The first tape I purchased featured three episodes of the *Lone Ranger* television show, including the pilot, "Enter the Lone Ranger." Life is circular, not linear. While B-westerns still nurtured me as they had when I was a boy, I saw them through the eyes of a grown man. The simple B-western plots and one-dimensional characters were not fully credible as before; however, they had personality, the music was still great, the action sequences were still thrilling, and they still resonated with honesty and fair play. I was reminded how the B-westerns had heart. I had renewed admiration for what the humble B-western accomplished on the edges of the Hollywood mainstream. The cowboy and horse connection was at their core. Remove horses and B-western films were not as engaging: no horse, no cowboy. With all Roy Rogers' charisma and talent, take Trigger away, and Rogers is not as compelling. Just as mustangs became noble symbols of the West with their free spirits and endurance, Trigger and his equine peers stood for all that was good in B-westerns: trust, bravery, loyalty, friendship, and grace.

Webster's defines *grace* by how it manifests itself outwardly and inwardly; beauty or charm of form, composition, movement, or expression. It has to do with a sense of what is right and proper; decency. Mother Teresa and Jacqueline Bouvier Kennedy Onassis were the personifications of grace. Fred Astaire had it. So did Grace Kelly. As did Roy Rogers and, yes, Trigger.

While researching this book I screened every Roy Rogers B-western that Republic Pictures made and was just as captivated as when I saw them as a kid. I was entertained again by old friends in their prime. How could one not like great characters like Gabby Hayes, Andy Devine, and Raymond Hatton? B-western clothes, with their colorful designs, were wonderful, especially the shirts. "Tumbling Tumbleweeds" and "Don't Fence Me In" are classic songs. Yes, B-westerns are naïve; still, there's a generosity of spirit in the simple black and white films. Sure, the early producers and players wanted to make a buck, but they didn't hit their fans over the head with things like product placement. Marketing was not as blatant or as diabolically efficient as it is today. If a kid came away with lessons in fair play, honesty and good conduct, what was the harm if he wanted to buy a comic book?

A cynic many be defined as a wounded idealist. I understand that all too well. I also understand how some parents may not want to raise their children with romantic notions of how the world should be. Whether they do or not, a price is paid. My passion for Trigger, and horses in general, represents an idealized view of life. As an adult, living in a world of terrorism, political scandals, corporate crime, built-in obsolescence, spin doctors, fast food, overt opulence, toxic narcissism, and a diminishing natural environment, it's an uphill battle to be optimistic. Good doesn't always triumph and sometimes crime pays. Trigger and Roy Rogers brought a sweet innocence into my life that, unfortunately, cannot exist the same way anymore. I lost a part of myself when they passed away.

In spite of my age, the cynicism of the times, and the discoveries I made regarding Trigger, I cherish the fantasy of this special horse and will be forever grateful for having lived at a time when I could believe it.

The "So What" Factor

One can't work on a subject such as Trigger without being aware of how out of sync it is with the times (kids today know Roy Rogers only as the name of a restaurant chain). A friend refers to this as the "so what" factor, and part of my task is to make an argument for why Trigger is still compelling. My main audience consists of people for whom the "so what" factor, regarding Roy Rogers, Trigger, and B-westerns, never enters their minds.

Heroes don't necessarily change; it's our perception of them that does. They take on nuances and contradictions over time.

Honesty, courage, and justice form the foundation of every healthy society. While cynical indifference seems to be the fashion today, the subject of this book called upon me to wear my heart on my sleeve. If I succeed, even to a limited degree, in reopening the door that has closed on the values and aspirations that B-western movies stood for, that would be great. Though the B-western era peaked 60-some years ago, the values found in the hero epics on which baby boomers were nurtured serve as a kind of distillation of cherished American and humanist values, and such values have always been best presented (and absorbed) through the popular media.

I submit that the story of Trigger and Roy Rogers is of value because our interests nourish us and we should, in turn, nourish them. Movies, television, even comic books, can sometimes be more than just entertainment. They give us a sense of being alive; they awaken us from our routines. They reaffirm and define our humanity.

Who Was Trigger?

Roy Rogers biographer and expert Robert W. Phillips spent hours scrutinizing Trigger related photos, text, films, and television shows; in the end, there were things about the horse that remained elusive and that made him cautious. When it comes to Hollywood, believe none of what you hear and only part of what you see. He and I agreed that there were some things we would never prove conclusively related to Trigger, certainly not to the satisfaction of every serious fan.

Robert W. Phillips never had firsthand knowledge of any "Trigger." Still, he was a meticulous investigator. He had a natural curiosity and loved research. He believed it was important to present as complete a story as possible, warts and all. In spite of all his accumulated knowledge of Trigger, Phillips was frustrated, and the following paragraphs from his personal correspondence explain why. In spite of his misgivings, his writings are filled with enthusiasm for his subject.

> How many "Triggers" are up there in the sky, that have helped keep the Roy Rogers legend alive? There are so many different accounts (regarding Trigger) both prior to my book and since then, that they all merge together. There is not one fiftieth of doubt in my mind that there are more Triggers, Champions, Silvers, Toppers (yes, Topper) as well, and many no-namers than we will ever see. And there is not one iota of doubt in my mind that Golden Cloud (aka Trigger) ran across the cameras in more films than we will ever determine.
>
> Hollywood created a mythical "Trigger." The machine went to work, with some ace people in position, the illusion machine, the publicity machine. Everything they released was meant for instant and immediate consumption and dissemination. Nothing was ever released, be it a statement or a photograph, for the purpose of anyone collecting them and comparing them. No film was ever made, no editing ever performed for someone to look at it frame by frame. If you do, you will see a lot of stuff that was not intended to be seen. You will see that which the editor knew you would not see with the frames in fast motion. This is a fiction in motion. Fantasy.
>
> And any magician is almost being a traitor to his profession, by dispelling the illusions of his trade, revealing the secrets of his proud profession, and contributing to the end of magic as entertainment, even in retirement. They spent a lifetime putting on shows, thrilling young and old alike, and they look back upon their work with pride, for they were damned good at what they did; they became a legend. Houdini, the great this or that, or "Roy Rogers," the great "King of the Cowboys." No way is this legend likely to ever sell out the happiness that he brought folks, who assumed that he brought the "Smartest Horse in the Movies," "Trigger," all the way from sunny California, to the state of Michigan, or Kentucky or Maine, to put on a show for their fans. All palominos with more or less identical markings, gold in color with a white mane and tail, and 1–4 white stockings. [Here Phillips imagines Roy Rogers providing details about his horses:] "And the one I rode in such and such parade belonged

to so and so who has a palomino ranch nearby, and I've ridden that horse in the parades every time I went to Fort Worth, etc. And we had this horse in the trailer that did such and such tricks, and for the next show, that horse in the trailer that did so and so tricks; and between shows my trainer was putting the next horse I would use through his tricks, and I have no earthly idea 'who' all those horses were, or who some of them even belonged to. When it came time for me to ride into that arena on a horse, I was 'Roy Rogers,' and that beautiful palomino was 'Trigger.'" It ain't gonna happen.

There were trainers who knew. There were horseman/friends/contractors/connections scattered all over the country who knew. But by and large the secrets and business transactions have all gone to the graves with the cowboys. And whatever secrets Roy Rogers can recall, will go the same way with him.

I am never, I am convinced, going to "prove" anything related to all these "Triggers." I am only going to be able to render opinions. It is almost impossible to search for and find reality and truth in a media that is meant in every detail, to deceive.[2]

Robert W. Phillips was, bless him, somewhat of a perfectionist. With respect to the study of history, loose ends are inevitable. The researcher is at the mercy of available resources and the mood of the times. It is a lucky historian who can corroborate his sources. Phillips would have loved to check his findings with Roy Rogers and trainer Glen Randall. However, he knew better than to ask them to explain a fantasy which took them decades to build. That would have been expecting too much.

One may wonder, why attempt to sort out the legend of Trigger when even an expert such as Phillips had his misgivings? Why publish anything that would be contrary to the publicity generated by Rogers and company regarding such a beautiful fantasy?

Again I say, it's a lot of fun. The fact that history can be elusive only makes it more fascinating. Readers are free to draw their own conclusions. It's highly doubtful Rogers, the directors he worked with, and the screenwriters who provided him with stories, thought in deep symbolic terms. Admittedly, Robert W. Phillips and I got pretty carried away and read more into Trigger than Roy Rogers intended. As kids, we were supposed to—and how could we not? Director Federico Fellini wisely advised, "Never lose your childhood enthusiasm." Fiction requires a suspension of disbelief and a leap of faith. Nevertheless, no matter how outrageous, fiction should be credible within the parameters of its genre. The audience should at least be entertained and not insulted. If something is learned about the human condition, all the better. Art is like that. While one can learn from an artist's intent, it's what one brings to an artwork that makes it resonate.

In the end, Phillips was pretty philosophical: "I understand your fascination with the legend of Roy Rogers, the legend of Trigger, etc. It's some story, decades long … involving many horses. Art Rush created one of the most intricate spider webs of a legend over the years, using Leonard Sly, that Ohio farm boy as 'Roy Rogers,' that ever came out of Hollywood, and it was everyone's desire to leave this world with it all intact … and they accomplished this. I cut through a lot of it, out of a natural curiosity, and a love for research … and most misinterpreted my intentions, seeing me as a traitor to something of value in their lives. So, continue spinning the web, keeping it around … for I enjoyed working on it for years."

The Great Contradiction

When children watched B-western movies in the 1940s and 1950s, they were ignorant of the filmmaking process. B-westerns were never discussed technically during their heyday. Fans believed what they saw on screen. Not much was known about look-alikes, stuntmen, or special effects. It never occurred to most fans that Rogers was riding Trigger doubles, although there were clues beyond differences in markings and conformation from horse to horse. The fact that the movies were black and white also gave them a special aura; they were already removed from reality in their own context. The black and white movie-making process gave Roy Rogers and Trigger an iconic stature. Film critic Roger Ebert hit the nail on the head with an insightful comment: "What black and white is, is the essence of something, whereas color is a particular example of it."[3]

Magic can be very fragile, especially as it applies to movies. That's ironic, because we live in a time when film technology can realize any scenario a screenwriter or a director can imagine. However, it's now commonplace for motion pictures to be released with extra features that explain production techniques and special effects. Magazines such as *Cinefex* and *American Cinematographer* are devoted to such things. All this is a mixed blessing. While the extra features that come with DVDs are great fun as well as educational, there's something to be said for not knowing anything about special effects. On the one hand, one's appreciation for the talent and hard work of moviemakers is enhanced. On the other, magic and mystery are sacrificed in degrees. Movies today are spectacular and great eye-candy, but there's no mystery to them anymore. After *2001: A Space Odyssey* (MGM, 1968) was completed, director Stanley Kubrick ordered all production plans and models sealed. Kubrick may have been doing fans a favor when he denied them access to the film techniques behind his science fiction masterpiece.

Fantasy and magic are almost synonymous; both have mystery at their core. One has to be careful when analyzing them. I was straddling both sides of the fence while writing this book. Take away mystery and they may not be as compelling. There's a fine line to be considered; deconstructing a fantasy may enhance and disempower. While it sounds like a contradiction, my goal is to celebrate the fantasy of Trigger via biography and analysis. The contradiction here is not as great as one might believe at first. Yes, there is something lost and something gained, but the scales are heavily weighted in favor of the latter. I am amazed by what Roy Rogers, his trainer Glenn Randall, and Trigger accomplished. If anything, I have more respect for them now than I had as a kid.

People become bored with fantasy that no longer stands up to their sophistication. Their taste changes as they grow. All that said, there is much that one doesn't outgrow, that one returns to again and again. Some magic is so potent that the secrets behind it are equally compelling. Some characters continue to grow as we do, and we never lose the affection we experienced from the start. For some, the potent fantasy of Roy Rogers and Trigger has not lost its luster, because the magic is not in the fantasy but in oneself.

A partnership such as that of Roy Rogers, Glenn Randall, and Trigger is formed almost by luck and great timing, but it does not survive that way. B-western players gave their fans magic with timeless music, classic characters, engaging stories, and impeccable horsemanship. The magicians who worked with Trigger are a very interesting bunch and are part of what this book is about. No apology is necessary for fleshing out the story of Trigger. It is a journey from wonder to appreciation. The Trigger fantasy is in no danger from this book. Many fans now have also been part way down this same path; my job is to take them the rest of the way. At the end of this book, the reader should have a clearer picture of how the fantasy of a wonder horse was accomplished, and the magic will still linger.[4]

This book is, finally, a personal acknowledgment of what Trigger meant. He was, after all, at the core of every little cowgirl's and cowboy's dreams. A special horse (especially a palomino in fancy show tack) set the tone of a scene by its presence and still symbolizes the romance of the West. Take note of how fan Jerry Dean feels after five decades:

> But, no matter what anyone ever says about Trigger, or what I think about the way he was farmed out to trainers and caretakers almost all of his life, I'm happiest about the fact that, in his films and TV shows, Roy was always riding him. You can't say that for any of the other western stars. Even sidekicks came and went, but, for as long as I watched them, and loved them, and pretended to be them with my plaster lathe horse and cap guns, I always saw Roy riding "Trigger." In my heart, and in my memory of those days ... riding "Trigger" down the canyon between the barn and the old Chevy truck where I suspected there might lurk my "bad guy" brother in ambush ... my "Trigger" never failed to warn me of the danger just in the nick of time and get us both to cover for the gun battle that followed. And, when it was my brother's turn to be "Roy" and I was the bad guy, no matter how carefully I hid my presence, "Trigger" managed to alert my brother, too. It's nice to know today that no matter which movie or TV show of theirs I watch, I still see the companionship I believed in then. It's always the two of them together, no matter who the supporting cast may be, and it always will be.[5]

Trigger was intelligent, beautiful, athletic, and charismatic. These qualities enabled him to add a great deal of ambience and mystique to a movie. Trigger transported Rogers and his fans to a West that never was, a place where horses could keep up with cars and trains, where guns fired more than six rounds, where people were shot but never bled. Most importantly, in the Roy Rogers version of the West, good always won over evil. B-western cowboys such as Roy Rogers, Gene Autry, and the Lone Ranger communicated a generosity of spirit partially through their horses. A silver-throated cowboy on a gorgeous horse, triumphing over the evils of the world with a gun, a guitar, and a faithful sidekick was a wonderful child's fantasy of how things should be.

Robert W. Phillips expressed what many have felt when he wrote, "Yes, it was all an illusion. It is still an illusion. But we're all the richer for it. We have a real need for illusions such as these, in the world today."

The Land of Eternal Youth

In one way or another, I've been chasing Trigger all my life. He existed in a romanticized West that I loved, and he still remains a symbol of a simpler place and time. In spite of all I've learned about his life—the workings behind the fantasy, the shaping of a corporate logo—it's a chase I continue to enjoy. I've heard it said many times that the journey is more important than the destination. I am reminded of cowboys in fiction who were obsessed with catching, training, and owning some special wild horse that they ultimately never catch. Remember the folk rock band the Byrds and their classic tune "Chestnut Mare," about an elusive horse and a never-ending pursuit for her? I see Robert W. Phillips that way. I have visions of him riding his own palomino, Thunder, with his lasso out and ready. Trigger is galloping ahead in the distance. With every hill and arroyo the golden stallion continues to maintain his distance while remaining in view. For Phillips and the rest of us, "Trigger" and the B-westerns he represents are constantly inspiring and yet always elusive. That's a great trail to have ahead and, with any luck, one that never ends.

In the 1993 film *Into the West* (Miramax) a grandfather tells his grandsons the legend of the Irish horse Tír na nÓg (tear-knee-no). As long as a rider stays on its back he will never age; if he ever dismounts or is thrown off, he will get old and die. When asked what the name Tír na nÓg meant, the old man replied, "the land of eternal youth."[6]

Dreaming on a dream horse: Roy Rogers (center), Gabby Hayes (second from left) and the Sons of the Pioneers serenade young Buzzy Henry (riding with Rogers) with "My Little Buckaroo" in *Rainbow Over Texas* **(1946).**

It would seem that I have my own particular white whale to chase.[7] It has taken the form of a palomino I first became infatuated with as a little boy and has resulted in this book. Nostalgia is a very powerful thing. I'm glad to say I'll never be a kid again, but all I have to do is look upon Trigger and the feelings of hope that so nourished me and were the best part of being a kid are mine again. When I watch B-westerns, I see individuals at their best. There are those who see B-westerns as arcane and naive. Historian Bobby Copeland was right when he said, "You cannot explain to the younger generation the fascination that we, who grew up in that era, have for B-western films." If you were there, no explanation is necessary, and if you weren't, no explanation will do. To anyone who cannot empathize with or has no time for a genre from days gone by, I say, "Tread softly because you tread on my dreams."[8] For the general public now, Trigger is, at the same time, a fond remembrance and a morbid artifact on display. For me he's much more than a corporate logo or marketing tool. I choose to see him as a symbol of hope and grace. He's Tír na nÓg, and as such, he'll always be the land of eternal youth.

Introduction: Once Upon a Time on a Horse

"Far back, far back in our dark soul the horse prances."
—D.H. Lawrence[1]

"We must never forget, every time we sit on a horse, what an extraordinary privilege it is: to be able to unite one's body with that of another sentient being, one that is stronger, faster and more agile by far than we are, and at the same time, brave, generous, and uncommonly forgiving."
—William Steinkraus, Olympic equestrian

Background

Horses are one of the most important animals humans have ever domesticated. It is hard to imagine how civilization, for better or worse, would have proceeded without them. From the moment horses were domesticated, humans exploited them. Certainly the two species were destined to intermingle. Whether as beasts of burden or transportation, in military campaigns or exploration, the horse made forward motion possible; civilization would have taken longer to develop had it not been for the horse. Science, language, philosophy, religion, art, information, et al., spread around the world on the backs of horses. Even something as common as the pants humans wear have to do with the domestication of equines for riding.

Countless books have been published about the bond between humans and horses. In our imagination, that bond is strongest when it binds horse to cowboy. Today the cowboy is seen at his best, as a symbol of rugged individualism, when he's on a horse. The romance of the cowboy and the allure of the horse—especially in our culture and with baby boomers in particular—is deeply seated and can be traced back to early humans.

As bonds were formed with horses, especially enlightened humans felt the connection between them was ultimately a connection to nature. Serious riders have experienced the harmony—and even spirituality—connecting them not only to their horse, but also to a universe extending beyond their own human state. Horses are not simple dumb brutes. Many an experienced horse person can recount situations when an animal has gone beyond the norm, beyond the expectations of even experts. For examples just study the careers of Seabiscuit and Secretariat.

What exactly is the romance and the allure of the cowboy's horse, and how did it

Rare photographs of the charismatic Trigger circa 1953 on the Randall Ranch, probably being cued off-camera by Glenn Randall (Roy Dillow collection).

figure into the cowboy's appeal? As horses played such critical roles in everything from war to recreation, they became symbols around the world of such diverse concepts as fear and beauty. The human-to-horse connection has always been great inspiration for literature, painting, and music. It is no wonder Hollywood films have glorified horses and national magazines devote pages to them every month. Human history is a great narrative for western movies, and horses are a key element. The Hollywood movie industry was built on the back of Western films. Along with that, the story of how horses were used in movies and live appearances, to the point where some became celebrities, is interesting in itself.

Horses and the Invention of the Motion Picture

Beyond their ubiquity and importance in history, horses were at the forefront during the invention of the motion picture. Movies would have been invented one way or another, magic lanterns were already in use, but horses can claim an influence.

In 1878 former California governor and railroad magnate Leland Stanford put his reputation and a considerable amount of money into proving all four legs of a horse came off the ground at any point in a gallop. Contrary to popular legend, there was never a bet, but Stanford offered photographer Eadweard Muybridge $2,000 to produce hard

Poetry in motion: Roy Rogers and Trigger at mid-gallop with all four of the palomino's feet off the ground (Roy Dillow collection).

evidence, on his Palo Alto Stock Farm in California. The project, which required a dozen of the finest cameras and the most advanced lenses, ended up costing some $50,000 and five years to get a satisfactory shot confirming Stanford's theory. Muybridge devised a crude shutter consisting of two slats, tripped by a string running at chest height. Stanford's own horse Occident broke the string at some 40 feet per second, a gap opened exposing the film.

Muybridge went on to produce the first sequential photos of rapid motion with a machine of his own invention that could project moving photographic images based on a popular children's toy called the zoetrope. He called his new machine the zoopraxiscope, a forerunner to the movie projector that many people could watch at once. By pursuing the secrets of equine gait, Stanford and Muybridge unknowingly laid the groundwork for the invention a decade later of the motion picture. When Edwin S. Porter directed *The Great Train Robb*ery (1903) in New Jersey, considered to be one of the first significant early narrative films to use new cinematic techniques to tell a sequential story, there they were again, running horses.

B-Westerns

The B in B-western stands for "budget," which is a polite way of saying, "produced for very little money." A-movies had A-list stars, well-crafted stories, and top-notch production values; aside from that, the primary difference between A-westerns and B-westerns was that the latter, like *My Pal Trigger* (1946), were usually geared towards children and were more of a fantasy of the West than their more expensive counterparts such as *The Searchers* (Warner Bros., 1956). And this is particularly true with regard to the representation of horses.

Anthropomorphism is the assignment of human characteristics to animals or inanimate objects. From the beginning, the B-western anthropomorphized horses to a degree far beyond their actual nature. Presented in almost magical terms, their connection to cowboys was amplified. B-western cowboys talked to their horses and considered them friends. Movie horses often rescued their masters from the clutches of evil by running for help, untying ropes, or even attacking villains. The net effect of anthropomorphism of horses is that it made them especially appealing to children, and that effect was long lasting.

Horses were used in western films not only as transportation and as draft animals

Roy Rogers and Trigger promotional giveaway photograph, shot in Lone Pine on the set of their first film together, *Under Western Stars* (1938). Note the Hudkins Bros. tack, complete with martingale but minus tapaderos (the martingale was not used after this film). Also note the tag line in the signature: "Many pleasant trails to you" (Roy Dillow collection).

but also as integral parts of the scenery and ambience. When a horse was a major element in an A-western story line, it was presented, for the most part, realistically—sometimes almost as an inanimate object, and certainly never with the same reverence as horses received in B-westerns. This was more true to life perhaps, but not as much fun and certainly not as inspiring.

In a press release written for CBS in 1958 titled "No Trick Horses for Me," James Arness, who played Matt Dillon on the *Gunsmoke* television series, stated: "In the real old West, horses were cheap and a cowboy—or a U.S. marshal—seldom had a favorite. He didn't keep a horse that long. He'd swap him off on a long trip for a fresh horse, or sell him between jobs knowing he could buy another when he needed to avoid stable bills."[2]

Silver screen cowboys and their horses were a rage from the 1920s through the 1960s, and reigned supreme in radio, movies, comic books, and eventually on television. They thrilled countless fans at rodeos, on auditorium stages, and at fairgrounds. From the start, the first cowboy superstars, William S. Hart and Tom Mix, realized what assets their four-legged partners, Fritz and Tony, were for their show business careers. Gene Autry knew what he was talking about when he stated, "In those days the horse was virtually the co-star. The kids all knew that the Lone Ranger's mount was Silver and Roy Rogers rode Trigger. But who could tell you, years later, the name of James Arness' horse or Paladin's or what the Cartwrights called theirs? ... Not for nothing were they called 'horse operas.'"[3]

Equine stars such as Trigger, Champion, and Silver were at the heart of B-westerns. Although these films may have been conceived as cheap entertainment and simple morality plays, the major players and their screen mounts became much more than one-dimensional characters on a movie screen. They became icons through their convictions and deeds.

From the first western film, directors quickly realized that the essence of the motion picture was action, and underlying that action were an individual's beliefs and the courage to back them up. The western lent itself very effectively to action and basic morals. B-westerns were light on plot and heavy on action, especially horse action. The horse was not only a symbol of the West, it helped drive a motion picture plot, and a cowboy's skill on horseback was mandatory if he were to prevail. Not only were moviegoers entertained, they were shown basic codes of good conduct: fair play, honesty, the value of hard work, and a respect for nature and age. All this they got from the back of a horse. It's no wonder adolescents who grew up in the 1940s and 1950s still respect B-western cowboys and their mounts.

Western movie fan Mike Johnson is correct when he says, "William S. Hart was the first movie cowboy to feature his horse by name, Fritz. Tom Mix was possibly the first to profile his horse, Tony, even to the extent of a screen of credit. The so-called B-western never really came into being until the sound era. By then Tony was well established in the minds of fans who followed the exploits of their cowboy heroes. Unlike any other genre, horses are without doubt the most important ingredient in a western, without them you have nothing."

Roy Rogers' Trigger is arguably the most famous equine movie star. The description of the *My Pal Trigger* (1946) movie on the Westerns Channel's schedule simply states, "About how Roy Rogers acquired the palomino." No other information is necessary. (The movie, by the way, rates three stars of a possible four.)

How Trigger's legend was created and nurtured via trainer Glenn Randall, a corral-full of palomino doubles, and Rogers' own expert horsemanship is an interesting story. The public relations material that the Rogers camp has propagated for decades regarding "Trigger" is the proverbial tip of the iceberg.

Trigger's contribution to the King of the Cowboys' success was immeasurable. Rogers was well aware that many fans were more interested in his horse than they were in him. Until the release of Robert W. Phillips' book *Roy Rogers*, information on "Trigger" was generic, carefully crafted public relations. It usually went something like this: "The mold was broken after Trigger was made. He could turn on a dime and give you nine cents change. He was in all of the Roy Rogers movies and television shows." The mold may have been broken when Trigger was made, but that didn't stop Roy Rogers and company from gluing it back together in hopes they could make more copies to use over and over as you will see.

Ground Rules

Cast horse—Term cast horse was used to describe the Golden Cloud when lead actors rode him on screen. Apparently the Hudkins brothers also used the term star horse. I prefer cast, as a star would more logically apply to a horse that was an actual character in a film, maybe even with screen credit. When lead players were riding the Golden Cloud he wasn't necessarily a star or a named character. Hudkins logbooks may have listed Trigger as "star horse," "Pistol," "Golden Cloud," or "GC."

Color in horses—Color when describing horses is very subjective and sometimes confusing. Scholars in both science and art have produced serious studies on horse color. Dr. Ben K. Green wrote an authoritative book titled *The Color of Horses* in 1974 (Northland). With wonderful paintings by Darol Dickinson to support his text, Green tells his readers how to identify color methodically and scientifically.

Art school students learn early on that a color is affected by adjacent colors and available light. Place identical one-inch squares of blue on a field of purple and a field of yellow and they will look different, because purple can bring out the red and yellow can bring out the green. Similarly, a one-inch square of blue under cool fluorescent lights looks different from the same square under warm incandescent light bulbs. The same goes for horses. Their color changes not only given the time of day, but by season and the horse's age. Even the weather and nutrition have an effect on color.

Trigger was palomino in color; Gene Autry's Champions came in various shades of chestnut and sorrel. A horse (also mules and jacks), regardless of breeding or type, that has a golden coat and a white or ivory mane and tail is considered a palomino. The name designates color only; there is no palomino breed and hence no typical conformation.

Many describe sorrel as too dark to be a palomino and too light to be a chestnut. According to Dr. Green, there are light, blonde, and bright sorrels, all very close to palomino. He describes palomino as the precise color of 22-carat gold. Dr. Green presents standard dark and chestnut sorrels that look chestnut.

According to the Palomino Horse Association, palomino coats range from a creamy buff to a deep copper. When the hair grows long, the palomino coat usually lightens in the winter and also usually dulls with age. A palomino should have black, dark brown, or hazel eyes, and the two eyes should match. Foals are almost never born with true palomino coloring but are mostly cream or honey color. They are not registered as palominos at birth because of the instability of their color. Before the Palomino Horse Association will register them, fillies must be at least yearlings and colts two years of age. Not all registries subscribe to this. Though the PHA was founded in 1936 and Trigger wasn't registered till 1937, his later registration doesn't seem to have any bearing on his coat coloring changing.

Some horses go through a stage of dapples—light spots all over the coat—during their early development. They can also be dappled depending on time of year, coat, and condition. Usually dapples are seen after the semi-annual shedding season. The age of the horse does not affect dapples.

Expert fan—Expert (or serious) fans are not professionals but have more than just a passing familiarity with Roy Rogers and Trigger. They are devoted and remained interested even though they have never been published. Expert fans I met through the Roy Rogers grapevine include Jerry Dean (Beloit, Kansas), Roy Dillow (Tazwell, Virginia), Mike Johnson (Toronto, Ontario, Canada), and Larry "Rocky" Roe (Knoxville, Tennessee). Each is cited where appropriate.

Horse primer—A horse is led, saddled, and mounted from its left or *near* side as opposed to its *far* or *off* side. When a horse is referred to as *at liberty*, that means it's without restraint, without a rope connecting it to a human. *Tack* is the equipment used to ride or drive a horse, such as a saddle, reins, harness, and so forth. *Tapaderos* are stirrup covers. (Roy Rogers' tapaderos usually sported the "RR" initials.) The *forelock* of a horse is the part of the mane and starts between the ears and drops over the forehead. A horse's height is measured from the base of the front foot to the top of its *withers*, the bump between the back and neck. Height is measured in *hands*, each held horizontally is equal to four inches. If a horse is 15.3 hands, it's $4 \times 15 + 3 = 63$ inches at the withers.

Movie titles—A movie title followed only by a date and not the name of its studio is a Republic Pictures production, where Roy Rogers and "Trigger" did the majority of their work.

Palomino—An American Spanish word derived from Latin *palumbinus* from *palumbes*, meaning ringdove. The Spanish word for pigeon or dove is *paloma*. The word, fairly common in Spain, was first used in California as a name for a golden horse with a white mane and tail. The Spanish term for a horse of milk-white color is *palomilla*, and as such there's a possibility that it could have been transformed to palomino to denote a darker color. "Yellow-stained shirt tail" is the colloquial meaning of palomino in Spanish.

Randall—Glenn Randall, Sr., seldom used "Sr." with his full name. Glenn Randall, Jr., used "Jr." and his nick name was J.R. They were often simply referred to as Glenn Sr. and Glenn Jr.

Trigger's names—there were four, depending on context and time line:

"Golden Cloud" versus "the Golden Cloud"—Trigger was first registered as "Golden Cloud" only. "The Golden Cloud" is optional and I use it both ways. Formal usage is not something horse people, cowboys wheeling and dealing in livestock, were concerned with.

Pistol—a name used by Hudkins Bros. Stable wranglers.

The Old Man—On movie sets Trigger was referred to as "the Old Man."

Sly to Slye—Roy Rogers was born Leonard Frank Sly. He was later referred to as Leonard Franklin Sly, and he also added the "e" at the end of Slye, although never filed a formal name change. He signed his first marriage certificate "Slye" when he married Lucile Ascolese.

"Trigger"—The use of quotation marks around the name "Trigger" I have adopted from Robert W. Phillips, who used them when referring to a character played by the numerous palomino doubles Roy Rogers used throughout his career (I will also use this device with Gene Autry's Champion). The name Trigger without quotation marks denotes the original animal. When Roy Rogers discussed his palomino, he was usually referring to it in quotation marks. Whichever horse a particular answer or context most readily applied to was the "Trigger" he was talking about. I will limit the use of quotation marks only for emphasis.

1

Remembering Trigger

*"There comes a point in your life when you need to stop reading
other people's books and write your own."*—Albert Einstein

To begin a study of "Trigger," a good place to start is to acknowledge what was said about him by two of Roy Rogers' children, Dusty and Cheryl; by Corky Randall, the son of "Trigger's" trainer Glenn Randall; and Roy Rogers himself. Glenn Randall's comments may be found throughout this book.

Dusty and Cheryl

Of Roy Rogers' eight children, Roy Rogers, Jr. ("Dusty"), and Cheryl Rogers-Barnett are the most public and the most responsible for promoting the image their famous father cultivated.[1] They have both written autobiographies, both discussed "Trigger." While I may not agree with everything they wrote, I understand their intentions.

People often make the mistake of assuming celebrity children know all about their parents' careers. Admittedly, Dusty and Cheryl do not have to back up their claims about "Trigger"; their stories are usually taken at face value. With all due respect, that doesn't mean they're completely accurate. While ordinary fans may not know intimate details about stars' personal lives, serious fans know a great deal about them as celebrities. Serious fans, from the time they were kids, absorbed all publicity and studied a star's body of work. The more discriminating ones eliminated the outrageous and drew their own conclusions. Fan scholarship has a fair claim to the truth, more than the principals care to admit. With regards to "Trigger," the public relations that the Rogers camp propagated for decades is only a small part of the whole; it's been the serious fans who have tried to address the real story.

If one accepts Dusty Rogers' book *Growing Up with Roy and Dale* as the truth with regards to his father's palomino, one is left to believe that there was only one Trigger and a few incidental doubles. The only significant anecdote Dusty added to the legend was his account of how his father kept Trigger's death from the family for twelve months: "When Trigger died in 1965 Dad was so broken up he never told anyone about it, not even us, for more than a year." He said the same thing on the *A&E's Biography* program during an episode on his father. The fact that Rogers was able to keep the news of Trigger's death from his children for a year demonstrates they were not particularly involved with the palomino.[2]

The incomparable Trigger from the cover of *Roy Rogers Comics* #43, 1948 (Roy Dillow collection).

Dusty Rogers also wrote in his autobiography that Trigger sired a son who was later used on tour as a trick horse: "One Easter morning we got a call from the stables where Trigger and most of Dad's other horses were kept. Trigger had sired a colt, and the foal looked just like him. We all went out to the stable before church to look at him. The colt never got to be as big as Trigger, but he was smart." The two horses Rogers used in public

Roy Rogers, Dale Evans, Cheryl, Linda Lou, and Dusty on the original Trigger. Although a stallion, Rogers trusted Trigger to tolerate five individuals (including a toddler) on his back, even without tack (Roy Dillow collection).

were Little Trigger and Trigger Jr. Neither was sired by the original Trigger. In fact, towards the end of his career Roy Rogers himself stated that the original Trigger never sired a foal. (See Chapter 5, "Trigger's Trail," the sections on "Trigger's Offspring" and on "Harvester-Trigger Breeding Business.")

Dusty Rogers also offered a humorous anecdote that's been cited many times since, having to do with how "Trigger" sometimes misbehaved in public. He would take off after playing dead, leaving Rogers alone in the middle of an arena. For reasons that will become apparent as you read, the horse Dusty was referring to was clearly Little Trigger.

Dusty Rogers followed in his father's footsteps as a singing cowboy. However, he has never publicly defined himself as a horseman and hasn't had to. There is no evidence he had any particular interest in horses. However, Rogers' daughter Cheryl Rogers-Barnett took after her father and liked to ride. Cheryl had a personal relationship with Trigger and has the pictures to prove it. Her anecdotes regarding Trigger are fun and one never gets tired of them.[3] She's the only member of the Rogers family who included a chapter on Trigger in her autobiography *Cowboy Princess*. Much to her credit, she acknowledged Little Trigger as no one in her family had before:

> Old Trigger remained Dad's favorite, but there were actually other Triggers. Dad bought Little Trigger a couple of years after he bought old Trigger. He purchased the second horse primarily to spare wear

and tear on old Trigger. He wanted a horse that he would take on the road; he only used old Trigger for the movies. Dad never publicly admitted that there was more than one Trigger. He always said that he didn't want to confuse the little kids who loved Trigger. The fans knew Trigger Jr.—the studio even had a contest to name him when Dad first got him—but Little Trigger was a "secret."

Even with Cheryl Rogers-Barnett's honest acknowledgment of Little Trigger, it would seem she (and her writing partner Frank Thompson) had only a partial knowledge of "Trigger." While she provided a fair background for the legendary palomino, it wasn't up to date. Rogers-Barnett erroneously claimed that the original Trigger appeared in every

Charming photograph of a proud love-struck Roy Rogers with his daughter Cheryl in her Sunday best, sitting on Trigger. Unlike her siblings, Cheryl remained an avid rider as an adult (Cheryl Rogers-Barnett collection).

one of Rogers' films except *Mackintosh and TJ* (Penland Productions, 1975). Roy Rogers also made the same claim over and over again: "I think I'm the only cowboy in history who started and finished his career with the same horse."[4] Trigger was present in all of the feature movies Roy Rogers made for Republic Pictures and in all the television episodes produced over six years. But it was only Little Trigger who starred with Rogers and Bob Hope in *Son of Paleface* (Paramount, 1952). Rogers-Barnett seemed to be of the impression that Little Trigger was used only on the road and the original Trigger was used on film, when in fact Little Trigger was in most Roy Rogers films after 1943 (refer to Chapter 6, "Little Trigger," and the "Movie Debut" section).

Cheryl Rogers-Barnett also presented information about Roy Rogers' purchase of Trigger that did not square with official documentation (more on this later in the section on Trigger's bill of sale).

The section on Trigger in Cheryl Rogers-Barnett's book *Cowboy Princess*, excerpted in *Cowboys and Indians* magazine,[5] for the most part stays within the public relations that Rogers' autobiography written with Carlton Stowers, *Happy Trails*, maintained. Of the five photos accompanying the text, only three are of the original Trigger, with no distinction made between him and Little Trigger. A full page shot of Trigger in the rearing position with Rogers in the saddle is printed in reverse changing the markings on his blaze. None of these photo errors were Rogers-Barnett's doing; blame them on poor editing.[6]

Cheryl Rogers-Barnett was born in 1940. Roy Dusty Rogers, Jr., was born in 1946. Their father's career was at its peak between 1942 and 1954; 1948 was Roy Rogers' biggest year. Cheryl and Dusty were 13 and 7 respectively when Roy Rogers' career was starting to level out. They were school children when their father, Glenn Randall, and "Trigger" were making movies and touring. It's doubtful Cheryl and Dusty were fully aware of how Trigger and his doubles were being used. It also has to be noted that Rogers' palominos were boarded on the Randall Ranch. (Dusty Rogers stated in his book, "Because Trigger was not a pet, dad kept him and all of his entertainment horses on a separate ranch.") Only if Cheryl and Dusty were on movie sets daily, keeping log books or diaries and asking Randall direct questions, would they have a solid idea of what he and their dad were up to with Trigger, Little Trigger, and all the palomino look-alikes.

Much to her credit, in her autobiographical sequel *Cowboy Princes Rides Again*, Cheryl Rogers-Barnett was even more objective and candid about the public relations that defined her father's career. I found Cheryl to be courteous, willing to share, and open to different points of view. While we may not agree one hundred percent, she certainly has my respect and gratitude.

Art Rush's vast collection of papers, photos, etc., were trashed after he passed away. According to Mike Johnson, 90 percent of what was destroyed were papers for Rush's only client at the time, Roy Rogers. Judging by Rogers' Victorville museum, he saved a lot. Official records like horse registration papers, bills of sale, and travel logs, may still exist. They could answer many questions and shed new light on "Trigger."

It could also be argued that the Rogers family is wasting its time trying to cater to children today who have no interest in a fantasy of a singing cowboy and his horse. While the Rogers family actually focuses mostly on older fans, there is still an expectation that longtime fans should be satisfied with the same incomplete stories they've read and heard hundreds of times. All this seems to be another example of the publicity becoming a hotly defended public stance long after many fans are curious for the truth. Serious fans have all grown up and no longer want to hear from official sources that every time Roy Rogers was pictured with a palomino, it was the original Trigger. If Trigger had done all that we saw him do on film, and in person, he would have indeed been a super horse. It's been noted in later interviews that Roy Rogers was a little less interested in promoting the image of his horse and more prone to telling the real story as best he could remember it. Many fans have acknowledged that while on visits to the Roy Rogers and Dale Evans Museum in Victorville they were able to ask Rogers very candid questions about his palominos. He was forthcoming with information on Little Trigger albeit off the record.

Buford "Corky" Randall

Most everyone who worked at close quarters with Roy Rogers and his "Triggers" is gone: the trainers, directors, stunt doubles, sidekicks, and Dale Evans. Buford Corky Randall, Glenn Randall's son, was one of the last people alive with a working knowledge and experience of Rogers' mounts. For Rogers' children, the different "Triggers" were just one aspect of their parents' lives. For Corky Randall's family, much of their income depended on Rogers' horses.

With his busy schedule running an empire, Roy Rogers did not have time to maintain a string of horses, and it made sense to board them at the Randall Ranch. Glenn Randall had immediate access to Trigger and his doubles. As their primary caregiver he attended to their conditioning and training. Cheryl Rogers-Barnett acknowledged in her biography that her father lived with the Randall family for a time around 1947 after his second wife, Arline, died.

Corky Randall was born in 1929. He started riding at an early age and was breaking in colts when he was in grade school. He learned how to train horses from his dad, as he put it, "from the get-go."[7]

Corky Randall actually handled Roy Rogers' palominos to a point far beyond just going on trail rides. He was about 14 when his father started working for Rogers. By the time Corky was in high school, he was already working in the motion picture industry, wrangling horses. He was 19 during Roy Rogers' heyday. Corky took care of the Randall stable when his dad was out of town touring with Rogers. It was not till his last year in high school that a barn man was hired, freeing Corky from some of his responsibilities. The year Glenn Randall was in Europe filming *Ben-Hur* (MGM, 1959), Corky toured with Rogers and Dale Evans. Corky was in his mid-twenties by then. Besides caring for Rogers' palominos, one of his duties was to drive the Rogers children from their hotels to where their parents were performing. By the time the Roy Rogers television show was going, Glenn Randall, was touring the country with separate horse acts. A very young Corky worked on *The Roy Rogers Show* on television under Johnny Brim, an old time wrangler who once worked at Hudkins Stables, Trigger's first Hollywood home.

While Corky Randall learned how to train horses from his father, it was Bill Jones, head wrangler and ramrod at Republic in the 1940s, who was his mentor in the movie business. Jones was in charge of recruiting horses and men, working with budgets, transportation, feeding livestock, etc. He taught Corky how scenes with horses were shot with respect to set-ups, angles, and such. A horse trainer's job was to provide an appropriate mount to do the required work and cue him accordingly.

As one of his father's assistants, Corky Randall not only hauled "Trigger" to different

Corky Randall looking splendid on Little Trigger, in the classic rearing pose circa 1945 (Corky Randall collection).

locations on occasion but even rode Trigger Jr. in horse shows, rodeos, fairs, and circuses under the palomino's first registered name, Golden Zephyr. He did so in order to acclimate the horse to crowds and all the distractions that confront an animal while performing in public. Although the horse belonged to Roy Rogers at the time, Rogers was not mentioned the as owner. By the time Rogers started to use the horse as Trigger Jr., the palomino was well-schooled in front of live audiences.

Corky Randall earned his living by what he could actually do with horses, not by self-promotion. He has nothing to gain by not telling the truth about what happened with his dad, Roy Rogers, and "Trigger."

Corky Randall was interviewed by telephone for this book on a number of occasions.[8] I tape-recorded him from his home in Newhall, California, where at 77 he was semi-retired. He was cordial, candid, generous with his time, and very forthcoming with information and rare photographs. Corky did not have a photographic memory and made no claims about knowing every detail. He was quick to say he did not intend to cast aspersions on anyone. From this writer's perspective, Corky's experience and knowledge of "Trigger" are not to be denied. Corky Randall was a man who could tell you what it was like to care for and ride Trigger and actually put him up on his hind legs in the classic rearing pose. As to credibility, that says it all.

Roy Rogers

In December of 1949, when his career was close to its zenith, Roy Rogers and writer Aaron Dudley produced an article for *Western Horseman* magazine titled "Trigger: First, Get a Good Horse." It appeared in volume 14, number 12, and ran five pages. Along with a cover portrait, four photographs were published, including three of Rogers grooming his beloved palomino. It's an important essay not only because it appeared in a well-respected magazine, but because it's a time capsule and offered Rogers the opportunity to present his four-legged partner exactly how he wished. The article was published the same year the *Golden Stallion* movie was released. Rogers and Republic Pictures had a horse and movie to promote.

What follows is a synopsis of the major points in the article. For reasons that will become apparent in the chapters that follow, Roy Rogers' *Western Horseman* article is true only if "Trigger" is viewed as a fictional character and a composite of several palominos.

1. Rogers implied that after he'd signed on as a movie cowboy and realized he needed a movie horse, he initiated a search. "It was as an obscure movie extra that I began visiting ranches, stables and hanging around rodeos looking for a horse." He went on to say that he finally heard about one from San Diego that Art Hudkins had just purchased.

2. Rogers gave the year he purchased Trigger and the palomino's age at the time: "It took a lot of doing, but I finally owned Trigger. That was in 1938, and it was the cheapest $2,500 I ever spent. He was a five year old then."

3. According to Rogers, trainer Glenn Randall appeared on the scene later. "About three years later after Trigger and I had worked several pictures, I met up with Glenn Randall." Rogers also stated that he'd already started training Trigger as a

trick horse: "Over the years, Randall helped me add 50 tricks to the meager ten I was putting on Trigger through in those early days."

4. Little Trigger was not mentioned when Rogers went on to note "Trigger's" prowess as a trick horse. "In addition to being a good all-around cow horse, Trigger today is considered the most versatile horse star in the motion picture business."

5. Rogers portrayed Trigger as a wonder horse, with great stamina, and capable of numerous tasks. "In the early days of our movie career, I worked the whole picture from start to finish with Trigger, close-ups, trick shots, running shots and all." While Trigger stand-ins were mentioned, the implication was that they didn't do that much: "Every leading actor in Hollywood has one or more doubles, so we have a couple of other palominos to do those long shots."

6. Rogers also discussed Trigger on tour: "We take him in hotels and theaters while on personal appearance tours."

7. Rogers also noted Trigger as a breeding sire. "There are only two genuine Trigger colts. The younger, a two-year-old, I own. The only other one I raised especially for a little girl in New England and presented to her as winner of a nation-wide contest."

2

Chasing Trigger

"This is the west, sir. When the legend becomes fact, print the legend."[1]
—from *The Man Who Shot Liberty Valance*

During his illustrious career Roy Rogers' name was paired in three different combinations: Roy Rogers and Dale Evans, Roy Rogers and the Sons of the Pioneers, and Roy Rogers and Trigger. It would seem that a pairing with his wife or the musical group that first brought him fame would be more important, but that is not so. For proof of Trigger's significance and popularity, one need only consider who was photographed with Roy Rogers more often and who received second billing in his films, television shows, and personal appearances. Whose name was set in cement with Rogers' at Grauman's Chinese Theatre in the heart of Hollywood? Trigger was truly an equal half of a magical team. Both man and horse remain powerful symbols of a place, a time, and even a state of mind. If Leonard Slye's formation of the Sons of the Pioneers is one of "his most significant contributions to the myth of the romantic west," as author Raymond White so insightfully states in his book *King of the Cowboys and Queen of the West*, the fantasy of a magical palomino was another.

To understand the full story of how the character of "Trigger, the Smartest Horse in the Movies" was created, even perpetrated, one has to consider a number of components. Surely there's no adult now with even a rudimentary knowledge of equines and film making, who could not guess it takes a number of animals and expert handlers to pull off the illusion of a single wonder horse.

Image, Public Relations and Controlling a Narrative

A Republic Pictures press release circa 1946 claimed, "Trigger, Roy Rogers' beautiful palomino, performs more than 70 tricks on cue. Rogers has trained the horse himself and Trigger goes through his repertoire of amazing tricks at children's and veterans' hospitals, on the stages of theatres, and at rodeos as well as in motion pictures." While this made nice copy, it was show business propaganda from the get-go and, by definition, a half-truth. "Trigger's" trainer Glenn Randall was not acknowledged; Roy Rogers and the public relations department at Republic Pictures were putting on a show.

Public relations (PR) is defined as "the professional maintenance of a favorable public image by a company or other organization or a famous person." Things are going

Trigger performed at liberty on a number of occasions, cued off camera by his trainer Glenn Randall. Here he evades captors in a running insert from *The Golden Stallion,* released in 1949 (Roy Dillow collection).

to be left out and put in all for the best possible effect. Truth is not the goal, though that's how PR wants to be perceived. Roy Rogers' brand of PR was at best a benign deception. In a show biz narrative no one is supposed to get hurt. Yes, it's misleading but the public tends to prefer gloss and glitter.

In 2005, author Bob Spitz cited an interview in *The Beatles: The Biography* in which Paul McCartney explained how the Fab Four and their manager, Brian Epstein, agreed on a "version of the facts" that would serve as their public story. The story was adhered to and embellished to suit their needs. Consequently, the Beatles' history was often laced with a lack of "reliable source material." Spitz went on to say, "Even in those remarkable cases where sources are offered, the accuracy remains suspect. Either memories were vague, tales were recycled, facts went unchecked, or circumstances were fabricated or obscured." Spitz even quoted Napoleon: "History is a set of lies agreed upon."

A February 25, 1950, letter by Al Rackin, publicity director for Roy Rogers, to Fred

W. Parnell of *Palomino Horses* magazine was laced with errors and falsehoods. "You might be interested in some facts about Trigger. He turned 17 January 1, 1950. Trained by Roy since 5 years old—memorized 52 tricks on cue—is known as 'The Smartest Horse in the Movies.' Has colt, Trigger Jr., introduced in pictures in *The Golden Stallion* and is now filming *Trigger Jr.* with Trigger and Roy. Trigger and Roy have worked together in nearly 100 western pictures—Trigger is a stallion—out of a Quarter mare and by a Thoroughbred stud—bought in 1938 for $2500."

Public relations and its by-products are nothing new of course. They've been a staple of entertainment, politics, business, etc., from the beginning of recorded history. Ingmar Bergman had a phrase for such contrivances, "a tissue of lies." Now there's fake news, while related it's much more malevolent. The pharaohs were aware of the power of image, as were Julius Caesar and the popes. Politicians like Teddy Roosevelt, John F. Kennedy, and Ronald Reagan put a great deal of effort into controlling their images. Outlaw bank robber Jesse James even went so far as to promote himself as a defiant Southern patriot by writing letters to newspapers defending his actions. He strove to create an image of a Robin Hood type figure who robbed the rich to give to the poor. Buffalo Bill was augmenting his image and the history of the West decades before Roy Rogers. Control over image is crucial whether one is trying to succeed in show business, rule a country, or run a corporation. Companies spend millions on advertising and promotion. As much as selling a product, they're selling a way of life. Roy Rogers spent his career trying to control his image and that of his horse. However, the truth catches up eventually.

Celebrities inevitably lose control over their own narrative and privacy even with studio and professional backing. Today, with the relentless focus and ubiquity of the Internet, they're practically impossible to keep. Gone are the days reporters would respectfully not address President Franklin Roosevelt's leg braces. Years before Elvis Presley lost control of his narrative, Frank Sinatra and Marilyn Monroe already had. Napoleon and Churchill lost theirs in time, as did King Tut. Powerful men like FBI head J. Edgar Hoover and newspaper magnate William Randolph Hearst couldn't keep their private lives private. Even the ultra-reclusive Howard Hughes and Greta Garbo couldn't keep certain aspects of their lives secret. Roy Rogers could never completely control his own narrative, much less that of his horse. For the most part he was able to maintain a chosen public persona when it counted, while his career was in full bloom.

"The King of the Cowboys" and "The Smartest Horse in the Movies" are all grandiose slogans designed to promote an image, hyperbole if you will. Hyperbole is long for hype. Hype and public relations are a two-headed monster. They are done for effect and are not subtle. Hyperbole is by definition an exaggeration and, depending on who's buying, very effective. Being young and susceptible, making allowances, accepting hyperbole at face value is one thing, but as an adult it's something else indeed. When grownups refuse to accept reality and common sense, or only gather information from one source (especially in an age of spin and short attention spans), there's no end to how much snake oil they'll swallow. Presidents have been elected through hyperbole.

One has to be very careful with memories, agenda, bias. Evidence is a starting point but it's best when corroborated with proof and common sense, two different sources if one is lucky. With respect to the big picture, Trigger's history is a lesson in the importance of image and the ubiquity of public relations.

Roy Rogers' knack for public relations was on display in countless live and print interviews. In a 1983 appearance on *The David Letterman Show*, within the space of a

Another rare appearance by the original Trigger, galloping into the Los Angeles Coliseum with the King of the Cowboys in the saddle. No western rider and horse partnership ever looked better (Roy Dillow collection).

few sentences, Rogers went seamlessly from talking about the original Trigger's history to clearly referencing the intelligence of his trick-horse double Little Trigger.

LETTERMAN: "Tell me a little bit about Trigger. How did you get him and he was a special horse wasn't he?"

ROY ROGERS: "He was without a doubt the greatest horse that ever came along. I got him when I
    made my first picture. He was four years old and before that, just the fall preceding that the first
    time he was ever in a picture was Olivia de Havilland rode him in Sherwood Forest in that pic-
    ture she made with Errol Flynn. And I made my first picture with him in January 1938 and we
    made 90 of our features and 101 of the half-hour TV shows plus appearances and he was like an
    iron horse."

LETTERMAN: "Yes, but he could do things?"

ROY ROGERS: "He could do anything. He was just, he was sharp, and you show him a few times and
    he would just do it on cue."

Celebrity is born out of publicity and by its very nature is subjective. In effect, cowboy
stars and their publicists were telling the truth under imaginary circumstances. Even a
fictional character, like a wonder horse, needed a background. However, on occasion the
subject of the publicity may blur the truth so much and for so long, he or she loses sight
of it. Some fans were also culpable, seeing only what they wanted and buying into any
and all publicity. There are adults who are still very dedicated to Roy Rogers and Trigger
and are very ambivalent towards any one who might tarnish the image they've held on
to since they were children. There are those who don't care if Rogers wanted to call every
palomino in the world "Trigger," as that was his choice. There were, after all, different
"Champions" and "Lassies," and fans loved them all, not knowing the difference. For
them it didn't matter which horse played "Trigger." The horse was a character in their
eyes just like the rider was. Fans loved the show that Roy Rogers and his team of professionals put on. They absorbed it and asked for more. Thousands paid money to see "Trigger," something they would recall for the rest of their lives. And don't try and tell them
they probably didn't see the original Trigger in person when they were young or you're
liable to have a fight on your hands.

B-western movies were fiction and their goal was wholesome entertainment. They
were optimistically sentimental facades, re-writes of history. If reality interfered with
what they were trying to accomplish, it was eliminated. Disheveled Gabby Hayes and his
bay Eddie looked more like a genuine cowboy and his horse in the early days of the Old
West than Roy Rogers and Trigger. Have you ever seen an archival photo of a genuine
cowboy who dressed like Rogers, riding a horse that wore tack like Trigger's? A working
cowboy back then would have most likely been riding a smaller horse, almost pony size,
like a mustang. It would have looked pretty mangy from work and hard riding outdoors
in all sorts of weather. Roy Rogers, Art Rush, and Republic Pictures wanted to fill movie
seats and sell merchandise. It's doubtful it occurred to them that fans would read more
into Rogers' myth and that of his horse than the obvious. And how could we not when
the palomino Roy Rogers used as his screen mount was so charismatic? Trigger added
a great deal of ambience with his regal looks and the way he carried himself. This was
his major strength and why he was critical for close-ups or running full out. Fans have
a mental picture of Trigger running during the opening credits of *The Roy Rogers Show*
on television and the voice-over: "Trigger, his golden Palomino!"

"He was beautiful with his flaxen mane and tail and proud arched neck. As I hit an
easy lope, then a fast gallop, I could feel that this boy was an athlete with power to spare
and a fine balance that would set him in good stead for chases over rocky grades and
down steep mountain slopes."[2]

When Trigger was being ridden down a road with Rogers singing a tune, the
palomino didn't just walk; he pranced, his mane and forelock flowing in the wind. Author

Richard Adams could have just as well been referring to Trigger in his book *Traveller* (Alfred A. Knopf, 1998), written from the point of view of General Robert E. Lee's great horse. In one section Traveller tells a barn cat friend about how he liked to carry himself when he was being ridden by his famous master: "It takes a durned good man to ride me, and I've no use for any other sort. I've got a lot of go in me, and I jest can't abide hanging around. I will walk, mind you, if a man really wants it and insists, but I always keep it fast and springy."

Rogers was very sensitive to every aspect of his public persona and that of his horse. Publicity photos of Trigger's striking signature pose, rearing in an almost perpendicular position with Rogers on his back, are almost always taken from the same side, the horse's right. Reading left to right, it's "Roy Rogers and Trigger."

In the book *My Brush with History,* famed portraitist Everett Raymond Kinstler (International Artist, 2005) wrote about his experiences painting famous people, including Roy Rogers and Dale Evans. Every time he asked them to pose, Rogers would move to his wife's right side, which put him first if one was "reading" left to right. When Kinstler asked him why he kept doing that, Rogers replied, "Well, it does read Roy and Dale."

Even Roy Rogers' romantic feelings towards his leading ladies had to be held in check for the sake of his image. "Cowboys weren't allowed to kiss girls in pictures, so one time I gave Dale a little peck on the forehead and we got a ton of letters to leave that mushy stuff out. So I had to kiss Trigger instead."[3]

An image, which can be a symbol, is a point of reference, a selling tool, and at times, a lot of fun. That's why so many fans embrace them. With regard to entertainment and art, it's best to trust art, not artists. It's also wise to take the same tack with symbols. Embrace the image if it nourishes you, but be aware of what the author's motives and message are. Trigger is at once a beloved memory of a more innocent time but he's also a corporate logo.

Trigger Doubles

It became obvious right away to Roy Rogers that Trigger could not retain his magnificence on the steady diet of movie work and personal appearance tours, which meant being cooped up in a trailer for weeks on end. Even with all his intelligence and athleticism, Trigger was still just a horse. So a horse referred to as "Little Trigger" took on the workload. Much more than a mere double, he was literally a second Trigger. However, as fantastic as Little Trigger was, he alone could not hold up to sustain a career as long as Rogers.' Shows being scheduled miles apart, time was tight, and physical endurance got pushed to the limit. A Roy Rogers tour in 1961 included 50 performances in 26 cities.[4]

During Roy Rogers' heyday the majority of his fans assumed Trigger was one horse, but it was common knowledge, and confirmed in interviews, that doubles were used for stunts and long shots. Rogers and trainer Glenn Randall chose not to reveal much publicly about "Trigger." While they acknowledged the use of palomino look-alikes, they did so almost in passing and only because they had to. Saying nothing at all would have been silly because some children and even horse-ignorant adults guessed that doubles were being used. Eventually Trigger Jr.—*not* Little Trigger—was introduced and promoted as Trigger's replacement. Little Trigger was Rogers' big secret, his personal appearance and trick-horse. Randall did not seem so dogged about keeping Little Trigger a secret, but no one suspected enough to ask. The Roy Rogers public relations machine was pretty animated, with its coverage of "Trigger" satisfying both the press and fans.

When asked how many "Triggers" there were, B-western director Joseph Kane replied, "Quite a few. After it got going, he had two or three. One for close-ups and stills, one for riding, and an extra one."[5]

Glenn Randall actually discussed Little Trigger in 1992. He was quoted in *Cowboy Magazine* in an article titled "He Spoke Horse" by Phil Spangenberger: "Actually, due to the grueling schedule of a superstar like Roy Rogers, it was necessary to train a trio of Triggers for the various films, and personal appearance tours and shows, including several trips abroad." As Randall also recalled, "Little Trigger was our personal appearance horse and, by God, he could do some of the most remarkable things."

Republic Pictures also agreed with Rogers not to risk two valuable palomino horses on hazardous movie stunts. Just as Rogers had stunt doubles, so did Trigger and Little Trigger. Different palominos were switched from scene to scene and sometimes from shot to shot depending on the requirements of a given situation. The original Trigger earned his oats and star treatment, but not anywhere near to the degree most of his fans were led to believe. Over the years, more palominos than will ever be known were used to keep Rogers and "Trigger" number one in the hearts of fans. Doreen M. Norton, in her book *The Palomino Horse*, wrote that "Trigger got a double to go on personal appearance tours. Eventually more doubles were obtained, because the main 'picture' Trigger was a horse too well trained to waste on any but the most important scenes, and other similar Triggers were obtained for stand-ins. These stand-ins pose while lights and camera are being adjusted, and a 'chase' Trigger does all the running in pictures."[6]

William Witney's claim that the original Trigger was taken on Rogers' tour for *Under Western Stars* (1938) is highly doubtful. It was Rogers' first movie in a leading role and he made almost every major city in the United States in about three months. Corky Randall maintained that the original Trigger did not like to travel. He did go as far as Oklahoma on movie locations when Yates was footing the bill. It would seem the horse appeared at only a few outings around Rogers' home base of Los Angeles. "Any time they ever saw Roy Rogers up close in person, it was Little Trigger. The old horse was never in anything but film and would have only been on a film company set."[7] However, for such high-profile events as the laying of hooves into wet cement at Hollywood's Grauman's Chinese Theater, the original Trigger was present in all his glory. Rogers was not going have any other palomino immortalized!

TRIGGER IN THE BIG APPLE

On page 18 of William Witney's book *Trigger Remembered*, there's a photo of Roy Rogers with the original Trigger (no date provided) that is particularly rare. According to the caption the shot was taken during "one of the few times that Trigger was used on personal appearances for Roy's first stint at New York's famed Madison Square Garden's Rodeo. Here Roy and Trigger delight the fans during a pre-rodeo parade on Fifth Avenue." Rocky Roe confirmed that the Gallen storefront (behind them to the left) was an East Coast manufacturer of women's clothing till the name was changed in the late 1940s. According to Roy Dillow, the saddle pictured was acquired by Rogers shortly after 1945 and his hat was of a style he used till early 1946. The 1946 date makes the most sense

Rare photograph of Roy Rogers with the original Trigger, taken in New York on Fifth Avenue circa 1946, the only known appearance of the palomino on the East Coast. Non-movie related photographs of the original Trigger outside of California are pretty much nonexistent (Roy Dillow collection).

though Robert Phillips placed Rogers at Madison Square Garden for the first time as early as 1942.

Gene Autry's Lindy Champion was the first horse to fly from California to New York in 1940 so it's likely Trigger made the same flight years later. It's doubtful the palomino toured across the country as no other photos have surfaced of him in any state other than on those occasions when he was making movies in the Southwest and West Coast. That Trigger was on the East Coast is unique and only happened once as far as this writer can determine, Corky Randall was correct. Beyond this very rare appearance, if you saw a performance by "the King of the Cowboys" and "the Smartest Horse in the Movies" outside of southern California, you more than likely did not see the original Trigger. With his limited bag of tricks, Rogers and Glenn Randall had no reason to trailer him far, especially since Little Trigger could do so much more in front of a live audience.

Roy Rogers and the Truth

Many fans start with the mistaken premise that it was only authors and journalists who embellished or were just plain inaccurate about Roy Rogers and Trigger, twisting things to suit their stories. Some fans actually believe anything of questionable accuracy was not Rogers' responsibility, but some journalist's concoction.

Roy Rogers' goal was entertainment. He is not thought of as a storyteller or myth-maker in the classic sense, but that is what he was. He played fast and loose with facts; he spoke to his advantage. In Hollywood image is everything, public relations is the common language, and Rogers spoke it fluently. He was not an anomaly, he was part of the studio system and that's the way the game was played. Recreating oneself was nothing new in the reel or real West by the time Leonard Slye tried it. Consider William H. Bonney, who was born Henry McCarty then became Billy the Kid, or Robert Leroy Parker, who died as Butch Cassidy.

As celebrities, Roy Rogers' and Trigger's public lives were shaped by the studio that represented them, by Rogers' publicist, by the press, and by Rogers himself.[8] Still, there is a difference between an subjective truth and an absolute truth. Author Tim "Tumbleweed" Lasiuta was very insightful when he said, "If we consider the Trigger dilemma, we can conclude that the spirit of the truth is more important than the substance. We all loved Trigger, but which one becomes the question."

As it turned out, even Roy Rogers' hardcore fans grew up and became less interested in his screen persona. The plot lines of *My Pal Trigger* and *Don't Fence Me In* were never going to remain as interesting as Rogers' and Trigger's real life stories or their behind the scenes rise to fame. Authorized biographies and public relations meet fan needs for a while but they will inevitably want more, something closer to the truth.

How could any serious fan make the argument that Roy Rogers was consistent and always accurate concerning "Trigger"? One would be hard pressed to find printed text or a video interview where Rogers discussed Little Trigger specifically. Author David Rothel claimed that Rogers was evasive when he talked to him on record about the use of backup Triggers. He said Rogers didn't really want to get into it.

An interview is only as good as the questions asked and the willingness of a subject to answer. For the most part the press didn't know what to ask Roy Rogers beyond the same obvious youth-oriented questions posed over and over. Rogers was not foolish enough to divulge more than he was asked. Had a real expert or even a serious fan interviewed Rogers off the record, there's no telling what might have been revealed about Trigger and his doubles.

If you want the truth about Roy Rogers and Trigger, you'll find some here. Though true objectivity doesn't exist, it doesn't mean this writer didn't try. Ultimately this book is speculation by a dedicated fan. I will present a lot of contradictory research then try to draw credible conclusions. These writings are a genuine attempt to sort out and construct a believable history, a counterpoint to Roy Rogers' subjectivity in public. When you're confused, go to the place where you started and begin again. As "Trigger" was show business sleight-of-hand, I had to re-evaluate a lot of what Rogers said on record.

Misinformation and Confusion

During the height of the hippie movement in 1967, Jerry Garcia, the lead guitarist for the Grateful Dead, was talking to a reporter about the quality of press coverage for the Summer of Love. Garcia was somewhat of an expert; he and his band mates were at ground zero living in the Haight-Ashbury section of San Francisco. He was amazed at how some very prestigious magazine and newspaper articles misled and did not truly represent the spirit of the movement or what it meant. It got him to thinking: if the press could not deliver an honest and truthful accounting, how could the general public trust stories about more important and complex topics like war, the economy, political scandals, or the environment?

I understand how, at a beginning, a fictional scenario is deemed necessary to promote a new star, but it's amazing how much misinformation has persisted decades after Trigger's death.

Roy Rogers and Glenn Randall apparently had a mutual agreement not to say much about "Trigger" during his heyday. Rogers' use of public relations throughout his career became second nature. After a while, at times unintentionally, he mixed up the facts. Rogers personally did not make any of Trigger's official records public, like his registration form or bill of sale, obviously so he could control the fantasy of one special horse.

When researching the lives of Roy Rogers, Trigger and his palomino doubles, one is easily overwhelmed by the number of interviews and other material from books, magazines, press releases, newsletters, and television documentaries. It's easy to see why the combined effect becomes confusing and at times contradictory. How could it not be, with Rogers using more than one palomino to play Trigger over his career? They were all "Trigger" when he rode them. He used a Tennessee Walker, a Quarter Horse, and a horse with Thoroughbred blood. One was descended from a great race horse. Some topped out at 16 hands; most averaged 15.2; one was 15 hands. They came from different breeders and different places; most were born from the mid-1930s on. Rogers used palominos he owned and some were provided on special occasions. Most were well mannered; one disliked women and children. Yet, over time, fans assumed all "Trigger" stories and information applied to one horse.

While Roy Rogers knew a great deal about the "Triggers" he used, there's no way even he could remember every detail with absolute certainty. After some 90 movies, 100 television shows, and even more live appearances, how could he be 100 percent accurate? That would have required a photographic memory or the keeping of detailed records in

The Magazine for Admirers of Stock Horse

Roy Rogers and Trigger

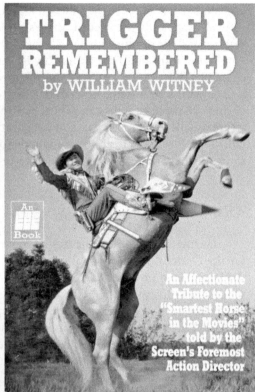

TRIGGER REMEMBERED
by WILLIAM WITNEY

An Book

An Affectionate Tribute to the "Smartest Horse in the Movies" told by the Screen's Foremost Action Director

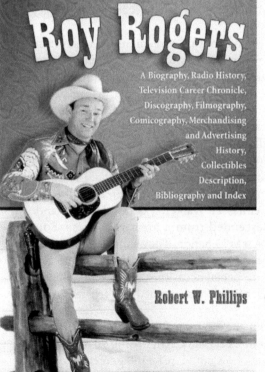

Roy Rogers

A Biography, Radio History, Television Career Chronicle, Discography, Filmography, Comicography, Merchandising and Advertising History, Collectibles Description, Bibliography and Index

Robert W. Phillips

The Old Cowboy Picture Show
"Celebrating The Great Western Heroes"

December 2000
Vol. 4, No. 12

In This Issue

Remembering Trigger
by Leo Pando
- - - - - - -
The Legend Of Trigger
by Robert W. Phillips
- - - - - - -
Howdy Saddle Pals
by George Coan
- - - - - - -
Collecting Toys And
Memorabilia Of
The Smartest Horse
In The Movies
by Robert W. Phillips
- - - - - - -
Trigger Markings
by Leo Pando
- - - - - - -
The Ultimate
B-Western Collectable
by Leo Pando
- - - - - - -
My Pal Trigger
A Review
by Leo Pando
- - - - - - -
Chasing The Palomino
by Robert W. Phillips
and Leo Pando
- - - - - - -
Performing Horses
and Me
by Roy Rogers

★ ★ ★

Copyright 2000
George Coan

a daily journal. However, it will become evident that even Rogers' seemingly contradictory statements make sense when seen chronologically and in the context of an entire career. Rogers had an empire to run, not to mention a personal life. As important as "Trigger" was to him and his public persona, he had to delegate the palomino's care and training to others. While Glenn Randall was "Trigger's" primary caregiver, even he was not present in every situation. Regrettably, Randall never wrote an autobiography and he never discussed "Trigger" in detail as only he could have. "Trigger" was by all accounts a very smart horse and at least one magazine article is attributed to him, the tongue-in-cheek "My Life with Roy" published in 1950 (publisher unknown).[9]

If one is trying to document Trigger's life, one is going to run into not only contradictions but lots of dead ends. The information that Roy Rogers and Glenn Randall once possessed between them is now gone. In the final analysis, they made some very shrewd decisions when it came to how Trigger and his doubles were used. The best way to manage Trigger's story is to present as many different sides as are credible and make judgments tempered by experience and common sense. No one person knows the complete story.

When B-westerns were in their heyday, no one—not Roy Rogers, Glenn Randall, or William Witney—could have predicted advances in technology, such as DVD players, that would allow millions of fans to own copies of their films, much less have the power to study them in detail and distinguish one palomino from another.

When William Witney first identified Little Trigger in his book *Trigger Remembered* as the most important Trigger double Rogers used, once again I thought, "Where there's smoke there's fire." Since the publication of Witney's book in 1989, many articles and books have discussed Little Trigger. Just as the use of Trigger look-alikes and palomino stunt doubles is no secret anymore, the existence of Little Trigger has been well known to serious fans for a long time now.

No one who has honestly tried to sort out which "Trigger" is which would be surprised by the difficulties separating fact from legend with regard to Roy Rogers' life. Leonard Slye really lived his role as Roy Rogers, King of the Cowboys. It's common knowledge, almost tradition, that many Hollywood actors changed their names, but not many went on to play the same character in every one of their films as well as in, television, radio and public appearances. As Robert W. Phillips noted, "Gene Autry initiated the practice of portraying himself on screen. Going a step further, Roy was now patterning his life as close as possible in every aspect to that of his film character." This second layer of publicity protection to Roy Rogers may be unique in the world of show business.[10] It also extended to his horse.[11]

Opposite: **Trigger print milestones:** *Western Horseman* **magazine cover article by Roy Rogers and writer Aaron Dudley (vol. 14, no. 12; December 1949)** • *Trigger Remembered* **by William Witney, the director's ode to the beloved palomino (Earl Blair Enterprises, 1989)** • *Roy Rogers* **by Robert W. Phillips, for which all 14 pages of Chapter 11 were devoted to "Trigger" (McFarland, 1995)** • *The Old Cowboy Picture Show,* **a newsletter devoted to Trigger by Robert W. Phillips, George Coan and Leo Pando (vol. 4, no. 12; December 2000).**

3

Trigger's Tale

"The true journey of discovery consists not in seeking new landscapes but in having fresh eyes."—Marcel Proust

Watching the original Trigger on film, noting all that's been said by those who knew him, and even making allowances for palomino look-alikes who stood in for him, it's easy to conclude that he was a very special horse. "Trigger was the best and I'll probably never find another like him," said Rogers on *The Merv Griffin Show* in 1982.[1] It's no wonder he was held in such high regard as a movie star that only Roy Rogers himself got higher billing on marquees and movie screens. Baby boomers cannot think on Roy Rogers without remembering "Trigger." Well over a quarter century after the palomino died, the King of the Cowboys was still signing autographs with "Roy Rogers and Trigger." Even U.S. President Bill Clinton remembered the palomino the morning after Roy Rogers passed away. In a press conference Clinton said, "Like most people my age, I grew up on Roy Rogers and Dale Evans and Trigger."[2]

It took many palominos to build the legend of "the Smartest Horse in the Movies," and even though the original Trigger didn't perform a great variety of tricks, he made up for it in charisma, screen presence, and beauty. He was much more than a mere glamour boy. But he could also rear up astonishingly high and run like the wind. He was every inch the movie star he was billed as. "Any cowboy worth his stuff owes half of what he gets to his horse," Roy Rogers was quoted as saying. He and Glenn Randall would have been foolish to endanger Trigger unnecessarily or to wear him out. Randall, horse doubles, and stunt riders were a strong support system for Trigger and Rogers. It took a great deal of work to pull off the illusion of a wonder horse, but no amount of work would have been enough without a great horse at the top.

Captain Larry Good and Roy F. Cloud, Jr.

Trigger was bred from stock owned by Captain Larry Good. Solid information on Captain Good is elusive. Chances are he lived in the San Diego area where the Golden Cloud/Trigger was foaled. It's home to a large naval base where senior officers retire. Could Good have been a Navy captain?

Roy Fletcher Cloud, Jr. (1881–1940) of Noblesville, Indiana, was Golden Cloud/Trigger's owner when the stud was registered in 1937. As a young man Cloud headed

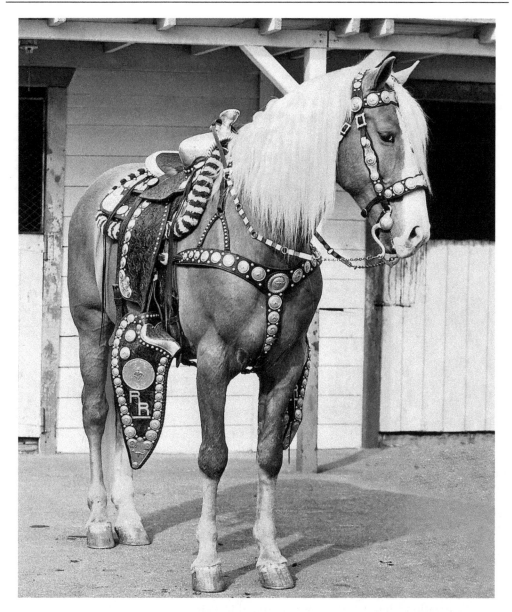

The original Trigger posing for a Schwinn bike advertisement. According to Corky Randall, this shot was taken at the Randall stables in Long Ridge circa 1947, the same year Roy Rogers lived on the property in quarters close to the barn in the background (Joel "Dutch" Dortch collection).

west sometime around 1900, working as a teamster. By 1904 he had enlisted in the army at Tulsa, Indian Territory (now Oklahoma), serving in the 17th Infantry Regiment until 1910. According to his World War I draft registration, Cloud worked as a barber at Camp Travis in San Antonio, Texas. No war service record has been found. In 1920, after the war, Cloud managed a hotel briefly in Comanche County, Texas, during an oil boom. It is believed he next worked as a border patrol agent. In 1927 he relocated to San Diego, California, becoming manager of the San Ysidro Stock Farm.

Roy F. Cloud, Jr. (left), on his palomino Golden Cloud (second rider and horse are unknown). This is the earliest known photograph of Trigger. It was taken circa 1936 probably in San Diego, California, when the horse was just over two. Provided to Robert W. Phillips from a family negative by Roy and Lexy Cloud of Sunnyvale, California, the nephew and niece of Roy F. Cloud, Jr. Before Phillips passed away from cancer in 2001 at only 57, he left the photograph in care of this writer.

Golden Cloud Registration Form—PHA

No palomino registry existed at the time of Trigger's birth in 1934. The Palomino Horse Association (PHA) registry was founded in 1936.

Roy Rogers gave 1932 as the date of Trigger's birth in interviews between 1957 and 1965. That would have meant he was 33 when he died in 1965 (something Rogers continued to maintain throughout his career). This was also stated on the plaque for Trigger at the Roy Rogers and Dale Evans Museum: "Trigger The Smartest Horse In The Movies Featured in 188 movies and TV shows. His sire was a Thoroughbred and his dam was a cold-blooded mare 15½ hands tall-original name Golden Cloud Foaled-1932 Died-1965."

Author David Rothel, in his book *Singing Cowboys*, stated that Trigger was three when Olivia de Havilland rode him in the Warner Bros. film *The Adventures of Robin Hood* (1938). Director William Witney indicated that the palomino was three or four during the filming of his first movie as Trigger, *Under Western Stars* (1938). Those dates made Trigger's birth year 1934.

Issued only to The San Ysidro Stock Farm to register one
stallion "Golden Cloud"   Signed *Dick Halliday, Sec*

Number 214 ----   Dated *March 25 – 1937*

*TRIGGER
(OLD MAN)*

The Palomino Horse Association and
Stud Book Registry

State if to be registered as a stallion?

APPLICATION FOR REGISTRATION

Date APril 1, 1937

I, Roy F. Cloud Jr. , apply for

registration for Golden Cloud
(Name of horse)

SEX Stallion

BRED BY Captain Larry Good
(Owner of dam at time of service)

SIRED BY Tarzan

DAM APac Li8ht Ch.

COLOR OF SIRE Golden Palomino

And DAM, IF KNOWN Li8ht ch.

FOALED July 4, 1934   July 3, 1965

NOW AGED 2 yrs. 8 mo. 27 d.

BODY COLOR Golden Palomino

COLOR OF MANE
AND TAIL white

ALL MARKINGS white Blaze Extendin8
From Above Eyes to nostrils.
Left hind white From AnKle to corhet

OWNED BY Roy F. Cloud Jr.

The above description is, to my knowledge and belief, correct.

SIGNED Roy F Cloud

ADDRESS BOx 323
San Ysidro
California

Registration Fee to
accompany each application.

Fee paid D H

Golden Cloud registration form filed and dated in 1937; the horse was three. One wonders who wrote "Trigger (Old Man)" (Palomino Horse Association, courtesy Steven and Patricia Rebuck).

According to the Golden Cloud registration form provided by Steve Rebuck, president of the Palomino Horse Association and Stud Book Registry, 1934 is the correct date of Trigger's birth.[3] The form (registry number 214) was signed and confirmed by then acting secretary Dick Halliday and dated March 25, 1937, in the upper right-hand corner. A second date, "April 1, 1937," appears with the body of the form. It reads:

> I, Roy F. Cloud, Jr., **apply for registration for** Golden Cloud. **Sex** Stallion. **Bred by** Captain Larry Good. **Sired by** Tarzan. **Dam** Apac. Light Ch. [This is the color of the dam, "light chestnut," apparently accidentally entered on this line; it is entered again below.] **Color of sire** Golden Palomino. **And dam, if known** Light ch.
>
> **Foaled** July 4, 1934. **Now aged** 2 yrs. 8 mo. 27 d. **Body color** Golden Palomino. **Color of mane and tail** White. **All markings** White blaze extending from above eyes to nostrils. Left hind white from ankle to cornet [coronet, i.e., an area just above the hoof]. **Owned by** Roy F. Cloud Jr.[4]

The lavish coffee table book *Roy Rogers: King of the Cowboys* by Georgia Morris and Mark Pollard quoted Rogers as saying, "Trigger made every picture. He was four and I was 26 when we made our first picture."[5] In this instance Rogers was right with regards to Trigger's age during the filming in 1938 of *Under Western Stars*. It means the palomino was born in 1934 and was 31 when he died in 1965. It remains a mystery as to why Rogers usually said Trigger died at age 33, which would have made the year of his death 1967, not 1965.

Trigger conformation poses probably taken at the Van Nuys wash, which ran adjacent to the Randall Ranch. While ideal equine proportions vary from breed to breed, a square look to the body is often preferred. The original Trigger was nicely built and that was reflected in his athleticism and endurance.

Bloodlines and Conformation

The Golden Cloud/Trigger's bloodlines were not confirmed by the Palomino Horse Association and Stud Book Registry and have always been a source of confusion. Information varies, and I was never able to find solid information on his sire, Tarzan, or his dam, Apac, from the PHA directly. Was either a Thoroughbred? Perhaps both horses were indeed unregistered? We know their names but not much beyond with any real certainty, nothing definite regarding bloodlines. Their background information and photos have never surfaced. Back then many unregistered horses raced in Caliente. Was Golden Cloud/Trigger one such animal? Are there records?

The Pedigree Online All Breed Data Base is not consistent with the PHA. It lists the following entries for Trigger as "(born) 1932–Color: palomino–Height; 15.3–PHA #214–'his sire was a Thoroughbred and his dam a grade (unregistered) mare who, like Trigger, was palomino…. Trigger's sire was not a registered Thoroughbred, he was a Thoroughbred cross, golden palomino per PHA records … his dam was APAC a light chestnut per PHA. The grandparents of Trigger/Golden Cloud are UNKNOWN!'" The online database further lists Tarzan and Apac as both born in 1922.

In *Trigger Remembered* by William Witney "Trigger's sire was a registered palomino and his dam was half cold blood and half thoroughbred." When discussing Trigger's origin in interviews, Roy Rogers usually claimed that he was "half Thoroughbred and half cold-blooded; his sire was a race horse at Caliente, and his dam was a cold-blooded palomino. He took the good parts from both of them."[6] It seems Rogers was incorrect with regards to the dam's color.

The original Trigger was to have inherited his color (as well as his speed) from his sire, and his fine conformation from his dam. Trigger's wide chest, short back, and powerful legs allowed him to rear safely straight up in his signature pose with Roy Rogers in the saddle.

Registry expert Pat Mefferd, stepdaughter of stunt man Fred Kennedy, who was around the original Trigger numerous times, makes a good point when she says, "If Trigger was a son of the Thoroughbred Tarzan, why would his breeder or owner at time of registration not put it down correctly; it would certainly enhance his pedigree." Mefferd further said, "I would not consider his conformation to be of the even fifty percent Thoroughbred, it was just not there, maybe one quarter."

Google a profile confirmation shot of a typical Thoroughbred and compare to a similar shot of Trigger. He was pretty compact in comparison with a smaller hindquarters, a shorter back and legs. A Thoroughbred head is narrower and tapers to the nose like its immediate ancestor the Arabian.

Roy Rogers referred to Trigger as a good "using" horse for chases and such. He claimed Trigger never had any ankles, hocks, or knees go wrong in all the chase sequences over rocks, mountains, down steep grades, and so forth. Rogers claimed he did running mounts and dismounts and never had any problems with Trigger.

There were those who claimed Trigger was a grandson of the great Sir Barton, the first Triple Crown winner. After Sir Barton's race career was over, he was purchased by the U.S. Remount Association in 1933 and sent to Wyoming Remount Station, where he was bred to many unregistered mares.[7] That is where he stayed until his death in 1937. In actual fact, it was Pal, a palomino look-alike Rogers and Dale Evans both rode, who was a descendent of Sir Barton. This was according to Wyoming veterinarian Dr. Jack

Ketcham and confirmed by trainer Orval Robinson, both of whom worked for Pal's former owner, Walt Rymill.

At one time the Tennessee Walking Horse Breeders Association ran national magazine ads stating that Trigger was a Tennessee Walking Horse. They were supported in an article by a horse expert who made the same assertion.[8] The problem with that claim, as is often the case when Trigger is discussed, is determining which horse they were referring to. This inconsistency may stem from the fact that Trigger Jr. was a registered Tennessee Walking Horse.

And to state the obvious: Trigger, Little Trigger, and Trigger Jr. were not related.

Golden's Cloud Registration Form—PHBA

The Palomino Horse Breeders of America (PHBA) was founded in 1941, two years after Roy Rogers bought Trigger from Hudkins Bros. Stables.

According to Dr. Floyd Branson, vice president of the Palomino Horse Breeders Heritage Foundation:

> Purebred in horses normally refers to those who meet certain breed specifics (for example Arabians bred to Arabians). Color registries like the PHBA take their registrations from certain approved breeds. In this method, horses are first purebred by their breeding and as recognized by their association. There are some associations that base their registry on only one parent of the two being purebred. Color breed horses must meet certain color requirements. So a half-breed has been half bred from two different (or more) breeds. For example, a Saddlebred stallion bred to a Quarter Horse mare results in half-breed offspring.
>
> "Grade" is a term given to a horse that has no registered history or official paperwork to verify its pedigree. Little Trigger would be a "grade" stallion. Again, the Color Breed Association determines what is appropriate to recognize and what is not. My information indicated that Trigger was out of a Steeldust quarter horse mare by a Thoroughbred or Morgan stud. Some literature can be found that says Thoroughbred/Morgan Stallion (*50th Anniversary Magazine of Palomino Horses* dated June 1991). Steeldust was a line of popular quarter horses. I don't think there is much question that Trigger was not from an identical breed line.

(Foaled in Kentucky in 1844, a palomino stud named Steel Dust was shipped to Texas as a yearling. The name Steel Dust came to identify an entire breed: heavy-muscled, with small ears, big jaw, intelligent with lightning speed in a quarter mile. Source: AQHA Breed History.)

Although not registered officially with the PHBA because he did not meet the aforementioned requirements for eligibility, Trigger was recognized with an honorary registry through a special exception clause. This type of registry is rarely done and only given to a horse of great accomplishment and renown. These records were a one-time acknowledgement, more ceremonial than functional, given to the owner and not filed with the PHBA. They were on display at the museum in Branson and are assumed to be among the Roy Rogers archive held by the Autry Center in Los Angeles. The palomino was referred to officially as Trigger, not Golden Cloud, on the form.

Roy Rogers and Dale Evans were given lifetime memberships to the PHBA in November 1976, "In recognition to their devotion to the palomino horse and for their part in advancing the breed."

Bing Crosby

Avid horseman Bing Crosby dressed in cowboy attire in a scene from *Rhythm on the Range* (Paramount Pictures, 1935), co-starring the Sons of the Pioneers (with Leonard Slye), released a year after Trigger was born.

In January of 1995 Robert W. Phillips received a letter from Roy and Lexy Cloud of Sunnyvale, California. Roy F. Cloud Jr., was their great uncle (they were the source for the rare photo negative of Roy F. Cloud on the Golden Cloud). In the letter the Clouds stated, " The son of a dairy farmer, Roy Cloud left his Noblesville, Indiana home at the age of thirteen following the death of his father. Roy ventured west and settled in Santa Ysidro, California just north of the Mexican border. His home was on a ranch which he managed. His time on the ranch was spent breeding and training palomino and race horses. One of Roy's major clients and part owner of the ranch was Bing Crosby. Roy was a major trainer of Bing's horses."

It's very possible Bing Crosby did indeed have partial ownership of the ranch where the Golden Cloud was born. This writer has not been able to contact a Crosby relative to confirm. Fan club members did not confirm either way. Did Crosby ever have partial owner ship of the San Ysidro ranch near San Diego, California? For all we know Crosby could have owned one alone and had partial ownership of a second in Ventura County. According to pedigree research expert Pat Mefferd, Crosby's ranch was indeed in Ventura County, and for many years his brother Bob owned a Thoroughbred farm in Hemet (San Jacinto Valley in Riverside County, California), so anything is possible.

Robert W. Phillips believed Trigger actually raced at the Caliente Race Track. There is a gap in the palomino's life of about 18 months between when Roy F. Cloud owned him and when he sold him to Hudkins Stables, so he could have run semi-professionally then. Granted, there could have been some match races pitting one horse against another in Mexico at Caliente as the entries were probably not registered.

Early Movie Stables

Roy Rogers and the original Trigger on location with a Republic Pictures movie crew on a camera truck modified to shoot running inserts. Like all animal actors, Trigger was accustomed to film equipment despite a natural flight instinct.

When Hollywood was still just a spot on the map, and studios were called "camps" or "colonies" operating out of makeshift locations such as abandoned barns, an enterprising individual named Clarence "Fat" Jones realized he could make money renting horses to the fledgling movie industry. This was circa 1912, when a company called Pathé began filming two-reeler westerns outside of Los Angeles. Jones was sure movies would develop into a major industry in California, and he built a stable with barns, corrals, and a blacksmith shop.[9] He purchased land in North Hollywood and started scouting the Southwest for all types of horse-related transport.[10] The Fat Jones stable became a magnet for real cowboys who came to Hollywood for jobs in pictures during the winter months when work was slow in ranch country. While the majority did not find permanent employment, a few stayed. Two of the most famous were the legendary western author Will James and character actor Ben Johnson.[11]

Studios paid from $5 to as high as $10 a day for extra or chase horses, and these animals made money consistently. It was rumored some cast horses, who did not work as often, commanded as much as $50 to $100 dollars a day.

According to an old newspaper promo piece for *Oklahoma Kid* (Warner Bros., 1939), the Hudkins brothers rated and described their horses by the on screen stature of the actors who rode them. Subsequently they would bill a studio as such (note the lower rates):

Two stars—$25 per day each,

Three featured—$15 per day each.

One bit—$7.50 per day.

Thirty-four mob: 11 at $5 per day each, 23 at $2:50 per day each.

> "We need forty head of horses at the Iverson Ranch in Chatsworth by 7 o'clock tomorrow morning," he says.
>
> "Forty head," agrees whichever one of the Hudkins brothers happens to answer the telephone. "How do you want them?"
>
> "Well, let's see," says the studio representative, consulting his animal cast sheet. "We need two star horses, three featured, one bit and the rest mob."
>
> "O.K.," says the Hudkins brother. "They'll be there."

Besides the Clarence "Fat" Jones stable located at 11300 Sherman Way, North Hollywood, two other large suppliers of rental horses and horse-drawn vehicles for the California film industry during the heyday of the B-western were the Ralph McCutcheon Stables located in Van Nuys and Hudkins Brothers. Stables, Inc., located at 7245 Coldwater Canyon Avenue, North Hollywood.

Hudkins Bros. Stables Inc.

At the same time Fat Jones was starting his business, four brothers, Ace, Art, Clyde and Ode Hudkins, ran a riding academy in the Los Angeles area. Ace and Art owned the stable. Ace, Ode and Clyde handled the day-to-day operations. At first they even assisted Jones, but soon they broadened their academy to a sales and rental business. They gained a reputation in the film industry for their stock company, which could furnish horses, cattle, western gear and horse-drawn vehicles; and eventually they became second only

Stuntman Fred Kennedy and the original Trigger at Hudkins Bros. Stables next to the Los Angeles River bed. Kennedy's stepdaughter and breed expert Pat Mefford of Cottonwood, California, claimed her mother took the photograph, "and in the photo album, the date shows, in her hand, 'Fred and Trigger 1940.'" Kennedy was a stuntman, bit player and 1982 Stuntmen's Hall of Fame inductee. The mount on the right was a Hudkins movie horse named Smoky, described by actress Peggy Stewart as part Arabian. Mefford claimed Kennedy rode the Golden Cloud/Pistol on a fairly regular basis during his association with Hudkins Bros. and further stated the horse belonged only to them through the early 1940s (Pat Mefford collection). Inserts: Ace Hudkins, left, the second man to own the Golden Cloud, and brother Clyde Hudkins, who discovered the palomino in San Diego.

to Jones. Even with all that, their real claim to fame would be one special palomino they acquired from a San Diego stock farm.

William Witney wrote that Clyde Hudkins first laid eyes on the Golden Cloud while on a horse-buying trip in San Diego where he was foaled. Clyde saw that the colt, with his great looks, would be perfect in movies. Horses with the best breeding and classiest markings were leased for the benefit of the star of a motion picture. The Golden Cloud was an obvious "cast horse"[12] and apparently part of a herd Ace Hudkins purchased all at once.[13]

As is common practice, the Golden Cloud would have been just over two when he was started under saddle. The earliest known picture of the Golden Cloud shows him being ridden by his then owner Roy F. Cloud, Jr. It is safe to assume that the animal was still on the San Ysidro ranch in 1936. Although the date is undocumented, it was around 1937 that the Golden Cloud was moved from the San Diego ranch to the Hudkins Bros. Stables in Los Angeles. Once there, he got movie work right away. With his golden color, great proportions and intelligence, he was a natural movie horse. By 1937 he was on the sets of *Cowboy from Brooklyn* (Warner Bros.) and *The Adventures of Robin Hood* (Warner Bros.). Trigger was sometimes referred to as the "Barrymore of horses"—a reference to John "the great profile" Barrymore, an actor from the silent movie days, noted not only for his skills as a thespian but for his classic looks.

The Hudkins Bros. Stables was originally located in Burbank where Forest Lawn Cemetery now stands. It was later relocated to North Hollywood and, finally, Coldwater Canyon. At one time, the Hudkins' and Glenn Randall's ranches were within a couple of blocks of each other in North Hollywood near Sherman Way. Both concerns were removed from that area due to zoning changes in the mid–1960s.

Of the Hudkins brothers, Ace was the most well-known, although he and Clyde ran the Hudkins Bros. Stables.

To describe Ace Hudkins as colorful would be an understatement. You could even call him notorious, especially as a young man. The Nebraska native was born in 1905 and boxed professionally until the age of 27, never losing by a knock out. With his brothers Clyde and Art as managers and with the nickname "the Nebraska Wildcat," Ace won several California state heavyweight titles and became southern California's biggest boxing draw in the 1920s. When his career as a prizefighter started to wane, his personal life spun out of control due to alcohol. Hudkins was arrested for a series of crimes including assault with a deadly weapon (the charges were dropped), public drunkenness, drunk driving, petty theft, speeding, and resisting arrest. The low point for Ace Hudkins came when he was shot twice in the chest during a brawl, leaving him in critical condition. He survived after several blood transfusions.

By the late 1930s Ace Hudkins had settled down and married. He found his calling after moving to Toluca Lake and buying a stable where he and his brother Art ran a string of racehorses. Along with brothers Clyde and Ode they started the Hudkins Bros. Stables, renting horses, wagons, and miscellaneous cowboy gear to studios for western films that were the rage. They even rented their land for location filming.

The Hudkins Bros. Stables also boarded horses for dozens of cowboy stars, Ace even did stunt work. Hudkins horses started appearing in dozens of Republic Pictures films, including a horse that Ace named Hi Yo Silver for the 1938 movie version of the Lone Ranger and a palomino called Target who was ridden by actress Gail Davis for the 1950s television show *Annie Oakley*.

Ace Hudkins was a hoarder, packrat, curmudgeon and a man of few words, except when he got angry (which was rumored to be often). In his 60s he looked like he was in his 80s or 90s. He eventually calmed down and was described as sweet in the end. Hudkins died of cancer at 68 in 1973 in Los Angeles and in 1995 was posthumously inducted into the World Boxing Hall of Fame.

The Hudkins brothers would typically begin work at about five in the morning. The wranglers arrived and checked a booking sheet for the day's rentals and locations. There would be a number of studios requiring the use of Hudkins stock. Horses were grained, cleaned up, and tacked accordingly. Horses and vintage wagons were loaded onto long Pullman trucks and driven to three possible destinations: a studio for interior shooting, a movie ranch location in north Hollywood, or on an extended trip that might cross state lines. Republic Studios was located at 4024 Radford Avenue, Studio City.[14]

Ace Hudkins would have had a hard time listing all the films for which he supplied horses. It was all in a day's work, whether supplying a cast horse, a dozen horse extras, or any combination a movie studio required. On any given day there might have been a request for a gentle mare for a star who wasn't much of a rider, or perhaps for a fancy, highly-schooled palomino who could make a movie star stand out.

Work was steady at Hudkins Bros. Stables. Wranglers and craftspeople were busy with any number of jobs, from training saddle horses to repairing and cleaning tack. With all the horses that needed to be shod and wagons needing maintenance and repair, the blacksmith shop was constantly busy. On top of all that activity, teaching actors how to ride properly was one of the most important functions of the stable.

Horses were a business for the Hudkins brothers. They didn't care which motion picture production company rented their stock, just so long as their animals were on location. For every week the Golden Cloud was a Hudkins rental horse, there was the probability he was on a film set.[15]

Hudkins Bros. Stable logbooks existed to keep track of a large complex business (containing names, dates, locations, and so on), a virtual history of movie horses. Unfortunately they were lost to water damage, according to Kristine Sader, niece to the brothers. The logbooks would have answered questions about the Golden Cloud's solo career pre–Roy Rogers.

Collateral Damage

Like all Hollywood livestock, Golden Cloud lived at the mercy of his owners and handlers. Many show business animals had precarious existences, dependent on their value to owners and studios that rented them. The silent version of *Ben-Hur* (MGM, 1925) was notorious for the number of horses maimed and killed during the filming of the chariot race. Second-unit director, B. Reeves Eason, was the man in charge. His directorial output was limited mainly to low-budget westerns and action pictures, including Gene Autry's starring debut sci-fi western serial *The Phantom Empire* (Republic, 1935). Eason is best known as an ace second-unit director and for spectacular action scenes in large-budget westerns. His nickname "Breezy" was acquired for his lax attitude towards safety while directing large involved action sequences. Eason directed the cavalry charge for *The Charge of the Light Brigade* (Warner Bros., 1936), where many horses were killed or summarily euthanized due to injuries received on the set. This was at the time when the infamous running–W was used, a rigging that was effective but inhumane.

When a scene called for groups of horses to drop and roll at a full gallop, the running-W was employed. A long line looped around a horse's front fetlocks, was fastened to an eye ring attached to a cinch. Two or more director's assistants allowed the line to play out as the horse moved forward in a quick gallop. On reaching the desired camera position they jerked the animal's legs from under him, sending the unsuspecting animal into a tumble. This outraged both the public and the Hollywood motion picture community. Among them was swashbuckler Errol Flynn, who complained to the ASPCA, urging studios to make sure animal actors were safe. From then on, beleaguered studios were compelled to provide access to American Humane Society representatives to monitor animal safety. The Humane Society eventually had the running-W banned on American films sets (foreign sets were not held to the same standards).

In 1939 the American Humane Society opened a Western Regional Office in Hollywood to fight animal abuse. By then the Golden Cloud had been working in Hollywood for about two years. If safety was precarious for livestock on A-movie sets, if some animals of lesser value were seen as collateral damage, one can only imagine what it was like on B-movie sets.

The Golden Cloud ran in the same Hollywood circles as some pretty notorious people. Many of the horses lost on the set of *The Charge of the Light Brigade* (Warner Bros., 1936) were Hudkins horses. The stable provided one thousand head for that film. At the end of the day, the Hudkins brothers saw their stock in business terms.

It was Michael Curtiz who directed *The Charge of the Light Brigade* and was ultimately responsible for the number of horses put in harm's way (estimates are between 25 and 200 injured or worse). Curtiz, who gave us such classics as *Casablanca* (Warner Bros., 1942), wasn't exactly sensitive to his cast or crew either. Though it has never been substantiated, an actress and some crew members were injured on the set of *Noah's Ark* (Warner Bros., 1928). Curtiz was determined to finish the film on time and cut a few crucial safety corners. Curtiz directed the Golden Cloud in *The Adventures of Robin Hood* (Warner Bros., 1938) with Breezy Eason as second-unit director.

As Roy Rogers wrote in a magazine article titled "Kindness Secret of Better Animal Actors" (date and publication unknown), "Hollywood's acting animals now are being trained through kindness not by brutality. Kindness definitely pays off in animal training–particularly in training a horse. A horse must work on cue—a cue learned only by hard work and patience. The running-W was a diabolical device for tripping a horse. Hollywood now recognizes this. For these various reforms, thanks must go to the various humane societies operating in America—humane groups which protested the treatment once accorded to animal actors."

Because of the Golden Cloud's regal beauty he was not at as much risk on a movie set, like most other horses for hire. Cheryl Rogers-Barnett many years later met a gentleman at a Golden Boot party who claimed he had been working for Ace Hudkins when Roy Rogers opened negotiations to buy Trigger. He said one of Ace Hudkins' brothers, after having been on the Lone Pine set of *Under Western Stars*, returned to the stables with advice to sell Trigger immediately if there was an offer. He warned that the palomino was being used to perform dangerous stunts and there was a good possibility he might be crippled. The Hudkins brothers surely did not want to lose a deal on a fancy palomino that might be injured and rendered worthless.

According to Corky Randall, Roy Rogers bought Trigger just in time. Randall maintained that his father, Glenn Sr., had become concerned over Trigger's welfare while he was still being rented out. Apparently the palomino was long overdue for a good trimming and new shoes. One would think that a glamorous horse for hire like Trigger would have been better taken care of. Unfortunately, rental horses were sometimes neglected perhaps due to busy schedules and poor record keeping. After Rogers bought the horse outright, Glenn Randall had the palomino's shoes removed and hooves trimmed. Trigger went without shoes until his hooves grew out. Corky Randall claimed Trigger made at least one movie without shoes (he couldn't recall which). Doubles were used for long running shots and over rocky terrain till Trigger could be shod again.

Like most Hollywood horses, the Golden Cloud was in a partially precarious situation until Roy Rogers and Glen Randall rescued him.

4

Dick Weston and the Golden Cloud

*"Perhaps it's impossible to wear an identity without becoming what
you pretend to be."*—Orson Scott Card, *Ender's Game*

A Western Star Is Born

Leonard Frank Sly (he added the "e" later)[1] was born in 1911 in Cincinnati, Ohio, and grew up on farm near Duck Run. After a move to Southern California in 1930, Len worked with a number of Western groups, eventually teaming with Tim Spencer and Bob Nolan of the Rocky Mountaineers, who evolved into the Pioneer Trio. They added fiddler Hugh Farr and his brother, guitarist Karl Farr, and were renamed the Sons of the Pioneers in 1934 (the same year the Golden Cloud was born in San Diego). During 1935 and 1936, the Sons of the Pioneers co-starred in movies for different studios, supporting Dick Foran, Gene Autry, Charles Starrett, and even Bing Crosby. Altogether Slye made about ten films using his given name.

Concerns over Gene Autry's possible departure because of a contract dispute had prompted Republic Pictures, specifically then acting studio head Sol Siegel (CEO Herb Yates would relocate from the East Coast and assume control later), to start looking for a replacement. Coincidentally, Len Slye also had other plans. While in a store getting his hat blocked, he heard about Republic's search for a singing cowboy and snuck on to the Republic lot for an audition. Sol Siegel was already very well aware of Slye's potential. Slye stood out in the Sons of the Pioneers, with good looks and a singing voice to match. In the 1936 movie *The Old Corral*, Slye had already been given a speaking role and shared a number of scenes with star Gene Autry. Slye passed the singing cowboy audition (probably as a formality); he would leave the Pioneers, and on October 13, 1937, signed a solo "stock" contact with Republic Pictures. It was conditional, not long-term or high paying. (That same year the Golden Cloud was discovered by Clyde Hudkins in San Diego, bought by his brother Ace, and transported to Hollywood).

The singing cowboy craze exploded under Sol Siegel, who had already decided Len Slye's name was not western enough and changed it to Dick Weston. Just as Gene Autry debuted with a cameo in a Ken Maynard movie, and Lash LaRue began in a supporting role to Eddie Dean, Weston was gradually being groomed by the studio possibly for a series of his own westerns. A Republic spokesman confirmed as much to the *Los Angeles Times*.

The first known publicity photos Len Slye made as Dick Weston featured him in a black shirt with white scarf under his collar and holding his very own OM-45 Deluxe

Above: The Sons of the Pioneers, in *The Old Wyoming Trail* (Columbia, 1937), ride in the background with, from left, Ray Whitley, Donald Grayson, and star Charles Starrett. Visible in the back row: Hugh Farr, Bob Nolan, and Len Slye. Just a few years later, the image of Roy Rogers and Trigger would become so ingrained in the hearts and minds of fans that he would never look quite right when not riding a palomino.

Left: Dick Weston publicity photographs, commissioned by Republic Pictures, featuring his own OM-45 Deluxe Martin 1930 guitar, among the company's most rare and coveted models (brand new in 1939: $225). In 2010 an anonymous bidder paid a whopping $460,000 for the guitar at Christie's auction in New York City. Rogers-Barnett said it was a gift from her dad's father who paid $19 for it (Roy Dillow collection).

Martin 1930 guitar. He would appear in supporting roles in two Republic films as Dick Weston: *Wild Horse Rodeo* (1937) with the Three Mesquiteers (not only did he have a speaking role but he was reviewed in *Variety* magazine for his perform-ance) and *The Old Barn Dance* (1938), the last film Gene Autry made before he did indeed go on strike. Turning Weston into Roy Rogers (Sol Siegel suggested this new name) and offering him Autry's leading part turned out to be premedi-tated show business savvy.[2] Thank you, Mr. Siegel.

Gene Autry went on strike on December 27, 1937.[3] He was quoted as say-ing, "I had a new picture

One of the first photographs of the future King of the Cowboys, circa 1938. The 27-year-old singer is pictured with Republic Pictures executive producer Sol Siegel, the man who oversaw Len Slye's name change to Dick Weston and finally to Roy Rogers. The new western star was wearing the same outfit featured in *The Roy Rogers Press Book* photographs that he took at the same time, probably the same day (Roy Dillow collection).

scheduled to start in two weeks, to be called *Washington Cowboy*."[4] Retitled *Under Western Stars*, it started filming with Roy Rogers in the lead in the middle of January 1937 (weather was apparently not a factor in Lone Pine that year). According to Robert Phillips, it took nine days to film (with a reported budget of $175,000). Archivist Bobby Copeland claimed the movie started filming March 15 and finished on March 29, 1938, 14 days total.[5] This writer tends to give more credence to the Phillips timeline, even though Republic was capable of fast-tracking a film, especially since *Under Western Stars* and Dick Weston were already in the pipeline when Autry walked. Reviews of *Under Western Stars* in *Variety* and *The Hollywood Reporter* were both published April 11, 1938, which means the movie was available to critics some ten days before it was released officially.

Subsequently, Republic may have had two and half months in post-production to ready *Under Western Stars* for its April 20, 1938, release date. All this makes a case for how quickly Dick Weston was turned into Roy Rogers at the beginning of 1938. Len Slye may have been born in 1911 but Roy Rogers was born 27 years later. The first promotional photos, brochure, and press books of the newly renamed Roy Rogers were by any usual standard rushed products. Republic after all was, when compared to the major studios, a finely tuned assembly line machine (*Billy the Kid Returns* began filming July 29, ended August 8, then was released September 4, 1938). Republic crews normally shot well over 30 scenes in a day, 10 times what bigger studios would do. Also *Under Western Stars* may have taken longer than normal in post-production because Roy Rogers had to be brought up to speed, though one could argue he hit the ground at a gallop.

Whether or not Gene Autry had gone on strike, Dick Weston would still have been given a shot as a singing cowboy. Republic was always grooming its stable of stars; Monte

Hale and Rex Allen came along later. Gene Autry's strike probably just advanced Weston sooner. When one considers how quickly Slye/Weston rose through the ranks (a brief four years between the founding of the Sons of the Pioneers and a leading movie role), his stardom seemed preordained (after arriving in Hollywood, the Golden Cloud was elevated to Trigger in less than one year).

The publicity department at Republic Pictures came up with a fictional biography for the newly christened Roy Rogers. He "was a true-blue son of the West, born in Cody, Wyoming, and raised on a sprawling cattle ranch." He was even supposed to have labored as a ranch hand in New Mexico for a while "before finally making his way to the bright lights of Hollywood."[6] With a suitable name and image, all the new singing cowboy needed was the right horse.

The Equine Audition

Just as movie studios had casting directors for actors, they had casting directors for animals. Filmmakers depended on them to find photogenic animals with even temperaments, able to perform on noisy movie sets. Bill Jones was head livestock man at Republic and had also worked at Hudkins Stables.[7] When Roy Rogers began to work on *Under Western Stars*, all the stables that leased livestock to the studios were allegedly asked to send cast horses. According to Rogers, about a half-dozen mounts were brought in for auditions. He rode a couple down the street and back. The third horse he tried was the Golden Cloud, and he never looked at the rest. Unfortunately the Hudkins wrangler who was handling stock that fateful day remains unknown. When he handed Golden Cloud's reins to Roy Rogers, he made one of the most important introductions in western film history.

One assumes a copy of the Golden Cloud's registration papers were transferred when Clyde Hudkins moved him to Hollywood from San Diego. According to Robert Phillips, Hudkins' wranglers were referring to the horse as Pistol when Rogers first met him. The word pistol is a slang term for "a remarkable person." Cowboy/wrangler types frequently used colloquial nomenclature when it suited an individual, two- or four-legged.

In a 1976 interview, Rogers recalled, "I knew I wanted a palomino to start with. The third horse they showed me was Trigger. I hadn't liked the first two, but when I took Ol' Trigger for a test ride, I told 'em he was the one I wanted. I didn't even look at any of the others."[8] Circa 1995 Rogers said the same thing on the *Horseworld* television show (in a nine-minute segment on Trigger) to host Larry Mahan. A champion rodeo rider, Mahan asked Rogers about first acquiring Trigger, and the King of the Cowboys answered, "I'll never forget the day they called me up to go over to pick out a horse. They had seven or eight of them there and I believe Trigger was the third one I got on. I never looked at the rest of them." After only a single test ride Rogers was quoted as saying, "it was like putting' on pants."[9]

The Roy Rogers Press Book—Ground Zero

The first known indoor and outdoor publicity photos of the short-lived Dick Weston as Roy Rogers seem to have been all taken at the same time, probably just as cameras

The Roy Rogers Press Book, an ultra-rare Republic Pictures promotional publication introducing "Roy Rogers, Republic's New Singing Western Star," 1938. Two of six panels were displayed at the Roy Rogers-Dale Evans Museum in Victorville. Here they are reassembled by Connecticut, graphic designer Jack Tom (with Roy Dillow photographs) using a low-quality online image file of the actual brochure as reference.

started rolling for *Under Western Stars*. Fourteen were featured in a press book with the headline "Roy Rogers Republic's New Singing Western Star" and the subtitle, "First Release Ready About April 15th–'*Under Western Stars*.'" It's important to note this promotional device was primarily aimed at the press, movie distributors, and theater owners. For the sake of brevity I will hereafter refer to it as *The Roy Rogers Press Book*. This writer was stopped in his tracks when he first saw it at the Roy Rogers-Dale Evans Museum in Victorville in 1998. It was printed double-sided and with six pages, and only two pages were displayed under glass (the staff did not accommodate my request for a complete hands-on inspection). Another copy surfaced online years later but was reproduced so small the photos were hard to make out, its quality too poor to reproduce here, but it has been a valuable resource. Of the 14 photos, super-collector Roy Dillow was able to come up with 10 from other sources.

Photos from *The Roy Rogers Press Book* have long been available separately in print and recently online, though not usually identified as to their source, chronology, or significance. Most fans (even most genre writers and historians) see them now as only a very young Roy Rogers, and don't acknowledge them as the very first shots of a soon-to-be iconic persona. Print, radio and movies drove the culture at the time; television, the Web, and cable did not exist. This press book is ground zero for Roy Rogers. The photos are distinguished not only by Rogers' youthful appearance but by the outfit he was wearing (neutral pants and shirt with trim around the yoke and pockets, he wore a similar shirt in a scene in *Under Western Stars*); his scarf under the collar (except for a

Before Trigger was selected by the future King of the Cowboys, three horses were featured in *The Roy Rogers Press Book*: a solid-colored palomino, a white horse, and a dark bay with a white star. The author created the montage with photographs from the Roy Dillow collection. Note the solid palomino did not have markings that would qualify as a blaze, certainly not one as pronounced as Trigger's. Super-collector Dillow had the foresight to win the shot of Rogers on the dark bay, via eBay, for a cool $200.

short fox hunting sequence in *Under Western Stars* Rogers rarely wore a scarf under his collar on screen); and, most importantly, because in one photo he was on a dark bay with a white star. Of the 14 press book photos, nine featured three different horses and none were the Golden Cloud. As well as the dark bay, a white horse was featured five times and a solid palomino without a blaze appeared in three photos. The other four panels, not on display, included one page of introductory public relations. Though a number of photos were shot, not all were used in the press book, including some with Rogers and Golden Cloud/Pistol, who was still wearing a Hudkins rig.

A few of the photos from *The Roy Rogers Press Book* were used again in the *Under Western Stars* press book (which was produced a little later) and miscellaneous promotional material as the movie was released. The *Under Western Stars* press book noted that Roy Rogers was "born on a ranch near Cody, Wyoming, Roy learned how to ride a horse about the same time he learned to walk." In a short piece on Trigger titled "'Trigger' New Western Film Thoroughbred" he was described as "light tan color, of Arabian descent, and as swift as the wind whistling through the trees and as gallant as the top blue-blood." One may assume *The Roy Rogers Press Book* had previously made the same claims.

Roy Rogers' claim that Hudkins Stables brought a string of horses to the studio, Golden Cloud/Pistol being the third horse he tried, may well be true but up to a point.

These are among the earliest known shots of Roy Rogers with the Golden Cloud/Pistol. Note Rogers' shirt with the tie under the collar and the thin bridle. The tack was a Hudkins Bros. rig used in their first feature together, *Under Western Stars* (the bridle was not). Rogers did not use the same clothing in the film. The photograph on the bottom left was used a number of times in *Under Western Stars* lobby cards. Note a variation of the pose in a movie poster (Roy Dillow collection).

The other mounts in that particular string can never be identified absolutely; still, the aforementioned dark bay, the white horse, and the solid palomino probably are the first horses Rogers tested. Rogers took photos with each, which also could have served as screen tests. Given Rogers' capacity to bend the truth, Republic's frugal ways, and *The Roy Rogers Press Book* photos themselves, the following scenario is just as feasible as anything fans have been led to believe. Republic had neither the time nor necessity to allow Rogers to audition horses from other stables. They had a long working relationship with Hudkins Bros. and could rely on them to suggest a string of qualified mounts: horses with screen presence, animals that knew their way around a movie set, and perhaps had a trick or two in their repertoire. *The Roy Rogers Press Book* was rushed into production. Photos with the dark bay, the white horse, and the solid palomino were published before Golden Cloud/Pistol was finally chosen and first featured in *Under Western Stars* press book, movie posters, lobby cards, and on screen.

One of the four press book photos of Roy Rogers on the white horse is of special interest because of how it was eventually used. First seen out of context, it seems to be merely an early image of Roy Rogers on a horse assumed to be Trigger in what would become their signature rearing pose. Originally thought to be high-contrast, the photo was incorrectly assumed to be washed out to the point the palomino looked white. The horse was not the original Trigger, and given Rogers' youth, it could not have been any

The newly renamed Roy Rogers astride a white horse in an early promotional photograph. Roy Rogers on the same mount but this time tinted to look palomino by Republic Pictures for the 1938 *Under Western Stars* debut movie poster (Roy Dillow collection).

Gabby Hayes, left, Dale Evans and Roy Rogers in the finale of fan favorite *Lights of Old Santa Fe*, released by Republic Pictures in 1944. Evans is riding Sunset Carson's horse, Cactus (Roy Dillow collection).

of Trigger's doubles (the timeline was too soon for Little Trigger). On closer inspection, the horse was indeed the same white horse that was later tinted to look palomino for use on the *Under Western Stars* poster!

Trigger expert Rocky Roe claims the white horse, Silver Chief, may have been the mount Republic Pictures used for the Bob Livingston serial, *The Lone Ranger Rides Again* (1939). Hudkins Stables acquired the animal from Buck Jones when it was originally called Silver B. Sunset Carson also used the steed in his movies where it was rechristened Cactus. Carson did not own the horse; after he left Republic he never saw the animal again (according to Roe who heard Carson speaking at a cowboy fest in Knoxville). Dale Evans rode Silver B at the end of *The Lights of Old Santa Fe* and in *Home in Oklahoma* (1946). Roe's claims are plausible because Republic provided its contract players with the same stock.

Of special note regarding Roy Rogers and the white horse was how he was already using the rearing pose, not something a novice rider would do. Rogers had been riding from a young age and continued to learn from Republic's top professionals (Yakima Canutt trained Gene Autry when he first became a movie star). There are also photos of Rogers rearing on Trigger during the production of *Under Western Stars*. He was obviously advanced as a rider and a natural on a horse.

The Roy Rogers Press Book images are of historical significance because they are among the first visual representations of a beloved cowboy icon and are rare before Trigger images. It was a magical few days indeed when 27-year-old aspiring singer/actor Dick Weston and four-year-old-cast-rental horse Golden Cloud/Pistol became Roy Rogers and Trigger. Len Slye/Dick Weston may have first become Roy Rogers in *The Roy Rogers Press Book*; but the future King of the Cowboys had not been finally paired with Trigger and was not quite complete without him.

The First Ride

How Roy Rogers came by Golden Cloud/Pistol is a story fans have heard hundreds of times, often from Rogers as the source. Only the pairing of Rex Allen with his stallion Koko had any resonance mostly because of the false rumor that Koko was originally intended for Dale Evans.

Did Roy Rogers alone pick the Golden Cloud/Pistol from a string of horses provided by Hudkins Stables? Given his capacity to bend the truth, one has to wonder. It's not out of the question to consider just how much freedom a studio like Republic would allow. Trainer Glenn Randall was not on the scene yet and picking out a horse is tricky business. Did a Republic or a Hudkins wrangler advise Rogers? Was Rogers accomplished enough as a horseman by then to make an informed choice? As the Golden Cloud/Pistol had screen experience before Rogers met him, did someone in the know recommend him? Rogers was not merely selecting a horse to ride on a Sunday outing. A cast horse had to be trained and behave accordingly given the precise work required on movie sets where time was money.

We want to believe that Roy Rogers, like any professional cowboy, was capable of judging good horseflesh. In point of fact, Rogers wasn't a professional cowboy yet though he had some riding chops. Remember Republic public relations then would have us believe Rogers was raised around horses on a Wyoming ranch. While he claimed he rode from an early age and had a pony named Babe, he probably spent more time with a guitar than on a horse. The same could be said of Gene Autry. Their singing got them into show business not their horsemanship. From what is known, Rogers didn't own a horse when he started filming *Under Western Stars*; he hadn't owned one for a long while though he'd been riding rented horses on movie sets.

At this point in Republic history a search for a movie horse was routine—not quite like David O. Selznick looking for a Scarlett O'Hara, though for some of us just as impactful. Just as Glenn Randall's job on some movie sets was to match actors to appropriate horses, Republic's wranglers probably guided Roy Rogers in his selection. At the very least he was provided with a preselected group of accomplished mounts to audition. It's obvious the dark bay, the white horse, and the solid palomino were chosen for their looks, temperament, training, and experience. It's not exactly the same story Rogers told time and again; it doesn't spin as well as him making the selection alone and unassisted. We're never going to know for sure, though in the end Roy Rogers most likely made the final choice.

The initial meeting between the cowboy and the horse was tantamount to when Stan Laurel met Oliver Hardy or when John Lennon met Paul McCartney. I've always loved the Roy Rogers/Golden Cloud/Pistol story and want to believe it, even to the point

The earliest known photograph of Roy Rogers riding Golden Cloud/Pistol. As these publicity shots were taken as *Under Western Stars* went into production, the stallion may have not yet been renamed Trigger. The legend is that Smiley Burnette suggested the name while on location. Judging by the look on Rogers' face, meeting the palomino for the first time was love at first sight (Roy Dillow collection).

of imagining how it played out. It's not hard to do and I suspect I'm not the only fan so inclined.[10]

The newly named Roy Rogers was on the Republic Pictures lot early that fateful day. He had so much on his mind after he'd been elevated to the star status of a singing cowboy. His first leading role was ahead and there was no end of things to do, one of the first being to choose a great equine screen partner. He'd been given the chance of a lifetime by Republic and he wasn't going to blow it. He knew a great horse was critical to his screen persona, now all he needed was for Lady Luck to be on his side.

The Hudkins Stables truck and trailer arrived on the Republic Pictures lot in a timely fashion and parked next to the stables. Rogers was alerted and greeted the driver and wranglers as he approached. "I'm Roy Rogers (he was still getting used to the name) and I'm told you have some horses for me to audition."

"Yes sir," the driver replied, "we've got a small string consisting of our best stock, first-rate cast horses."

"Great! Lets see what you've got!" Rogers answered enthusiastically.

"I need to find a good horse. I've got some promotional pictures lined up and we're due on the set before you know it. I'd also like to spend whatever time I can manage getting to know a new mount before we start production."

"That's not going to be a problem. Once you pick a horse we can work out the scheduling details," the wrangler replied.

As the Hudkins wranglers unloaded and tacked horses, the young screen hopeful mounted each in turn. He'd been riding off and on most of his life, even in supporting roles on camera. He wasn't at the top of his game yet but he had the raw talent and athleticism to be good, even great, given time.

Rogers rode the first couple of equine prospects up and down the Republic lot pretty much uneventfully. They were nice, well schooled but nothing special.

A third horse was unloaded. Rogers froze spellbound in his tracks. As the animal was being saddled, Rogers slowly circled inspecting the vision before his eyes, a tall striking fellow with thick silky mane and long silvery tail. His handsome head was adorned by a long white blaze. The horse was well built with great square conformation and one distinct white rear stocking. The horse looked at the cowboy with a kind brown eye. He was graceful, sleek, in a word: stunning. And, as if that wasn't enough, he was a golden palomino with a coat that shone like a new penny.

Rogers took a deep breath, blinked his eyes, his heart skipped a beat and he thought, "Man oh man, is he a beauty. Now if only he has the temperament and talent to match his looks!"

"He's really a looker," Rogers commented aloud.

"You bet," the wrangler agreed. "He's one of our best. He's already been used around town and even been featured on the big screen. He's a stud, well behaved, and the camera loves him."

"How is he under saddle?" Rogers inquired hopefully.

"Judge for yourself, I doubt you'll be disappointed," came the reply.

Rogers checked the cinch, made sure the tack was on correctly, gave a nod to the wrangler, took the reins and carefully placed his boot in the stirrup. He mounted then sat calmly, the palomino stood waiting for a cue to move. That was a good sign. With a slight squeeze of his legs, Rogers started the stallion in a slow walk down the street.

The Republic lot was busy that morning, lots of commotion, noisy as one would expect. None of that seemed to bother his horse. Rogers cued the stud into a trot. A few of the Republic crew and some extras couldn't help but notice the pair. They were a great match. That horse could make anybody look good but Rogers didn't need any help. He was young, handsome and had presence to match.

Rogers put the horse in a lope. He turned him left and turned him right; they moved in a few circles. The palomino was flawless. He was smooth as silk and very sensitive to cues. It didn't take Rogers time or effort to sync up with the palomino; they were one.

After a few minutes that seemed like seconds the pair headed back towards the Hudkins truck.

"Well, what do you think?" the wrangler asked, with the grin of a man who already knew the answer.

"He's the one!" Rogers replied. "He's like a dream and I bet he's fast too. I don't need to see the others. From what I can tell, this palomino's got it all—looks, brains, solid as a rock. And what moves! He can turn on a dime and give you nine cents change!"

"What's his name?" Rogers inquired.

"He came to us registered as the Golden Cloud but we call him Pistol."

"That's fitting," Rogers mused, "but I'm sure we can come up with something even better."

Rogers handed the reins over to the wrangler, patted the big stallion lightly on the neck and whispered, "I've got a good feeling about you, my handsome friend. If I've got any chance of being a singing cowboy star, you're the one I'm going to do it with. I'll be seeing you again and I mean soon."

Rogers thanked the wranglers and extended his hand. They responded in kind and one remarked, "A horse like this doesn't come along that often. You made the right choice here today, cowboy."

Roy Rogers let out a sigh of relief; he knew he'd literally struck gold. He looked skyward and winked in gratitude as if to good old Lady Luck herself.

Under Western Stars began filming in Lone Pine, Independence and the Republic Pictures backlot in January of 1938.[11] During a 1983 appearance on *The David Letterman Show* Roy Rogers claimed Trigger had been used in the fall of 1937 in *The Adventures of Robin Hood*. Roy Rogers and Trigger would in time eventually get the titles "King of the Cowboys" and "the Smartest Horse in the Movies" but they had to earn them first.

5

Trigger's Trail

*"Truth is like the sun. You can shut it out for a time,
but it's not going to go away."*—Elvis Presley

Bill of Sale, Purchase Timeline and Contracts

Under Western Stars, the first B-western to premiere on Broadway,[1] was a hit. Even the *New York Times* reviewed the film, which it never did for B-westerns. The movie and Roy Rogers both received glowing reviews all around. *The Hollywood Reporter* referred to Republic's new singing cowboy as "a studio-manufactured star (who) lived up to expectations and advance notices."

Though Trigger was not mentioned in early reviews, according to William Witney, audiences would ask for him everywhere Rogers toured. The beautiful palomino had quickly become important to Roy Rogers's image—and Rogers had his heart set on him. He was not in a position to take the palomino on personal appearances because he didn't own him. It was obvious he had to make some kind of commitment to owning the horse or a talented look-alike in his place.

The public relations timeline in which Roy Rogers purchased the Golden Cloud/Trigger is confusing and contradictory. Sources differ, and sorting through everything between 1937 to 1943 requires effort. There are professional factors to consider regarding not only timing but also motives, some not so obvious, some a little controversial.

REPUBLIC PICTURES

The official studio version from Republic Pictures was that Rogers bought Trigger after he rode him in *Under Western Stars* in 1938. Director William Witney claimed that Rogers asked Clyde Hudkins directly if he would sell Trigger to him. Hudkins, seeing potential in Rogers and Trigger, made a counteroffer. Hudkins would take care of the horse until Rogers was in a position where he could pay him a little at a time. Numerous published articles even stated that Rogers used a guitar as part of the down payment.

ROY ROGERS AND FAMILY

The Roy Rogers camp always maintained Trigger was purchased with time payments right after he started using him. One of the earliest biographies on Roy Rogers and Dale

The Golden Cloud, aka Pistol, aka the Old Man, aka Trigger, rearing at liberty. Roy Rogers was hand-painted out, note the rope disappearing behind the mane (Rocky Roe collection).

Smiley Burnette, aka Frog Millhouse, on Ring-Eyed Nellie and Roy Rogers in *Under Western Stars* (1938). Burnette was said to have suggested the name "Trigger" after seeing the palomino run (Roy Dillow collection).

Evans, *The Answer Is God*, gives 1940 as the year Trigger was purchased.[2] Another popular story is that Rogers bought Trigger right after he came back from the first tour for *Under Western Stars*. In *Liberty* magazine (December 1946) Rogers was quoted as saying he bought Trigger in 1937 on the installment plan. "About the second or third picture, I went to Hudkins Stables and bought him from them." The standard line was that Rogers and Hudkins apparently worked out some kind of deal, part of which was the exclusive use of Hudkins stock in all his films. This would serve Rogers well in future negotiations with Republic bosses who were apparently unaware of the transaction.

Writer Sam Henderson stated, "Roy raised Trigger from a colt, and scrimped and saved to buy him, feed him and train him." In his autobiography *Happy Trails*, Rogers claimed, "We rented my palomino from Hudkins, one of the stables Republic did considerable business with. So I drove out there one day and, after quite a bit of horse trading, bought him for twenty-five hundred dollars."

In her autobiography *Cowboy Princess*, Cheryl Rogers-Barnett claimed her father bought Trigger in 1938 for two thousand dollars on time payments after their third film together: "Dad and Ace Hudkins had struck up a deal for Dad to make payments while Ace continued to rent Trigger to Republic—but he wouldn't let them put another cowboy on him—until the last payment had been made."

Cheryl Rogers-Barnett later offered a quote from her dad, printed in the *HappyTrails* book by Michael Stern, (Simon & Schuster, 1994, page 103). "During the three months after … *Under Western Stars* was released … I realized that I couldn't take him (Trigger) out a personal appearance tour … it also meant that they could lease him to another cowboy actor…. When I returned from the tour I went to see Clyde Hudkins. I found him in the barn. Sell the palomino to me,' I said, 'and if I hit this jackpot, I'll make sure Hudkins horses are on the set.' Mr. Hudkins considered my proposition … then he named his price: $2,500. Remember I was making seventy-five dollars a week…. I took a deep breath and held out my hand to shake…. I paid him off on time, just like you would a bedroom set."

BILL OF SALE

Roy Rogers' son Dusty eventually made Trigger's actual bill of sale available to Joel "Dutch" Dortch, executive director of the Happy Trails Children's Foundation, who in turn made it public.[3] It revealed that Rogers purchased Trigger from the Hudkins Brothers for $2,500. Trigger's bill of sale is dated September 18, 1943, and reads, "Sold to Roy Rogers, one palomino stallion named "Trigger" for the sum of Twenty-five Hundred Dollars. ($2500.00) Five Hundred Dollars has been paid down and the balance, $2000.00 to be paid on Roy Rogers return from New York."

Ray White referenced the bill of sale and 1943 purchase date for Trigger in the June 2001 issue of *Western Horseman* magazine in an article titled "B-western Horses." Eventually the second bill of sale surfaced for the $2000 balance dated four months later. Two official paper documents state Trigger was purchased outright in 1943 over two payments. Neither bill of sale says who transacted the deal. It is not known if they were between Roy Rogers and Ace Hudkins, or between Hudkins Stables and Glenn Randall acting on Rogers' behalf.

According to *DollarTimes*, a web site that calculates relative worth of money in the past versus the present, the $2,500 Trigger was valued at in 1938 translates to $43,617 in 2019. Roy Rogers was making $75 a week at the time, which translates to $1,309 in 2019. By 1939 Gene Autry's more established Champion was reportedly worth $25,000 (*Gene Autry Westerns* by Boyd Magers, p. 434), or $449,000 in 2019.

HANDSHAKES, INFLUENCE AND CONTROL

Cheryl Rogers-Barnett believes her father bought Trigger on a handshake, just as he sealed an agreement with his agent Art Rush (they never had a formal contract). Back then, that was a gentleman's way of doing things, your word was your bond. She also said that "Dad always said that every time he was to get a contractual raise, the Old Man (Mr. Yates) would find some way of not honoring the contract. As to how Dad would get money to pay for Trigger, he did rodeos, he was on radio, he was still taking gigs with the Sons of the Pioneers and making personal appearances. He did everything he could to make money. He also had a western store in Studio City in 1940 called Roy Rogers' Ranger Post."

As far as the two existing bills of sale, September 1943 and December 1943, Rogers-Barnett believes "they were simply done to memorialize the purchase. It may well have taken Dad that long to make the final payment but according to what I read and what

HUDKINS STABLES

MOTION PICTURE EQUIPMENT
3744 Barham Blvd.
Hollywood, Calif.
Phone HOllywood 9078

DATE Sept. 18, 1943
INVOICE NO.
ORDER NO.
PICTURE NO.

TERMS: NET CASH, NO DISCOUNT monthly
account payable on or before 10th of following month

Sold to Roy Rogers, one palomino stallion

named "Trigger" for the sum of Twenty-five Hundred

Dollars. ($2500.00) Five Hundred Dollars has been

paid down and the balance, $2000.00 to be paid on

Roy Rogers return from New York.

HUDKINS STABLES

MOTION PICTURE EQUIPMENT
3744 Barham Blvd.
Hollywood, Calif.
Phone HOllywood 9078

DATE Dec. 6, 1943
INVOICE NO.
ORDER NO.
PICTURE NO.

TERMS: NET CASH, NO DISCOUNT monthly
account payable on or before 10th of following month

Received of Roy Rogers Two Thousand Dollars, ($2000.00.)

Payment in full for one palomino stallion named "Trigger".

Art Hudkins
(By) Helen Myers

Trigger bills of sale from Hudkins Stables, both dated 1943. Top: $500 down payment (courtesy Joel Dutch Dortch). Bottom: $2000 balance paid in full.

Dad always said, he entered into negotiations as soon as he returned from Lone Pine in 1938."

Although Roy Rogers had two bills of sale in his possession with purchase dates in 1943, this writer has not come across one print or video interview where Roy Rogers said he bought Trigger that year. There's a good chance Rogers was aware of Trigger's solo performances in other movies between 1938 and 1943 but did not acknowledge them because it would have meant explaining why other movie studios had access to a horse he was thought to own.

Though Cheryl Rogers-Barnett's take on Trigger's purchase timeline comes directly from what her father told her, the scenario asks us to believe Roy Rogers had influence with studio boss Herb Yates when it came to production costs. Again, remember Roy Rogers was a 27-year-old newcomer undergoing a studio system makeover and Yates was 58-year-old seasoned studio head used to giving orders. Who had influence over whom? Republic Pictures was the boss and a penny-pinching one at that. Roy Rogers was a hired hand. Since their relationship ended in a lawsuit, one may assume Rogers' influence did not carry weight with studio executives. According to Cheryl Rogers-Barnett, the only Republic players immune to Yates' threats were Gene Autry and John Wayne. Herb Yates wasn't about to involve himself with new singing cowboy and risk exposing himself and the studio again to the same problems he had with Autry.

The Roy Rogers–Hudkins handshake locked in a deal and granted Rogers first option to buy Trigger. That's all it did. Was there an understanding between both parties that Trigger could be rented but not sold to anyone else? It seems it was not stipulated that Trigger could not be used elsewhere. Either that or the Hudkins brothers misled Rogers. At first Cheryl Rogers-Barnett honestly thought no other cowboy used Trigger while her father was buying him.

For the sake of argument, let's say Roy Rogers had been paying on Trigger from 1938 on, that would have come to about $7 and change a month for five years, $100 per year. That would have given him the down payment of $500 by 1943. It's possible but it still didn't give him control over a $2500 palomino that he only owned a fifth of. Are we to believe Hudkins provided Trigger room and board because Rogers was paying $100 a year to keep him on retainer? Hudkins had a business to run; they expected their stock to earn their keep. There is ample evidence they still hired Trigger out—he was too big an asset as a cast horse.

No documented evidence has ever surfaced regarding any arrangements between Hudkins and Republic or Rogers for Trigger's services between the time Rogers first started riding him and the time he actually bought him.

It was never written into Roy Rogers' contracts with Republic that only horses from Hudkins stables were to be used in his films, those on set were there because they represented the best deal for the studio. Juxtapose what Roy Rogers said versus what Republic Pictures did. He may have liked the Hudkins brothers but he surely cared more about the Sons of the Pioneers and Gabby Hayes. He'd have done as much or more for them, so why were they eventually let go? To save money Republic replaced the six Pioneers by the four Riders of the Purple Sage, who were later replaced by generic singers. Gabby Hayes, arguably the best sidekick in the genre, was replaced by lesser personalities including the likes of Pinky Lee.

SALARY AND CONTRACTS

When Roy Rogers was considering buying Trigger, he wasn't being paid a lot by Republic Pictures and was under a term players contract from October 13, 1937, through December 3, 1948.[4] His initial weekly salary of $75.00, which amounted to $3,600 a year (by 1940 it had been doubled to $150 or $7,200 a year), was certainly not enough to buy, transport, outfit and maintain a horse. Of course the record of Trigger's purchase in 1943 dispels the myth that Roy Rogers bought him when he was making only $75 a week in 1938. However, by 1943 Rogers was making good money with personal appearances, radio and rodeos.[5] One may assume payments on Trigger could have cost him close to half a year's earnings (and that doesn't cover costs for care and a trainer).

Although his first movies were successful, the young Roy Rogers may not have been sure he could sustain a career as a singing cowboy. A movie cowboy's fortune back then could change at the drop of a Stetson, and if Rogers felt he was constantly just shy of having to rejoin the Sons of the Pioneers, it was not without reason. After an eight-year run, even the popular Hopalong Cassidy films had begun to wane. Some of the older cowboy stars were taking lesser roles as heavies and supporting characters. Some had moved on to unrelated businesses. Roy Rogers would likely have noticed all that going on around him and undoubtedly wondered if he really should buy an expensive horse. Roy Rogers wasn't the only screen cowboy who rode a rented horse; Sunset Carson and Clayton Moore

Roy Rogers' long-time agent Art Rush goes over a contract for the original Trigger to sign. In reality the horse was not under any formal arrangement with Republic Pictures (Roy Dillow collection).

also used horses they did not own. Some of their peers didn't need a horse outside of a movie set; they did not want the extra expense; and they weren't particularly horse-oriented to begin with.

The purchase date of 1943 on the bill of sale is remarkable because it means Roy Rogers was riding a horse he did not own for five full years after appearing with Trigger in *Under Western Stars*! Trigger also appeared in over a half-dozen other films that we know in that same period (more on that in Chapter 8, "Golden Stallion, Silver Screen"). Obviously Rogers did not have exclusive use of the palomino; Hudkins Stables was controlling where and when Trigger worked. It's safe to assume that Rogers was rightfully concerned Trigger was up for grabs to anyone who could afford to rent him. It's understandable how in later biographies and interviews, the publicity-conscious Rogers avoided making it known that he was ever riding someone else's horse. This was not how Rogers or his family wanted the public to picture the relationship between himself and Trigger.

While no record of any arrangement has come to light, one could reasonably accept that Roy Rogers and Hudkins reached an oral agreement—as often described by the singing cowboy—which was then sealed with a handshake. We kids did our part too, by accepting every palomino Rogers rode as "Trigger." At the time, there seemed to be no pressing need for Rogers to own the original Trigger.

Trigger was never under contract with Republic, in spite of early reports to the contrary. Doreen M. Norton, in her 1949 book *The Palomino Horse*, wrote, "Trigger's contract stipulates that he be given equal billing with Roy Rogers, and that in each picture he have at least three close-ups." Rogers is quoted in Elise Miller Davis' 1955 biography *The Answer Is God*: "Trigger shares top billing with me. And he has a contract that calls for three close-ups and a direct part in motivating the plot in each picture. He gets his own fan mail and his own salary." Nevertheless, when author David Rothel asked Rogers in the 1980s whether Trigger's contract called for three close-ups in each film, equal billing, and scripts showing him helping to motivate the story, Rogers replied that was nonsense, some publicity guy's daydream. Trigger did not get a salary, not even scale. He was part of a package deal with Rogers.

Why didn't anyone else buy Trigger? It doesn't seem to have occurred to Herb Yates, president of Republic Pictures. Fans just assumed Rogers owned the horse. Perhaps there were offers made to Hudkins but turned down because of the agreement with Rogers? If he didn't have the resources to buy the palomino, there were many cowboy stars who did. Rogers' regular use of Trigger during his filming period may have limited the palomino's availability for rental to other studios for big chunks of the year, to the point where there was no chance another western movie star would use the horse enough to become established with him in the public's mind.

After Dick Weston became Roy Rogers at Republic and the Golden Cloud became Trigger, Rogers kept the rights to his new name and likeness. What about Trigger? Look what happened to Smiley "Frog Milhouse" Burnette when he left Republic, his character name didn't go with him. He was simply Smiley Burnette when he became sidekick to Charles Starrett at Columbia.

As Trigger was a Republic character, it would seem Rogers owned the palomino's name and likeness outright, or how else how was he able to merchandise him later? Republic may have included Trigger's name and likeness when they allowed Rogers to keep his. If Yates had originally bought Trigger and therefore his name and likeness, Roy Rogers could well have been forced to create another horse character with a different name if he wanted its rights if he ever left Republic.

We now have the benefit of hindsight and know what a huge star Roy Rogers became, but back then he could only have hoped for the best. What he had was a dream, a plan, and lots of talent. He also had great timing and luck. He was sharp enough to take ownership of his image and his new name from shortsighted studio head Herb Yates. This would serve him well as Rogers would eventually make most of his income from personal appearances and merchandising. Still, he had to gamble on a business that was fickle at best—that alone was reason not to buy Trigger at first, though he surely wanted to.

REPUBLIC PICTURES AND WORLD WAR II

When considering the circumstances surrounding the timing of Rogers' purchase of Trigger, his contractual relationship with Republic must be taken into account. And, there was a war going on and it, too, played a part in creating the legend of Roy Rogers, the King of the Cowboys, and Trigger his golden palomino.

When he enlisted in the Air Force in 1942 Gene Autry was Republic's leading cowboy star. It was likely a blow to Republic, so much so that Autry claimed Herb Yates offered to call in some favors to keep him out of military service but Autry refused. Yates threatened to throw Republic Pictures' resources into building up Rogers, which he did. Rogers' career went into high gear. He soon became the number one box office western star.

It's been theorized that Republic Pictures initially used Roy Rogers to scare Gene Autry into signing a contract after he went on strike. An old press clipping from Bobby Copeland (no periodical or year noted) reads, "Republic Is Not Sign-

Ultra-rare shot of Roy Rogers, Little Trigger, and Flight Officer Gene Autry in uniform during a Republic celebration at the Hotel Astor Grand Ballroom in New York in 1943 (from a newspaper story titled "Trigger's in Town," no periodical noted). A specially built corral was constructed for the occasion.

ing Autry Successor-Siegel—Moe J. Siegel, president of Republic Productions, Inc., now in New York, said yesterday that reports published elsewhere that the company had signed Roy Rogers of radio as a 'successor' to Gene Autry, western star, were without foundation. Rogers had been taken on for a single pix, Siegel said, adding that Autry's series would be resumed when the star reported back to the studio. Autry and Republic are apart on terms."

With or without the Gene Autry versus Republic Pictures dispute, trying out a new unknown face was potentially risky for the studio. Had Roy Rogers bombed with only a one-picture deal, they wouldn't have any contract problems to worry about when letting him go. And if Rogers was just signed for one picture, it does not support his claim about paying on Trigger while *Under Western Stars* was in production or after its initial release. It more than likely he shook hands over Trigger's sale shortly after the movie was a success and there was a real possibility he might actually become successful.

Conversely, in all probability Republic was watching all the angles. The studio had indeed spent money turning Dick Weston into Roy Rogers and promoting his first film.

It's a good bet they wanted a little more for their investment than one movie. The fact that Roy Rogers and Trigger had a great deal of potential from the get-go was just an added luck for Republic, as the studio ended up with the two biggest singing cowboy stars of all time. Roy Rogers and Trigger went right into production on their next film.

Success certainly gave Roy Rogers the confidence to think that he might have a sustained future, and he knew darn well that Roy Rogers wasn't Roy Rogers without Trigger. In *My Weekly Reader*, a newsletter distributed to schoolchildren (April 1954), Rogers was quoted as saying, "Some children like Trigger more than they do me. They write letters to Trigger. I am glad that they like my horse."

Roy Rogers and Trigger were so closely linked that Rogers did not look right on a horse if it wasn't a palomino. On those rare occasions when a script put him on another mount—for example, when Trigger was stolen in *Under California Stars* (1948) and Rogers was forced to ride a chestnut—he looked out of place. Roy Rogers was not complete without Trigger—but it was a two-way street. Had Herb Yates or some other movie person purchased Trigger, the horse might have had only a short career as attractive equine transportation. Trigger needed Roy too.

During the war years in America, 1941 to 1945, Rogers' status jumped around. According to Robert W. Phillips' book *Roy Rogers*—at first he was enlisting, then he wasn't. In 1943 Rogers' draft status was 3-A (sole surviving son, married with children). As the war got hotter and manpower scarcer, men were reclassified, and Rogers received notice that he had been reclassified 1-A. Republic nervously began grooming Monte Hale to take his place.[6] By that time, Rogers had already purchased Trigger. In 1945 Rogers was reclassified 3-A because of a change in the deferment age. As it turned out, the war ended before Rogers' number ever came up.

Like John Wayne and so many others who never actually saw combat or active duty, Rogers did a tremendous amount for the war effort, giving freely of his time. According to publicity, he could flat outsell most entertainers when it came to war bond drives. Wrote Joel Dortch, "Roy was a patriot who loved his flag and country. He sold millions of dollars worth of War Bonds during World War II and made numerous USO tours of military bases with 'Trigger,' performing for the men and women in uniform. During one record setting tour of Texas bases, Roy and Trigger made 136 performances in just 20 days! Years later he made a tour of Vietnam to cheer up the troops fighting there."[7]

Being drafted would have certainly had an influence on Rogers' decision to buy Trigger. Would he have made a major purchase that would only be useful to him as a civilian if he were going off to war, perhaps never to return? It does not make sense that he would unless he was darn sure he was going to be around. It seems safe to assume Rogers did not believe he was going to serve in the military when he decided to buy Trigger. Why and how he got out of military service—whether it resulted from his having kids, or being 31 years old at the time, or some other reason—is not known. At any rate, Rogers wouldn't have spent $2,500 on a horse if he hadn't been fairly certain of his future as a movie cowboy.

Rogers' contract status was coming up for renewal in 1944. Perhaps he could have reasoned that buying Trigger in 1943 would give him better leverage in contract talks between his agent, Art Rush, and Yates. Rogers wanted his negotiating bases covered. If Rogers owned Trigger, Rush could offer Republic Pictures a package deal. If things didn't work out with Republic, he could take his package deal to other studios, and Yates would realize it. Since Rogers owned his name and image, he could shop around.[8] (Rogers always

Selections from "A Pattern for Pubic Service" brochure commemorating "The remarkable pictorial record of an entertainment tour through the State of Texas by a Great American Cowboy, Roy Rogers, whose sole purpose was to bring happiness to the men of the service and to those who serve on the home front." The morale-building wartime tour was sponsored by the Eighth Service Command of the Southwest, the State of Texas, Interstate Theatre Circuit, The Theatre Owners of Texas, and Republic Pictures. Photographs: Little Trigger featured and quoted on the back cover of the brochure, "I am proud to do my part in helping Roy Rogers entertain the men of the service and the boys and girls of America—our friends." • Texas Governor Coke R. Stevenson on Little Trigger in Austin. • Roy Rogers and Little Trigger entertain troops at Sheppard Field in Wichita Falls (Roy Dillow collection).

claimed that his dispute with Yates was not over his contract, but over money for secretaries needed to help deal with the tons of fan mail he was receiving. He had to hire help out of his own pocket to handle bags of letters arriving weekly.)

Roy Rogers claimed in his book *Happy Trails*, "Republic was planning to shoot a movie entitled *Front Page*, and Yates wanted me to play the part of a cocky newspaper reporter. It just didn't make sense to me to suddenly switch my image just after I had begun to establish myself in Westerns. So we got into a pretty heated argument which resulted in me telling him in no uncertain terms that I wasn't going to do the part. 'In that case,' he said, 'maybe we'll just have to put some other cowboy on Trigger and let him do your next movie.' 'You may get someone to do the next picture,' I told him, 'but he won't be riding Trigger. I bought him.' Once aware that the horse belonged to me, Mr. Yates signed Lloyd Nolan for the part in *Front Page*, and I went on about my business of being a singing cowboy."[9]

Fortunately Yates was slow to recognize how important Trigger was to Roy Rogers' career; otherwise he might have even pressured Hudkins to sell and then teamed the animal with anyone he wished. Rogers was honest about the reason for buying Trigger; he just altered the time frame to fit his public image. Rogers didn't want it known that he waited five years. It makes sense that he bought Trigger when he did. Underscoring all of this was the fact that Rogers may have gone for a few years at first not knowing for sure whether he would actually get to own Trigger in the end.

Republic contracts did not run only seven years, as has been often assumed. According to Jack Mathis in his 1992 book *Republic Confidential: The Players*, "Security—the primary personal inducement in these alliances—was fleeting for most players, with nearly 60% contracted for one year or less before they were terminated while only 26 endured for more than three years. Of the top 11 whose options were repeatedly renewed, Roy Rogers was extended for over 11 years.... Termination did not necessarily spell an end to Republic appearances, however, since many of the 146 either converted to multiple-picture arrangements as did Rogers and Gene Autry or returned in single films as free-lancers."[10]

On page three of *Republic Confidential: The Players*, there's a box showing Roy Rogers' term contract ran from October 13, 1937, to December 3, 1948. The exact terms and conditions obviously underwent changes during this period. Unless the Rogers family chooses to make that information public, we simply cannot know the details of those changes. It can be assumed that the purchase of Trigger would have been an advantage to Rogers' position with the studio, whenever it happened.

The impression from reading Roy Rogers' many biographies was that he made very few financial moves without consulting his managers, and the business aspects of purchasing Trigger would have had to be a driving force in the decision. As Dusty Rogers has pointed out, Trigger was not a pet. Rogers and his team surely realized that losing the association of "Roy Rogers and Trigger" was not a wise business decision. Trigger eventually started sharing top billing with Rogers in all the films, and it wouldn't have looked good to splash the horse's name all over the place and then have some other cowboy ride off on him.

Is it a mere coincidence that 1943, the year Roy Rogers bought Trigger outright, happened to be the same year Republic released *Hands Across the Border*, the first film with a plot line built around the palomino? Thirty-nine movies into his career, Rogers knew for sure his horse was a real star. After 1943 Trigger was probably not being boarded at Hudkins stables anymore.

ROY ROGERS' CHRISTMAS PRESENT TO HIMSELF

Rocky Roe theorized that Roy Rogers probably learned Trigger was used in 1943 for Columbia's movie *Silver City Raiders* and that knowledge impelled Rogers to buy the horse. While it will never be proven conclusively, consider the following. It's obvious Rogers loved Trigger, he knew how popular the horse was with fans, and he had even bought a silver saddle. Rogers' agreement with Hudkins Stables could have continued status quo; it wasn't absolutely imperative that he buy Trigger then. Republic Studios was renting the horse for him, and he'd already bought Little Trigger. However, the bottom line was that he had no control over how Trigger was used or who could ride him. Republic Pictures may not have cared as long as they could get the palomino for Rogers' movies. Trigger's conspicuous appearance with Russ Hayden in *Silver City Raiders* was the last straw.

"Trigger was still owned by the Hudkins Stables, which meant that I couldn't take him out on a personal appearance tour if I wanted to; it also meant they could lease him to another cowboy actor if they wanted to."[11]

If Rocky Roe is correct about Roy Rogers knowing that Columbia and Russell Hayden were using Trigger in *Silver City Raiders*, it's a safe bet that it was at this point in time when the King of the Cowboys made up his mind to buy the palomino outright. *Silver City Raiders* was released on November 4, 1943.[12] Rogers went to Hudkins and finalized the deal, and the last bill of sale was dated December 6. After that, nobody had control over Trigger but Rogers; the palomino cannot be found solo in a non–Roy Rogers film thereafter (he's with Rogers in *The Kid from Gower Gulch*). Circumstantial evidence and the bill of sale complement each other. Golden Cloud/Pistol, a Hudkins Bros. palomino-for-hire, ceased to exist and only Trigger, the celebrity horse, remained.

Tag Lines and Screen Billing

Trigger didn't get billing alongside Roy Rogers on movie posters and screens till the early 1940s. Posters from 1938 and 1939 did not bear his name. By the time Dale Evans starred in *The Cowboy and the Senorita* (1944), Trigger was well established, and his name appeared right below Rogers' and above everyone else's in the cast for the remainder of his career at Republic Pictures. What's more, Trigger's name was printed in the same size as Rogers' and larger than the names of the other cast members.

Trigger was not the first horse to be so honored. Roy Rogers was still one of the Sons of the Pioneers when the group appeared in the Dick Foran western *The California Mail* in 1936. Foran's beautiful palomino Smoke received star billing and the tag line "the wonder horse." Smoke was instrumental in driving the plot; he even killed two of the villains. Years later, when Rogers became a star and finally chose his own palomino, he may have thought back on Smoke.[13]

Many horses were dubbed "the wonder horse," beginning with the temperamental black Morgan stallion, Rex, who achieved stardom in the early days of film. Tom Mix was the first cowboy to use the tag line "the King of the Cowboys." Mix's horse, Tony, was called "the wonder horse"; so was Ken Maynard's horse, Tarzan. Autry's horse, Champion, was referred to as "the world's wonder horse." A popular comic book produced by Charleton in the 1950s and 1960s titled *Black Fury* used the "wonder horse" tag on its covers. Even Trigger was referred to as "the wonder horse" on toys occasionally, and one of the three versions of the National Safety Council statuettes awarded annually by Rogers read, "Official Roy Rogers' Trigger the Wonder Horse."

Roy Rogers and Republic started using the tag line "King of the Cowboys" shortly after the film of the same title. In the last scene Rogers was referred to as "King of Cowboys." In the film that followed, *Song of Texas*, Rogers was introduced at a rodeo as "the King of the Cowboys." The posters seem to be different; Rogers and Trigger may have gotten their tag lines on posters before they got them on screen. Trigger received no screen billing up through *Song of Texas*, released by Republic in June of 1943. However, in the film that followed in August of that same year, *Silver Spurs*, the line "Trigger, the Smartest Horse in the Movies" appeared right under Rogers' name. Perhaps after Republic, Rogers and Art Rush decided to use the "King of the Cowboys" title, giving Trigger his own tag line was a natural next step. In *Shine On Harvest Moon* (1938), Rogers referred to Trigger not only by name but described him as "the smartest horse I've ever had." Trigger even got billing along with Rogers in his cameo appearance in *Hit Parade of 1947*, the Republic musical extravaganza, along with stars Eddie Albert and Constance Moore. Trigger got fourth billing under Bob Hope, Jane Russell, and Roy Rogers in *Son of Paleface* (Paramount, 1952). During the film's opening credits, when Trigger's name appeared, the sound of a neighing horse was heard.

According to *Variety*, in order to make Rogers "king," a publicity campaign in 1944 placed 192 billboards across the country carrying 24-sheet movie posters featuring Rogers and Trigger and announcing that he was "King of the Cowboys" and Trigger was "the Smartest Horse in the Movies." The budget for the campaign has been estimated from $100,000 to $500,000. Nothing like this was ever done for another B-western cowboy, but Republic was determined to make Rogers number one. While there may have been resentment from the other cowboys after Rogers was christened "King of the Cowboys," he never referred to himself that way.

When *Time* magazine acknowledged Dale Evans' death in February of 2001, it was noted that despite her popularity, Trigger out-billed her in Roy Rogers' films. Said Bill Whitaker of the *Abilene Reporter News*, "When I interviewed her 15 years ago, she recalled with humor how Trigger—Rogers' famous horse—'used to get billing over me.' Eventually the Uvalde native graduated to the point she got billing over Gabby Hayes, Rogers' wizened, bearded, ever-cantankerous sidekick. But more often than not, Trigger still got more attention than she did, both in film credits and in the film itself. 'It never bothered me that much,' she said, 'but it bothered my agent.'"

Trigger's Name

Roy Rogers claimed that sidekick Smiley "Frog Milhouse" Burnette first suggested the name "Trigger" on the set of *Under Western Stars* after commenting, "As fast as that horse is, you ought to call him 'Trigger.' You know, quick-on-the-trigger?" This scenario was sort of appropriated in the film *My Pal Trigger* (1946). After Trigger's dam, Lady, gave birth to him, Rogers noted that the colt was delivered quickly, saying, "You're kinda quick on the trigger, son." Then he's asked, "What are you going to name him, Roy?" To which he replied, "I just did: 'Trigger.'"

In point of fact, the palomino Roy Rogers rode to fame underwent a couple of name changes before he was called "Trigger." He'd already been given the name Golden Cloud as a colt in San Diego and kept it for a time after Hudkins Stables bought him. According to legend, on the fateful day Rogers discovered him among the string of horses Hudkins Stables brought to audition, the wrangler in charge referred to the palomino as "Pistol."[14] William Witney claimed in his book *Trigger Remembered* that the horse was renamed "Trigger" the same day in 1937 that Leonard Slye's name was changed to "Roy Rogers."[15] Rogers, an avid hunter and outdoorsman, liked naming his animals after items related to firearms. Remember his dog Bullet?

It has been suggested that Ace Hudkins may have named "Trigger." E.J. Fleming wrote in an International Movie Database biography that Roy Rogers went to Hudkins Stables looking for a horse to use in his first starring vehicle *Under the Western Stars*. "After the lengthy ride Rogers and the horse had become instantly attached, and although Rogers was only making $75 a week at the time, he agreed to pay Ace $2,500 for the horse. It took him several years to pay for his new partner, whom Ace had named 'Trigger.'" It's unclear by this text whether Ace Hudkins made the claim himself or if Fleming made it for him. As Ace Hudkins was a colorful and even notorious character, his credibility suffers. Roy Rogers mostly recalled that a number of rental stables took horses to Republic Pictures for him to try out, not that he went to any place in particular looking for one.

Another source for the origin of Trigger's name comes from the book *King of the Bs* by Todd McCarthy and Charles Flynn. They quote Joe Kane, who directed many of Rogers' films: "While we were on location on that picture (*Under Western Stars*, 1938), they sent word up that he was going to be called Roy Rogers, and they wanted a name for his horse. We were getting ready to shoot a scene with a revolver, so I said, "Why don't we call him Trigger? They took the name, and he became Trigger."[16]

It is uncertain who really named Trigger. It's a bit of the Trigger legend that has been lost to time. B-western historian Bobby Copeland stated, "I'm going along with Joe Kane on the naming of Trigger. Roy always said, I 'believe' or I 'think' it was Smiley. Kane said, without reservation, that it was he [Kane] who named the horse."

Many prefer to believe it was indeed Smiley Burnette who named Trigger. Burnette was very creative and wrote hundreds of songs. With his gift for clever lyrics, he may well have come up with an appropriate name.

It will never be known whether Roy Rogers and the script writer for the movie *Come On, Rangers* (1938) were having fun and making a veiled reference to Trigger's first name, but in that film, when the King of the Cowboys is asked by sidekick Raymond Hatton how he's going to get out of jail, Rogers replies, "I'm going to ride out on a cloud."

William Witney in *Trigger Remembered* claimed that Trigger was nicknamed the "Old Man" on movie sets. Apparently this was for two reasons: to distinguish Trigger from his doubles and to denote the horse's age and wisdom. Wrote Witney, "It has been shown that Trigger was relied upon for years to get Roy and the producers out of tough filming situations. They would have the doubles on the scenes for certain stunts, but there were some stunts they just couldn't film, despite numerous attempts, because the horses were afraid. They could always depend on the 'Old Man,' as they called him, to bail them out, however. The horse had quite a reputation with everyone on the set for being fearless. How much of this is fact and how much publicity, we will probably never know, but it's a beautiful story." Here Witney is referring to a chase sequence in *Far Frontier* (1948), where Trigger narrowly avoids barrels thrown from a truck by bad guy Roy Barcroft. Dodging those barrels was something stunt horses on the set refused to do.

Yet another story of the origin for Trigger's name came from a Roy Rogers comic book special section titled "My Pal Trigger" (reprinted in *Roy Rogers Western Classics*, no. 3; AC Collector Classics, 1990). "The day I found Trigger was just about the luckiest day of my life. He was only a romping colt then, but, today, he is one of the greatest trick horses in the world. I started right away to train him, and he learned so many tricks so fast that I named him Trigger, because he could think 'quick on the trigger.'"

Finally, we know Roy Cloud registered the palomino in 1937 with the Palomino Horse Association as Golden Cloud. We also know that Roy Rogers bought him in two payments in 1943 and both bills of sale refers to him as "one palomino stallion named Trigger." The PHA had no such record for Rogers officially changing Golden Cloud's name to Trigger in their archives, neither did the PHBA.

According to Cheryl Rogers-Barnett her father didn't change Trigger's name "officially" that she could recall. (Roy Rogers didn't change his own name officially till 1942, four years after *Under Western Stars*.) Subsequently, Golden Cloud first became Trigger officially on his bills of sale.

Trigger's Offspring

Rogers referred to "Trigger" as a stallion and that's the image fans wanted to believe. Rogers also always described "Trigger" as well mannered and gentle in spite of being one. On a few occasions, he claimed that he had a number of his children on "Trigger" all at the same time. "Trigger has a different personality," he said. "He was a stallion, but you'd never know it, he was so gentle and kind. And he had a great rein on him as a cow pony. I've had several of my kids on him at one time, from his ears back to his tail and would just … aw, he was a fabulous horse."[17]

There are many photos of Rogers and "Trigger" in their signature rearing pose where the horse looks gelded. However, in some pictures the horse is complete. When he looked gelded, the photos were doctored.[18]

As to any offspring of the "real" Trigger, the most famous horse in the world, it's very doubtful whether Rogers would have allowed anyone but himself to have kept the foal. Perhaps he wanted to breed Trigger to maintain his bloodline but didn't for fear it would change the palomino's disposition; in that case, he surely wouldn't have bred Trigger for someone else. Promoter that he was, he would have made the biggest deal in the world had Trigger really sired a foal. Fans would have known about it.

In *My Pal Trigger*, Trigger sired two identical colts at the end of the film.[19] In the *Golden Stallion*, he sired Trigger Jr. These are fictional scenarios, of course, but children, understandably, wanted to believe them. The Rogers publicity machine got carried away on occasion with regard to Buttermilk's gender. It was once reported that the gelding was a mare and gave birth to one of Trigger's offsprings.

A multitude of conflicting stories about Trigger's offspring have appeared in print through the years. Rogers himself related many stories in radio interviews and television guest appearances. A mythical Trigger foal appeared in advertising from time to time, sometimes in contests under such headlines as "name the son of Trigger." In some

Roy Rogers and a "Win a Pony" palomino, circa 1954. A number of contests were offered with mini-Triggers as top prizes. According to Cheryl Rogers-Barnett, her dad did not own the ponies; contest sponsors supplied them.

instances, actual winners were identified or alluded to as having received an offspring or descendant of Trigger. Quaker Oats sponsored a "Name the Son of Trigger" contest; first prize for the youngster with the winning entry was a week with Roy Rogers.

Trigger's alleged offspring were offered to fans in contests advertised in national magazines. In November of 1947 *Movie Star Parade* magazine devoted a couple of pages to such a contest. The headline read, "Win a Wee Trigger!" The tag went on to exclaim,

"Hurry, Hurry, Hurry, Here's your last chance to win a real live colt, sired by Trigger, Smartest Horse in the Movies." The copy went on, "Roy Rogers has offered two live colts, sired by the one and only Trigger, to two alert MSP readers." Showing four still photos from a Rogers film, the contest ad instructed readers to identify the film and to finish a Roy and Trigger limerick.

An April 16, 1952, issue of the *Dispatch News Services* featured a picture of Roy Rogers standing next to "Trigger" and a newborn colt who had been named Easter. The caption read that Trigger "has just become the father of a little colt and Trigger looks down admiring at his offspring."

In 1946 a number of articles placed Rogers in the horse breeding business with the slogan "Colts By Trigger." Published reports claimed that Mr. J. B. Ferguson, a wealthy Texas oilman, tried but failed to purchase Trigger in 1951 and had to accept one of his specially bred colts. In a televised interview it was claimed that a Pennsylvania girl was the recipient of the only colt Trigger ever sired. In 1990 country singer Randy Travis allegedly purchased the "grandson" of Trigger. All these stories delighted fans and were great public relations.[20]

Palomino Horse Breeding Business

Around the time *My Pal Trigger* was released in 1946, it was reported in a number of fan magazines that Roy Rogers tried to get into the palomino horse breeding business. Writer Len Simpson claimed Rogers decided to breed palominos "on a large scale." According to Simpson the King of the Cowboys went so far as to purchase five palomino stallions and twenty-five chestnut brood mares. Rogers supposedly had a 560-acre ranch located seven and a half miles west of Las Vegas.

The inspiration for the palomino horse breeding venture was supposed to have come to Roy Rogers on the *My Pal Trigger* set during the filming of the last scene when the title character is about to become a father. Simpson even made the farfetched claim, "For the first time, the actual birth of a palomino colt was recorded for the screen." Apparently this article was written before the movie was released. While there is a birth scene in the movie, the actual act is not shown. The colt's name was Golden Hours, and the article includes a photo of him with Rogers. It's from the scene where Rogers has to shoot Trigger's mother, Lady, after she has been attacked by a mountain lion.[21] (Refer to Chapter 6, "Golden Stallion, Silver Screen.")

An article by Don Allen makes many of the same claims Simpson's article does: "Horse lovers wrote to Roy asking how they could buy Trigger colts. Rogers was glad to oblige. Soon, however, the demands began to pile up and Roy saw the possibilities of a good business in breeding palomino colts. Today Rogers' ranch in Van Nuys, California, proves Roy had a profitable idea. His farm has 24 brood mares, with 17 of them in foal. Each Trigger colt's value is from $1,000 to $2,000, proof that Roy can make money either riding or selling horses."[22]

Don Allen even wrote about breeding for the golden palomino color: "For breeding purposes, sorrel mares are used entirely. This is because a palomino foal usually is the result of a union between a palomino stallion and a sorrel mare. An albino colt result from palomino stallion and a palomino mare."[23] This differs from Simpson's article, which claims, "For his breeding farm, Roy largely is giving the break to the method he feels is

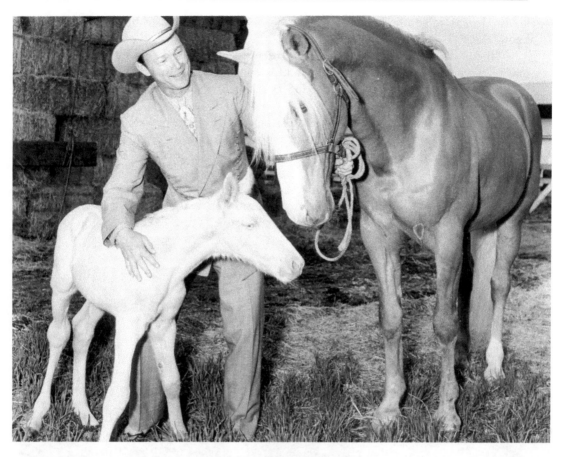

Roy Rogers and the original Trigger greet a new-born foal born on Easter Sunday at the cowboy's ranch in Chatsworth. The baby was not sired by Trigger. It was probably a Harvester-Trigger offspring and named accordingly "Easter" (Roy Dillow collection).

most successful—breeding of chestnut mares to palomino stallions. Statistics point out that in such cases approximately seventy per cent of the colts are palominos."

Rogers finally came clean about breeding Trigger and had the last word on the subject. According to entertainment industry writer John Chadwell, Roy Rogers said in an interview, "Not so." Chadwell went on to state, "He (Rogers) felt that since Trigger was so unusually gentle for a stallion, he didn't want to take the risk that he (Trigger) might change if he were put out to stud."[24]

When asked by Sam Henderson for an article in *Western Horse* magazine why he never bred Trigger, Rogers noted that for him, the best palomino horse coloring came when he bred his all-white, quarter-type (but nevertheless "grade") stallion to quality dark bay quarter horse mares. When it came time for a replacement, Roy Rogers' famous horse bowed once again to a stand-in—a quiet-mannered grade stallion named Whitey.[25]

Champion rodeo rider Larry Mahan, host of the *Horseworld* television show (circa 1995), asked Rogers about breeding Trigger. Rogers answered: "Some horses, if you breed them they get mean and so old Trigger was so gentle. I've got pictures of all my kids on him, I had seven of them at this time, clear from his ears back to his tail, you know. He was so gentle, he'd just stand there. He knew he had to be responsible, you know."

"Today there are no descendants of Trigger. Roy believed that fatherhood might make Trigger less gentle to people. 'My kids could walk right under his belly and it wouldn't bother him.' Roy explained. 'He was real gentle, and I wanted to keep him that way.'"[26]

Corky Randall claimed Trigger, Little Trigger, and Trigger Jr. were all stallions. Only Trigger Jr. was ever used to breed (recent reports claim he sired five palominos out of nine registered foals). All the equine prizes for "name Trigger's colt" contests were from other sources, not the real thing.[27]

For those wanting to purchase a descendant, Trigger Jr.'s production records are on file and copies are available for a fee from Tennessee Walking Horse Breeders' and Exhibitors' Association® according to Walter Chism (Acting Executive Director) and Rory R. Williams (Executive Director).

Roy Rogers with Jim Fagan. Fagan and his wife, Edna, ran the Palomino Association and bred palomino horses in Chatsworth. Their stallion Harvester was a champion parade horse and sired television's Mr. Ed, aka Bamboo-Harvester. Trigger stands next to a young palomino acquired as a breeding stud that Rogers would refer to as Harvester-Trigger (Chatsworth Historical Society collection).

Harvester-Trigger

Roy Rogers and friend Mel Williams, owner of Mel's Dodge dealership in Marysville, California (they met when Rogers was being sponsored by Dodge), bought a ranch in Yuba City, California, to raise cattle and palominos. Their foundation sire was named Harvester, Rogers referred to him as Harvester-Trigger. He was featured on the cover of Roy Rogers Comic #5 and back cover of #12 (both Dell, 1948).

The Chatsworth Historical Society acknowledged a well-known stallion named Harvester (foaled in 1938) bred by James Fagan at Harvester Farms. Harvester was a golden palomino who sired over 100 registered offspring including television star Mr. Ed played by Bamboo-Harvester. Being a California palomino, he was also registered with PHA. Bamboo Harvester/Mr. Ed was foaled in 1949 in El Monte; his dam was name Zetna. He was trained by Lester Hilton who apprenticed under Will Rogers. Hilton also worked with mules in the *Francis the Talking Mule* movies. Mr. Ed's touring/display double was named Pumpkin and was marked almost identical to Mr. Ed.

James and his wife, Edna, moved to Reseda in 1943 where they bred and trained palominos. After James died in 1952, Edna moved eight miles away to Harvester Farms in Chatsworth circa 1953. Roy Rogers and his business partner more than likely bought one of the Fagan Harvester colts and gave it the name Harvester-Trigger to acknowledge its pedigree. According to Mike Johnson, "All of Roy's palominos had a Trigger reference attached to their names. He once showed me his billfold, and where other people have pictures of their kids and grandkids, Roy's wallet contained pictures of all his palominos!"

It was during this time Roy Rogers sponsored a contest (either for a cereal brand or his fan club) that awarded the winner one of "Trigger's" foals. Because Rogers always spoke in public relations terms, that meant Harvester-Trigger who sired the offspring. Years later Roy Rogers and another friend, Tony Agnello, bought a descendant of Harvester-Trigger's and raised palominos again just a few miles from Apple Valley in Oro Grande, California, according to Cheryl Rogers-Barnett.

Rogers and the Republic publicity went all-out to promote *My Pal Trigger* including a feature article that touted a palomino breeding business the singing cowboy planned to run. In hindsight, it sounds like pure public relations. According to author Len Simpson in a magazine article titled "Trigger Man" (periodical and date unknown) promoting *My Pal Trigger*, "Roy Rogers started a 560 acre breeding farm and dude ranch seven and a half miles west on the outskirts of Las Vegas. Allegedly Rogers went into palomino breeding on a large scale. Almost over night he purchased five palomino stallions at prices ranging from one thousand to twenty-five hundred dollars, along with twenty-five chestnut mares. Roy has amassed a lot of information about palominos. Some of it he got out of books. The rest he obtained on lonely nights around the prairie camp fire."

Coda

A favorite story among Trigger fans had to do with the circumstances by which Roy Rogers proposed to Dale Evans. In 1947 the couple were headlining a rodeo at the Chicago Stadium. As they were waiting on horseback to be introduced, Rogers popped the question. While that story has been refuted for another with a more pedestrian breakfast

Dale Evans on Pal and Roy Rogers on Trigger. Unique shot in that each horse was wearing differently styled tack, the former in plastic and the latter in traditional leather. Note how large the plastic tapaderos were (Roy Dillow collection).

setting, it's the story most fans prefer. For a cowboy proposing to his lady love, what better place than on his horse?

"There was one other part of that bargain Dale had to learn to love: my horse. Maybe it sounds odd that I proposed marriage to her on horseback—not too romantic. He was my partner and my pal, and part of nearly everything I did."[28]

6

Little Trigger

*"That horse probably had more tricks on him than any other horse
in the world."*—Corky Randall describing Little Trigger.[1]

The original Trigger seemed to have had it all. According to Roy Rogers, "He was
an iron horse. And smart! He just would do anything, and he had a rein on him as good
as any cow pony you've ever seen. He would stop on a dime and give you nine cents
change."[2]

Trigger was blessed with great looks, an even disposition, fine conformation, athleticism, and perfect timing. When Roy Rogers selected him from a string of rental horses
as his movie co-star, the palomino was more than ready to make his mark in show business. Beyond his assets, all Trigger needed for the challenge that lay ahead was a first-
rate support team: a great trainer and a special double horse to perform a variety of tricks
on movie sets and on tour. Enter Glenn Randall to handle training duties and an extraordinary palomino look-alike named Little Trigger.

As previously noted, Corky Randall claimed that the only traveling Trigger did was
to movie locations in states neighboring California: Utah, Nevada, and Arizona. He was
groomed like a Hollywood starlet. His main jobs were to be seen and photographed; to
perform a couple of tricks; to run at full speed with Rogers on his back; and to rear up.
For just about everything else, he had doubles.

Rogers needed not only a second "Trigger" with similar looks, but also a horse with
intelligence and endurance because the demands on him would be great. While Little
Trigger was not as beautiful as the original Trigger, he could do things like dance, count,
pull sheets off a bed, and sign an X on a hotel registry. According to Cheryl Barnett-
Rogers, Little Trigger was extremely smart, a quick study, and did not forget tricks. Little
Trigger would eventually go on to double Trigger Jr. as well. It was Little Trigger who
secured the title "the Smartest Horse in the Movies."

Little Trigger was not a stunt horse; he was a trick horse. When he performed in
rodeo arenas, fair grounds, parades, hospital rooms, and hotel lobbies, he had to endure
public adulation to the point where parts of his mane and tail were clipped by enthusiastic
fans as souvenirs. Rogers even used soldiers and policemen to guard him. He claimed
that the pilfering became such a problem that "Trigger" was sometimes forced to wear
a toupee till his mane and tail grew out. Rogers and Randall eventually resorted to the
use of display Triggers.

Although Little Trigger was seen in public by more people than any other palomino

Little Trigger prancing. The palomino could do many dressage steps with or without a rider in the saddle cuing him (Robert Phillips collection).

Roy Rogers used, much more is known about Trigger Jr. and even Dale Evans' palomino, Pal. When researching Little Trigger one mostly encounters theories, hearsay, and colorful anecdotes. What one doesn't run across are official documents. Little Trigger's place of birth, date of birth, breed, and breeder are all unknown. Sadly, even the date of Little Trigger's death was never acknowledged. Corky Randall said Little Trigger was not papered. Little Trigger was considered a grade stallion, a horse with no registered history or official paperwork verifying pedigree. When asked by Joel Dutch Dortch of the Happy Trails Foundation in May 2006, Dave Koch, the Internet administrator for the Roy Rogers and Dale Evans Museum and Dusty Rogers' son-in-law, replied, "Little Trigger was purchased ... for stunt purposes to protect Trigger. We have no information on when or where Roy purchased him, or his birth and death dates."[3] Even if papers did exist, it's doubtful he would have been referred to as "Little Trigger" officially. One would have to rely on the description of the animal on the registration form for identification and hope that Rogers didn't own more than one small stocky palomino. It's a shame Roy Rogers didn't keep better records for Little Trigger—and it's strange, really, because of his tendency to hang on to things.[4]

As one would expect, stories regarding Little Trigger are laced with contradictions. Roy Rogers and Glenn Randall covered their tracks, and, with very rare exceptions, neither acknowledged the horse as an individual to the press. One exception was when Randall was quoted in an article titled "He Spoke Horse" which appeared in the summer of 1992 in *Cowboy Magazine*: "Little Trigger was our personal appearance horse and, by God, he could do some of the most remarkable things."

During Roy Roger's career, however, Little Trigger's name was not used publicly and was kept out of most published matter. Little Trigger was never recognized as a character in his own right, like Trigger Jr., Buttermilk, Bullet, or even sidekick Pat Brady's jeep, Nellybelle. Little Trigger was never the subject of any of Rogers' films like Trigger and Trigger Jr. were. He existed only as a double for them.

It's never been known exactly how many "Trigger" doubles Roy Rogers used. One 1946 article claimed, "So valuable is Trigger that he has four stand-ins who also double for him in hazardous shots. Trigger is capable of performing any spectacular stunt, but Rogers and Republic Pictures prefer to use the other four horses, each a specialist in running, jumping, or talking falls for any trick action scenes. Trigger is there for the human interest, devotion-of-master-to-horse scenes. The stand-ins are raised on the Rogers ranch."[5] Corky Randall claimed that Rogers didn't own many Trigger doubles and further claimed that during many personal appearances anonymous palominos were provided by either Republic or whoever was sponsoring a particular event.[6] This happened at the beginning of his career and especially towards the end.

Previous Owner

Although official papers have never surfaced, it's very possible Roy Rogers may have purchased one or maybe two palominos from cowboy star Ray "Crash" Corrigan. Little Trigger may have been one of them.

Ray Corrigan maintained a living by promoting himself; therefore, some fans thought he was just being a publicity hound when he claimed to have sold "Trigger" to Roy Rogers. No matter how shaky the underlying facts were, Corrigan did not draw a distinction between the original Trigger and Little Trigger. However, there are ear-witness accounts to what Roy Rogers said when asked from whom he got Little Trigger. In 1993, longtime Rogers fan Carol Johnson noted,

> I asked him where he bought Little Trigger. He said, "As a matter of fact from Ray Corrigan." I think both are telling the truth but talking about different Triggers. I then asked him if he purchased another horse at the same time and he said, "No, that was later but that one didn't turn out as good as Little

Roy Rogers and Little Trigger circa 1939–1940, in what is believed to be one of the earliest known photographs of the palomino. Roy Dillow dates the picture by the style of tall, round-top hat Rogers was wearing. The future King of the Cowboy's gun holster, still nice and new in this photograph, would soon show wear and tear from use (Jerry Dean collection).

> Trigger." Then I asked him about the one time that Trigger was used as a stud and what happened to the foal. He told me about the close friend of his trainers that talked him into using Trigger and how the owner of the mare couldn't wait to go on tour with the offspring. He whispered to me that he wasn't very happy about that. Roy did also say on one of the *Happy Trails Theater* shows that Trigger was used once at stud. I have that on tape.[7]

This may also be corroborated in the Frank Rasky biography *Roy Rogers: King of the Cowboys*. Rasky goes into detail about how Rogers bought "Trigger" from Corrigan.[8] There are diehard Roy Rogers fans who believe it was Little Trigger that Rasky, unknowingly, was referencing.

Ray Corrigan also claimed he sold Trigger to Rogers for $250. "I sold Roy two palominos for $500—that's for both of them—$250 apiece. A millionaire from Texas later offered $50,000 for the one with the four white stockings, the horse you know as Trigger. The second horse had only three white stockings so when it doubled the other palomino they painted his leg with white paint. Roy named both of the horses Trigger—and folks, until this day he still owes me $250!"[9]

During the 1975 Nashville Film Festival, Ray Corrigan recalled the following conversation with Roy Rogers: "'Ray, if I ever get a horse I want to call him Trigger.' At that time, I had thirty-one horses. Among those were three beautiful palominos. Two of the palominos looked almost exactly alike. One of them had four white stocking feet, and the other had three white stocking feet."[10]

The Rasky biography of Rogers was clearly written for the youth market, and it made a number of outrageous claims, even though it seemed to have had Roy Rogers' blessing. While it still remains within reason that Rogers could have indeed purchased Little Trigger from Ray Corrigan, if one is going to trust the Rasky book, one has to consider the following inconsistencies. Rasky noted (page 98) that Roy Rogers bought a palomino at one-and-a-half years of age from Corrigan in 1938 for $360. This was not the original Trigger (who was four at the time) because the palomino's first film, *Under Western Stars*, was shot the same year. On page 102, Rasky wrote that trainer Glenn Randall, Sr., worked Trigger "between twelve and fourteen hours a day, alternating between twenty minutes of training and twenty minutes of rest." Horses do not have a long attention span and; that much training would not only be counter-productive but ultimately very stressful. Rasky also claimed it was Rogers who originally named Trigger, foregoing the Smiley Burnette claim. Rasky does not mention Jimmy Griffin, Rogers' first trainer. Rasky also stated the palomino Rogers bought from Corrigan was "fifteen and a half hands" (15.2). It is generally agreed that Little Trigger was about 15 hands, and he may have looked bigger because he was more of a bulldog-type quarter horse, very stocky compared to the original Trigger.

In all probability Roy Rogers realized that he needed a horse for touring, bought one from Ray Corrigan and used the horse in movies too. Absent a bill of sale, this is a good theory, and the scenario fits the pattern of the Rogers public relations machine, adjusting the facts enough to release the best-sounding story.

The palomino Rasky mentioned was bought in 1938. Roy Rogers biographer Robert W. Phillips gave 1940 as the year Little

Little Trigger on tour: Author Robert W. Phillips found this photograph (circa 1947) hanging in the Longhorn Bar-B-Q Restaurant in Tulsa, Oklahoma, and bought it on the spot from owners Tom and Carol Nimmo. Phillips tore a wall loose with a borrowed hammer and saw because the photograph was glued directly to the surface.

Trigger was bought at age 18 months.[11] If one goes by the timeline provided by Roy Rogers spokespersons, Little Trigger died in 1965 at around age 25. This would mean he was born in 1940 and the Phillips date is incorrect. However, it is very unlikely Little Trigger was born in 1940, because he would have been too young to have been doubling Trigger and performing fancy tricks in front of cameras at age three. Little Trigger appeared for the first time in a Roy Rogers movie in 1943. Horses, by rule, are started under saddle at two and are performing more complicated tricks at four or five years. The Lipizzaner stallions from the Spanish Riding School of Vienna are started at four or five and aren't put into advanced training until they are eight or nine!

In February 1944, "How I Trained Trigger" by Roy Rogers (as told to Adrienne Ames) was published in *Motion Picture* magazine. Rogers said, "I bought Trigger in Santa Susanna, California, for $350, and that was on-time, no money down…. He was only a year and a half old." It sounds like Rogers is talking about Little Trigger in this case, and it may well corroborate the Corrigan connection. Ironically the Golden Cloud wasn't a trick horse like Little Trigger, making the latter of equal screen value.

According to a June 1991 column on Trigger in *Palomino Horses* magazine, Roy Rogers purchased him in 1938 at the Corrigan ranch in Santa Susana, California, from Ray Corrigan for $360. Rogers paid $200 down and the balance in installments. The essay goes on to say Rogers was "delighted to find that his colt had an exceptional I.Q., and reacted 'as quick as a trigger.'" This article was also probably referring to Little Trigger.

A very likely scenario is that Rogers may have tried to nip the Corrigan/Little Trigger connection in the bud because he wanted to maintain the fantasy of Trigger as one horse. In later years, after William Witney first mentioned Little Trigger in his *Trigger Remembered* book and fans started to ask questions about him, Rogers may have decided to acknowledge the Corrigan connection to Little Trigger. Once again Roy Rogers and his family may have been spinning facts for best effect. Rogers may have thought it was good public relations, like Trigger's appearance in *The Adventures of Robin Hood* movie, to associate Little Trigger with an action hero like Ray "Crash" Corrigan—one of the Three Mesquiteers, no less.[12]

Rocky Roe noted, "Roy Rogers knew Jimmy Griffin through Crash Corrigan. Rogers didn't meet Glenn Randall until later at the Hudkins ranch." And that lends credence to Griffin as Rogers' first trainer and Corrigan as Little Trigger's seller. If it's true Little Trigger was indeed sold by Corrigan, subsequently Jimmy Griffin would have been around when Roy Rogers was making the buy. As noted previously, Corky Randall claimed Rogers already owned Little Trigger when his dad Glenn Randall, Sr., took over.

The confusion over whom Roy Rogers purchased Little Trigger from has a lot to do with Rogers himself. It goes back to his habit of referring to all horses as "Trigger," a mix of public relations, convenience, and oversight. Rogers is on record stating he bought the palomino from Crash Corrigan and many times stating he did not. If a fan asked Rogers if he bought Trigger from Corrigan he would, of course, say "no." If a fan asked Rogers if he bought Trigger from Corrigan and Rogers thought the fan was referring to Little Trigger, he would answer "yes." That doesn't get fans any closer to Little Trigger's origin but it sure makes a case for the Corrigan connection.

In the end this writer cannot state categorically that Roy Rogers bought Little Trigger from Ray Corrigan. There is no official documentation and both men used public relations as it suited them.

According to author Merrill T. McCord in his book *Brothers of the West* (Alhambra, 2003), when Ray Corrigan claimed that he'd helped Roy Rogers with his career it took his Three Mesquiteers co-star Bob Livingston by surprise. It's well known that there was no love lost between Corrigan and Livingston. When told of Corrigan's claim that he had a hand in Rogers being signed by Republic Pictures, Livingston categorically stated, "That's a lot of bunk.... Corrigan at that time couldn't help anybody do anything. He was having too much trouble holding his own job."[13]

Like Corrigan, Livingston also claimed to have had a hand in the uniting of Roy Rogers and Trigger. He stated: "I was walking from the back lot up to the front office one day. This was the beginning of Roy Rogers' career. He said, 'Hey Bob, do me a favor will you? They want me to pick a horse out of this bunch (they had about five horses there) to ride in the picture. I wish you'd help me pick one out.' So I'm in a big hurry. I'm not much interested in this routine anyway because I know the background of it.... I said (sarcastically), 'Oh, that's a beauty! That palomino there. That's the one!' And I went on my merry way."[14]

Birth Date

A few news releases from the mid-1940s may offer clues to Little Trigger's birth year. the *New York Times* published a short press release on October 7, 1943. It reported that a celebration for "Trigger" was being held in the Plantation Room of the Hotel Dixie in Manhattan: "Smartest Horse in the Movies will be seven years old today."[15] It's safe to assume it was Little Trigger touring with Rogers at the time. The *New York Times* date would make Little Trigger's birth year 1936. (As previously stated, the original Trigger's registration gave July 4, 1934, as his date of birth.) A similar story published in May of 1943 in the *Junior Rodeo Fans* newsletter claimed that a "rodeo tour 'Trigger' was not at home for his sixth birthday but was honored with his own party in the main dining room of a Boston hotel." This would mean the horse mentioned was born in 1937. Again, most likely it was Little Trigger who was being referenced. It also needs to be understood, with regards to the New York celebration especially, that a phony birth date may have been concocted as a publicity stunt to promote Rogers' appearance at Madison Square Garden.[16]

A Roy Rogers comic book special section titled "My Pal Trigger" stated, "Trigger, a palomino stallion, weighs 1,100 pounds and stands 15 hands. His birthday is March 17." This description matches Little Trigger's, in which case March 17 might be his date of birth. However, the same paragraph also contains the erroneous claim, "He has sired numerous colts, but one in particular, Trigger Junior, is almost a perfect likeness of his father."[17]

In the 1944 *Motion Picture* article "How I Trained Trigger," credited to Roy Rogers ("as told to Adrienne Ames"), it was reported that "Trigger" "made his 'stage' debut about three years ago in Tulare, California, when Roy made a personal appearance there, and (Trigger) was very bad in the first show. But after a few performances, he began to like it." That would put the debut in 1941. If Little Trigger is the horse being mentioned, and he's around three or four, that too would put his year of birth at 1936 or 1937.

In an article titled "That Horse, Trigger" which appeared in *Pageant* magazine (February 1947), Stephen Strassberg wrote, "Tricks, however, are Trigger's main claim to fame.

Since buying him for $350 in 1935, Rogers has taught him more than 50." Given the price paid, this again sounds like a reference to Little Trigger, but the date would mean he was born before the original Trigger.

If we accept Robert W. Phillips' claim that Little Trigger was purchased in 1940 at age 18 months, then the palomino was born in 1937. Little Trigger's first appearance was in *Song of Texas*, released in 1943. Prior to 1943, "Trigger's" tricks on film were limited. Trigger was hardly seen in *King of the Cowboys*, the movie released right before *Song of Texas*. When Little Trigger arrived on the scene, all of a sudden there was dancing, bowing, and more. We know that a horse is started under saddle at two, and that by three or four a trick horse is moved along to more complicated tricks. Using 1943 as a point to count back from, it's reasonable to say that Little Trigger was born between 1936 and 1939. It's doubtful Roy Rogers and Glenn Randall, Sr., needed to wait until Little Trigger was six before he was ready to appear in a film. This writer will split the difference and place his likely birth year at 1937.

Four Color Roy Rogers Comics number 86 was issued by Dell in 1945 and sports one of the earliest photos of Little Trigger according to Rocky Roe.

Movie Debut

In *Song of Texas* (1943) Roy Rogers, playing a rodeo star, visited the Texas Springs Hospital and took Little Trigger into a children's ward packed with recovering patients, most of them lying in beds. The first time Little Trigger appeared on camera in a movie was when he was walking down a corridor with Rogers and the Sons of the Pioneers right before they entered the children's ward. Apparently the palomino had been given a full beauty treatment in order to pass as the original Trigger. His forelock was teased and he was immaculate. While the Sons of the Pioneers played "Git Along Little Dogies," Rogers hopped up on Little Trigger and they performed a short dance. Rogers even cued the horse to rear up, which he did quickly and in a very confined space. Little Trigger also threw a kiss to the adoring children.

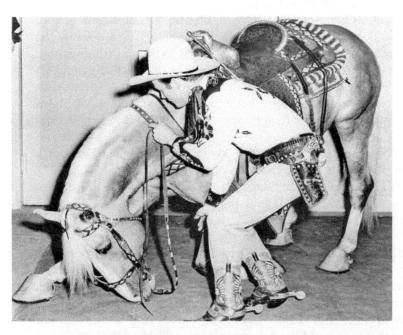

Little Trigger (wearing rubber hoof covers) rehearsing indoors with Roy Rogers on the set of *Song of Texas*, the palomino's movie debut (Roy Dillow collection).

This sequence—in which Little Trigger truly shone—was typical of how he was to be used to enhance the "Trigger" legend. The sequence was more or less an abbreviated version of the show Rogers, Little Trigger, and the Sons of the Pioneers put on a year later in *The Hollywood Canteen* (Warner Bros., 1944).

Purchase Time Line

We know that Rogers bought the original Trigger in 1943. The question becomes, why did he buy Little Trigger before the original? Probably because he had first priority use of Trigger with Hudkins Stables, and also had a probable first option to buy. Rogers either came to this conclusion on his own or was advised that having Little Trigger as a touring trick horse was more important than owning the original Trigger because he did not travel well and wasn't a trick horse. Before Rogers owned him, Herb Yates and Republic most likely weren't going to pay his rental fees on tour in any case. Little Trigger, as a double with a bag full of tricks, may have been viewed as more of a necessity, a higher priority. The ever practical Rogers saw "Trigger" as a prop as much as a partner. He obviously wanted a personal appearance "Trigger" of his own, and was able to get Little Trigger for less money than the original Trigger.

Since Jimmy Griffin was Little Trigger's first trainer, it eliminates the idea that Glenn Randall, Sr., may have found Little Trigger for Rogers as some have thought.

Temperament and Personality

For those who have made an effort to learn about Little Trigger, his reputation for being unpleasant is common knowledge. According to Corky Randall, Little Trigger eventually became quite impatient with fans while on tour and could be aggressive if they got near him. One couldn't blame the horse. Any animal that's over stimulated by too much hands-on attention, especially from strangers, has a breaking point. Little Trigger had to tolerate an enormous amount of traveling, sleeping in different locations every night. Cheryl Rogers-Barnett claimed that "much of Little Trigger's sour temperament surfaced because he was so smart and got easily bored. Having to do the same tricks and routines night after night wore thin. He would misbehave at times out of frustration and also because of so much attention and overstimulation from adoring fans." In addition, Little Trigger was the first horse to be house broken; in other words, even something as natural as relieving himself was regimented. Insuring the "Trigger" character the position of "the Smartest Horse in the Movies" came at a price and it was Little Trigger who paid it.

A 1943 *Song of Texas* press release claimed that Rogers and "Trigger" gave 136 performances in 20 days. With a schedule like that, it's astonishing that Little Trigger actually behaved most of the time. One is amazed not only by what tricks the palomino mastered, but also by the many different situations he was asked to perform in.

Mike Johnson claimed Roy Rogers never appeared to have that much affection for Little Trigger. "It was obvious Rogers loved the original Trigger more than any other horse, but in spite of Little Trigger's personality it's hard to believe that after all the touring, movies, etc., that they shared, Rogers wouldn't have had some kind of affection

A stunned Dale Evans witnesses Little Trigger misbehaving during a performance at the Iowa State Fair. Roy Rogers is pictured with his back to the camera; Glenn Randall has fallen clear; the Sons of the Pioneers play on. From a Des Moines, Iowa, newspaper clipping, year unknown.

for the animal. In reality he probably spent as much time with the trick horse as he did with the original Trigger. Rogers stated that Little Trigger was more of a ham, and was certainly more temperamental. That in itself is not surprising when, unlike Trigger, Little Trigger was constantly working, and on the road a lot of the time. Paraphrasing one of Rogers' favorite expressions, "Is it any wonder that the horse might occasionally be guilty of losing his pretty ways?"

Along with his reputation for being impatient with strangers, Little Trigger was by nature temperamental. He was a stallion, after all, and not allowed to procreate. Cheryl Rogers-Barnett described him as being like an ornery little kid: "Little Trigger hated women, and he didn't much care for kids except for when Dad had him under saddle and bridle. He wasn't one you would let out in the paddock for little kids to go and pat."[18]

The following anecdotes cannot be connected to Little Trigger absolutely, but they sound very much like him. After all, when it came to personal appearances, he was on the front lines.

There were occasions when Roy Rogers was in the center of an arena singing a hymn and "Trigger" came up behind him and grabbed a piece of his shirt in his mouth along with a good chunk of his shoulder. The audience thought the palomino was giving his master an affectionate nuzzle, but in reality it hurt like crazy. "Trigger" seemed to know Rogers could not acknowledge his pain in the middle of the hymn. During rehearsals when there was no audience the horse never attempted the same stunt. Little Trigger sometimes left teeth marks along Roger's forearms. In her *Cowboy Princess* book, Cheryl Rogers-Barnett even recounts a time when her dad mockingly threatened to discipline the diminutive palomino with a baseball bat.

In the 1944, article "How I Trained Trigger," Rogers admitted to author Adrience Ames, "'And sometimes he even goes so far as to give me a nip. If you don't believe me, I'll show you.' And with that he rolled up his sleeve and showed me his arm, with some 'gentle' reminders of Trigger's temperament."

It was noted in the pages of *Esquire* magazine (December 1975) that fans were shocked by a certain exchange between Roy Rogers and his four-legged partner: "He (Trigger) and his master had more than one set-to over his penchant for scene stealing. After one such episode at the Earle Theater in Washington, Roy stormed off the stage and announced, "Someday I'm going to shoot that god damn horse right between the eyes."

In August of 1956 Roy Rogers, Dale Evans, and the Sons of the Pioneers were appearing at the Iowa State Fair in Des Moines. A local newspaper published a photo of Rogers and a handler (probably Glenn Randall) moving clear of "Trigger" as he rolled on the ground. In all fairness, even the most highly trained horse can spook, but this appears to be deliberate misbehavior. A horse should not roll while being handled, especially while wearing a saddle. The accompanying caption read: "Des Moines, Aug. 31—Roy and Trigger part company—Dale Evans (mounted, background) holds a hand over her mouth in apprehension as her husband Roy Rogers (left) and a handler (right) fall clear of Rogers' sprawling horse Trigger at the Iowa State Fair yesterday. Trigger, for reasons unknown, reared, twisted and fell as Rogers started to mount him on the muddy infield in front of the fair grandstand. The western movie star moments later mounted without trouble and rode away."

Corky Randall recounted a similar rolling incident by Trigger Jr. that took place in Canada. His dad Glenn Sr. was holding the palomino with a finger looped through one of the rings on the bit. Then for some unknown reason the horse spooked, raised his head almost taking Randall's finger, everyone panicked; the palomino got even more scared and fell over backwards then proceeded to roll before getting up.

In 1952, in Los Angeles, actress Mabel Smeyne (aka Mable Smaney) filed a lawsuit against Roy Rogers Enterprises seeking $186,000 plus court costs and general relief. She alleged that Rogers and others recklessly failed to control "Trigger" on the movie set of *Son of Paleface*, allowing him to kick her. She claimed permanent internal and external injuries to the head, chest, and breast. The trial did not begin until October 1954. Rogers spoke for himself and "Trigger." On October 29 the jury was out only 39 minutes and rendered a verdict in favor of Rogers and "Trigger." To win the case, Smeyne was required to prove the accident happened because Rogers was negligent. She was unable to do so. The Mabel Smeyne case was finally dismissed on appeal in 1955.

Little Trigger worked at close quarters with Bob Hope during *Son of Paleface*. It's rumored Hope, a novice with horses, was nervous. It's safe to assume Roy Rogers and Glenn Randall, Sr., were monitoring the situation very carefully and it says a lot for their expertise.

Don "Jug" Reynolds, one time pre-teen wrangler on the Randall Ranch, got the full measure of Little Trigger purely by accident. Reynolds had been around horses all his life. Little Trigger had been taught to stand in a far corner of his stall when someone entered, but once while mucking out Reynolds inadvertently cued the horse into an action that must have been terrifying. By merely waving his shovel, the stud, ears back and teeth bared, lunged at Reynolds full on. Fortunately the experienced and quick thinking youngster, startled though he was, recognized the behavior and raised his hands bringing the stallion back into a quiet state.

When not doing stable chores, Reynold got to watch Glenn Randall, Corky, and his own father Fess Reynolds train horses. He actually saw Randall Sr., teach Little Trigger a number of tricks, some by physically cuing the animal on certain parts of his body and some with hand and whip signals at a distance. According to Cheryl Rogers-Barnett, "Jug is the only person I know who rode Little Trigger other than Glenn Sr., Corky, and Junior Randall, dad's doubles on the movie sets, and the men who worked for Glenn. It was dangerous for anyone else as every where you touched Little Trigger, he would perform a trick."

Mike Johnson confided that "Roy had no problem talking about Little Trigger privately but not for public consumption. As you know (director William) Witney did acknowledge the other Triggers in his book *Trigger Remembered*. Some facts in the book were wrong, but the long and short of it was that the book was an affectionate tribute. Roy refused to autograph, or have anything to do with the book. That was partly because Witney had (presumably, in Roy's opinion) shattered the myth of just the one Trigger, but also because Witney hadn't consulted with him, or even mentioned that he was writing a book. It would appear Roy Rogers probably saw it as a betrayal of sorts. After four decades creating and perpetuating a myth, I have real doubts Roy would have given it up so easy." (It's reasonable to assume this book would not have thrilled Rogers either.)

Kids of the 40s and 50s saw most things in black and white, or as right and wrong. Roy recognized this and, being a person who had respect for his young audience, possibly thought that identifying multiple horses might confuse and disappoint those kids. I think that he viewed all of us adult fans as just kids at heart. To Roy it never became necessary to destroy the myth of Trigger any more than it would have made sense to destroy his own myth. In Roy's mind the legend of Roy and Trigger were one and the same.

The fact that Roy had considerably less affection for Little Trigger than he did for the Old Man is obviously true but nevertheless surprising. After all, the thousands of fans who saw Roy and Trigger at personal appearances, etc., during the 1940s and 1950s only ever got to see Little Trigger. Personally I would have preferred to see Little Trigger mounted instead of Trigger Jr.; though beautiful and talented, Trigger Jr. never really helped towards creating the single Trigger story."

Touring with Little Trigger

Both Little Trigger and his tack were kept immaculate and in top condition. Corky Randall also confirmed that he and his dad actually drove "Trigger's" touring trailer. Roy

Glenn Randall and Little Trigger (with fans and flight crew) about to depart for yet another personal appearance.

Rogers was not involved in the day-to-day care of his horse while on the road because he was too busy attending to miscellaneous business and promotion. Corky also claimed that if Rogers had checked in on his mount after hours, he would have been mobbed. The Randalls handed "Trigger" to the King of the Cowboys right outside a performance arena. When the show was over, the palomino was returned, and Rogers was either off to his hotel or involved in more promotion and tour business.

Roy Rogers realized early on how a touring horse was critical to his budding career. When Gene Autry could not fulfill all his tour bookings, he advised Roy Rogers to create a rodeo and even recommended him. Subsequently Republic Pictures and its two major singing cowboys had the sense never to overlap their movies or personal appearances. When Autry was filming, Rogers was touring and vice versa.

The Display Trigger

"Trigger" achieved such fame that while on tour he was often on exhibit in full tack in front of an arena. Not only was this great publicity and an incentive to go into the show, but it was done so that kids who couldn't afford tickets could at least see the beautiful palomino.

"Boys and girls like Trigger so much that I tried to station him and his fancy trailer

Roy Rogers, Dale Evans, and Little Trigger arrive in England for a tour. As a publicity gimmick, the palomino presented a passport.

outside each auditorium for a few hours before a performance. I figured that this was a way for those who didn't have enough money for a ticket to get a chance to see him."[19]

Cheryl Rogers-Barnett confided, "Glenn [Randall] often had a second palomino in the trailer when on the road. This was a display Trigger, a horse that could be stabled where the public could see and touch him. "He was not Trigger! He did not do tricks. He was just a palomino that was safe to put people up on." The "Trigger" audiences saw in a small corral outside an area before the show, the horse fans were photographed with or got close to backstage, was the display Trigger. He was a probably a gelding. Pal, California, or Monarch all traveled with Randall and may have been used as well as a palomino from Randall's own Liberty Horse Act.

If you saw "Trigger" outside of California, if you had your picture taken on or next to him during a tour, it was probably Little Trigger or any one of the display Triggers. If you clipped his mane and tail hair as a souvenir, you did not disfigure the original Trigger. If you were allowed to groom "Trigger" before a public appearance, it was probably a display Trigger you were working on. In point of fact Little Trigger was carefully handled in public because adoring crowds would over stimulated him when he needed to be mentally predisposed to perform. His ornery and even dangerous ways were inappropriate for a novice to be around unattended.

Picture Proof

Not surprisingly, there are few existing photos that show the original Trigger with his doubles. Professional publicity shots showing them together would not have fostered the image of Trigger as a single horse. Nor are there many amateur shots. The cast and crew on movie sets were sure to have seen Randall and Rogers off-camera with two or three palominos in fancy show tack, but Republic probably had rules against taking certain pictures behind the scenes. My guess is that Roy Rogers did not allow it either, though he posed for shots with Trigger and with Trigger Jr. when he was promoting the latter. Even shots of Little Trigger with Trigger Jr. exist. No candid on set photos have emerged of Trigger along side of his doubles waiting for cameras to roll. As Glenn Randall surely trailered however many palominos necessary to a film location, they had to be tacked together and ready to perform. (There are shots of Gene Autry with Champion and his doubles on movies sets.) A photograph of Trigger standing in the ready next to Little Trigger, Monarch, or California is as rare as a shot of Roy Rogers and Joe Yrigoyen together in identical clothing. That was an illusion B-western cowboys would rarely break.

Photos showing the original Trigger with Little Trigger are rarest of all. Only one such photo is known. Published in *Pic* magazine in July 1946 over the caption "Trigger and His Doubles," it shows Trigger, Monarch, California, Pal, and Little Trigger. It was probably taken on the Randall Ranch.

Little Trigger was the cast horse in the movie *Son of Paleface*, making him the last "Trigger" to star in a motion picture. The original Trigger was nowhere to be found in the production despite the King of the Cowboy's claims that he was in every Roy Rogers film. Corky Randall's simple and obvious explanation was that the script called for a trick horse that would be called upon to perform in most every scene he was in. Only Little Trigger was up to the task. *My Pal Trigger* and *The Golden Stallion* included, no other Roy Rogers movie required more tricks of "Trigger" than *Son of Paleface*.

Markings and Color

A number of palominos were featured in Western movies from the 1930s to the 1950s. Johnny Mack Brown, Eddie Dean, Hoot Gibson, Russell Hayden, and Ken Maynard all rode them at one time or another. From time to time, some well-meaning fan claims to have made a Trigger sighting in a non–Roy Rogers movie; however, most of the time the palomino in question doesn't hold up to close scrutiny. Horses may resemble each other closely, but individuals have their own unique markings and conformation.

THE ORIGINAL TRIGGER

Two important things to keep in mind about the original Trigger are that he had a very wide blaze (white marking on his face) and only one white half-stocking, on his left hind leg (some published photos are reversed). His blaze extended from the left side of his face, jutting out over his left eye with a notch cut out, to the right side, covering his entire right nostril and the top part of the mouth. Above his left eye, the blaze returned, with a jagged edge, to the center of his face, resulting in a very large white area on his forehead. One of the best unobstructed frontal views of Trigger's blaze can be seen during the horseback square dance in *My Pal Trigger* (1946). Because of the English tack Trigger carries, the top of his blaze is exposed; one can see how it ends in a pyramid shape at the top of his forehead and how at that location it covers more of his left side (over his eye) than his right side. Viewed from his right side, the blaze ran straight up, considerably away from his eye, to the high part of his forehead, where it turned in. The white area well below the right nostril, made a 90-degree right turn and, with a jagged edge, continued toward the mouth. It is really this formation that most prominently distinguishes the original Trigger from his doubles.

In 1952 Trigger weighed 1100 pounds according to *Western Horseman* (April 1961) and *Movie Fan* (March 1953). David Rothel's *Roy Rogers Book*[20] gives Trigger's height as 15.3 hands. Bobby Copeland wrote in his book, *Silent Hoofbeats,*[21] that the original Trigger was 16 hands and weighed 1150 lbs. Corky Randall claimed the original Trigger was 16 hands.

Almost every artist's rendition of Trigger shows him with four white stockings—flashier than the single stocking he actually had. This was Rogers' reason for requesting that four white stockings be painted on the 23.5' fiberglass statue of Trigger for the front of his museum. According to the Tennessee Walking Horse Association, as with any breed of horse, a palomino's coat can bleach out under lots of sun. But true socks are white and permanent, making them a useful aid to identification. They are not considered socks if they are simply a lightening of the hair from exposure to the sun and are not visible year round.

In some photos even the original Trigger's front legs look white. It is entirely possible that photos may have been doctored and makeup used to lighten Trigger's legs in some instances. There are even those who claim that Trigger sometimes appeared with four white stockings because his legs were intentionally bleached. This is absurd; however, it is likely that peroxide was used on "Trigger's" mane and tail to keep them white. It has also been reported that makeup artists polished "Trigger's" hoofs and used extra long lashes on his eyes.[22]

On a horse's stifle joint (analogous to the human knee), the flesh covering the area makes a bulge with a slight indent below. Trigger's stifle on his off side was more pronounced than on his near side, and some use it as a way to identify him.[23]

One of the problems in finding a good copy of Trigger was that he had brown eyes. Most palominos have blue eyes. When looking for palomino doubles, Glenn Randall, Sr., had to get around that little quirk. For example, Loco, the palomino Leo Carrillo used in the *Cisco Kid* television show, could not double Trigger because of his blue eyes. In some running scenes, however, he would have been a pretty close match.

LITTLE TRIGGER AND TRIGGER JR.

The Encyclopedia of TV Pets describes Little Trigger as a Quarter Horse. Corky Randall thought he looked like a Morgan.

Little Trigger had four nearly matching white stockings and a black line across his back. He had a very narrow blaze at top of the forehead, which gradually widened to approximately 2–3" as it ran downward, along the center of his face. The blaze widened to approximately 3–4" at the bridle, where it began to angle towards his right nostril. Only the top part of the right nostril was covered as the blaze worked its way toward the

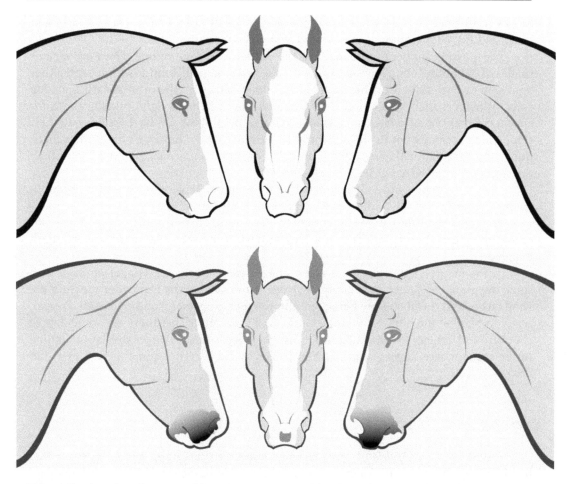

Trigger (top) and Little Trigger blaze diagrams created by the author. Note the dark area around Little Trigger's muzzle.

center of his mouth. Even with the area just below the top part of the nostril, there was a noticeable quarter-sized dark spot. The white area under his nose, near the top center of his mouth, had a large notch, which was very visible. Little Trigger's blaze ran narrow and straight up the left center of his face. Only the top part of the left nostril was covered. Little Trigger was also very dark around his nostrils and mouth.

In the *Son of Paleface* (Paramount, 1952) sequence where Little Trigger chased Bob Hope into a hotel and up a flight of stairs, the palomino stuck his head out a window, eyeing Hope as the comedian tried to shimmy down a drainpipe. As the horse wasn't wearing a bridle, his blaze was very visible. The window curtains parted his forelock, and one can see his blaze peak at the top of his forehead. In a later sequence when Little Trigger is sharing a bed with Bob Hope, one can see all his facial markings quite well.[24]

The drawings of Trigger and Little Trigger shown on these pages are intended to help the reader attempt to distinguish their facial markings—which are only one aspect of identification. At best the drawings are simple diagrams. The horse heads are generic, just like the ones horse owners would find on an equine registration form; they do not address conformation or head type. Those are entirely different subjects. Determining a horse's conformation is a science and is possible only with complete access to a particular horse and full cooperation of the owner for specific measurements.

The illustrations here do not address the subtleties of color or hue. There are various shades of palomino, often having to do with age and season. Palominos come with either light skin or dark skin. Most have dark skin, which makes for the most beautiful golden color. Whatever their skin color, their fine hair may catch the light, making the color appear different in alternate shots. (Light-skinned palominos can have freckles on their skin, which are more apt to show during the summer when they don't have thick coats; unlike the dark-skinned ones, light-skinned palominos can be darker in the winter than the summer. They have lighter eye color, too.)

Little Trigger was not only smaller than the original Trigger but was also lighter in color. Trigger Jr. was the darkest of Rogers' three main palominos.

Trigger Jr. had four white stockings to the knees. He had a blaze, but it was not nearly as wide as the original Trigger's. He was perfect in body color and was sometimes dappled.

In the movie *Trigger Jr.,* there is a scene where the original Trigger appears with some dapple spots. Rogers and company have just arrived at the Harkrider ranch in the wind storm and the horses are being led into the tent. Rogers is standing beside Trigger, ready to blanket the horse. Looking closely, one may notice that there are some dapple spots around Trigger's stomach area. In *My Pal Trigger* Little Trigger displays dappling in the scene where Rogers returned him to Gabby Hayes. The animal is tied to a stall door.[25]

Serafix and "Trigger"

A 1984 article in *Arabian Horse* magazine noted a British stallion named Serafix that had been purchased by an American breeder for more money than had ever been paid for a stallion imported to the States at the time happened to share an airplane with Roy Rogers and Little Trigger on one occasion. Serafix had structure and balance—an overall look that gave Arabian horse experts chills. When fans compared Serafix to "Trigger" the palomino got shortchanged. Alongside Serafix he was described as "coarse and clumsy." In all honesty he probably looked like a draft horse in comparison. Although he did not have show-quality looks, he had enough eye appeal to stand in for one of the most beautiful horses in Hollywood history, he fooled fans for decades. This sleight of hand was aided by shifting attention from Little Trigger's looks to his talent and athleticism.

Obit

Corky Randall stated categorically that although he could not recall the exact date, Little Trigger died years before the original Trigger, sometime before the Rogers family moved to Hidden Valley in 1963.

Cheryl Rogers-Barnett maintained that Little Trigger actually died at her father's ranch in Hidden Valley, which was between Malibu and Thousand Oaks. "Dad and Mom never lived at that ranch as it only had a one bedroom house while Dad owned it," she wrote. "He planned on adding on to it but Debbie (another daughter) died and Dad

Little Trigger being led down a ramp after an airplane flight. Roy Rogers was literally bringing up the rear (Corky Randall collection).

wanted to move away. Anyway, he had the horses out there (that is where the Old Man died as well) when Little Trigger died and he had a pit dug and buried him there (in an unknown location on his property). With the old horse, Dad and Mom had already moved to Apple Valley but Dad didn't have a barn and worked a deal with the new owner of the Hidden Valley ranch to keep Old Trigger and his thoroughbreds there until Dad had a place for them."

Corky Randall could not recall if Little Trigger died of old age or was put down. It's no wonder he did not live as long as the original Trigger; he worked harder and in more stressful situations. Corky said the horse developed severe problems with his knees when he got old as a result of all the traveling he did in trailers. "His knees bucked. Now you know how a bow-legged guy's knees buck out? His bucked forward." This happened because of the stopping and starting during the trailer rides. (Horse trailers are now designed to haul horses sideways, not straight on, to avoid such problems.)

Little Trigger was also ridden in a number of situations, such as parades, where he had to walk on hard surfaces. This probably also contributed to the problems he eventually developed with his legs.

Little Trigger Coda

As Roy Rogers never discussed Little Trigger on record, it's been rumored the King of the Cowboys regretted not having him mounted. He probably did not want to have to explain the little palomino as Trigger's trick horse double.

The inimitable Little Trigger bowing at liberty, photographed for *Who's Who in Western Stars* magazine for Dell Publishing in 1953 (Roy Dillow collection).

Roy Rogers and the original Trigger built their careers on Little Trigger's back. Corky Randall's claim that his dad and Rogers didn't use very many trick horse doubles means Little Trigger worked harder than most people have ever imagined. As well cared for as Little Trigger was and as glamorous as his job seemed to be, he was a work horse. On days when he and Roy Rogers weren't in the mood to perform, they were still out there. Fans just saw the glory; they did not see the blood, sweat, or tears. Little Trigger was on the front lines and it took a toll on the palomino's psychology and health.

The more one researches Little Trigger and makes a conscious effort to locate him in movies and personal appearance footage, the more one understands his importance and how he was as critical to Roy Rogers' career as the original Trigger. Little Trigger was truly a wonder horse, and he earned the honor of being photographed with Rogers for the cover of *Life* magazine. A more accurate billing on movie marquees and posters should have been, "Roy Rogers, Trigger and Little Trigger."

While a great deal is known about the original Trigger, there's much that remains unresolved about the most important horse that doubled him. By not discussing Little Trigger, Roy Rogers and Glenn Randall unintentionally added to his mystery, and that's ultimately what makes him so compelling. Not being able to tie up important facts leaves Trigger's story open-ended. This book is as much about Little Trigger as it is about the original Trigger. Little Trigger was the real deal, the real Professor of Triggernometry, he was also the first palomino Roy Rogers ever owned. For all his shenanigans and notorious temperament, Little Trigger was, in a word: extraordinary.

7

Trigger Jr. and the Roy Rogers Remuda

*"When he visited a horse farm during this quest the horseman
would nearly always ask him: 'Well, sir, just what kind of horse are
you looking for?' Roy would explain that he wanted a fine western stock
horse, with a good rein and preferably a palomino."*—William Roper[1]

The notion of one-man-one-horse is a complete fantasy, especially as it applies to western movies. Real working cowboys rode a number of horses over time. Some horses excelled at only certain disciplines; they varied in color and temperament. A cowboy owned a few, borrowed when he had to, and rode stock owned by his employers. A cattle drive required each cowboy to use a string of up to six horses per day, changing a fresh mount every two or three hours. *Remuda*, originally a Spanish word, means the stable of working horses that an outfit owns. To pull off the illusion of one spectacular animal, Roy Rogers also required a remuda, in his case, palominos that looked like Trigger.

Movie cowboys riding through big country on screen were identified by their clothes and mounts. The four leads on television's *Bonanza* (NBC, 1959–1973) never changed clothes or horses; neither did most television cowboys of the day. Audiences needed to identify them from scene to scene. Film crews also shot all outdoor sequences for different episodes at the same time to save money. Changing clothes and using horses of different colors would have been expensive and a continuity nightmare.

Apart from Little Trigger, Corky Randall could confirm only three other doubles: Pal, California, and Monarch. He also stated that many of the palominos that doubled Trigger were not owned by Roy Rogers but were provided by Hudkins Stables.[2]

Trigger Jr. and Paul K. Fisher

"During the shooting of the picture *My Pal Trigger*, one scene called for the birth of a colt. The studio arranged to rent one from a California horse breeder, and the rancher

Opposite, top: **One of a kind shot of Roy Rogers and Dale Evans with the original Trigger and four of his palomino doubles. From left: Monarch, Trigger, California, Pal, and Little Trigger. This photograph, with the caption "Trigger and his doubles," appeared in *PIC*, "a magazine for young men," in July 1946. Rogers would not own Trigger Jr. until 1950 (Roy Dillow collection).** *Bottom:* **Roy Rogers and Trigger Jr. Corky Randall described the dappled palomino as "elegant." The Tennessee Walker had wonderful conformation, great looks, and was the only purebred in the Rogers remuda. Paul Fisher used the palomino as a breeding sire though Rogers did not (Janey Miller collection).**

was so pleased with the deal that he gave the colt to Roy when the picture was completed. Roy began training the young horse to become Trigger's understudy. He named him Trigger Junior. Later, Roy and Glenn Randall took over the training, and Trigger Junior appeared in two pictures as Trigger's son."

This charming account of Trigger Jr.'s origin from the book *Roy Rogers: King of the Cowboys* by William Roper made a nice story for young fans. Unfortunately, like the two foals that were sired by Trigger in *My Pal Trigger*, the story is a fantasy.

As the second palomino Roy Rogers acknowledged in public, Trigger Jr. was also subject to public relations, particularly in regards to his seller. Trigger Jr. was born in 1941 and died 28 years later in 1969.[3] The Roy Rogers publicity machine would have fans believe the singing cowboy purchased him from well-known breeder Paul K. Fisher of Souderton, Pennsylvania. However, records show it was a John Ewell of East Earl Township in Lancaster County, Pennsylvania, who sold the Tennessee Walker stud to Rogers.

According to a May 2003 essay posted in 2019 on *Lancaster Online* by reporter Jack Brubaker, John Ewell had a large farm along Butter Road where he operated a milk transportation business along side the raising and training of palomino Tennessee Walking Horses. Ewell sold one to show business impresario Ted Mack and another to television personality Arthur Godfrey. The most famous horse he sold was Trigger Jr. to Roy Rogers.

Trigger Jr. registration papers filed in 1943, the same year Roy Rogers bought the original Trigger from Hudkins Bros. Stables (copyright and compliments of the Tennessee Walking Horse Breeders' and Exhibitors' Association, Lewisburg, TN).

The horse was born in Souderton at Fisher Farms. Ewell bought him as a young colt and sold him at age five. Ewell met Rogers several times in New York and Philadelphia according to his daughter Harriet Sheaffer of New Holland. Tom Hunt of New Holland trained Trigger Jr. before Rogers purchased him in 1954 (that date is not in line with official records).

A form on file with the PHBA dated September 30, 1947, noted a transfer of ownership for Allen's Gold Zephyr to John Ewell by seller P.K. Fisher. The PHBA also provided a July 7, 1950, letter to Roy Rogers from Texas official Dr. Arthur Zappe with a "transfer certificate of registration on the stallion, Allen's Golden Zephyr, PHBA 4055, which has been transferred from John Ewell, East Earl, PA to you [Roy Rogers]." Endorsed on the back by seller Mr. Ewell to Roy Rogers.

It is reasonable to assume John Ewell wasn't mentioned publicly because Allen's Gold Zephyr's purchase from the nationally known P.K. Fisher at Fisher Farms was better public relations. Roy Rogers was too media savvy to let that go. Glenn Randall. purchased the horse as Rogers' agent.

Though no bill of sale was found between Mr. John Ewell and Roy Rogers, the PHBA provided a certificate of registration dated July 12, 1950 to certify Trigger Jr. was owned by Roy Rogers of Hollywood, California. There also exists an April 21, 1950, Roy Rogers Enterprise letter to Fred W. Parnell of Palomino Horses (PHBA) in Mineral Wells, Texas, with a check for $16 to cover the cost of re-registering the palomino Allen's Golden Zephyr (PHBA 4055) with the new name Trigger Jr., signed by Roy Rogers.

According to the Palomino Horse Breeders of America Trigger Jr. was originally foaled under the auspices of breeder C.O. Barker of Readyville, Tennessee; owned by Paul K. Fisher of Souderton, Pennsylvania, and registered with the PHBA as Allen's Gold Zephyr. The horse was also registered with the Tennessee Walking Horse Association (TWHA) and the PHA.

Allen's Gold Zephyr was sired by Barker's Moonbeam (TWHBA, color: yellow) and he by foundation Tennessee Walker stallion Golden Sunshine. Zephyr's dam was Fisher's Gray Maud (registered TWHBA, color: gray) and she by Curlee's Spotted Allen out of Susie Hill. At five years of age Allen's Gold Zephyr stood 15.3 hands tall and weighed about 1050 lbs. He was described as dark eyes and dark skin; dark golden in body coat color; evenly matched white stocking on all four legs; blaze extending into left nostril; white mane and tail.

Trigger Jr. received billing on personal appearance tours. Marquees read, "Roy Rogers, Trigger, and Trigger, Jr." Glenn Randall taught Trigger Jr. a few crowd-pleasing tricks. Beyond the movie that bears his name in the title, Trigger Jr. was not used in films, but appeared extensively in personal appearances throughout the 1950s and 1960s. On certain occasions he was used as a double for Trigger. Copies of an old Perry Como television show are in circulation with an appearance by Roy Rogers, Dale Evans, and "Trigger." It's in fact Trigger Jr. standing in. When author David Rothel asked Rogers about using Trigger Jr. in movies, he replied, "Very little, we used him for personal appearances. He wasn't worth a nickel as a cowboy horse, but he could do a beautiful dance routine."[4]

Paul K. Fisher, "P.K." to his friends, was a walking encyclopedia when it came to palominos. He was on the PHA board of directors from the early 1940s when the organization began. At one time Fisher Farms was considered one of the largest palomino breeding facilities in the United States—1,700 acres in Souderton. Fisher eventually started breeding Tennessee Walkers mostly because of their even dispositions. He finally acquired

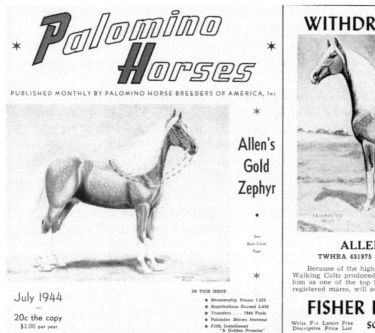

Before Allen's Gold Zephyr became Trigger Jr., he was featured on the cover of *Palomino Horses* magazine published by the PHBA (July 1944). A second portrait appeared inside (also by Elizabeth Bell of Rochester, New York), part of a sacrifice sale ad sponsored by Fisher Palomino Farms. Apparently the facility had to reduce its stock by more than half due to a hired help shortage. Allen's Gold Zephyr was not part of the sale because of the high percentage of quality colts he had sired (Roy Dillow collection).

enough to build a breeding program that blossomed into one of the largest herds in the world, over 200 registered mares. He would also eventually breed American Saddlebred and Arabian palominos. Articles appeared in newspapers across the country, and Fisher's horses were the subjects of many a magazine feature, including a 1948 issue of *LIFE* magazine. He passed away October 1991 at age 91 in Harleysville, Pennsylvania.

Before Roy Rogers, Hoot Gibson and Tom Mix had been Paul K. Fisher customers. Fisher often took his horses to Madison Square Garden Rodeo to show and sell. According to Roy Rogers, Fisher's palominos were in great demand, as Rogers found out when he tried to buy Allen's Gold Zephyr. Rogers stated that it took him six years to buy the stud. Fisher had many offers besides the one from Rogers. At first Fisher refused because the horse was so important to his breeding program.[5] Rogers really fell in love with Trigger Jr. during the filming of the movie that bears the palomino's name. Apparently the stud was still owned and on loan by Fisher who did not agree to sell him. Fisher allowed Rogers to use Trigger Jr. in personal appearances, according to Corky Randall. Fisher was finally forced to sell the stud after a well-publicized dispersal sale in 1947, to John Ewell, not to Roy Rogers.

According to Cheryl Rogers-Barnett, one Mel Marion, as a very young man, ran the stables next to the Apple Valley Inn where Trigger Jr. and Buttermilk were kept after her father built the first museum in 1966. There early visitors got to see them in the flesh.[6] The horses were on display at the museum during the day and locked up at night. Trigger

Rare shot of Paul K. Fisher on Trigger Jr. in front of Roy Rogers' custom-made touring van. The singing cowboy was touring in the East Coast, most likely Pennsylvania circa 1951 (PHBA collection).

One of the earliest known shots of Glenn Randall with Trigger Jr. Judging by the coat the trainer was wearing, this photograph may have been taken in the East Coast fall or winter perhaps during a visit to Pennsylvania. (Roy Dillow collection).

Jr. and Buttermilk only lived a couple of years after the move. According Marion, Roy Rogers never bred Trigger Jr. while at the Apple Valley location. As Cheryl Rogers-Barnett confirmed, "The only horse Dad bred early on was Harvester Trigger. Trigger Jr. had been bred before Dad got him but he was Golden Zephyr then."

Triggerson, the horse that actor Val Kilmer led on stage as a tribute to Roy Rogers and his B-western cowboy peers during the Academy Awards show in March 1999, was reportedly a descendent of Trigger.[7] Since Trigger was never bred, this horse—if descended from any of Rogers' horses—was most likely one of the palomino studs from Rogers' Happy Trails Ranch in Oro Grande or a descendant of Harvester-Trigger, the stallion from Yuba City in northern California. Trigger Jr. did not live long enough to be at the Oro Grande ranch.

For many years, Rogers also raised and trained Thoroughbred racehorses at his Happy Trails Ranch, such as Run Trigger Run, who took first place in his maiden race. Another Rogers race horse was called Triggaro. In October 1993, Rogers auctioned the last of his herd, which included grandsons and granddaughters of Trigger Jr. The palomino sired several foals that were registered with TWHBA, and his bloodline continues today.[8]

In recognition of their devotion to the palomino horse and for their part in advancing the breed, Roy Rogers and Dale Evans were presented with lifetime memberships in the PHBA. They were declared "ambassadors of good will for palomino horses the world over and now duly recognized for their contributions." The award was given in Oklahoma during a benefit premiere showing of Rogers' film *MacIntosh and T.J.* and noted by Robert Shiflet in *Palomino Horses* magazine in 1976.

Pal O' Mine

In *The Bells of San Angelo* (1946) and *The Golden Stallion* (1949), Dale Evans rode a brown and white pinto. It seemed she and Rogers decided she needed a regular horse and had started looking. It's no surprise they tried to match Evans at first with another palomino. Around 1950 she was using one named Pal for personal appearances. Evans rode him in the pilot episode of her television series, *Queen of the West*. The show never aired (it is included in the DVD release *The Rogers Family Presents: TV Collection, Pilots & Rarities*) because Evans joined her husband in the highly successful and long-running *The Roy Rogers Show* in 1951. She didn't use Pal in that particular show because he looked too much like Trigger. It was thought that the audience would get the two horses confused. In *Rainbow Over Texas* (1946) Rogers rode Pal in a pony express race where one rider used a string of horses. Pal was the first mount Rogers rode to compete in the event. Pal also doubled as Trigger on occasion during personal appearances.

Dale Evans rode a very young Pal during a brief sequence in *My Pal Trigger*. In the

Dale Evans on Pal and Roy Rogers on the original Trigger in front of a crowd of more than 100,000 at the Sheriff's Rodeo at the Los Angeles Coliseum in 1949 (Roy Dillow collection).

scene, after Rogers discovers Trigger's sire, the Golden Sovereign, dead in a corral, Evans rides up on Pal.

Pal's original name was Pal O' Mine and he was foaled on a ranch owned by Joe and Mary Reynolds in Douglas, Wyoming. Pal O' Mine's dam was a buckskin mare named Steel-Dust. His sire was a bay stallion named Temple Boy, the son of Sir Barton and Temple Girl. As noted earlier, this has led some to believe it was the original Trigger who was a descendant of the famous Sir Barton.[9]

Pal O' Mine was first sold to a rancher named Walt Rymill, who employed Orval Robinson, a trainer and former jockey, on his ranch. Glenn Randall, a native of the Lusk-Torrington area, was acquainted with Rymill. In the 1940s, when Randall was looking for horse to double Trigger, he called Rymill and was invited to see Pal O' Mine at the Rymill Ranch. Robinson happened to be riding the horse when Randall arrived. Immediately Randall was struck by Pal O' Mine's resemblance to Trigger, except that he had white stockings on both hind legs and the front left. Randall bought the horse for $2,500.[10]

The Lusk Herald dated May 25, 1944, printed the statement: "It is understood Rogers gave $2000 for the horse. He intends to train him to take the place of Trigger, who is getting a little too old to follow the strenuous life of a movie actor." At first it was assumed that Pal O' Mine became Trigger Jr., but this was not the case. Darryl Manring of Lusk, while visiting the Roy Rogers Museum in Victorville in May of 1993, was able to speak to Rogers about Pal O' Mine. The King of the Cowboys was very candid about the horse. He verified that Pal O' Mine became a star in certain ways. He called the horse versatile and talented. He acknowledged that Pal O' Mine was in some of his movies, was Dale Evans' mount during public appearances for a time, and was Rogers' favorite trail horse.[11]

Cheryl Rogers-Barnett wrote in *Cowboy Princess Rides Again*, "Dad had bought Pal for Mom to ride in their films but he looked too much like Trigger, so I got to have him." She included a photo of herself on Pal at the family's Encino ranch.[12] She also claimed her father eventually sold Pal to a trick rider from Encino, California, circa 1954.

California and Monarch

Corky Randall recalled another Trigger double named California and claimed Roy Rogers bought him at a California horse show. During our first conversations, Corky could not remember the horse's name, but eventually he recalled it in a dream. The palomino had a narrow blaze, shaped almost like a diamond up on his forehead that narrowed down to his muzzle. As with many of the more anonymous doubles, records on this particular horse have not surfaced. When he was still in junior college, Corky used the horse in a San Francisco college rodeo during a calf roping competition. California often doubled for Trigger in *The Roy Rogers Show*.

In the second fight sequence from *Trigger Jr.*, California was the stunt "Trigger." Director William Witney said that the horses were not injured doing these scenes because wires were used to pull and guide them off one another.[13]

The last Trigger double Corky Randall was able to identify was a tall palomino named Monarch. Rocky Roe identified the horse in William Witney's book *Trigger Remembered*.[14] According to Roe, Dale Evans rode Monarch (along with Trigger) during a dressage sequence in *My Pal Trigger* (1946). She also rode him shortly afterward in an

Left: **Roy Rogers on Monarch in** *Pals of the Golden West* **(1951). Right: Rogers on Monarch from** *In Old Amarillo* **(1951). The palomino had a striking resemblance to the original Trigger, more than Little Trigger or Trigger Jr. had (Roy Dillow collection).**

equine square dance scene. Monarch acted up when Roy Rogers rode up on his mare, Lady. Rogers also rode Monarch in some of the climactic racing footage at the end of *My Pal Trigger*. Monarch was used sometimes as a stunt double. He appeared in *Home in Oklahoma* (1946) and was ridden by stuntman Joe Yrigoyen in *North of the Great Divide* (1950).

Monarch was a close match to the original Trigger in head type and size, but with white socks in the rear and pale socks in front. According to Rocky Roe, Monarch's blaze was similar to Trigger's. It was wide and had a similar drop on both sides of the face, the difference being Monarch's blaze came to a slight point high up on the forehead and on the nose (especially the right side). The white line continued through the nose whereas Trigger's line dropped off before it got to the nostril. On their left nostrils Monarch's and Trigger's blaze lines were similar, both extended through the nostril. Up on Trigger's forehead was where the blazes differed. Trigger's blaze was broad and more rounded where as Monarch's was narrow and had a slight peak.

Rocky Roe also spotted both California and Monarch in two Spade Cooley low-budget westerns, *The Silver Bandit* (Friedgen, 1947) and *The Kid from Gower Gulch* (Friedgen/Aster, 1950).

In *The Silver Bandit,* California (all decked out in fancy parade tack) was ridden by the title character. Monarch was ridden by Spade Cooley when he chased the Silver Bandit, who was trying to escape in a wagon.

Roy Rogers converses with border patrolman Pat Brady in *Pals of the Golden West* (1951) with Monarch standing behind. Visible to keep the palomino in place are string hobbles on his two front legs midway up the cannon bones (Roy Dillow collection).

In *The Kid from Gower Gulch*, protagonist Craig Morgan and female lead Peggy Andrews both rode California. Shorty, a little cowboy, rode Monarch during a calf-roping demonstration. Spade Cooley climbed on board the palomino in a brief sequence right before three cowboys pursued him in a long chase sequence.

Monarch was used very effectively in a few of Roy Rogers' later films, none better than *The Golden Stallion*. Again, he was ridden for the most part by stuntman Joe Yrigoyen. Early on when Roy Rogers jumps Trigger over a fence to save Dale Evans, it was Yrigoyen on Monarch. When Trigger jumps a fence and runs off with the Belle Mare, cowboys were chasing Monarch and Lady.

According to Rocky Roe, "In *Pals of the Golden West*, Rogers' last movie at Republic, Trigger was used in only one scene. Monarch looked so much like Trigger, though he didn't have the same conformation nor was he as handsome, one has to look very closely to tell the difference. This drove Robert W. Phillips crazy. He knew Roy Rogers had

Opposite, top: **Roy Rogers roping a calf on Trigger double California in front of Fess Reynolds' property next to the Randall Ranch (Roy Dillow collection).** *Bottom:* **Fight sequence from the color movie *Trigger Jr.* (1950). Stunt double California stood in for the title character during this confrontation with a trained stallion named Phantom.**

another palomino look-alike who was really close in looks to the Old Man, way more so than Little Trigger or Trigger Jr. All along it was Monarch." Because Monarch was gelded and Trigger was not, that just added to the confusion. As it turned out, Trigger was in only one scene in *Pals of the Golden West*, riding through the Circle S gate. Monarch and other doubles played him throughout the rest of movie. Because this was Roy Rogers' last film for Republic Pictures and Herbert Yates, the singing cowboy was apparently saving Trigger for his television show.

As Monarch and California belonged to Glenn Randall, who was in the horse business and rented to whomever, it's possible they were used as cast horses in the *Bat Masterson* television show. Rocky Roe claims they were. Roy Rogers' television series ended June 9, 1957; Monarch and California would have been available for the Masterson shows early- to mid-1960 until late 1961, probably the third season. The blazes on the Masterson horses are the same as the ones in Rogers' movies. Every Palomino has its own distinct blaze, no two alike; as with fingerprints they may be similar but no are two identical.

Cheryl Rogers-Barnett believes Monarch and California were never owned by her father (contrary to what Corky Randall claimed) and didn't recall ever seeing them in Hidden Valley where Little Trigger and Trigger died years later. She didn't know for sure but guessed Monarch and California were gelded. Monarch was a dressage horse that Glenn Randall's wife, Minnie, used on the horse show circuit in California.

Trigger Doubles and Continuity

For a fairly decent view of Trigger and most of his doubles try watching *Rainbow Over Texas*. As with all B-movies it's made of pieces from other sources and some shots

Roy Rogers riding an anonymous Hudkins Trigger double in a scene from *Under Western Stars*, released in 1938 (Roy Dillow collection).

created especially for the production. If one were looking to make sense of a Republic story sequence from shot to shot, good luck. Republic employed "script girls" on set to keep things in order but only up to a point. Lax continuity and incongruous editing was Republic's style by default. On any B-western set for that matter; continuity wasn't going to get in the way of telling a story: shoot fast, edit whatever works, and above all work cheap. Work progressed in high gear, with the clock ticking. Republic Pictures maintained its existence with very sparse budgets; the overall image was everything, continuity be damned, and it showed. Conversely, that often made for some thrilling sequences and darn interesting behind-the-scenes stories.

The final sections of *Rainbow Over Texas* consisted of the preparation and participation in a relay race. Roy Rogers used a team of palominos of course. The sharp-eyed Rocky Roe sorted out the Rogers string as well as possible given the quality of the film. The race sequence used footage from other Roy Rogers movies.

In the stable sequence when Gabby Hayes, Dale Evans, and Roy Rogers first inspect the palominos in preparation for the race, four are lined up in stalls. Rocky Roe believes, "The first one is Monarch, the second is Pal, third horse looks somewhat like Little Trigger, the fourth one unknown, not California because the blaze is too wide, and definitely not Trigger Jr. The relay race continuity, with some shots taken from *Hands Across the Border*, is best described as a horse-to-horse hodgepodge.

Liberty Palomino Act

At one time Roy Rogers performed on tour with a string of eight highly trained palominos in a ring without halters or reins, the kind of act one would see at a circus. The horses were owned by Glenn Randall and referred to as the Roy Rogers Liberty Horse Act. On occasion the King of the Cowboys used them on personal appearances at rodeos and state fairs for a couple of summers. Individual horses came and went. Corky

The Roy Rogers Liberty Horse act, owned and trained by Glenn Randall (Joel "Dutch" Dortch collection).

Randall recalled a particular palomino named Tiger, who was out of an Oklahoma stallion named Phillips 66, as being very difficult. Satin was the first lead horse. Tiger later became lead and was followed by Murphy, Chalk Eye, Dick, Sonny, Pal, Rex and Elmer. When Glenn Randall was putting the act together, he purchased horses in groups. Koko, the stallion who was eventually teamed with Rex Allen, was bought as part of such a group, but because of his chocolate color, he was never considered for the Liberty Horse Act.

Witnesses to the Glenn Randall Liberty Horse Act were amazed by what they were trained to do with voice and whip cues. The climax of the act had all the horses standing with front legs-on a raised platform performance circle. Given a certain command, all turned their heads half-way to the left (they were moving counter-clockwise) at the same split second, an exact amount of turn, then a stop. It was procession like no one had ever seen, all palominos turning their heads and stopping together like robots set to a thousandth of a second.

In 2015, an episode of the *Roy Rogers Chevy Show* from 1959 (complete with commercials) was posted on YouTube. The Roy Rogers Liberty Horse Act was featured at the 37-minute mark performing an entire routine, The King of the Cowboys was center ring with seven palominos circling in unison (Glenn Randall was also present in a dark suit and white hat). It is a masterful joy to behold.

Buttermilk

Trigger had a number of four-legged sidekicks. Frog Millhouse's mare, Ring-Eyed Nellie, and Raymond Hatton's little mule, Dinah, were the first. Gabby Hayes' bay, Eddie, was probably his most regular sidekick. Roy Rogers' German shepherd, Bullet, was probably his best known, along with Dale Evans' light buckskin, Buttermilk.

According to Ken Beck and Jim Clark's *Encyclopedia of TV Pets*, Buttermilk was born in 1941. It was trainer Glenn Randall who found the buckskin Quarter Horse gelding with dark points. That Buttermilk survived his early life and made it to Hollywood is a story in itself. As a colt, Buttermilk had been severely abused and was consequently very mean. He was bought as a colt from a horse trader as he was being taken to slaughter. The cattle farmer who rescued him named him Taffy and began training him as a cutting and roping competition horse. With patience and kindness, Taffy eventually developed a friendly disposition. Randall, always looking for animals to train, noticed Taffy in a competition at the miniature rodeo in Nebraska and purchased the little buckskin, originally for Corky. Later he thought the horse would make a good mount for Dale Evans. Buddy Sherwood, a wrangler on the set of *The Roy Rogers Show*, suggested the name Soda. Evans named the gelding Buttermilk, from a Hoagie Carmichael tune, "Ole Buttermilk Sky."

According to author Vivian H. Whitlock in his essay "Buttermilk and Trigger," for the September 1960 issue of *Western Horseman*, Glenn Randall found the "handsome six-year-old buckskin gelding on a ranch in Angora, Nebraska, near Alliance. He was a trim and fast Quarter Horse, being used as a working pony on the ranch for cutting and roping. His smallness, plus his vivid coloring of black mane and tail against the palest of buckskin coats, made him an excellent contrast to the big golden Trigger."

Dale Evans first rode Buttermilk on screen in 1950 in *Twilight in the Sierras*. Actress Penny Edwards rode Buttermilk when she co-starred with Rogers in *Spoilers of the Plains*

Dale Evans with her Quarter Horse gelding, Buttermilk, a handsome duo (Ray White collection).

and *Heart of the Rockies*, both released in 1951. Evans was on maternity leave at the time, having just given birth to her baby Robin.

Buttermilk was even noted in Dale Evans' comic book. While Evans was switching her publisher from DC to Dell, her horse was given the name Soda for the last few issues. So Pal was in the DC series at first, then Soda came next for a brief stint, then Buttermilk in the Dell series.

Buttermilk appeared in all but six *Roy Rogers Show* episodes that aired from 1951 to 1957. Many people associated with Rogers and Evans commented that Buttermilk was a hard ride; it was rumored that the diminutive horse even managed to unseat Glenn Randall one time.

Trigger could outrun any horse on the set. But you had to be "with him" whenever you gave him a cue to go left or right or he'd spin right out from under you. However, quarter horses are bred for a quick takeoff and Buttermilk was actually faster in short distances than Trigger. This irritated Rogers and often required retakes of scenes when Buttermilk broke away sooner.

According to Corky Randall, the light buckskinned Buttermilk did not have a double per se. Although he appeared on most of the episodes of *The Roy Rogers Show*, he wasn't ridden hard. On rare occasions, when a double was necessary, a grey horse was used for long shots.

Corky Randall also claimed that his father, Glenn, eventually gave Buttermilk to Dale Evans after *The Roy Rogers Show* had been canceled on television. Buttermilk died in 1972. Like the original Trigger, he lived to 31 years of age.

Trigger doubles: Trigger Jr. was used for live and televised appearances for basic tricks, dressage and photo shoots (the only Rogers horse that used a double-bridle). Little Trigger's specialities were tricks, dressage, also photo shoots. Monarch and California were used for stunts and running inserts. Both Rogers and Evans rode Pal briefly in movies. Evans used him in a television pilot and photo shoots. Monarch, California, Pal and other Randall stock were used as display "Triggers" on tour. Miscellaneous Hudkins palominos were used for action sequences.

8

Golden Stallion, Silver Screen

*"About nineteen years ago, Trigger was a colt romping around on a San Diego ranch,
when a movie talent scout saw him and brought him to the Ace Hudkins Stables in
North Hollywood for training. He had appeared in quite a few movies and was six years
old when we met."*—Roy Rogers[1]

Roy Rogers and Republic Pictures capitalized on the original Trigger's great looks, camera presence, and intelligence, and used him to maximum effect. This was a gradual process. First Rogers had to become established with the movie-going public. Then as Trigger's popularity increased, more attention was given to him. At the beginning, the original Trigger was primarily used to give Rogers a beautiful and charismatic horse to ride (if most kids were like yours truly, their eyes were focused on him). However, whenever the opportunity arose, the "Trigger" character was referred to by name or at least acknowledged even when he did not have a significant role. In time, movie plots were influenced by Trigger, as when he ran for help as in *Spoilers of the Plains* (1951) or *Bells of San Angelo* (1947). Rogers, a diligent promoter, even referred to Trigger in songs.

Eventually Trigger was held in such high esteem, that not only was he billed just below Rogers, six movies were produced around him, more than any other B-western horse, including Gene Autry's Champion.

Regrettably, uncut copies of Roy Rogers' movies broadcast on television are rare. The films were trimmed for syndication from around 70 minutes to just over 50 in order to fill a one-hour slot with commercials. It is therefore possible special scenes with "Trigger" were lost.

Trigger's Movie Persona

Trigger's role changed from film to film. In some movies he actively protected his master; on other occasions, he was like any other horse, just transportation. In *Utah* (1945) he actually saved Gabby Hayes from bad guy Wally Wales (Hal Taliaferro). At the end of *San Fernando Valley* (1944) Rogers ran down bad guys Kenne Duncan and Leroy Mason. Forced to fight both men, Rogers lost the upper hand and was knocked out. Duncan grabbed a large dead branch to finish him off. Little Trigger came to the rescue and attacked Duncan as Rogers regained consciousness. In *Sunset in the West* (1950), however, Trigger stood by as a bound and blindfolded Rogers was nearly thrown off a cliff by a

A middle-aged 15-year-old Trigger in an outtake from the *Golden Stallion* (1949). He was so well trained and accustomed to movie sets that he often worked at liberty (Roy Dillow collection).

couple of crooks. In *South of Caliente* (1951) Trigger also stood passively as Rogers fought two gypsies. After they overpowered him and departed, Trigger nuzzled Rogers as he lay in the dirt.

"Trigger" seemed to have been able to run at a full gallop without ever tiring. After many long chases Rogers never once changed him for a fresh mount. One would be hard pressed to find an instance in any Rogers movies where he ever said that his horse needed a rest. In *Heart of the Golden West* (1942), after Rogers and the Sons of the Pioneers lost the trail of a gang of cattle thieves, Rogers suggested that they get fresh horses and resume the search in the morning. The next day, however, he was on Trigger again. In *The Gay Ranchero* (1948), Rogers mounted up and rode off to rendezvous with, of all things, an airplane. At a full gallop over miles, horse and rider reached an appointed rendezvous spot only to find that the pilot and passengers had been attacked after landing near a gang of bad guys on horseback. Rogers put Trigger into high gear again and proceeded to chase the crooks. Trigger was fresh as a daisy, never breaking a sweat, catching up to horses who hadn't been running all afternoon.[2]

Trigger as Shield

Realism aside, some fans were surprised and a little disappointed when Rogers hid behind Trigger to avoid gunfire. Many a time Rogers was seen ducking behind the palomino as they pursued bad guys who were returning fire as they fled. Rogers did it in chase sequences in *On the Old Spanish Trail* (1947), *The Gay Ranchero*, *The Far Frontier* (1948), and *Sunset in the West*. Trigger is used the same way in the last movie Rogers made for Republic Pictures, *Pals of the Golden West* (1951). Rogers was not, however, the last cowboy to use this tactic. Augustus McCrea (Robert Duvall) in *Lonesome Dove* (Motown Productions, 1989) stabbed his horse in the neck, killing it instantly, to create a barrier to hide behind as a gang of thugs was closing in on him. Shocking, but close to how it must have been in the Old West.

Not only did Rogers use Trigger as a shield, but he also gambled that the palomino wouldn't get shot during many a difficult situation. At the end of *The Gay Ranchero*, Rogers cornered bad guy Leroy Mason in a cabin. Rogers approached

Much to the chagrin of some fans, the King of the Cowboys sometimes used his palomino as a shield while dodging bullets.

on foot and then tried to draw Mason out by stomping on the front porch. Mason shot through the front door and Rogers ducked for cover. He then whistled for Trigger, who approached, turned around and started mule kicking the same door to break it down. Luckily for the palomino, instead of shooting through the door again, Mason panicked and hid.

In *Home in Oklahoma* (1946), Rogers and Gabby Hayes used their mounts as shields when they charged through a line of rifle men. In today's westerns, that stunt wouldn't work because marksmen would simply shoot the horses. In the 1994 Warner Bros. motion picture *Wyatt Earp*, actor Kevin Costner told his partner to shoot the horses being ridden by a gang of outlaws who were pursuing them. "Shoot the horse. Shoot the lead horse. You can shoot a horse, can't ya?" No self-respecting B-western cowboy would have ever uttered such a line, and he would have been deserted by his fans if he had.

Considering all the gun fights Trigger was exposed to on screen, it's a wonder he wasn't shot more often. In *Frontier Pony Express* (1939) Rogers was cautioned by sidekick Raymond Hatton not to take "Trigger" into a gunfight. The palomino finally took a bullet in *Twilight in the Sierras* (1950). Veterinarian Sparrow Biffle, played by Pat Brady, attended to his wound while Rogers calmed the horse down.

Golden Cloud Solo Roles

The Golden Cloud/Trigger was in Hollywood earning his oats for Hudkins Bros. Stables by 1937. With his striking looks, it didn't take the palomino long to find work in motion pictures. Between 1937 and 1943 the Golden Cloud/Trigger was in demand, doing double duty as a Hudkins stable cast horse and Roy Rogers' screen partner.

Going by release date, April 20, 1938, *Under Western Stars* was Trigger's first known screen appearance. In 1938 he was in six that are on record, and of those, only four were made with Roy Rogers at Republic Pictures. The other two were made for Warner Bros.: *The Adventures of Robin Hood* and *Cowboy from Brooklyn*.

Beyond traditional westerns, the Golden Cloud would be used in history, adventure, and comedy movies. The palomino not only appeared in Republic movies but ones produced by Warner Brothers, MGM, Columbia, and 20th Century–Fox. It's noteworthy how from the start, the Golden Cloud was paired with lead actors; he wasn't just background or part of a posse (except for a walk-on in *Gone With the Wind*). The Golden Cloud shared scenes with an impressive number of A-list actors of the day. The only other Hollywood horse peers who were his equal in that regard were Dice, Steel, and Highland Dale/Fury. Steel, a big chestnut with a white blaze out of the Fat Jones stables, was in his share of A-westerns. He was ridden by the likes of Clark Gable, Joel McCrea, Robert Mitchum, Randolph Scott, Ben Johnson and Henry Fonda.

THE ADVENTURES OF ROBIN HOOD

The Golden Cloud's first known appearance without Roy Rogers in a movie was in *The Adventures of Robin Hood*. It was based on the well-known English legend of Robin of Locksley, a nobleman forced to become an outlaw when evil Prince John took the throne from his absent brother Richard I, who was off fighting in the Crusades. Along the way Robin Hood defended the throne for Richard I and won the heart of Maid Marian.

Much press has been devoted to Golden Cloud and his role as actress Olivia de Havilland's mount in *The Adventures of Robin Hood*. This is undoubtedly the most famous of his film appearances without Roy Rogers and the only one ever officially acknowledged by the King of the Cowboys.

From a production standpoint, *The Adventures of Robin Hood* is arguably the best film Golden Cloud ever appeared in. It was a big-budget motion picture, shot in glorious Technicolor, and featured Errol Flynn at the head of an A-list cast. It is generally considered a classic, and in 2003 Warner Bros. issued a special edition DVD.

Along with the restored version of the film, the special edition DVD includes a documentary titled *Welcome to Sherwood Forest*. During the section on casting, Rogers fan and film historian Leonard Maltin pointed out that although many of the cast members were movie veterans at the time the film, there was one rookie: Trigger. He went on to say that the palomino was at the beginning of "a long and distinguished career" and described Trigger as "one of the greatest horses in the history of movies, and apparently, from all accounts, an exceptionally smart horse." He noted that the palomino was then called Golden Cloud. There are even a couple of behind-the-scenes shots of Olivia de Havilland on Trigger.

It has never been revealed how Roy Rogers learned of Trigger's appearance in *The*

Olivia de Havilland (Maid Marian) on the Golden Cloud, standing next to Errol Flynn (Robin Hood) on the set of *The Adventures of Robin Hood* **filmed in Chico, California (Warner Bros., 1938). Insert: Stand-in Dorothy Ändre on the Golden Cloud (Roy Dillow collection).**

Adventures of Robin Hood. Some business associate or friend may have spotted the horse and told him. Glenn Randall, Sr., or Rogers may have been told by one of the Hudkins brothers as the palomino was being used at about the same time in *Under Western Stars.*

Rogers obviously liked the story of Trigger's appearance in *The Adventures of Robin Hood* and repeated it often. When the publicity folks followed suit, it became part of the "Trigger" legend. Trigger's appearance in *The Adventures of Robin Hood* is so well known that when the film was shown on the Turner Movie Classics Channel, host Robert Osborne acknowledged Golden Cloud/Trigger.

The golden palomino appeared for the first time about 35 minutes into *The Adventures of Robin Hood*. Robin Hood (Flynn) and his men overpowered the Sheriff of Nottingham (Basil Rathbone), his company of soldiers, and Maid Marian (De Havilland) riding the Golden Cloud (possibly on a side-saddle). As Robin Hood and his men led the royal company back to their secret camp, the Golden Cloud was in full view briefly in the same frame as De Havilland, Flynn, and Rathbone. Flynn was on foot leading the palomino. The Sherwood Forest sequence ended when De Havilland and company were released, at which point Flynn once again led the Golden Cloud, carrying De Havilland, to a clearing at the edge of his secret camp. De Havilland and the palomino were last seen from behind as they galloped off.

COWBOY FROM BROOKLYN

The musical comedy titled *Cowboy from Brooklyn* featured an all-star cast of Hollywood celebrities including Dick Powell, Priscilla Lane, Pat O'Brien and future U.S. president Ronald Reagan.[3] Dick Foran appeared as the heavy; later he would go on to make a few singing cowboy westerns with his own palomino, Smoke.

A typical fish-out-of-water story, *Cowboy from Brooklyn* concerned a Brooklynite (Powell) who became a cowboy in spite of himself. After drifting into a small western town, he met a cowgirl (Lane), who offered him a ranch job. He was a gifted singer and attracted the attention of a talent scout (O'Brien). Before long, he became America's favorite singing cowboy but was hard-pressed to prove his western skills, especially as he was afraid of horses.

The Golden Cloud appeared very briefly in the first five minutes of *Cowboy from Brooklyn* when actress Priscilla Lane rode him while leading a posse of cowgirls. They approached a ranch house, where Lane dismounted and handed Golden Cloud over to a wrangler, who led him away. The blaze across his nose (dropping on his far side and ending at his lip) is obvious with a frame-by-frame inspection.

The Golden Cloud ridden by an anonymous stunt-woman doubling for actress Priscilla Lane in this brief sequence from the western musical comedy *Cowboy from Brooklyn* (Warner Bros., 1938).

Later, Lane mounted Golden Cloud quickly to pursue star Dick Powell who'd been running away from an angry donkey. Here the palomino's appearance was even briefer than before.

JUAREZ

Juarez (Warner Bros., 1939) is a weighty costume epic about the 19th-century Mexican revolutionary Benito Juarez. It's sizeable, not only for a running time of 132 minutes,

Actor Gilbert Roland, on the Golden Cloud, leads an honor guard for Emperor Maxmilian of Mexico (Brian Aherne) in *Juarez* (Warner Bros. 1939).

but with 1,000 extras and 54 massive sets. *Juarez* was as ambitious a production as *The Adventures of Robin Hood*, but it never attained the same status as a classic. The legendary Bette Davis played Carlota von Habsburg, the wife of Emperor Maximilian; John Garfield portrayed General Porfirio Diaz, and Claude Rains played Emperor Louis Napoleon III. Paul Muni starred as the title character, Don Benito Pablo Juarez. As

Actor Gilbert Roland, as Colonel Miguel Lopez, on the Golden Cloud on the set of the 1939 Warner Bros. motion picture *Juarez*.

president of Mexico, Juarez led his beloved country in its fight for independence in the 1860s when France was trying to colonize it.

In the film, the newly named emperor Maximilian (Brian Aherne) and his wife Carlota arrived in Mexico to clash head on with the popular sentiment that favored Benito Juarez and democracy. It is in the first part of the film, when actor Gilbert Roland, as Colonel Miguel Lopez, may be seen riding Golden Cloud. Lopez and his men were escorting the royal couple from their docked ship to the emperor's castle. Emperor Maximilian and Lopez engaged in a brief dialogue, Maximilian from the window of the royal coach and Lopez riding Golden Cloud alongside. It's a brief sequence but long enough to get a good look at the palomino's distinctive blaze.

The bizarre gag bit/curb bit the Golden Cloud was wearing may have been because he was a young stud carrying a novice rider. The Golden Cloud rarely used a tie-down much less a double bridle.

THE RAINS CAME

The Rains Came (20th Century–Fox, 1939), starred Tyrone Power, Myrna Loy, and Nigel Bruce, and the plot involved a romantic triangle between an Indian doctor, a British woman and her former flame.

Myrna Loy (Lady Edwina Esketh) and Tyrone Power (Major Rama Safti) return from a riding date in *The Rains Came* (20th Century–Fox, 1939). One gets only a glimpse of the Golden Cloud in this brief sequence. Of four palominos, he was assigned to Powers, the lead actor (Roy Dillow collection).

Tyrone Power on Golden Cloud on location alongside Myrna Loy in *The Rains Came* (20th Century–Fox, 1939). In this candid shot the blaze on the palomino's right side is unmistakable (Roy Dillow collection).

Lady Edwina Esketh (Loy) set out to seduce but gradually fell in love with Major Rama Safti (Power). It's on a riding date with the two characters when one gets a very brief glimpse of the Golden Cloud. The palomino stood out coming down a street just in the way he held his head. As Power dismounted, the Cloud's long flowing tail was visible in a side view. One can see how his blaze dropped a little to the left, then goes back up and down through his left nostril. This was followed by a hindquarters shot looking towards Golden Cloud's head with his wavy mane flowing on his right side. A final shot followed with Power and Loy running onto a porch to get out of the rain after which a handler led the Golden Cloud off-camera.

GONE WITH THE WIND

The most audacious claim in this book is that the Golden Cloud appeared in one of the greatest films Hollywood ever produced, *Gone with the Wind* (MGM, 1939). When considered together, a quick cameo and rare behind the scenes footage are credible. Between these two short corroborating segments, this writer and his Trigger experts are convinced.

Scott Coleman from Edmond, Oklahoma, gets credit for the discovery of a five minute YouTube clip, "Gone with the Wind & Vivien Leigh home video footage discovered!" (www.youtube.com/watch?v=2E4-KR86LnY), from NBC's *Today Show* circa 1999 hosted by news anchor Katie Couric. She interviewed Herb Bridges, owner of one of the largest *Gone with the Wind* collections in the world and co-writer of several books on the iconic film (*Gone with the Wind, The Definitive Illustrated History of the Book, the Movie and the Legend*, Fireside by Simon and Schuster, 1989). They discussed the then recently discovered home video footage by one Howard Hall filmed on the set of the Wilkes barbecue/Twelve Oaks sequence at Busch Gardens (California circa 1939).

Apparently Howard Hall had set access through his friend Paul Robinson, whose wife Ann was stand-in for Olivia de Havilland. Most of the footage shows director Victor Fleming and stars Clark Gable, Vivien Leigh, Olivia de Havilland, and Leslie Howard in antebellum costumes sitting by their trailers, smoking and waiting to film their scenes. Three minutes into the clip the home video features a beautiful palomino with a white rear left sock bearing a more than striking resemblance to Golden Cloud. Even the mane is on the correct side and its countenance feels correct. The Golden Cloud may be seen from the rear under English saddle moving from screen right to left. Trigger expert Rocky Roe agrees, "In this clip you can see a slight shot of the forelock and it's long; the hind quarters and the animal's movements are a dead giveaway. I was able to slow the clip down frame for frame and I'm ready to bet it is the Golden Cloud."

In *Gone with the Wind* movie itself, Golden Cloud appears after the Wilkes barbecue and the Civil War has been declared. Men are leaving to join fighting regiments amidst much commotion. Ashley Wilkes mounts his Tennessee Walker to ride off to war, three horses pass in the background, two dark mounts and a palomino (probably rear-projection, combining foreground performances with pre-filmed backgrounds). The sequence lasts only seconds and happens while Scarlett O'Hara and her beau watch through a large window. Although the image is in soft focus and fast, with a DVR and the replay feature, the palomino in question is the Golden Cloud. I would stake my Trigger lunch box on it!

Why have no photos surfaced of the Golden Cloud on the set of *Gone with the Wind*? In all his other movie cameos he was a cast horse, and a lead player was riding him. Clark Gable and Leslie Howard, as one might expect of Southern gentlemen, were riding Tennessee Walkers and such. A number set photos exist of them with their screen mounts. Regarding *Gone with the Wind*, the best one could say of the Golden Cloud is that he was hired for a day as an equine extra and relegated to the background.

As the premiere stock rental stable in Hollywood, it's very possible Hudkins Bros. Stables would have furnished horses for *Gone with the Wind*. The 1938–1939 production timeline works with the Golden Cloud's availability. Roy Rogers made approximately four movies with Republic in the first half of 1939, each having production schedules of two to three weeks, leaving more than enough time for MGM to have access to the horse. You can bet Hudkins would have supplied its best stock if approached by MGM for a blockbuster like *Gone with the Wind*. Seen alone, the Golden Cloud in *Gone with the Wind* could be argued by a skeptical onlooker; seen in concert with the home movie footage and a strong case can be made. Regardless of whether the Golden Cloud had actual *Gone with the Wind* screen time or not, just placing him on the set in home movie footage of this iconic film is a tantalizing bit of Hollywood history.

SHUT MY BIG MOUTH

Shut My Big Mouth (Columbia, 1942) is the story of a timid horticulturist named Wellington Holmes, played by comedian Joe E. Brown, and his adventures in the small western town of Big Bluff. About two minutes into the western comedy, Golden Cloud appeared in a brief sequence with villain Buckskin Bill (Victor Jory) riding him in fancy show saddle and all. (Roy Rogers' movie *South of Santa Fe*, released February 17, 1942, was shot around the same time as *Shut My Big Mouth*. Columbia used the same tack that Rogers had.) Jory and his men dismounted under a stand of trees to wait for the coach carrying Wellington Holmes. The Golden Cloud may be seen in close up waiting next to Jory. The remaining shots are of the palomino in motion, usually from a distance.[4] Approximately 17 minutes later, Wellington Holmes escaped Big Bluff disguised as a woman, when Buckskin Bill again held up his stage. Golden Cloud was very striking in this brief sequence among the other horses, which were all bays. The palomino is not on screen again after the first 20 minutes of *Shut My Big Mouth*—a pity, because his cameo appearance is the only redeeming thing in this silly movie.

Golden Cloud with villain Victor Jory in a scene from the Joe E. Brown comedy *Shut My Big Mouth* (Columbia, 1942). Jory was best known to serial fans as *The Shadow* (Columbia, 1940).

BAD MEN OF THE HILLS

While *The Adventures of Robin Hood* may have been the most prestigious film the Golden Cloud appeared in without Roy Rogers, one of the palomino's most involved non–"Trigger" roles was in an obscure Charles Starrett western titled *Bad Men of the Hills* (Columbia, 1942).[5] The 58-minute, black and white B-western was released one month after Republic released its thirtieth Roy Rogers movie, *Sons of the Pioneers*. Consequently, it's reasonable to assume people at Columbia knew the beautiful palomino they had leased for the *Bad Men of the Hills* production was Trigger. Columbia was probably not allowed to give him a screen credit or refer to him as Trigger, but director William A. Berke certainly used him for more than just beautiful transportation. The palomino figured into the plot of *Bad Men of the Hills* from the beginning. Golden Cloud played the part of a nameless horse first owned by Marshal Dave Upjohn (played by John Shay). He was later given to Lucky Shelton (Russell Hayden). Ironically, neither man actually rode the Golden Cloud on screen in *Bad Men of the Hills*; he was ridden only briefly by an unidentified stuntman in an early sequence.[6]

Charles Starrett played Marshal Steve Carlton, who had been sent to investigate after Upjohn was murdered. Carlton ended up in Chimney Hole, where he ran into Harmony Haines (Cliff "Ukulele Ike" Edwards) and Lucky Shelton. Shelton was now the owner of Marshal Upjohn's palomino, who was found roaming the hills. Shelton tied Golden Cloud up and asked Haines to look after him. Apparently the palomino had an attitude problem and misbehaved by stamping on the ground when Haines approached him. Carlton offered to help settle him. (At this point Golden Cloud turns toward the camera and, because his forelock is parted to one side, we get a great look at how his wide blaze ends at the top of his forehead and goes straight up on his far side and makes an arrow shape on his near side). Carlton even cradled Golden Cloud's head affectionately in his arms, causing his own horse, Raider, to let out a jealous neigh. Golden Cloud's mane was combed to the left side of his neck in some shots but his mane naturally flowed to the right.

Golden Cloud's third appearance took place at night. When Carlton returned to the barn after some late night investigating, the palomino started stomping again and woke Haines, who was asleep in a bunk. Carlton went to the horse to calm him. Haines described the horse as "one

Charles Starrett, left, and Cliff "Ukulele Ike" Edwards share a scene with Golden Cloud in *Bad Men of the Hills* (Columbia, 1942). Edwards' considerable vocal talents were featured in the Disney animated classic *Pinocchio* (1940) as the voice of Jiminy Cricket.

of the meanest critters I've ever seen." Carlton questioned Haines as to the palomino's origins, trying to find out what a horse that belonged to his murdered friend Marshal Upjohn was doing in Lucky Shelton's possession.

In a scene taking place the next morning, the Golden Cloud appeared for one last time. He was still in his stall; Carlton was tacking Raider up next to him. Before Carlton left he asked Haines to watch his horse and stepped out. Haines looked at Golden Cloud, pointed to the well-behaved Raider, and asked, "Why don't you act like him?" The Golden Cloud began to misbehave again and stomped on the ground. Haines threatened the horse but the palomino continued to stomp.

SILVER CITY RAIDERS

Golden Cloud/Trigger was in seven movies in 1943, one that we know of with Russell Hayden and six with Roy Rogers,who by then had made 39 movies post–Dick Weston.

Silver City Raiders (1943) was the first in a series of movies featuring Russell Hayden as the star at Columbia. He played Lucky Harlan, the same type of character he'd played in the Hopalong Cassidy movies.[7] The plot revolved around Hayden attempting to prove that a crooked land baron, played by Paul Sutton, didn't have prior claim on an entire territory. After legal methods failed to produce conclusive results, Hayden and his pals, Dub "Cannonball" Taylor and Bob Wills (both veterans from Charles Starrett's series of movies), used more effective methods to deal with Sutton and his thugs.

As he had in *Bad Men of the Hills*, director William A. Berke used the Golden Cloud to maximum effect. It's obvious the cast and crew knew they had a very special celebrity horse on the set so they featured him for all he was worth, taking every opportunity to show him off. Golden Cloud seemed to play a more pivotal role in *Silver City Raiders* than he did in many of Rogers' own movies. Almost all the running shots, from close up to medium, were actually done by the Golden Cloud. It could be argued that the folks at Columbia were having fun at Rogers' expense. It was one thing to rent the Golden Cloud for use in period pieces like *The Adventures of Robin Hood* and *Juarez* when Rogers was new to the movies, but it was something else again to rent him to another B-western movie cowboy when Rogers was the number one. Hayden started the movie in a dark hat but was later given a white hat to wear. One could speculate that this was intentional and meant as a visual cue to Rogers.

Seeing Hayden riding the Golden Cloud—and he did plenty of it—is astonishing because Rogers' family maintained that no other cowboy was allowed on him. Hayden was taller than Rogers, but not too big for Trigger.

The Golden Cloud did not make an appearance till about 30 minutes into *Silver City Raiders*, when Lucky Harlan decided to go to Santa Fe for the official records that would save all the ranches in the valley. For his ride to the train station he changed mounts. As he dismounted from the dark sorrel he'd been riding, he removed the saddle and ordered one of his saddle pals, "Bring me Comanche." Out came Golden Cloud. Harlan saddled him up and rode off.

In a later sequence Harlan was riding fast over a hill on "Comanche" when three bad guys started shooting. Harlan pulled up, evaluated the situation and cued the horse to move on. He spun to one side to shoot, then spun to the other side to take off running. It was here that the palomino was featured in a nice profile shot. Golden Cloud never looked better.

Golden Cloud as Comanche, Russ Hayden's mount in *Silver City Raiders*, released by Columbia Pictures in 1943 featuring Bob Wills and the Texas Playboys (Bobby Copeland collection).

Harlan eventually pulled up behind some rocks and started returning fire, with the horse looking over Harlan's shoulder. This is the same shot used on a lobby card. It's a comic book cover shot if ever there was one.[8]

When Lucky Harlan returned from Santa Fe, his enemies were waiting at the train station and got the drop on him. They forced him at gunpoint into a barn where "Comanche" was stabled. As they commenced to threaten Harlan, the palomino backed out of his stall, knocking down one of the thugs and giving Harlan the opportunity to relieve him of his gun. Finally in control, Harlan ordered his adversaries to bring his horse out of his stall and saddle him up. The palomino was filmed center stage.

In the next scene Lucky Harland was riding down a road with a bad guy on each side, the Golden Cloud was prancing like he was leading a parade. Bob Wills caught up to them and they all continued. By the time Harlan and company reached town, with no explanation Russell Hayden was back on the sorrel he began the movie on.

As B-westerns go, *Silver City Raiders* is pretty good. Bob Wills and the Texas Playboys provide great musical interludes and there's plenty of action. It's certainly on a par with some of the King of the Cowboy's movies, except that even riding the Golden Cloud Russell Hayden was no Roy Rogers.[9]

Trigger Stock Footage

As was common practice, Republic Pictures used stock and available footage to save money, subsequently Trigger may be seen in other non–Roy Rogers productions. A palomino in Bohlin tack is hard to miss among a herd of bays.

From *The Carson City Kid* (1940). This photograph was also used very briefly in the Gene Autry movie *Ride Tenderfoot Ride* (1940) with a picture of actress Mary Lee collaged over Rogers (Roy Dillow collection).

Ride Tenderfoot Ride (1940): In this Gene Autry movie, Trigger appeared in a photograph rearing with actress Mary Kay on his back. Autry noticed the photo on her dresser. On closer inspection, her face and upper body looked bigger and out of proportion. They were pasted over Roy Rogers in a publicity shot from *Carson City Kid* (1940).

Rancho Grande (1940): Trigger may also be seen in stock footage from this Gene Autry movie towards the end during a chase sequence. An anonymous cowboy is after a bad guy; he catches up and performs the old reliable bulldog stunt, a rider leaping from his horse to tackle a second rider on another mount. On this occasion the stunt man doing the honors was riding none other than Trigger.

Navajo Trail Riders (1949): Rocky Roe spotted Trigger in: Rocky Lane's *Navajo Trail Riders*, about outlaw gangs plundering freight supply lines. During one sequence a hatless Roy Rogers may be seen on Trigger being chased in a running gun battle. The pair, along with three or four other riders is leading wagons. In a second quick shot, Rogers riding Trigger shoots back at his pursuers.

Border Saddlemates (1952): Also according to Rocky Roe, Republic used stock footage during the Rex Allen movie *Border Saddlemates*. Republic bad guy Roy Barcroft was transporting counterfeit bills across the border in the bottom of fox cages. In a sequence where foxes are being chased through trees, Rogers may be seen out front on Trigger in footage from *Twilight in the Sierras* (1950).

Russell Hayden

Russell Hayden first appeared in the Hopalong Cassidy film *Bar 20 Rides Again* in 1936. A year later he was cast as sidekick Lucky Jenkins in *Hills of Old Wyoming*. During his tenure as Jenkins, he rode palominos, but Trigger is nowhere to be seen in a Hopalong Cassidy movie.

Russell Hayden went on to star in his own series at Columbia filmed after 1943, the same year Rogers bought Trigger.[10] Trigger could have appeared in other Russell Hayden Columbia movies.[11]

Halfway through Russell Hayden's movie *Knights of the Range*, released by Paramount years earlier in 1940, one gets a good look at his palomino. The animal had more than one white stocking and the blaze on the far side of his head did not match Trigger's. This horse might well be the same palomino Victor Jory rode in *Lights of Western Stars*, also released by Paramount in 1940. Hayden and leading lady Jo Ann Sayers shared a beautiful palomino named Pal who was featured prominently. Pal had four white socks. The blaze running down his nose did not match Trigger's. (This was not the same Pal Dale Evans rode.)

Russell Hayden was associated with the two most famous horses in B-westerns. Not only was he the only other cowboy to star in a western using Trigger as his horse; he also (briefly) rode Gene Autry's television Champion. In a *Gene Autry Show* episode titled "The Peacemaker," Hayden played a heavy who stole the sorrel and tried to ride away. Champion refused to leave Autry and bucked the Hayden character off, killing him in the fall. (George "Gabby" Hayes rode the original Trigger in *Robin Hood of the Pecos* and Gene Autry's original Champion during the rousing climax of *In Old Monterey* (1939).)

Movies About Trigger

Six motion pictures were produced around Trigger: *Hands Across the Border, My Pal Trigger, The Lights of Old Santa Fe, Under California Stars, The Golden Stallion*, and *Trigger, Jr.*

In *Hands Across the Border* (1943) Rogers plays a wrangler looking for a job when he first meets Trigger on a ranch owned by entertainer Kim Adams (Ruth Terry), daughter of rancher Jeff Adams (Joseph Crehan), who raises prize horses for the army. The palomino was part of a herd Adams caught and was hoping to train and sell as army remounts. Kim's dad loved "Trigger" but got thrown and killed when he tried to ride

Duncan Renaldo (left), before his role as the Cisco Kid, aided Roy Rogers (center) and sidekick Guinn "Big Boy" Williams in their quest to save Trigger after a price was put on his head in *Hands Across the Border*, 1943.

him. It fell on Rogers to befriend the palomino and save him from being destroyed by the villainous Brock Danvers (Onslow Stevens) who wished to marry Kim, take over her ranch, and monopolize the local remount business.

Trigger escapes back into the wild, but Rogers captures him with the help of sidekick Guinn "Big Boy" Williams and ranch foreman Duncan "the Cisco Kid" Renaldo. The three friends hide Trigger and Rogers sets to work training him. Rogers eventually shows Kim how valuable the palomino would be to her horse business. After she is convinced, she realizes she can carry on her dad's work with horses and win a valuable contract supplying the army remounts (the palomino even got to kiss her on the cheek). Trigger redeems himself by winning a race for the army remount contract against Danvers' horses.

Roy Rogers acknowledged *My Pal Trigger* (1946) as the favorite of his own movies. ("Roy, commenting later on his own role in the picture featuring Trigger, said that while he was virtually playing 'a supporting role to a horse,' it was one of his favorites."[12]) It is

Gabby Hayes, Dale Evans, and Roy Rogers in *My Pal Trigger* (1946). Evans is riding Trigger in English tack. The palomino was playing his own sire, the Golden Sovereign. Rogers' mount Lady also played the Belle Mare in *The Golden Stallion* (1949) (Roy Dillow collection).

certainly one of his best known and ranks as a fan favorite. Serious Roy Rogers fans remember the first time they saw it as children, sitting enthralled as the opening film credits crawl over a shot of Trigger in the back of a horse trailer. The movie begins as Rogers drives under a sign that reads "Golden Horse Ranch—Home of Golden Sovereign." Rogers, in a voice-over says, "Golden horse: that's what they call the palomino. And palominos have quite a history. You know, the history of my palomino begins right here at this ranch. If I hadn't gone through that gate a few years back, I'd never have gotten my pal Trigger."

My Pal Trigger featured a top-notch cast headed by Roy Rogers, Gabby Hayes, and Dale Evans. They were followed by the best gang of villains in B-westerns: Roy Barcroft, Leroy Mason, Kenne Duncan, William Haade, Fred Graham, and Jack Holt. For musical support the Sons of the Pioneers were on board featuring Bob Nolan.

My Pal Trigger was filmed at the Kentucky Park farm located west of Lake Sherwood at the eastern end of Hidden Valley. From Los Angeles it's due north off the Hollywood (101) Freeway. The ranch is now called Ventura Farms and its current owner raises thoroughbred horses. The race track has since been removed but the stable and paddock remain. *San Fernando Valley* (1944) was also filmed there.

The story of how Rogers got "Trigger" had been touched on, firstly, in *Come On Rangers* (1938), which included a sequence where Rogers got Trigger after his first owner (Rogers' brother) was slain. However, there is no argument that *My Pal Trigger* is the definitive fictional origin story. Rogers was cast as a traveling horse trader who wanted to breed his mare, Lady, to the Golden Sovereign, a prize palomino stud on Gabby Hayes' Golden Horse Ranch. Gambling house operator Jack Holt had similar plans for his brood mares. Hayes made it known that the Sovereign wasn't for stud at any price, even a million dollars. Holt, with the help of heavies LeRoy Mason and Roy Barcroft, steals the Golden Sovereign. The stallion escapes and, in turn, runs off with Rogers' Lady. After a romantic equine interlude on the open range, Holt shoots the Golden Sovereign. Rogers gets blamed and, with his beloved Lady, who was carrying the Golden Sovereign's foal, becomes a fugitive. While on the run Lady gives birth to Trigger; then, months later, she dies after a cougar attacks her.

Roy Rogers raises Trigger, the only son of the Golden Sovereign. (The name of the colt playing Trigger as a yearling was Golden Hours). Rogers returns him to Hayes, who refuses to acknowledge the animal. Rogers is sent to jail, then loses Trigger in an auction to cover his debts. Holt buys Trigger secretly to race him against Hayes' prized Golden

The original Trigger, Roy Rogers, and Dale Evans in the closing scene from *My Pal Trigger* (1946). The beautiful palomino was about to become a father in this charming sequence (Roy Dillow collection).

Empress. Upon his release from prison, Rogers learns Holt owns the palomino and signs on as his trainer. The movie climaxes in a race between Trigger and the Golden Empress. Holt is revealed as the killer of the Golden Sovereign and Rogers is exonerated.

A number of unusual elements make *My Pal Trigger* atypical of the Roy Rogers movies. First of all, Roy had no real sidekick; only the ever-loyal Bob Nolan came close. He defended Rogers against the false accusation that he stole and killed the Golden Sovereign. Rogers was a loner, with only a good horse for companionship. Second, the original Trigger, playing the Golden Sovereign in an early sequence, could be seen for the first and only time on film in English tack during a dressage demonstration with Evans. (In the first shot, Evans appeared to be on the palomino double, Monarch.)[13] As Evans approached Rogers on the sideline, she was on the original Trigger. In an equine square dance that followed, it's the original Trigger throughout. Third, although Evans and Rogers clearly had eyes for each other—they even sang a duet—there was no romance between them. The love story in this outing is between Rogers and Lady, then Rogers and Trigger. Fourth, Gabby Hayes, as Evans' father, plays a sour individual, a man who gambles too much. "Your hatred of Roy has become an obsession, it's dominating your whole life," Evans lectures him. Through most of the movie, Hayes is an enemy of Rogers and refers to him as "a hoss killer and a skunk." He calls Trigger a half-breed. In an interview Hayes noted, "My favorite is *My Pal Trigger*. They gave me the best acting part of any picture I've done. I played it straight all the way through. No funny stuff in that movie." Fifth, Rogers rides two other horses in *My Pal Trigger*, the chestnut mare (and Champion look-alike) Lady and a dark bay horse in a sequence while searching for Lady. Sixth, two lead horses die violently in this movie: Lady and the Golden Sovereign. Seventh, Rogers' voice-over. He narrated the introduction and the sequences before and after Lady's death.

In spite of being one of the best of Roy Rogers' movies, *My Pal Trigger* has a number of holes in the plot. It isn't *High Noon*, after all. As it was made for children, such holes may be forgiven. First, Rogers is accused of killing the Golden Sovereign, when it was villain Jack Holt who shot the animal with a rifle. By simply digging out the bullet it would have been easily determined that the slug did not come from Rogers' six-shooter. Second, Bob Nolan and the Sons of the Pioneers beat confessions out of Jack Holt's henchmen, LeRoy Mason and Roy Barcroft. How legal could that have been? Third, palomino couplings rarely produce a palomino. Palominos may be bred from chestnuts and grays, grays and palominos and (preferably) from chestnut and palominos—although none of these couplings guarantees a palomino either. However, breeding a palomino to a palomino often makes a cremello.[14]

During most of his career, Rogers followed in Gene Autry's footsteps. With *My Pal Trigger*, the tables were reversed. Years later Autry filmed *Strawberry Roan* (Columbia Pictures, 1948), a fictional account of how he got Champion. While not an exact copy of *My Pal Trigger*, *Strawberry Roan* was clearly in the same vein. The Rogers film is far superior to Autry's. Rogers was in his prime, with all his supporting players still in place and Republic Pictures solidly behind him.

Gene Autry got the jump on Rogers, however, with the song "Ole Faithful," a tune Gene Autry sang to Champion in *The Big Show* (1937). Rogers sang it to his beloved Lady later in *My Pal Trigger*. (According to Roy Dillow it's one of the few rare scenes in a Roy Rogers movie where he's wearing chaps.)

It's fitting that the best stuntman in the movie business, Yakima Canutt, was called in as second unit director for *My Pal Trigger*. His hand was clearly visible in a staged fight sequence between the Golden Sovereign and a wild black stallion, and later in a race between Roy Rogers on "Trigger" versus Dale Evans on the Golden Empress. Evans did her own riding, much to the displeasure of insurance minded Republic Pictures executives.

Like most Roy Rogers movies, *My Pal Trigger* was a showcase for Little Trigger's talents. The film could not have been made without him. There's no better example of this than the training sequence staged after Rogers went to work for Holt. Trigger and Little Trigger were used flawlessly from shot to shot, giving the illusion of one horse. Little Trigger retrieved Rogers' hat; Trigger reared up on command; Trigger carried Rogers at a full-out gallop; Little Trigger reared up on command with Rogers on his back, then bowed after Rogers dismounted; Little Trigger walked on his hind legs and, after he stopped, kissed Rogers.

After Rogers raises Trigger, he returned him to Hayes. It is Little Trigger that Hayes first sees in his barn and confuses for the Golden Sovereign. Hayes refuses the colt, unties him, and sends him back to Rogers. Little Trigger also stands in for the original Trigger as he is being auctioned off to cover Rogers' legal expenses after he is falsely accused of killing the Golden Sovereign. It is Little Trigger again in the sequence when he escapes from Holt's ranch and heads into town looking for Rogers.

Republic Pictures publicity shot intended for newspapers, movie reviews, etc. "While a camera crew sits around, Minnie, the mare, who was supposed to have had a date with the stork over a week ago, calmly awaits developments in Hollywood, Los Angeles, March 17, 1946. The colt that she will foal is necessary to the story of *My Pal, Trigger*, a Roy Rogers picture. The first hours of the colt's life will be filmed and incorporated into the picture" (Roy Dillow collection).

In the climactic race between "Trigger" and the Golden Empress, the original Trigger is seen in some cuts at a full-out gallop. In the closing scene, when Golden Empress gives birth to "Trigger's" twin sons, it is the original Trigger pacing in his stall. After the vet announces the birth of the second twin, it is Little Trigger who sits in astonishment (any time "Trigger" was in a seated pose it was more than likely Little Trigger performing the trick).

One of the last shots in *My Pal Trigger* was not what it seemed: The frame with Trigger's twin sons is a simple double exposure of the same palomino colt. (Note the foal on the left whose left rear leg disappears into the hay bedding.) It was magic to children. (The chance of a horse pregnant with twins successfully carrying to full-term is rare. Human twins occur 1 in every 67 pregnancies, horse twins occur 1 in every 10,000.)

A promotional photograph that appeared in print at the same time shows a Republic Pictures film crew waiting patiently for one Minnie the mare to give birth to a palomino foal. It makes one to wonder just how the *My Pal, Trigger* twin foal scenario actually transpired.

According to author Len Simpson in a magazine article titled "Trigger Man" (periodical and date unknown) promoting *My Pal Trigger*, "For the first time, the actual birth of a palomino colt was recorded. It cost, 12,000 to put the scene on film and the hero of it all was a wobbly-legged little fellow, with the world's smartest horse for his papa." The colt was named Golden Hours.

This may be taken with a grain, even a boulder, of salt. Republic had a reputation for producing great sequences on modest budgets. Between what the Lydecker brothers accomplished with special effects and what the crack stunt department produced, Republic pulled off great cinematic slights of hand time and time again. The birth of palomino foals was hardly beyond the studio's technical and financial resources.

Republic got what it needed, a newborn baby palomino on camera. Beyond the double exposure to produce twins, there were no special effects—that was a real foal not more than an hour old. One never sees a human in the frame while the baby is on camera. Roy Rogers and company were filmed at another place at another time, probably doing reaction shots. The same foal was used earlier in the film when Trigger was born to Roy Rogers' chestnut mare Lady. Again one never sees a human in the frame while the baby is on camera.

Press releases claimed Trigger's first offspring would make its film debut in *My Pal Trigger*. One thousand dollars in cash prizes were offered by Republic Pictures for winning names for the twin colts sired by Trigger who had acquired 24 mares, 17 were in foal. Rogers offered the use of the first born for the part and a camera crew was sent to his ranch to photograph the new arrival.

Most likely savvy horse people on the Republic payroll suggested a situation with better odds for producing a palomino, as predicting a foal's arrival is a guess at best. While palominos can produce palomino foals, breeders realized it is a crapshoot because mating one palomino to another frequently resulted in diluted coloring. More likely Republic found a breeding facility where a number of mares (bays, chestnuts and grays) were in foal (babies tend to come in early spring and late at night) hoping one would drop a palomino. Keeping their options open would have been wise for the studio to insure success. Palominos to chestnuts seem to produce the best results thought it's not always guaranteed.

While the Minnie the mare photo may indeed have been a publicity shot used to

Formal portrait of three of the best-looking individuals in Hollywood movies of the 1940s: Roy Rogers, Dale Evans, and the original Trigger. All were in their primes when they starred in the *Lights of Old Santa Fe* in 1944, a year before the end of World War II.

promote *My Pal, Trigger*—Republic and Roy Rogers himself were not past concocting the scenario. It's hard to believe Republic would pay a small film crew to sit around and wait for a mare to drop a foal. It's even unlikely the particular palomino mare (Minnie) pictured is the actual mother of Trigger's foal. While fun, the shot is more likely a simple gimmick set up to enhance the Trigger fantasy, for if ever a film is pure fantasy, it's *My Pal Trigger*.

Although *The Lights of Old Santa Fe* (1944) was not built around Trigger per se, he was the focus of attention. Rogers and Trigger played themselves in the film; they were a star attraction rodeo act and a coup for anyone who could book them. They were a team, a package deal, and it was clear on screen as in real life that the palomino was instrumental to Rogers' celebrity.

In the film Rogers decides to hire on with the Brooks International Rodeo show, which is owned by Dale Evans and managed by Gabby Hayes. Before he hires Rogers, Trigger, and the Sons of the Pioneers, Hayes inspects Trigger closely. He checks his top line and croup, picks up his feet, then stands back, smiles and sighs. Hayes then refers to the palomino as "that magnificent specimen of horse flesh."

In a later attempt to convince Evans to keep the rodeo going, Hayes takes her to meet "Trigger." Hayes, his face aglow with pride and smiling from ear to ear, leads the palomino in a small circle to show him off. Evans too is transfixed and declares Trigger "a beautiful animal." As she and Hayes continue the scene, she stands next to Trigger, cheek to cheek. Fans were treated to a close look at the palomino's beautiful face and markings. He was indeed a breathtaking sight.

Later in the film Dale Evans borrows Trigger to go to a nearby lake with villain Tom Keene, the owner of a competing rodeo show. Rogers is upset when he finds out that she is using Trigger and asks Bob Nolan to drive him out to retrieve "a valuable horse." Not only does he get Trigger back, but Rogers throws Keene in the lake. Evans is left on foot and has to walk home. With cues from Rogers, Trigger encourages her to start walking with a nudge. This affords Rogers the opportunity to sing the Tim Spencer tune "Trigger Doesn't Have a Purty Figure."

In a later sequence, henchman Roy Barcroft wreaks havoc at Hayes' rodeo campsite. He turns stock loose and sets wagons on fire. He ties his rawhide rope on "Trigger" (Monarch and Little Trigger actually) but the palomino breaks free. "Trigger" runs into camp with a cut rawhide rope around his neck. A couple of scenes later, Trigger spots Barcroft's horse in town and alerts Rogers, who finds the remaining rawhide rope still tied to the saddle.

In the closing sequence of the film, Rogers and Evans share a duet of the ethereal title song. The short sequence is sublime. *The Lights of Old Santa Fe* is a very satisfying movie and one of Rogers' best.

Under California Stars (1948) was released in Trucolor. The plot centered on the kidnapping of "Trigger." Roy Rogers and Trigger again played themselves, a movie star cowboy with a famous and valuable horse. The implication was that Rogers was as much a hero and cowboy in real life as he was on movie screens. Art imitating life. The tag line for *Under California Stars* "Horse Nappers Have Gone Too Far—They've Got Trigger!"

Under California Stars opened with a brief look at the Republic Pictures back lot in Studio City, California, where Rogers is completing a movie. He is anxious for a break and has made plans to drive to his Double R Ranch.[15] His friend Cookie Bullfincher, played by Andy Devine, manages the place with the help of the Sons of the Pioneers (in an early sequence Little Trigger helps Pat Brady play a hand of cards against the rest of the Pioneers). When Rogers and Trigger arrive they find Bullfincher has hired some of his relatives including his cousin Caroline (Jane Frazee) as a horse trainer.

Rogers, Devine, and the Sons of the Pioneers soon find themselves forced to fight a gang who are hunting range horses. The brains behind these crooks is Pop Jordan (George Lloyd), who along with his muscle, Lige McFarland (Wade Crosby), change their focus and decided there is money in kidnapping Trigger. Young Ted Conover (Michael Chapin), McFarland's innocent stepson, and his dog Tramp run away and are taken in by Rogers. Pop Jordan enlists the young Conover as a spy at the Rogers homestead.

In order to kidnap "Trigger," the kidnappers coax him out of his stall with a mare. Once outside and on an open road, he is ambushed by a couple of wranglers who manage

Trigger attacks one of his kidnappers in a scene from *Under California Stars* (1948). During this sequence the palomino reared up and fell over backwards. It wasn't a double horse and had to have been an accident. Everyone on the set must have been relieved when the palomino stood up unharmed. Horses can break their necks during such dangerous mishaps.

to rope him. One clubs him with a rifle butt and, sadly, the palomino goes down (in this heartbreaking sequence, "Trigger" was played by Little Trigger). "Trigger" is taken to a secret hideout. His abduction is headline news all over the country. The *Victorville Tribune* runs a front-page story titled "Movie Horse Abducted."[16] Pop Jordan demands a $100,000 ransom.

Trigger is roughed up by his captors, but he gets his revenge by crippling one (ironically named Glenn). Young Ted Conover, who would do anything to recover the imperiled "Trigger," goes to the palomino's aid as McFarland is about to destroy him. Conover's dog Tramp saves the day by leading Rogers to Conover at the secret hideout. Pop Jordan, Lige McFarland, and the rest of the gang try to escape during a fierce gun battle.

In a final chase, Rogers reunites with "Trigger" and rides him bareback in pursuit of villain McFarland. When they catch up, Rogers fights McFarland, and "Trigger" fights McFarland's horse. In the climactic shoot-out, villains Jordan and McFarland end up betraying and killing each other.

This film had young fans on the edge of their seats, concerned over the fate of Trigger. It made a deep impression and was a little traumatic.

The Golden Stallion (1949) was released in Trucolor. Directed by prolific B-movie and serial specialist William Witney, *The Golden Stallion* begins as Roy Rogers and the Riders of the Purple Sage are trying to fill a contract with a large western stock company that supplies rodeo horses. Hoping to capture a fine wild herd that roams back and forth

Lobby card from Republic Pictures' *The Golden Stallion*, released in color in the fall of 1944. Trigger returned to the wild and assumed leadership of a herd of mustangs (Roy Dillow collection).

across the Mexican border, Rogers leases the Circle B Ranch from Stormy Billings (Dale Evans) to use as his headquarters. The wild herd, led by a specially trained horse referred to as the Bell Mare,[17] is being used by smugglers to transport diamonds, wearing a specially made hollow shoe, from Mexico to the U.S.

After Roy Rogers and his men round up the herd he unsaddles Trigger and lets him loose among the frightened horses in the hope he can settle them down. Just as the Bell Mare takes a shine to Trigger, the diamond smugglers scatter the herd and all the horses, including Trigger, run off. Later that night, Trigger drives the Bell Mare back to the Rogers ranch. Trigger puts on a nice performance—at liberty, no less—when he first leads the wild Bell Mare into a corral after Rogers cues him with a whistle. Still later, one of the smugglers sneaks on to the property to retrieve the mare. The mare kills him and runs away. The sheriff, believing Trigger is the killer, demands he be destroyed. Rogers confesses to the murder to save his horse and is sentenced to prison.

Trigger is put up for auction to cover Rogers' expenses. The smugglers win the palomino, thinking they can train him to drive the herd back and forth to Mexico since they could not find the Bell Mare. Awhile later she is caught outside of their secret hideout, but she and Trigger escape once again. She goes into hiding and Trigger returns to the wild herd. The Bell Mare gives birth to Trigger's son, Trigger Jr., but dies in the process. Again Trigger puts on a nice performance at liberty as he discovers the Bell Mare's body. Trigger leads his son back to the Evans ranch for safekeeping and returns to the wild herd.

Lady and the Belle Mare were the same horse and featured in both *My Pal Trigger* and *The Golden Stallion*, first as Trigger's mother and then as his girl friend. A closer look at the blaze and it's the same animal. In some shots in *My Pal Trigger* she looks like

Roy Rogers takes blame for a murder that Trigger was falsely accused of in this emotional scene from *The Golden Stallion* (1949). Left to right: Frank Fenton, Douglas Evans, Pat Brady, Roy Rogers, Trigger, Dale Evans, Al Sloey, Johnny Paul, Estelita Rodriguez, and Foy Willing (Roy Dillow collection).

a dark chestnut perhaps due to the black and white film stock. Corky Randall could not recall Lady/Belle Mare. If Rogers had owned her, the Randalls would have been her caregivers. Since she was not, the mare could have been owned the Hudkins brothers. In either case her real name is lost to history. It obvious by her performance in *Golden Stallion,* she was trained to perform tricks.

While Rogers serves time in prison, the diamond smugglers train "Trigger" as the new leader of the herd. Little Trigger plays "Trigger Jr." for the first time in a film in a brief dance sequence with Evans riding him. When Rogers is freed, he enlists the sheriff to help capture the smugglers.

Trigger remains wild and is still leading a herd. Riding Little Trigger, again playing "Trigger Jr.," Rogers corners the original Trigger among some rocks. He dismounts and lets Little Trigger approach Trigger. The two palominos acknowledge head-to-head and for a brief moment both are together in the same frame. Rogers approaches and, standing between the two horses that made him a star, greets Trigger after their long separation. For serious Trigger fans this brief scene is a treasure.

While the *Golden Stallion* is considered one of Rogers' more mature efforts, like all his movies, it exaggerated horse behavior where necessary to tell a story. It's great fun and sets up the only Rogers movie that even comes close to being called a sequel, *Trigger, Jr.*, which was released just one year later.

Although *The Golden Stallion* wouldn't seem to hold much appeal for the maverick filmmaker of *Pulp Fiction* (Miramax, 1994), Quentin Tarantino, it is one of his favorite movies. He referred to *The Golden Stallion* on record in the *New York Times*' celebrated "Watching Movies" series of 2000.[18] *The Golden Stallion* was a bold choice and helped to call attention to the long career of the film's director, Republic Pictures' veteran action specialist, William Witney. Tarantino praised Witney's direction and Roy Rogers' performance. Tarantino found the relationship between Rogers and Trigger particularly moving, "You know, in some movies, a cowboy might go to jail to save his best friend from being shot down dead. Well, Trigger is Roy's best friend. It's the easiest leap to have him do that here, yet it's so powerful and so unexpected. What's great is that you buy it, you absolutely buy it, and I don't know that I really would buy it from anybody else but Roy and Trigger."

Quentin Tarantino also acknowledged Trigger twice at the end in his opus *Kill Bill 2* (Miramax, 2004). David Carradine played the title character, leader of a group of assassins for hire. He is attracted to blondes, Uma Thurman in particular. He'd been obsessed with them all his life. Tarantino used footage from *The Golden Stallion*, a movie about a blonde

After being auctioned off to a gang of smugglers, Trigger returns to Roy Rogers in this scene from *The Golden Stallion* (1949). Insert: Little Trigger (left, wearing bridle), playing "Trigger Jr.," face to face with the original Trigger in *The Golden Stallion* (1949). This is the only instance when both palominos appeared together on screen.

Trigger Jr. with dappling on his coat, circa 1950, on the set of the movie that bore his name (Roy Dillow collection).

horse, as an accent.[19] In one scene, Thurman is at Carradine's home lying in bed with her daughter. A Breyer Trigger figure is standing on the night table close by. During a later conversation between Carradine and Thurman, a television is tuned to *The Golden Stallion*. It's no coincidence that the sequence on screen is the same one Tarantino discussed in the *New York Times* essay. While Carradine and Thurman discuss the chain of events that led to their reunion, Rogers is sacrificing himself to save his beloved horse. Tarantino included an R.I.P. dedication at the end of the credits, and William Witney's name was among those listed.

In Quentin Tarantino's homage to the spaghetti western, *Django Unchained* (Columbia Pictures, 2012), the director/actor indulged himself with a small roll as a heavy named Frankie. It's no coincidence the horse he chose to ride was a palomino with a white blaze. Later, during Dan Rather's *Big Interview* show, Tarantino commented about how Django and his mount do a short dance routine, "so at the end when Jamie [Foxx] is on that horse and is doing his little Roy Rogers and Trigger dance he has become this cowboy hero that's kind of fantastical."

Trigger, Jr. (1950) is one of a handful of movies that was featured on the *Happy Trails Theatre* television show taped in Knoxville, Tennessee, in 1986. Hosts Roy Rogers and

Dale Evans introduced it with great anecdotes and were pretty candid about the actual Trigger Jr. It was obvious Rogers was very attached to the palomino. He said that the stallion was three when he first saw him. Rogers was doing a show at Madison Square Garden when the horse was brought from Pennsylvania for him to look at. Rogers also noted that he had a difficult time buying him; he claimed that it took nine years. Rogers also acknowledged trainer Glenn Randall Sr. and how he trained Trigger Jr. to do a number of dance routines.

Directed by William Witney, *Trigger, Jr.* was released in Trucolor and features Rogers, Trigger, Trigger Jr., sidekicks Gordon Jones and Pat Brady, Foy Willing and the Riders of the Purple Sage. In the film, Rogers' circus and wild west show is headed towards its winter quarters, a ranch owned by wheelchair-bound Colonel Harkrider (George Cleveland), his daughter Kay (Dale Evans), and grandson Larry (Peter Miles). Larry's mother, a circus bareback rider, was killed during a performance; consequently, the boy had a paralyzing fear of horses.

Trigger, Jr. is an odd film and plays pretty fast and loose with both human and horse behavior. At the time of its release it was considered one of Rogers' more sophisticated outings, but in retrospect, while it may be seen as a well-intended lesson in finding courage and growing up, by today's standards it is very naive. Nevertheless, it did attempt some serious character development. Both Colonel Harkrider and Larry were wrestling with problems. We learned that the Colonel's reliance on the wheelchair was psychosomatic and that he was verbally abusing Larry for being fearful and the no-account son of a drifter, leaving the boy constantly afraid and miserable.

Villain Grant Withers and his so-called range patrol, which were supposed to keep rancher's horses from straying onto neighboring ranges and prevent wild horses from making off with their herds, had accomplished nothing yet were charging the ranchers exorbitant fees. Withers uses a vicious wild stallion, an equine killing machine named the Phantom, to terrorize the area's horse-breeders.

The main action is fast and begins with both Trigger and Trigger Jr. losing fights with the Phantom. A lucky blow the Phantom delivered to Trigger's head causes the palomino to go blind when the optic nerve is paralyzed. (Poor Trigger spent half the movie sidelined and wore a pair of protective goggles.) Rogers attempts to uncover the foul doings but is ambushed by Grant Withers' patrol. He and sidekick Jones keep them at bay, hoping they'll get rescued.

Back at the ranch, the Phantom goes on a killing rampage and attacks Colonel Harkrider in his wheelchair. The rogue horse next goes after Trigger confined in a corral. Once again he lands a couple of blows to "Trigger's" head and the blind palomino goes down. Trigger Jr. comes to his father's rescue and also goes down. Trigger's sight is restored when his optic nerve is struck again. Trigger chases off the Phantom, and Larry finds the courage to ride Trigger Jr. to rescue Rogers and Jones, who remain surrounded by bad guy Grant Withers and his men.

Larry on Trigger Jr. finds Dale Evans and the Riders of the Purple Sage. He leads them to Rogers and Jones and saves the day. In the meantime Trigger had chased the Phantom towards Rogers, who dispatches the Phantom with a bullet to the head—not a pleasant thing to see, and an extreme plot solution for a movie aimed at children. Larry overcomes his fear of horses and is cured. Colonel Harkrider overcomes his psychological attachment to his wheelchair.

Trigger, Jr. is unique among Roy Rogers movies because the three major horses used in his career were present: the original Trigger, Trigger Jr., and Little Trigger. Trigger Jr. is not hard to identify in the movie that bears his name; at the time his dappled coat was very distinctive. Trigger and Trigger Jr. first appear side by side in a dramatic shot on a hilltop. Trigger Jr. mischievously runs off, scattering a herd of horses. Rogers whistles for Trigger and mounts up bareback, and takes after Trigger Jr. Stuntman Joe Yrigoyen, substituting for Rogers, did some fancy riding among the herd of horses and got a rope around Trigger Jr. For a brief instance Rogers may be seen riding Trigger bareback at a gallop.

Even Little Trigger got into the action when he substituted for Trigger during his last fight with the Phantom. He was the palomino seen in close-up chasing the Phantom out of the corral where they were fighting. A few scenes later Little Trigger substituted for Trigger Jr. as he stopped a stampeding herd of horses. He cuts across the foreground of the picture frame.

William Witney

Luckily for Roy Rogers, Republic Pictures had some excellent directors on its payroll, including Joseph Kane, John English, and Frank McDonald. At the end of his motion picture career he was teamed with one of the best action directors of all time, William Witney. Like Rogers, Witney loved the outdoors and was an experienced horseman, which made him especially adept at action and stunts. Of all the directors Rogers worked with, Witney was especially drawn to Trigger and it makes sense that he directed three movies with the palomino at the center of the plot: *Under California Stars, The Golden Stallion*, and *Trigger, Jr.*

Between 1937 and 1946, William Witney directed or co-directed 23 of Republic Pictures' greatest cliffhanger serials, including *Adventures of Captain Marvel, Dick Tracy vs. Crime, Inc., The Lone Ranger, Spy Smasher,* and *Zorro's Fighting Legion.* (Witney's serials inspired Steven Spielberg's Indiana Jones movies of the 1980s.) From 1946 to 1951 Witney directed 27 Roy Rogers westerns that marked a dramatic change in content and style, cutting back on the musical aspects in favor of more action driven stories.

William Witney was one of the first directors to rehearse fight scenes. He had never been satisfied with how movie fights were filmed, much less how they looked—a stuntman free-for-all in front of a camera. "The fights always seemed to be okay for the first punch. Then the stuntmen were always out of place for the next punch. By the time three or four minutes had passed, the stuntmen were out of breath, scattered all over the set and seemed to be staggering around waiting for someone to hit them."[20] After watching choreographer-turned-director Busby Berkeley rehearse a dance sequence with 40 dancers at Warner Bros., Witney learned a valuable lesson. He saw how Berkeley lined up the dancers to execute one tiny movement, over and over until it was perfect. He shot that movement, then went on the rehearse another. When that next movement was perfect, he shot again. Eventually he shot some close-ups to fill in between the dance shots.

Using Berkeley's method, Witney started staging and filming fight sequences, breaking them into fragments, mixing camera angles and even using close-ups. With good editing, this had a huge impact on movie audiences. Witney's technique has since become an industry standard.

William Witney appeared on the *Happy Trails Theater Show* (Cintel) in 1987 (the "Far Frontier" episode) and promoted his book *Trigger Remembered.*

Trigger's Special Scenes

Trigger eventually became important not only as ambience and transportation, but also as a supporting character that sometimes affected plot lines.

Roy Rogers first called Trigger by name in his second film, *Billy the Kid Returns* (1938). Trigger didn't do any fancy tricks, just snorted in response when Rogers spoke to him. At one point he neighed to warn Rogers of trouble. The most spectacular horse stunt in this early film was performed by a palomino double and a stuntman when they jumped off a cliff into a lake and swam across to the other side. This footage was used a number of times in Republic movies.

In *Come On, Rangers* (1938), when Rogers was caught on foot spying on renegades, one of the gang was ordered to retrieve Trigger. The palomino was roped but did not submit; he pulled free and fled. A little later sidekick Raymond Hatton, who was out looking for his partner Rogers, saw Trigger running loose and proceeded to pick him up. Rogers' character didn't even own Trigger at the beginning of *Come On, Rangers*; his older brother, played by Lane Chandler, did. The two men and Raymond Hatton were Texas Rangers (in an early scene three actors who were in the first Lone Ranger serial may be seen around a campfire: Lee Powell, Lane Chandler, and George Montgomery). White men disguised as Indians attacked Chandler's farm. He's killed and his house and barn were set on fire. Rogers arrived in time to pull Trigger out of his burning stall.

Trigger really started to shine in *Frontier Pony Express* (1939); he was the fastest horse working for the company. Roy Rogers rode the dangerous California-to-Kansas-City route while the Civil War raged in the East. For the climax of the film, while carrying important Union vouchers, Rogers was ambushed and wounded by a gang of Confederate thugs and tried to make an escape. Weakened by a bullet in the arm, he fell from Trigger. The faithful palomino returned for him but Rogers signaled the horse to keep running. The Confederates ignored Rogers and pursued Trigger, hoping to take the vouchers. Trigger was forced to jump off a cliff into a lake and swim for the other side. A diving sequence from *Billy the Kid Returns* was reused. (The original Trigger is easily identifiable in the chase sequences. As he was about to run off the cliff, an unidentified palomino double made the jump and swam across the lake.) It was at this point that Raymond Hatton caught Trigger with his speedy little mule, Dinah. Hatton made a transfer from mule to horse and continued on with the vouchers. Later, Trigger reared up, surprising his diminutive rider; but the B-western veteran stayed with the palomino and continued his escape. A running joke in *Frontier Pony Express* was how Hatton, a trader of goods, would offer Trigger's horseshoes as bonus items.

Roy Rogers asked Trigger to buck him off as a ruse to speak to actress Pauline Moore in *Days of Jesse James* (1939). A stunt man and stunt horse completed the scene.

In *Rough Riders' Roundup* (1939), Raymond Hatton's mule Dinah again outran "Trigger" in a friendly race. Hatton used his catch phrase, "Hi Ho, Dinah,"[21] throughout the film. The little mule was clearly given much more attention than Trigger in this outing.

In *Ridin' Down the Canyon* (1942), young Bobby Blake (Buzzy Henry) got to experience every little saddle pal's fantasy: He rode Trigger surrounded by the Sons of the Pioneers with Roy Rogers on Pat Brady's horse. Bobby idolized Rogers and even named his own pinto pony Trigger Jr.

The original Trigger was pretty much on his own in *Silver Spurs* (1943); Little Trigger was nowhere in sight. There were a couple of exciting stunt sequences in the film, including one where an unidentified stuntman and palomino slid down a hill into a river, then swam to the opposite shore. Trigger showed his cow horse training by standing firm after Roy Rogers tied a rope to the pommel of his saddle then lowered himself down a hill. When Rogers wanted an assist, he yelled to Trigger to back up and Rogers, holding the rope, made the climb.

The closing musical number of *Don't Fence Me In* (1945), a reprise of the title track, began with dancers performing on a stage in front of a movie screen. As they parted, Roy Rogers and Trigger appeared, riding full towards the camera, eventually bursting though the screen itself. Rogers was riding Trigger towards the camera in the outdoor footage; after they broke through the screen, he was on Little Trigger. The four white-stockinged feet were clearly visible as the animal reared up onstage. The palomino was wearing rubber boots over his hooves to keep from slipping. In one of the last shots of the sequence, Little Trigger blew a kiss towards the camera, and the black spot on his muzzle was in plain view.

In *Utah* (1945) Trigger was pretty much a typical cowboy's horse till the climax of the movie. Roy Rogers and Gabby Hayes chased bad guys Grant Withers and Hal Taliaferro (aka Wally Wales) from Utah to the Chicago stockyards. Rogers disposed of Withers after "Trigger" helped run him down. As Rogers put the final touches on Withers with his fists, from out of nowhere Trigger took it upon himself to look after Hayes, who had caught up to Taliaferro. Hayes was holding his own, but as the younger Taliaferro was about to get the upper hand, Trigger (Little Trigger) attacked. Taliaferro ended up cowering on the ground for fear of his life. Rogers arrived, called the palomino off.

Heldorado (1946) is noteworthy for a number of reasons. Even though Trigger was mostly used as transportation, he was depicted as a local celebrity along with Roy Rogers who worked for the state (on his salary he mysteriously could afford a very expensive saddle and a highly trained horse). During the Heldorado Days celebration shown in the film, Rogers appeared in a parade on Little Trigger. He also used Little Trigger during a rodeo performance. He rode into an arena; Little Trigger reared up; Rogers dismounted and handed him over to Glenn Randall Sr. After Rogers sang "My Saddle Pals and I" with the Sons of the Pioneers, Randall brought Little Trigger back for Rogers to use in a dance routine.

Rainbow Over Texas (1946) is very interesting from a horse-watcher's point of view. Three of the most well known palominos Roy Rogers used were present. The original Trigger was, of course, dominant and was mentioned by name throughout. Roy Rogers was sort of playing himself, a famous western entertainer. Dale Evans played the rebellious daughter of a very rich easterner who owned a ranch. At one point Evans stole Trigger, leaving Rogers no choice but to chase her in a wagon. During the chase the cinch on "Trigger's" saddle came loose (it had not been cinched correctly). Evans panicked but could not slow down the palomino. Rogers cut her off and made a flying leap from the wagon, dismounting Evans from Trigger, saddle and all. After they dusted themselves off, they loaded the saddle onto the wagon, climbed aboard, and headed into town with Trigger following behind. After they got back to town, the palomino, still without his saddle, started following Rogers down a sidewalk until he was told not to.

Rainbow Over Texas includes a climactic Pony Express race. Riders were allowed a string of horses stationed over a long course. Roy Rogers rode palominos from Evans' father's ranch. For the race itself, Pal was the first of the string of horses Rogers used. Before the riders mounted up, fiddler Hugh Farr walked Pal to the starting line and handed the horse to Rogers. Pal's three white stockings were easy to spot, as was his unique blaze, which exploded halfway down his face on his off side. One got a better look at Pal's facial markings when Rogers mounted up right before the race began.

Trigger was a beautiful sight when he ran for help in *Bells of San Angelo* (1947) and reared up amidst the Sons of the Pioneers, alerting them that Roy Rogers and Dale Evans were in trouble.

In *Springtime in the Sierras* (1947), Roy Rogers and "Trigger" chased down villain Roy Barcroft. Both men used their empty rifles like clubs while still on horseback. Rogers was eventually knocked to the ground and Barcroft, hoping to finish off the King of the Cowboys, went after him while still mounted. Rogers yelled to Trigger to shield him, and the palomino reared up in front of Barcroft, giving Rogers the opportunity to go on the offensive.

In *Night Time in Nevada* (1948) two city gals bumped into Trigger and one referred to him as a "blonde horse." One even asked Roy Rogers what he used to make Trigger's mane so white; then she leaned against the palomino and draped his mane over her head to simulate a wig. Rogers replied, "Not a thing, ma'am, he was born that way." Later, after Rogers stopped villain Grant Withers with a punch to the jaw, he asked Trigger to stand guard over him and not let him get away.

In *Eyes of Texas* (1948) villain Roy Barcroft tried to run Trigger out of his barn when the palomino wandered in to get a drink from a water trough. When Barcroft went after Trigger with a pitchfork, the horse attacked him. Roy Rogers called Trigger off, but Barcroft came after the King of the Cowboys with a whip. As Rogers and Barcroft mixed it up with their fists, Trigger joined in. Twice he head-butted Barcroft into Rogers' fists.

The plot of *Eyes of Texas* centered on a pack of dogs trained to kill on command by villain Nana Bryant. Eventually one was wounded and left for dead. Roy Rogers later found him, but the half-starved and half-wild animal wouldn't let him come near. It was Trigger who was able to break through to the frightened dog.

In another sequence Rogers was kidnapped by Barcroft and his gang. They threw Roy Rogers on the ground, bound his feet, tied the rope to the saddle of another horse and whipped the horse into a run. It dragged Rogers down a dirt road. Trigger, seeing his master in trouble, followed and intercepted the horse, stopping him long enough for Rogers to untie his feet. He hopped up on Trigger and eluded Barcroft and his gang.

In *The Far Frontier* (1948), Trigger got Roy Rogers in trouble with leading lady Gail Davis. The palomino accidentally bumped Rogers, knocking a package out of his hand. It fell into a puddle of mud and splashed all over Davis. Trigger was most impressive later on in a chase sequence where he actually jumped over and narrowly avoided a barrel thrown from a truck by bad guy Roy Barcroft.[22]

During the gunfight climax of *Down Dakota Way* (1949), Little Trigger attacked a bad guy and kept him at bay.

In *Susanna Pass* (1949) Trigger was noted for his speed. When the boss villain made a quick escape during the film's climax, Roy Rogers was forced to take after him on another horse. Standing at a distance, Trigger noticed and took off after his master. As Rogers proceeded, he discovered the horse he'd borrowed was very slow. The King of the Cowboys yelled, "Is this all you've got, fella?" Shortly after he noticed Trigger coming on strong behind him. He shouted to his palomino and, a few seconds later, made a switch as Trigger caught up.

In *North of the Great Divide* (1950), Trigger (Little Trigger) saved Roy Rogers and his Indian friend Dacona (Keith Richards) from a wolf attack. After killing the lupine with his teeth, the palomino backed off. In the nearby brush Rogers found a wolf pup, which he adopted and raised.

About forty minutes into *Twilight in the Sierras* (1950), Trigger gets shot while a posse and a pack of hunting dogs were pursuing Roy Rogers. The palomino ran till he eventually began to limp. Rogers dismounted and was forced to hide. After checking Trigger closely, Rogers saw that the horse had taken a bullet in the shoulder. Rogers removed the palomino's saddle to lessen the weight he was carrying and made for a stream to disguise his scent from the dogs that were tracking them. The original Trigger did a very convincing limp as Rogers led him to a marshy area. It was Little Trigger who stepped in when Rogers cued him to lie down. The cowboy and his horse lay motionless in tall grass while the posse and hunting dogs passed them by. After they were gone, Rogers cued Little Trigger to stand, and they departed for a drier hiding place. Rogers contacted the local veterinarian, Sparrow Biffle, played by Pat Brady. As Trigger lay alone and wounded, a mountain lion spotted him and started to close in, but retreated as Rogers and Brady approached. Rogers held Little Trigger by the head to calm him as Brady removed the slug. The dark spot on Little Trigger's muzzle was clearly visible. The bullet, fortunately, was not deep and only pinching a nerve. "Trigger" was fine and able to stand right after the bullet was removed.

The Trail of Robin Hood (1950) is significant because of guest appearances by several cowboy stars, including Monte Hale, Crash Corrigan, Tom Tyler, and Kermit Maynard. Rex Allen and Rocky Lane appeared as well with their famous horses Koko and Black Jack. Regrettably, a great opportunity was lost to film the three celebrity horses together. No publicity shot exists of the event, although there were some good group shots of the cowboys on foot. At one point, Trigger and Koko shared a scene. It's unfortunate the sequence wasn't blocked differently to show both horses.

Dale Evans (a stuntwoman most likely) rode Trigger sidesaddle in *Bells of Colorado* (1950). Little Trigger bit and tossed a thug (a dummy actually) who Roy Rogers was fighting.

The plot of *South of Caliente* (1951) is built around horses, and Trigger drove the plot as much as any human in the cast. Rogers owned a horse transporting business. Sidekicks Pat Brady and Pinky Lee worked for him. Dale Evans played the owner of a Thoroughbred breeding ranch. She hired Rogers to take some very valuable horses down to Mexico, including her prized mare, Miss Glory. Trigger raced Miss Glory to a dead heat and clearly had eyes for her.

Roy Rogers, Trigger, Little Trigger, Joe Yrigoyen and a couple of Trigger doubles put on quite a show about 15 minutes into *South of Caliente* when the truck transporting horses (including Trigger) was hijacked, leaving the wranglers on foot in the Mexican desert. After thieves made their getaway, they stopped to unload the stolen horses. Trigger got loose, attacked a couple of rustlers and escaped. Once empty of its valuable equine cargo, Rogers' truck was put in neutral gear and was sent careening down a dirt road. Trigger ran back to Rogers, who was in pursuit on foot. Rogers mounted up and, riding bareback, continued the chase. Rogers and Trigger were actually filmed in this following sequence, riding at a full gallop without a saddle. As they approached the driverless truck, a stuntman and a palomino double closed in till the rider made a transfer into the cab and stopped the vehicle.

In *Spoilers of the Plains* (1951) Roy Rogers was ambushed and shot in the shoulder.

He tried to escape on Trigger but was too wounded to ride. He eventually slipped off, allowing his assailants to catch up, but it was his German shepherd, Bullet, who tried to protect him.[23] He too was shot and it was left to Trigger to run for help. He found Penny Edwards, who followed him (on Buttermilk) back to his fallen master and canine friend.

Later Roy Rogers was captured by villain Grant Withers and his gang. While the gang was transporting Rogers by wagon with some stolen equipment, sidekick Gordon Jones and the Riders of the Purple Sage chased them down in a second wagon. Trigger also ran along at a distance, shadowing his master. What followed was a thrilling sequence, as dangerous as any Republic Pictures ever filmed. The two wagons, drawn by teams of six horses, started racing side by side down a dirt road. Men from both started jumping from wagon to wagon in a huge brawl. At one point Withers jumped onto his team of horses and Rogers followed. Rogers can actually be seen standing on the tongue of the wagon between the galloping team of horses. Withers freed his pair of horses and sped up. Rogers did the same and stayed in pursuit. The riderless Trigger moved in, and Rogers switched to the palomino and continued the chase.[24]

Trigger was mostly beautiful transportation in the 1951 movie *In Old Amarillo*. It's only during the closing moments that he was featured in a special sequence. Stuntman Joe Yrigoyen stepped over four bay horses tied to a hitching rail and standing in a row. He mounted Trigger, who was standing at the opposite end, and rode off.

Comedian Bob Hope and Little Trigger shared a bed in this funny and charming sequence from *Son of Paleface*, released by Paramount in 1952 (Roy Dillow collection).

Little Trigger was the equine star of Rogers' last feature film, *Son of Paleface* (Paramount, 1952). Trigger got fourth billing under the names of his master, comedian Bob Hope and actress Jane Russell. Little Trigger was featured prominently throughout *Son of Paleface.*

In *Son of Paleface* Little Trigger performed a number of gags. He untied Roy Rogers and Bob Hope while they were bound together in a barber's chair. He chased Hope into a hotel, then popped his head out of a second story window to catch Hope trying to escape down a drainpipe. Little Trigger ran back down the stairs, exited the building, ran to the pipe, and loosened it, dropping Hope into a barrel of water below.

Little Trigger was used in many sequences in *Son of Paleface*, but other doubles appeared as well. A stuntman (either Buddy Van Horn or Joe Yrigoyen) dropped from a tree on to Monarch and galloped off. Roy Rogers rode Monarch in an interior sequence that may have been shot on a treadmill. While on his galloping horse, he placed a wheel on Bob Hope's moving automobile.

The most famous sequence involving "Trigger" in *Son of Paleface* occurred midway through the movie after Hope, wishing to use the palomino for an escape, disguised himself as Roy Rogers. He walked toward the animal carrying a guitar and singing "Four-legged Friend," then mounted up, only to have Little Trigger run him back into an abandoned hotel, trot up a series of stairs, and pitch him onto a bed. Later, Rogers, Hope, and Trigger were sleeping—Rogers in one bed, Hope and Little Trigger sharing the other. What commenced was a fight between the comedian and the palomino over the bed sheets. Here the blaze and black spot on Little Trigger's muzzle are plain to see, especially by freezing key frames on a DVD player. Harpo Marx had filmed a similar sequence with a horse in the Marx Brothers comedy *Duck Soup* (Paramount, 1933).

The last scene of *Son of Paleface* featured Roy Rogers and Trigger in their signature pose: the palomino reared and the cowboy waved goodbye. This, appropriately, was the last shot of the last movie Roy Rogers and Trigger appeared in together. Little Trigger was about 14 years old when he performed in *Son of Paleface.*

Trigger, Beautiful Transportation

Trigger's first appearance with Roy Rogers in *Under Western Stars* (1938) was inauspicious at best. In point of fact, it was another horse that had a more important role: sidekick Frog Milhouse's white mare, Ring-eyed Nellie. It seems she was a former fire horse who was trained to follow the sound of a ringing bell. *Under Western Stars* closed with Milhouse helplessly aboard Ring-eyed Nellie, chasing after the sound of a bell from a passing truck.[25]

Although Trigger's appearance in *Under Western Stars* was pretty low key, it offered a hint of things to come. His first scene with Roy Rogers opened as the cowboy was repairing a barbwire fence. Trigger was standing next to Milhouse, who was mounted on Ring-eyed Nellie. Distant gunfire drew their attention and they all decided to investigate. Rogers mounted up quickly. As he turned Trigger to move out, the palomino reared up ever so slightly.

In a later scene Trigger performed his first trick in a Roy Rogers film. While Rogers was rehearsing a speech he was planning to give before a political rival, Trigger, acting as his audience, gave a simple nod.

Bob Nolan, a master composer of cowboy music, on Trigger in a scene from *Utah* (Roy Dillow collection).

Trigger was not mentioned by name in *Under Western Stars* but fans got a very good look at him. In a short sequence after Rogers rescued starlet Carolyn Hughes, Rogers and Hughes ended up walking together with Trigger in between. It's safe to assume there were many fans who saw this film when it premiered in 1938 and gladly paid another nickel the next time a Roy Rogers film was in theaters just to look at Trigger again.

A quarter of Trigger's movie appearances were spent simply as beautiful transportation, examples being: *Wall Street Cowboy* (1939), *The Arizona Kid* (1939), *South of Santa Fe* (1942), *Sons of the Pioneers* (1942), *Idaho* (1943), and *Pals of the Golden West* (1951). Beyond serving as any horse would, he did nothing out of the ordinary to affect the plot of a movie. In *Young Bill Hickok*, Trigger was never referred to by name, only as Roy Rogers' horse. In *Sunset Serenade* (1942) Trigger functioned for the most part as transportation;

however, during the climax of the film, Rogers tied a rope to Trigger's saddle horn, then lowered himself into a deep canyon to rescue an injured man. Rogers hoisted the man onto his back and whistled to Trigger. The palomino started backing up, helping Rogers walk back up the steep incline with the injured man in tow.

Although Trigger was considered a one-man horse, many rode the famous palomino in Roy Rogers' movies: Gabby Hayes in *Robin Hood of the Pecos*, Lane Chandler in *Come On, Rangers*, Gale Storm in *Red River Valley*, Bob Nolan in *Utah*, Adele Mara in *Night Time in Nevada*, Raymond Hatton in *Frontier Pony Express*, Gordon Jones in *Trigger, Jr.*, Jane Frazee in *On the Old Spanish Trail*, Jack Rockwell in *Shine On Harvest Moon*, and Buzzy Henry in *Ridin' Down the Canyon* (Rogers rides Daisy, Pat Brady's horse with the wide blaze). Even villains got to ride the palomino: Frank McDonald in *The Carson City Kid* and Bradley Page in *Sons of the Pioneers*. Dale Evans rode Trigger in three movies: *Rainbow Over Texas*, *Bells of San Angelo* and *Bells of Colorado*. She rode Little Trigger in *The Golden Stallion*. Bob Hope rode Little Trigger in *Son of Paleface*. Publicity shots exist of Roy Rogers, Bob Hope, and Jane Russell riding triple on Little Trigger. Sidekick Pat Brady and the young John Meek both rode Trigger in the television episode titled *Fighting Sire*.

Trigger Cameo Appearances

Like Roy Rogers, Trigger made cameo appearances as himself in other movies: *Hollywood Canteen* (Warner Bros., 1944), *Out California Way* (Republic, 1946), *Hit Parade of 1947* (Republic, 1947), and *Melody Time* (RKO Radio Pictures, 1948).

Roy Rogers and Little Trigger delivered a short and flawless cameo performance in *The Hollywood Canteen*. The sequence opened with the Sons of the Pioneers singing Bob Nolan's immortal "Tumbling Tumbleweeds." Next, Rogers entered the hall filled with G.I.s, a bevy of young ladies, and dozens of motion picture celebrities. The crowd parted as the pair entered. Little Trigger reared up in the middle of the dance floor; then Rogers dismounted. He introduced the palomino who, took a bow, then blew a kiss to the crowd. When the Sons of the Pioneers started to play Cole Porter's classic "Don't Fence Me In," Rogers handed Little Trigger over to Tim Spencer and joined the Pioneers on stage and sang a couple of verses. When he got to the "on my cayuse" line, he turned towards Little Trigger and smiled. One can see the pride on Rogers' face as he serenaded his palomino. As the instrumental break began, Rogers handed his guitar to Spencer and quickly mounted Little Trigger again. They went into a dance routine as the song played out. Right before they left the room, Little Trigger reared up. The entire sequence lasts about five minutes. One is amazed by how easily it all went down. Rogers was as smooth fronting a band as he was on horseback. Little Trigger wasn't even wearing rubber boots!

In the Monte Hale picture *Out California Way*, Roy Rogers, Dale Evans and Trigger made a cameo appearance as themselves. Rogers and Evans sang "Ridin' Down the Sunset Trail." Evans rode a jet-black horse during the sequence—not a good complement to Trigger's golden color or Evans' image.

In *Hit Parade of 1947* "Trigger" shared a scene with Roy Rogers, the Sons of the Pioneers, and star Eddie Albert who was giving friends a tour of Hyperion Studios. Rogers and company sang "Out California Way" while Little Trigger stood behind all decked out in his fancy show tack. Minutes later actor Gil Lamb shared a solo scene with the

Trigger (and a rider believed to be Roy Rogers) in a sequence from the Spade Cooley B-western *The Kid from Gower Gulch,* released by Friedgen/Aster in 1950 (Roy Dillow collection).

original Trigger. Lamb exclaimed, "What a horse! What a horse! Trigger, you look like a two year old! How old are you?" Trigger counted by pawing on the ground, to which Lamb replied, "Look, a talking horse!"

In the "Pecos Bill" sequence of *Melody Time*, the original Trigger stood calmly next to a campfire and added so much ambience with his beauty and regal countenance. Roy Rogers and the Sons of the Pioneers recounted in song the ballad of Pecos Bill animated brilliantly by the Walt Disney studios. Trigger even got screen credit and added his two cents by neighing, reminding Rogers about Pecos Bill's horse, Widow Maker, depicted as a palomino with a white blaze.

Roy Rogers expert Roy Dillow found Trigger in a secret cameo appearance in a very obscure B-western titled *The Kid from Gower Gulch* (Friedgen/Aster, 1950). Director Oliver Drake filmed the minor musical on a shoestring budget at his own ranch near Pearblossom, California. The star of the movie was one of the "Kings of Western Swing," Spade Cooley. Dillow claims the original Trigger was used in a long chase sequence mid-way through the film. Freezing the DVD frame by frame, it's impossible to see the blaze clearly; there's simply too much motion blur. However, the palomino in question bears a striking resemblance to the original Trigger (Rocky Roe concurs).

Roy Dillow further claims that Roy Rogers actually did some of the riding in the chase sequence. Despite the rider's attempt to look like an amateur, the riding style was classic Roy Rogers. Rocky Roe stated, "There was no one who ad-libbed on a horse like Rogers, the way he looked back, the way he moved from side to side of Trigger's head and neck. Running inserts were a Rogers forte. There wasn't a horse in the world who looked as good running full out as the original Trigger, the way he held his head back and close to his neck."

The *Kid from Gower Gulch* was produced by Raymond Friedgen in 1947 and released in 1950. As has already been established, Roy Rogers made the final payments on Trigger in 1943. The question becomes, why would he loan a major asset like Trigger to a professional bandleader making an obscure budget western? Rogers and Spade Cooley were friends and worked together on occasion. *The Kid from Gower Gulch* was a low-budget movie and it's possible Rogers, still under contract to Republic Pictures, may have loaned his horse and even his own services simply as a favor for a friend.

Jamboree is described as a pleasant, high-gloss rock and roll musical about two singing hopefuls trying to succeed in show business. It includes musical interludes throughout by such talents as Fats Domino, Jerry Lee Lewis, Carl Perkins, Connie Francis, Frankie Avalon, and Roy Rogers and Trigger. Directed by Roy Lockwood for Warner Bros., it was released in 1957 with a running time of 86 minutes.

In 1976 Paul Heller and Fred Weintraub produced an 86-minute color documentary for United Artists titled *It's Showtime*. The tagline on posters was, "Not all the great movie stars were people. Some of the greatest stars were animals!" Animal movie stars were the focus. Among the performances were those of Asta, the dog from *The Thin Man* series, and Cheetah, the chimpanzee from the Tarzan movies. Little Trigger was in a great company, which included Champion, Silver, Tony, and Topper.

Trigger the Magazine Model

While the Golden Cloud/Trigger was still owned by Hudkins his work was not limited to films. With his good looks and temperament, he was an obvious choice for still photography assignments. Two examples have surfaced both are from 1941. Because photographers commonly shoot roles of film in order to insure a near perfect shot, there are probably dozens of never before seen photos of the Golden Cloud/Trigger in forgotten archives.

Olivia de Havilland and Golden Cloud/Trigger were photographed together for a publicity photo used to promote her Warner Bros. film *Strawberry Blonde*. Directed by Raoul Walsh, it's a turn-of-the-century story of dentist James Cagney infatuated with gold-digger Rita Hayworth, and his subsequent marriage to Olivia de Havilland. The Golden Cloud/Trigger was not in the film. The only cameo of significance was that of future television Superman, George Reeves.

The caption with the photos reads, "Olivia de Havilland, Warner Bros. star soon appearing in *Strawberry Blonde,* wonders why her beautiful western palomino won't move. Little does she suspect that the horse doesn't want to risk throwing off such a lovely rider. Olivia vacations at a friend's farm near Hollywood." That the Golden Cloud/Trigger (wearing Hudkins brothers tack) was a four-year-old stallion with a valuable studio property on his back, says a lot about his training and temperament. He was also not identified by name by the studio. Warner Bros. management either assumed he was just a "beautiful western palomino" or may have remembered him when he and de Havilland were paired three years earlier in *The Adventures of Robin Hood*.

Trigger also appeared on the cover of *Flash Photos* magazine. He was ridden by model Jean Albert and photographed by Earl Theisen, a famed photo-reporter for *LOOK* magazine. It was published by Heiland Research Corp., Denver, Colorado; there was not an accompanying article. Albert and Trigger were both identified on the front and inside

Olivia de Havilland and Golden Cloud/Trigger in a publicity photograph to promote her film *Strawberry Blonde* (Warner Bros., 1941). The four-year-old palomino, wearing Hudkins Bros. tack, was still owned by the stable.

PERFECT

Flash Photos

Made Easy

PROFESSIONAL SECRETS OF AMERICA'S OUTSTANDING PHOTOGRAPHERS

Contents:

THE FLASH IN COLOR
By Earl Theisen
*LOOK Magazine's Ace
Photo-Reporter*

GLAMOUR IN A FLASH
By Elmer Fryer
*Portrait Photographer,
Warner Bros. Studios*

FLASHES IN FASHION
By Ric Conde'
*Fashion Illustrator,
Director of Film Center*

**TIPS FROM A NEWS
PHOTOGRAPHER**
By George Yates
*Chief Photographer,
Des Moines Register and Tribune*

ON YOUR TOES
By Torkel Korling
*Well Known Baby
Portrait Photographer*

**AN EDITOR'S TIPS ON
MAGAZINE PICTURES**
By Norman C. Lipton
*Editor, Good Photography,
Photography Handbook*

PUBLICITY FLASHES
By Bill Sumits
*Chief Photographer,
Transcontinental and Western Airlines*

COWBOY PICTURES
By Charles J. Belden
Wyoming Rancher-Photographer

MY "MOST FRAMED" PICTURES
By Ed M. Hunter**

**PLUS OTHER ARTICLES AND
DOZENS OF PICTURES BY
FAMOUS PHOTOGRAPHERS**

*Cover Picture—Jean Albert on "Trigger"
By Earl Theisen*

Price **25ᶜ**

Trigger ridden by model Jean Albert and photographed by Earl Theisen on the cover of *Flash Photos* magazine, published by Heiland Research Corp., 1941.

covers. It appears the magazine was a one-shot publication with a cover price of .25 cents. Though Hudkins Stables was free to hire the palomino out for photo shoots, Roy Rogers may have agreed to the use of the name "Trigger" with Republic's blessing as good publicity.

Electric Horseman

Could a successful, entertaining, family-oriented, Roy Rogers-and-Trigger-styled movie still be made? Yes. Warner Bros. released a very successful comedy in 1974 in the tradition of *Son of Paleface* titled *Blazing Saddles*. In 1985 Paramount Pictures offered an homage to B-westerns, *Rustlers' Rhapsody* starring Tom Berenger. It was in 1979 that Columbia Pictures produced a movie that could easily be seen as a vehicle for the King of the Cowboys and his horse, *Electric Horseman*. Even now, almost forty years later, beyond dated clothes and hairstyles, *Electric Horseman* is fresh enough especially given Hollywood's tendency to reboot everything.

Set in the contemporary West, *Electric Horseman* is an adventure-comedy-romance with a conscience. Roy Rogers would have been 68 in 1979, just right for the role a western star at the end of his career. As Hollywood usually doesn't allow women to age as it does men, Dale Evans would have probably been replaced by a younger actress in a part familiar to the Queen of the West, a duck-out-of-water big-city reporter after a story.

Electric Horseman is about a former rodeo champion relegated to the role of a western pitchman and corporate stooge. Attired in a Nudie Cohn-styled cowboy outfit covered in lights, he's expected to hawk cornflakes across the country with a tour finale in Las Vegas. When he discovers that the $12 million dollar race horse he'll be using had been drugged by the corporation in order to hide an injury, he absconds with the stud, hoping to release it in a remote wild horse canyon. The stud was a bay but could have easily been a palomino. A perky female reporter, sensing a story, catches up with the pair. She ends up helping them when the malevolent food corporation, hoping to quiet the story so as not to compromise its brand, comes after its horse, in effect its corporate logo.

Electric Horseman is about a disillusioned man who'd reluctantly accepted his fate. Seeing a champion racer in the same denigrating position through no choice of his own, the cowboy finds his conscience and a purpose. He will not allow an evil conglomerate to defile something as regal and pure as a horse.

While *Electric Horseman* may be seen as a diatribe against unbridled corporate power and an attempt to make people aware of big business injustices and animal rights, it's fundamentally about self-redemption. And if that isn't enough, it's a cautionary tale about branding and image. The cowboy finds his dignity, the reporter gets her big story, and the horse is given its freedom. They fade into the sunset albeit in three different directions. *Electric Horseman* makes for a pretty good Roy Rogers and Trigger movie and with a few modern twists included.

Trigger's Movie Reviews

Trigger always fared well with the critics as one can see in quotes from reviews:

Trigger, Jr.: "Trigger and Trigger Jr. display their fine training in amazingly good performances." *The Hollywood Reporter*, June 29, 1950.

Under California Stars: "Golden palomino, incidentally, shows up beautifully in Trucolor." "The shots of Trigger in full pursuit of a mare and of his fights with the men who are trying to pacify him are quite exciting." "The device of giving Trigger, a truly gifted and photogenic horse, considerably more to do than in the past, will bring this film home the same winner as the others in the series." *Variety*, May 6, 1948.

Son of Paleface: "Parody often makes for strange bedfellows but whoever thought of putting Bob Hope in the sack with Roy Rogers' famed mount Trigger deserves the iconoclasm award of 1952! In a thorough milking of the Hollywood western, Trigger has all the finest anthropomorphized attributes—like brains—while our boy Roy appears as a wooden figure of a sheriff." *Pacific Film Archive*, September, 1987.

The Golden Stallion: "Trigger shines as his master's co-star with every trick in the book." "Members of the cast are all excellent, but it is Trigger and the other four-footed actors who steal many of the honors." *The Hollywood Reporter*, October 25, 1949.

Palomino Pal of Mine

Much of Roy Rogers' appeal was musical. Along with the Sons of the Pioneers and the Riders of the Purple Sage, he left a legacy of great western songs, and he acknowledged Trigger in quite a few. Rogers recorded "A Lonely Ranger Am I" in 1938 for ARC.[26] He mentioned Trigger in the tune, possibly for the first time in any song. An accomplished

Roy Rogers wisely mentioned Trigger in songs when given the opportunity (Roy Dillow collection).

singer and yodeler, Rogers also tried his hand at composing and came up with a few pretty nice songs, notably "My Saddle Pals and I," "I've Sold My Saddle for an Old Guitar" (with Fleming Allan), "Heldorado," "The Man in the Moon Is a Cowhand," "My Heart Went That-a-way" (with Dale Evans), and "May the Good Lord Take a Likin' to You" (with Peter Tinturin). He never wrote anything on a par with fellow Pioneer Bob Nolan, such as the immortal "Tumbling Tumbleweeds." Dale Evans eclipsed Rogers as a songwriter when she came up with "Happy Trails." That one song guaranteed her a place in western music history. Ironically it was Evans, not Rogers, who wrote a song about Trigger: "Don't Ever Fall in Love with a Cowboy" (*Happy Trails: The Roy Rogers Collection* [1937–1990], Rhino Entertainment Company, 1999). With tongue in cheek, Evans dealt with Trigger being higher on the pecking order than she, both on movie posters and in her husband's heart. Ironically, it was released around the time they announced their engagement to be married.

When Roy Rogers made a cameo appearance in *Hollywood Canteen*, he sang "Don't Fence Me In" and at the end of the tune mentioned his palomino by name. He did the same in "Four-Legged Friend" (Jack "That's Amore" Brooks and Lyn Murray) from *Son of Paleface* (Paramount, 1952). (Little Trigger was at his peak as he danced to the tune in an early sequence). Found on *Roy Rogers and the Sons of the Pioneers: King of the Cowboys* (Bear Family Records; RCA, 1983) and *Happy Trails: The Roy Rogers Collection* (1937–1990) (Rhino Entertainment Company, 1999), the tune was a hit for Rogers in England.

Roy Rogers also shouted "Whoa, Trigger" during the long "Lore of the West" title track number he did with Gabby Hayes. Dale Evans got into the act by mentioning her horse, Buttermilk, twice on the track "Texas for Me" from the same compilation (*Lore of the West* released on CD in 1996 by ESX Entertainment, Inc.).

Roy Rogers had a minor hit on the ARC label titled "Hi-Yo Silver." In June of 1938 it reached number 13 on the popular charts. "Hi-Yo Silver" was a tribute to the Lone Ranger's gallant mount, of course. The Lone Ranger was never mentioned by name in the song, and Tonto makes only a brief appearance in the last verse. "Hi-Yo Silver" was credited to De Leath and Erickson as co-writers and may be found on a recording titled *Roy Rogers: King of the Cowboys* (Living Era; ASV Ltd.; England, 1998).

Trigger was mentioned in "Who Taught You Everything?" (Ghost Town, RR 181) and in the tune "Singing Down the Road" by Charles Tobias and Raymond Scott from *Bells of Rosarita* (1945).

Bob Nolan never lent his skills as a songsmith to writing a tune about Trigger, but his fellow Pioneer Tim Spencer composed "Trigger Hasn't Got a Purty Figure" for the film *The Lights of Old Santa Fe* (1947). Roy Rogers sang it to Dale Evans, hoping to coax her into riding double.

Oddly enough, a song perfectly suited for Trigger, "That Palomino Pal of Mine," was not performed by Roy Rogers in any of his movies. The Kingsley and Kenwood song was recorded by Rogers for RCA Victor on December 1, 1947. It is available on a CD, *Lore of the West* (released on CD in 1996 by ESX Entertainment, Inc.). It is also found on *The Best of Roy Rogers* LP (RCA Camden).

There are two different songs with similar titles. The first, "Palamino Pal of Mine" (Fleming Allan/Dick Foran) is from *Dick Foran's Song Folio No. 1: 20 Original West Songs* (Cross Music, 1943). Foran's publisher spelled it as "palamino." The song makes a reference to Smoke, the horse Foran rode in his westerns. Circa 1950 Wilf Carter (Montana Slim) recorded "Palomino Pal of Mine" (Canadian Victor). At about the same time Eddie Dean recorded the song on Standard Transcriptions. Dean rode a palomino named White Cloud and a sorrel named Copper in his films.

The title track from the *Golden Stallion* movie of 1949, with ethereal lyrics written by Foy Willing and Sid Robin, was about Trigger and tailor-made to promote him as a magical animal. Trigger was also mentioned in the tune from the same movie titled "Night on the Prairie" by Nathan Gluck and Anne Parentean.

In the song "Roy Rogers, King of the Cowboys" by Jack Elliot from *Under California Stars* (1948), Andy Devine sang a line that referred to Trigger. In a later sequence, Rogers tucked young Michael Chapin into bed with a lullaby titled "Little Saddle Pal" (Jack Elliot), which also referred to his golden palomino.

Spade Cooley added a sweet violin during the original recording session for "Make Believe Cowboy" (Carroll Lucas), a lullaby for Rogers' son Dusty. (78 rpm recording reissued on R*oy Rogers: King of the Cowboys*, Living Era; ASV LTD; 1998). Roger referenced his horse in the last verse.

The closest Rogers ever got to singing a song about Trigger Jr. was when he recorded "Tennessee Stud" (*Happy Trails to You: Roy Rogers*, 20th Century Records; 1973). The tune was, in all likelihood, chosen on its own merits, but it's safe to assume that Rogers must have been pleased by the coincidence, as Trigger Jr. was a Tennessee walker stallion.

Even British rocker Elton John honored Trigger in song. "Roy Rogers" was a tune he and songwriting partner Bernie Taupin wrote for the album *Goodbye Yellow Brick Road* (Polydor, 1973).

Trigger was mentioned in the "Cowboy Heaven" track written by singing cowboy Eddie Dean and his partner Hal Sothern (*Happy Trails to You*, LP; 20th Century–Fox, 1975; Nostalgia Merchant Records).

Rogers wasn't going to complete the *Roy Rogers Tribute* CD without mentioning Trigger. He did so in the autobiographical tune titled "Alive and Kickin'" (RCA, 1991; also featured on the *Happy Trails: The Roy Rogers Collection* (1937–1990) (Rhino Entertainment Company, 1999).

Rogers' son Roy Rogers, Jr. ("Dusty"), contributed the song "King of the Cowboys" (Roy Rogers, Jr., and Larry Carney) to the *Roy Rogers Tribute* CD (BMG Music, 1991). Trigger was acknowledged in the line that refers to a golden palomino.

Rex Allen, Jr., mentioned Roy Rogers and Trigger in his own composition, "Last of the Silverscreen Cowboys," from his 1995 album *Singing Cowboys*.

In the comedy track "A Letter to Roy" by J. Nunnally and G. Nunnally (*Roy Rogers: A Musical Anthology*, A&E—Biography; 1998; Capitol Records Inc.), Rogers read a letter from a fan with questionable motives and a loose grasp of the facts. Trigger wasn't mentioned, but his main equine rival, Champion, was. A Spike Jones novelty song titled "Morpheus" by Eddie Maxwell, RCA Victor 1950, sported lyrics with a nod to Trigger.

Jimmy Webb, lyricist to such '60s hits as "By the Time I Get To Phoenix," referred to Trigger as being "stuffed and dried" in his song "P.F. Sloan" (*Words And Music*, 1970) about the line of communication between writers and their public. Sloan was the composer of "Eve of Destruction" and "Secret Agent Man."

Country star Lyle Lovett tipped his hat to Trigger in the tune "If I Had a Boat" (*Live in Texas*, MCA, 1999 and *Anthology, Vol. 1: Cowboy Man*, MCA/ Nashville, 2001).

Leighton B. Watts composed and performed "The Day That Trigger Died," a tribute to Roy Rogers and Trigger uploaded to YouTube in 2008.

Roy Rogers and Dale Evans were also radio celebrities, of course. Sixty-five half-hour episodes were packaged onto an audio CD in 2004. Along with musical numbers, short dramatic stories were featured. In these "Trigger "was played by a number of anonymous sound technicians to full effect. One episode was titled "Trigger Has Been Stolen."

9

Trigger Filmography

The following list includes all the movies Trigger made at Republic Pictures with Roy Rogers, movies the palomino made solo at other studios, and cameo appearances they made together. They are arranged according to release date.

Under Western Stars (Republic, 1938)
The Adventures of Robin Hood (Warner Bros., 1938) (solo no. 1)
Cowboy from Brooklyn (Warner Bros., 1938) (solo no. 2)
Billy the Kid Returns (Republic, 1938)
Come On, Rangers (Republic, 1938)
Shine On, Harvest Moon (Republic, 1938)
Juarez (Warner Bros., 1939) (solo no. 3)
Rough Riders' Roundup (Republic, 1939)
Frontier Pony Express (Republic, 1939)
Southward Ho! (Republic, 1939)
In Old Caliente (Republic, 1939)
Wall Street Cowboy (Republic, 1939)
The Rains Came (20th Century–Fox, 1939) (solo no. 4)
The Arizona Kid (Republic, 1939)
Gone with the Wind (MGM, 1939) (solo no. 5)
Saga of Death Valley (Republic, 1939)
Days of Jesse James (Republic, 1939)
Young Buffalo Bill (Republic, 1940)
The Carson City Kid (Republic, 1940)
The Ranger and the Lady (Republic, 1940)
Colorado (Republic, 1940)
Young Bill Hickok (Republic, 1940)
The Border Legion aka *West of the Badlands* (Republic, 1940)
Robin Hood of the Pecos (Republic, 1941)
In Old Cheyenne (Republic, 1941)
Sheriff of Tombstone (Republic, 1941)
Nevada City (Republic, 1941)
Badman of Deadwood (Republic, 1941)
Jesse James at Bay (Republic, 1941)
Red River Valley (Republic, 1941)
Bad Men of the Hills (Columbia, 1942) (solo no. 6)

The Golden Cloud/Pistol makes his film debut in 1938 as Trigger in a scene from *Under Western Stars*.

Man from Cheyenne (Republic, 1942)
South of Santa Fe (Republic, 1942)
Shut My Big Mouth (Columbia, 1942) (solo no. 7)
Sunset on the Desert (Republic, 1942)
Romance on the Range (Republic, 1942)
Sons of the Pioneers (Republic, 1942)
Sunset Serenade (Republic, 1942)
Heart of the Golden West (Republic, 1942)
Ridin' Down the Canyon (Republic, 1942)
Idaho (Republic, 1943)
King of the Cowboys (Republic, 1943)
Song of Texas (Republic, 1943)
Silver Spurs (Republic, 1943)
Silver City Raiders (Columbia, 1943) (solo no. 8)
Man from Music Mountain aka *Texas Legionnaires* (Republic, 1943)
Hands Across the Border (Republic, 1944)
The Cowboy and the Senorita (Republic, 1944)
The Yellow Rose of Texas (Republic, 1944)

Song of Nevada (Republic, 1944)
San Fernando Valley (Republic, 1944)
Lights of Old Santa Fe (Republic, 1944)
Hollywood Canteen (Warner Bros., 1944) (cameo no. 1)
Utah (Republic, 1945)
Bells of Rosarita (Republic, 1945)
The Man from Oklahoma (Republic, 1945)
Sunset in El Dorado (Republic, 1945)
Don't Fence Me In (Republic, 1945)
Along the Navajo Trail (Republic, 1945)
Song of Arizona (Republic, 1946)
Rainbow Over Texas (Republic, 1946)
My Pal Trigger (Republic, 1946)
Under Nevada Skies (Republic, 1946)
Roll On Texas Moon (Republic, 1946)
Home in Oklahoma (Republic, 1946)
Out California Way (Republic, 1946) (cameo no. 2)
Heldorado (Republic, 1946)
Apache Rose (Republic, 1947)
Hit Parade of 1947 (Republic, 1947) (cameo no. 3)
Bells of San Angelo (Republic, 1947)
Springtime in the Sierras (Republic, 1947)
On the Old Spanish Trail (Republic, 1947)
The Gay Ranchero (Republic, 1948)
Under California Stars (Republic, 1948)
Melody Time (RKO Radio Pictures, 1948) (cameo no. 4)
Eyes of Texas (Republic, 1948)
Night Time in Nevada (Republic, 1948)
Grand Canyon Trail (Republic, 1948)
The Far Frontier (Republic, 1948)
Susanna Pass (Republic, 1949)
Down Dakota Way (Republic, 1949)
The Golden Stallion (Republic, 1949)
Bells of Coronado (Republic, 1950)
The Kid from Gower Gulch (Friedgen/Aster, 1950) (cameo no. 5)
Twilight in the Sierras (Republic, 1950)
Trigger, Jr. (Republic, 1950)
Sunset in the West (Republic, 1950)
North of the Great Divide (Republic, 1950)
The Trail of Robin Hood (Republic, 1950)
Spoilers of the Plains (Republic, 1951)
Heart of the Rockies (Republic, 1951)
In Old Amarillo (Republic, 1951)
South of Caliente (Republic, 1951)
Pals of the Golden West (Republic, 1951)
Son of Paleface (Paramount, 1952)
Jamboree (Exploitation Productions, 1954) (cameo no. 6)
It's Showtime (United Artists, 1976) (cameo no. 7 a rerun of old footage)

10

Trigger Television

*"The war horse, the plow horse and the ranch horse all fell from view,
but in their stead came a far grander version of the horse to fire our
imaginations and keep the horse-human bond alive: the heroic
horse of the silver screen and the TV screen."*—Lawrence Scanlan[1]

The Roy Rogers Show

By the 1950s Roy Rogers' best movies were arguably behind him and the changes were obvious. The Sons of the Pioneers were replaced by the Riders of the Purple Sage.[2] Great sidekicks like Gabby Hayes, Smiley Burnette, and Raymond Hatton had been replaced by the overbearing Gordon Jones and obnoxious Pinky Lee. The only Rogers sidekick in his later films worthy of Hayes and Burnette was Andy Devine. B-westerns began to wind down as budgets and fan interest started to slip. Hopalong Cassidy and Gene Autry moved onto television in 1949 and 1950 respectively. In 1951, Roy Rogers followed.

His own Frontier Productions produced *The Roy Rogers Show* on television. It was set on the Double R Bar ranch in Paradise Valley, not far from Mineral City, where Dale Evans owned the Eureka Cafe. The half-hour black-and-white show aired initially on Sunday evenings on NBC from 1951 to 1957. Between 1958 and 1961 it was syndicated on mostly NBC affiliate stations on Saturday mornings. Reruns were broadcast on CBS on Saturday mornings from 1961 until 1964.

The two main assets Roy Rogers took when he made the move to television were his wife and his horse (Corky Randall, rather than his father, worked on *The Roy Rogers Show* under Hudkins wranglers Johnny Brim and Buddy Sherwood), but still the King of the Cowboy's small-screen adventures paled in comparison to those on the big screen. Rogers and company worked within such tight budgets that only his charisma and loyal fan base sustained his show. Had Republic Pictures backed Rogers, if Republic CEO Herb Yates hadn't been so fearful of television, *The Roy Rogers Show* could have been greatly improved. Beyond "Happy Trails" sung over the closing credits, the singing cowboy almost never sang on the show—no music, no royalties to pay—and because Dale Evans wrote the iconic theme; its royalties stayed with the family.

Gene Autry's television episodes were better produced than Roy Rogers', who simply didn't have the same resources. Still, Autry's show had the feel of dinner theatre productions with small ensemble casts and sparse settings. Action sequences, a Republic trade-

Trigger's blaze was not symmetrical and his mane fell on his right side (Roy Dillow collection).

mark, were not as involved or complex. Nevertheless, broadcast on a weekly basis in the 1950s and coupled with the novelty of the new medium of television, the small-screen Western succeeded. Today, watching daily reruns on Western cable channels, one can see how formulaic B-western television shows were. In all fairness, they were never meant to be seen back to back; it's unfair to subject them to a great deal of scrutiny. And in spite of everything, there were magic moments, though admittedly few and far between.

Although he got second billing on *The Roy Rogers Show,* Trigger didn't get nearly the attention that he received in movies. Trigger was already so well established in the hearts and minds of fans (the television short titled *Trigger Tricks* was already in production) that the King of the Cowboys seems to have decided to focus as much attention on his German shepherd Bullet, and sidekick Pat Brady's jeep Nellybelle. Bullet's importance may have had a little influence on *The Adventures of Rin Tin Tin* and *Lassie* television shows, which both came along in 1954.

Although Bullet had already appeared in a few of Roy Rogers' movies, it was on the television show that he really blossomed. In many episodes, Bullet either attacked a villain or tracked him down. Rogers even used a motorboat instead of Trigger during a chase sequence in "Mountain Pirates" (11/56). It stands to reason Roy Rogers would use what he had available to fill out story lines since he was producing his shows. Why not use

Roy Rogers on Trigger and Dale Evans riding Buttermilk. This formal portrait was taken during the height of their popularity on television. Evans had ridden both pintos and palominos before settling on a light buckskin—clearly a good choice and a fine complement to Trigger (Roy Dillow collection).

things he wouldn't have to rent? Rogers may have also wanted to get Bullet and Nellybelle established with youngsters the way Trigger was in order to add to their merchandising potential.

Synopses of every episode of *The Roy Rogers Show* are available in *The Roy Rogers Book* by David Rothel and *Roy Rogers, King of the Cowboys: A Film Guide* by Bob Carman and Dan Scapperotti. One may conclude from these two sources that none of the shows were built around Trigger, and only a few ever featured him in any special way. Conversely, Gene Autry produced two of his television show episodes around Champion: "Six-Shooter Sweepstakes" and "Horse Sense." It's odd Rogers did not do the same for Trigger. It may have been that the tighter budgets did not allow Trigger to have as many special scenes as he did in movies. Scenes where animals perform special routines require more time to rehearse and shoot. Time, especially on television, is money.

When it came to television, Gene Autry's sorrel Champion was clearly ahead of Trigger. A spin-off series from *The Gene Autry Show*, *The Adventures of Champion* was a natural manifestation of the horse's popularity with fans. Produced by Gene Autry, 26 episodes ran from 1955 to 1956.

Some episodes of *The Roy Rogers Show*, like "Ghost Town Gold," open with Roy Rogers on Little Trigger rearing up in front of the Double R Bar ranch sign. Rogers says, "Well riders, Trigger here is raring to go, so let's get started with today's story."[3] In a later sequence Trigger comes to Rogers's aid after bad guy Marshal Reed ropes him. Little Trigger attacks Reed before he can drag Rogers down the road with his own horse. The sequence lasts only a few moments, with many cuts.

"The Phantom Rustlers" is one of the most interesting television show episodes, thanks to Little Trigger. It opens with Roy Rogers putting the palomino through a routine of tricks including lying down on his side and sitting down. Later, Rogers is shot as he's riding down a dirt road. Because he's too weak to get up, he cues Little Trigger to lie down beside him. Rogers slides over the saddle, and the horse rises back up and carries him back to his ranch.

"Ambush" featured both Trigger and Little Trigger working at liberty: the former running solo to Roy Rogers' ranch and the latter rearing in a barn as Rogers fights a bad guy. Rocky Roe also noted special scenes with Trigger in "Go for Your Guns," "Carnival Killer," "Silver Fox," "Gun Trouble," "M Stands for Murder," "Gun Trouble," "Morse Mix Up," "Dead End Trail," "Boy's Day in Paradise Valley," "Backfire" "Bad Neighbors," and "Miller from Medicine Creek."

Trigger Jr. appeared in a television commercial with Rogers for the chocolate drink, Nestle's Quik. The palomino, in a red, white, and blue show saddle and matching bridle, did a short dance and bow.

Dale Evans Queen of the West

In 1950 Dale Evans filmed a television pilot for the *Dale Evans, Queen of the West* show titled "Slip of the Gun." Pal was the horse she used. Fans got a very good look at the palomino with his three white stockings and unique blaze. Evans even mentioned the horse in the opening song, "Lo De, Lo Di." She rode him in very showy tack, which included ridiculously large tapaderos.

Pal was used in the Dale Evans pilot just as Trigger and Little Trigger had been used in Rogers' movies before. At one point, while exchanging gunfire with a gang of thugs, Evans ducked behind Pal, using him as a shield as she rode off. As Evans was being pursued she dismounted and cued Pal to lie down and hide with her in some tall grass as the bad guys rode past.

There are also some beautiful shots of the palomino double California substituting

Dale Evans on Pal during the production of her own weekly television series, *Queen of the West*. Only a pilot episode was filmed (Roy Dillow collection).

for Pal in *Dale Evans, Queen of the West*. During one sequence where two bad guys were waiting for Evans, her horse acted up as a way of warning her; it was California she was riding.[4]

Trigger Tricks

Just as Dale Evans filmed a pilot for a television series, Trigger was up for his own show as well. It was to be sponsored by Quaker Oats and titled *Trigger Tricks*. It seems to have been planned as a 15-minute show, common in the early days of television, to showcase Trigger's famous rodeo and personal appearance stunts. *Trigger Tricks* ended up being one-minute segments.

Roy Rogers would sue Republic Pictures to keep his movies off the air. He wanted a television show like Hopalong Cassidy's and Gene Autry's, but he couldn't get sponsors. Republic didn't want a show that would compete against Rogers' old movies, which they were planning to syndicate on television. *Trigger Tricks* was a way to establish a television presence and a stopgap measure used to keep Rogers' name affiliated with a sponsor, so if an impending court battle was ruled in his favor, he would immediately be ready to get *The Roy Rogers* Show on the air.

Trigger Tricks and the pilot for the Dale Evans television show (with Pat Brady as the comic relief) were ready to go if Republic had won the lawsuit. After Republic lost, *Trigger Tricks* and Dale Evans' shows were scrapped. *The Roy Rogers Show* was put on the air quickly that same year, in the event that Republic might win on appeal. After about two years the appeal was successful, but that was enough time for *The Roy Rogers Show* to become well established.

Trigger Tricks marked Roy Rogers' first network television appearance, which happened on *The Gabby Hayes Show* in 1950. Dale Evans sang a solo, Roy Rogers and Little Trigger performed a few tricks, and Bullet was also present. A week before the show, *Life* magazine did a feature about Trigger (Little Trigger) and featured Glenn Randall, Sr., grooming the horse.

The Gabby Hayes Show was sponsored by Quaker Oats and contained two or three commercials featuring Rogers and "Trigger" performing different tricks. The show was mentioned in Roy Rogers rodeo souvenir programs of the time: "Trigger made his debut on television in a series sponsored by Quaker Oats titled *Trigger Tricks*, which shows all of his famous rodeo and personal appearance stunts. For once, he easily steals the show from Roy."

Roy Rogers even thanked Republic CEO Herbert Yates for allowing him to appear on television. Obviously this was done prior to his fight with Yates over the making of his own television movies.

Bullet Von Berge, Little Bullet and the Pack

Several Bullets were used at Republic Pictures and later in *The Roy Rogers Show* on NBC television from 1951–57 and CBS from 1961–64. The German shepherds were billed collectively as "Bullet the Wonder Dog."

The original Bullet was an AKC registered German shepherd, with the typically ostentatious breeder's name Bullet Von Berge (born November 9, 1949; breeder, Earl W. Johnson; sire, Ch. York of San Miguel; dam, Pogie Bait; death, unknown). He first appeared in the Roy Rogers film *Spoiler's of the Plains* (1951). He was not owned by Rogers; neither were any of the several Bullets used at Republic Pictures. However, later on television; Rogers' own personal Bullet, the smaller of the dogs, was used to perform tricks. The dog's real name was Max.

It's believed the first television Bullet died while the television series was in production. A second Bullet was brought in and died years later after Trigger passed. Neither dog was mounted for the museum. Max had that dubious honor, the same dog Rogers

The original Trigger taking it easy with his German shepherd pal, Bullet (Larry Roe collection).

owned. Max's mounted body was eventually auctioned at Christies. It was never described as the original Bullet by the auction house though that was the assumption.

Sadly one of the touring Bullets was killed while being transported with Little Trigger and another palomino double in the large custom-made hauler and trailer. The circumstances are vague. Depending on speed and turns horses are required to balance standing while in transport. They are haltered, tied and separated by a cross bar. Apparently the dog got loose and, despite the room, got a little too close and was kicked. Whether this horrible turn of events was due to negligence by one of Glenn Randall's assistants, is pure speculation. As an animal lover Roy Rogers was no doubt mortified and should not be faulted for never discussing this unpleasant episode publicly.

Miscellaneous Trigger Television Appearances

Beyond his role on *The Roy Rogers Show*, the original Trigger rarely if ever appeared on television. He was retired in 1957 at age 23 to Rogers' ranch in Chatsworth, California.

Over the course of their careers, Roy Rogers and Dale Evans made a number of guest appearances together and solo on television. Rogers and Evans even hosted their own variety hours; some were taped performances at rodeo and fairs.

The opening episode of *The Roy Rogers Show* on NBC television was more of an introductory half-hour special featuring Bob Hope, Dale Evans, the Whippoorwills, Pat Brady, and Little Trigger. It was also used to promote the movie *Son of Paleface* (Paramount, 1952). NBC and Post Cereals aired the special and first episode live from the El Capitan theater in downtown Hollywood on December 30, 1951. Little Trigger was showcased in a sequence playing cards around a table with Hope, Roy Rogers, and trainer Glenn Randall, Sr. Little Trigger's cards were held on a wire stand. Said Rogers, "We did a sketch in which Bob, I, and Trigger were all supposed to be playing poker together.

Roy Rogers and Bob Hope played a hand of cards with Little Trigger during a television special promoting their film *Son of Paleface* (Paramount Pictures, 1954). Glenn Randall was seated directly behind the palomino with his hand on the bridle (Roy Dillow collection).

When Trigger spots Bob trying to pull an ace from his sleeve, he knocks over the table with his nose and pushes him offstage."[5] The segment was rebroadcast on *The Bob Hope Chevy Hour* in February of 1955.

Beyond their weekly adventure program, Rogers and Evans starred in a number of *Roy Rogers Rodeo: TV Special* shows including one broadcast from the San Antonio, Texas, Coliseum in 1955. The one-hour show featured Little Trigger and Trigger Jr.

Roy Rogers, Dale Evans, and Trigger Jr. appeared on *The Perry Como Show* in 1956. Trigger Jr., doubling for Trigger, got a good deal of screen time. Roy Rogers, Trigger Jr., and even Glenn Randall Sr. first appeared among the studio audience. Como called Rogers and Trigger Jr. on stage, where he asked the cowboy to introduce him to his horse. What followed was a little routine where Como offered the palomino a lump of sugar. One gets a close look at the animal in this sequence and can see that he is immaculately groomed; he was beautiful. Rogers effortlessly did a step mount onto Trigger Jr. and cued him to extend his front leg to Como as a parting gesture. Later, Trigger Jr. was featured in a western setting. Como, a former barber, offered to trim the palomino's forelock, but Rogers objected. In a closing sequence, Rogers brought the palomino out and performed a short dance routine. If anything the appearance demonstrated how ably Trigger Jr. filled in for his legendary predecessor.

In the fall of 1960 Roy Rogers and Dale Evans hosted the *Grand National Championship Rodeo* from the San Francisco Cow Palace. The show was broadcast on their own *Chevy Show* on NBC. Trigger's trainer, Glenn Randall was one of the guests.

Little Trigger appeared with Roy Rogers and Dale Evans in the winter of 1961 at the Championship Rodeo at San Antonio, Texas. The program was also broadcast on the *Chevy Show*.

The original Trigger does not seem to have appeared in the *Roy Rogers and Dale Evans Show* variety hour produced by ABC in 1962. Little Trigger stood

Roy Rogers and Dale Evans on borrowed horses at Texas A&M Stadium in College Station, 90 miles northwest of Houston. All of Rogers' palomino string was long gone by this time (Roy Dillow collection).

Trigger Jr. and Roy Rogers make a guest appearance on *The Dinah Shore Show*. Both Rogers and Shore hosted hour-long variety shows sponsored by Chevrolet in the 1950s (Roy Dillow collection).

in for Trigger on the *This Is Your Life* episode dedicated to Roy Rogers in 1953. The program was hosted by Ralph Edwards, who introduced the palomino by saying, "No show on Roy Rogers would be complete without Trigger. We can't forget Trigger. We couldn't tell the story of your life without Trigger sharing the spotlight.... Trigger, thank you for the part you played in Roy's life." The palomino appeared from behind a curtain and gave Rogers a kiss before being led off stage.

Little Trigger appeared with Rogers and Dale Evans on the *Hollywood Palace* show on ABC in February of 1964 and February of 1965.

Roy Rogers and Dale Evans also rode in a number of parades across the country, many of which were televised, including the Tournament of Roses Parade held on New Year's Day in Pasadena (in 1977, they were selected as grand marshals). When they weren't riding Little Trigger, Pal, or Buttermilk, they rode elaborate floats.

Actor John Ritter hosted a documentary salute to B-western cowboys titled *The Singing Cowboys Ride Again* which aired in October 1979 on HBO. "Trigger" and "Champion" were featured in clips from their movies. Also the same year, Roy Rogers discussed Trigger on *The Phil Donahue Show*.

In 1982 on *The John Davidson Show* Roy Rogers talked about Trigger, and Dale Evans added anecdotes about her days at Republic Pictures trying to improve her horseback riding skills. Also in 1982, *The Merv Griffin Show* (NBC) was taped at record producer Snuff Garrett's ranch. Griffin devoted the entire show to B-westerns and interviewed Gene Autry, Rex Allen, Yakima Canutt, and Roy Rogers. The King of the Cowboys told Griffin that he first started teaching Trigger tricks but later hired Glenn Randall.

Sometime in 1989 or 1990, Roy Rogers and Dale Evans appeared on *The Pat Sajak Show* (CBS). Sajak asked a few questions about Trigger, which Rogers dealt with in the same fashion he did in countless interviews. He said Trigger was four when he first worked with him in *Under Western Stars*. When Sajak asked Rogers what he thought of current Western movies, the King of the Cowboys responded as he had so many times before, saying there were some done in such poor taste he wouldn't even let Trigger watch.

In 1994 on *The Late Late Show with Tom Snyder* (NBC), Roy Rogers and Dale Evans talked about Trigger and Buttermilk.

A nine-minute segment on Trigger for the *Horseworld* television show was broadcast circa 1995 and included a visit to the Roy Rogers and Dale Evans Museum in Victorville. It was hosted by champion rodeo rider Larry Mahan.

Roy Rogers' horse Trigger was featured on the Outdoor Life Channel program *Complete Rider*. The segment lasted about five minutes and began with a brief biography. Dusty Rogers, Jr., spoke about how his dad was hoping to find an equine partner with a more interesting color than black, bay, or white when he began at Republic Pictures.

Towards the end of his career, Roy Rogers rode a palomino (in a standard western stock saddle) in a Randy Travis 60-minute television special for the Nashville Network (TNN) titled *Randy Travis—Happy Trails* (1990). Rogers made a dramatic entrance riding in at a full gallop. He accounted for himself pretty well considering his advanced age. As he slowed down and dismounted, he was holding on to the saddle horn, something he never did in his films or television shows.

Roy Rogers and "Trigger" first appeared on the television show *The Fall Guy* in January of 1983 in an episode titled "Happy Trails." The last appearance of "Trigger" on television occurred on *The Fall Guy* in 1984 in episode #65, titled "King of the Cowboys." Rogers and former television cowboy stars John Russell (*Lawman*), Peter Breck (*The Big Valley*), and Jock Mahoney (*Range Rider*) joined series star Lee Majors and Dusty to track a gang of diamond smugglers. Rogers rode a gorgeous Trigger look-alike for the occasion.

In March of 1999 actor Val Kilmer appeared on the Academy Awards show with a "Trigger" double to introduce a B-western cowboy tribute commemorating the deaths of Roy Rogers and Gene Autry the previous year. Kilmer at one point referred to the palomino as "Trigger." One source claimed the horse was the grandson of Trigger Jr.[6]

Roy Rogers on the last horse to play "Trigger" on screen in an episode of *The Fall Guy* television show, 1984. The beautiful palomino look-alike was on loan (Roy Dillow collection).

The History Channel program *America's Lost and Found* featured a short segment on Trigger, following his life and career all the way up to when he was mounted and put on display at the Roy Rogers and Dale Evans Museum in Victorville.

In January of 2005 the Animal Planet cable show presented a two-hour program on the 50 greatest animal stars. Trigger was 39th on the list. Toto from *The Wizard of Oz* (MGM, 1939) was number one. This was obviously more an acknowledgment of the movie than the animal. When one accounts for the countless performances on film by Rin Tin Tin, Lassie, Rex, etc., Toto is pretty small potatoes in comparison.

In 2005, Trigger was mentioned in the "Taxidermy" episode of the History Channel's weekly program *Modern Marvels*.

Trigger Documentaries and Cameos

When Roy Rogers was the subject of a documentary Trigger was mentioned, of course, but in the same way he had always been, in public relations terms. No mention was made of Little Trigger, and palomino doubles were acknowledged only in passing. Three documentaries of note are *A&E Biography Roy Rogers* (2001) and *Roy Rogers: King of the Cowboys* (Republic/AMC/Galen Films, 1992). The AMC network also produced a fabulous documentary titled *The Republic Pictures Story* in 1990 featuring interviews with Rogers.

Cowboys of the Saturday Matinee, a 76-minute documentary on "Hollywood legends of the old west," was produced in 1984. It was produced and written by Ken Shapiro, directed by Jerry Kramer, and narrated by James Coburn. Referring to Roy Rogers, Coburn states, "He was the King of the Cowboys. Now I don't know who named him that, but it was probably Trigger. After all, he was the smartest horse in the movies."

In 1992 Thys Ockersen, a fan from Holland, wrote and directed a documentary titled *Roy Rogers: King of the Cowboys*. It was released through Scorpio Film Productions Ltd., Nos Television, Holland. Ockersen had incredible access to the Rogers family and the Republic movie archive. *Roy Rogers: King of the Cowboys* begins with an interview of Mindy Peterson, the granddaughter of Dale Evans from a previous marriage. As it happened she was living in Amsterdam in 1981 and working with the International Mission Organization. She told Ockersen about how she and her siblings often went out to the Rogers ranch and rode Trigger and Buttermilk. She recalled one instance when she was riding Trigger and inadvertently miscued him to rear up on his hind legs. Her grandfather rescued her from the predicament.

Certainly the most moving segment in Thys Ockersen's documentary occurred while he was interviewing former Republic director William Witney who talked about the stunts Trigger, the Old Man, would do on movie sets that professional stunt horses would not.

William Witney got very emotional when he reminisced about the last time he saw the original Trigger. Witney happened to be directing an episode of the old *Sky King* (NBC, 1951–1962) television show near Roy Rogers' ranch in Chatsworth. During a lunch break he drove over to see the palomino, whose eyesight was failing. As he approached the stall, he called out. Trigger's ears perked up and he moved towards the director. Witney's eyes started to tear up as he described the aged palomino. That was the last time he saw the horse alive. One can see why Witney devoted a book to the horse; he was clearly very attached to him.

The William Witney interview is the high point of the Thys Ockersen documentary. For all the access he had, Ockersen asked the same tired questions that had been asked before. Roy Rogers, Dale Evans, and Dusty Rogers gave the same generic responses they'd given time and time again. Nothing new was revealed. As it is one of the last glimpses into Roy Rogers' world during the final years of his life, the Ockersen documentary is worth viewing. There's even a sequence at the Roy Rogers celebration in Portsmouth and a visit to Rogers' boyhood home.

The History Channel presented a two-hour documentary on western movies titled *When Cowboys Were King* in 2004. Narrated by veteran character actor Eli Wallach, *When Cowboys Were King* not only explored the popularity of Westerns, but examined their impact on American culture. It won a 2004 Golden Boot Award for outstanding contribution to Western movie heritage. *When Cowboys Were King* was produced for the History Channel by Lou Reda Productions. The documentary featured extensive film clips and interviews with such Western film veterans as Tom Selleck, Ernest Borgnine, Peggy Stewart, and Morgan Woodward. Even the children of cowboy stars were interviewed: John Ritter, Dusty Rogers, and Cheryl Rogers-Barnett. Trigger and Tom Mix's Tony were the only horses singled out in *When Cowboys Were King*. It was erroneously stated that Republic Studios owned Trigger at the time Rogers insisted on buying him.

William S. Hart's pinto Fritz was the only horse hero mentioned by name in the 90-minute documentary *Golden Saddles, Silver Spurs: The History of Movie Westerns* (2006), although other four-legged stars, like Tony, Champion, and Trigger were shown.

11

Glenn Randall and the Randall Ranch

"A bus load of fans drove out once to where they were filming an episode and somebody
asked Roy, 'To what do you attribute your success?'
Roy walked over to Trigger, and he took Glenn Randall's hand,
and he said, 'These two right here.'"—Bill Catching[1]

Roy Rogers was close to a few people: his manager Art Rush; a few of the men who played his sidekicks (especially Gabby Hayes and Pat Brady); the original Sons of the Pioneers (specifically Tim Spencer); and the man who cared for and trained his horses, Glenn Randall. When one studies how Rogers and Randall worked together, it's easy to conclude that their relationship transcended that of client and trainer to that of confidant and mentor. Both men spent hours together training, and traveling all over the United States and parts of Europe. After speaking to Randall's son Corky, it's easy to conclude they were almost family. When Corky spoke about Roy Rogers, he said, "He was like a father to me." Cheryl Rogers-Barnett says that her father even lived at the Randall Ranch for a while some time around 1947: "He stayed at the home of Glenn Randall, his good friend and Trigger's trainer, which was also practically right around the corner from Republic."[2]

During the golden age of Hollywood, only movie headliners, and certain people in production who worked in such areas as special effects, set design, and wardrobe, were given screen credit. There was no acknowledgment of stuntmen, horse trainers, or wranglers—the people who had the most dangerous jobs. Today, every crewmember gets a screen credit, even drivers and caterers. But, credited or not, great trainers are all-important for animals that spent as much time before the public as Trigger and his doubles.

Before Glenn Randall arrived on the scene, three men are known to have had a hand in training the original Trigger. Under the auspices of his first owner, Roy Cloud, Trigger was started under saddle when he was around two years of age. According to Corky Randall, a trainer named Johnny Goodwin finished horses at Hudkins Stables, and it's safe to assume that Goodwin probably continued Trigger's training, preparing him for work on a movie set.[3] After Rogers started riding Trigger, he hired his first trainer, a cowboy named Jimmy Griffin. According to Republic director William Witney, Griffin was not only responsible for care and training of Trigger and Little Trigger, but he transported them wherever necessary.

Biographer Robert W. Phillips claimed Jimmy Griffin was hired in 1939, a year before

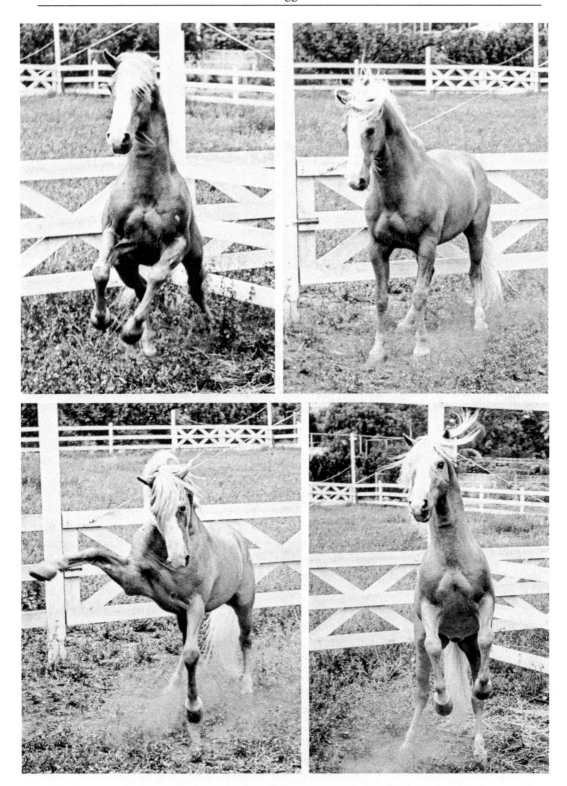

The regal Trigger at home at the Randall Ranch (Roy Dillow collection).

Trigger poses at liberty with his caretaker and trainer, Glenn Randall (Roy Dillow collection).

Roy Rogers hired his personal manager W. Arthur (Art) Rush. It would seem getting his horse squared away was more of a priority than his own personal management. Griffith didn't seem to be around long enough to play a big part in Trigger's training as it turned out and may have been more of a handler/caretaker. He left Rogers' employ sometime in 1941 to work in the defense industry. According to author David Rothel, Glenn Randall claimed to have started working with Trigger, replacing Griffin, that same year. Randall would work with Rogers' horses for the next 24 years.

Corky did not recall Jimmy Griffin. Corky remembered Rogers already in possession of Little Trigger when he started working with his father. Rogers needed the palomino trained for a forthcoming appearance at Madison Square Garden.

Glenn Randall's Early Years

Glenn Randall was born on Christmas Day, 1909, in western Nebraska. His family homesteaded in the area around Melbeta, and he grew up farming with his dad's stock. He always loved horses and began training them at an early age. The very first horse

Randall owned and trained was a little mustang named Rags. When Randall was only nine years old, he trained and sold a black-and-white half–Shetland/American Saddlebred paint mare to the Sells-Floto Circus. "My people were horse people," he explained. "I used to go to all the circuses and horse shows and [watch the] stunts, and I'd always see a horse do something and go home and try it on my pony."[4]

In the early 1930s, Randall's first job away from home was breaking horses for the cavalry and artillery. After that he also worked for the mayor of Torrington, Wyoming, training his standardbred trotters and pacers. He worked for movie cowboy Tim McCoy's Wild West Show, handling 250 horses. Randall went on to train remount horses and mules for the cavalry at Fort Robinson, Nebraska, and worked at the Oregon Trail Days celebrations near Gering. He trained horses for the government at Ft. Warren, Wyoming. Randall eventually left his military job and followed the professional rodeo circuit, where he rode bucking horses and worked as a rodeo clown.

By the late 1930s, Glenn Randall moved to California, where he managed a thoroughbred breeding facility owned by Elmer Houchins outside Bakersfield, in Arvin. It was here that Randall branched out and started his own training stable at the Arvin facility. He eventually ran across the Hudkins brothers who would introduce him to the horse and client who would change his life.

Randall Takes Over

Clyde Hudkins, brother to Ace and Art Hudkins, recommended Glenn Randall to Roy Rogers after Jimmy Griffin departed. Hudkins told Rogers of a young man naturally gifted at handling equines who lived outside of Bakersfield. According to Corky, Art Hudkins brought Roy Rogers to Bakersfield to meet Glenn Sr. at his rented ranch in Weedpatch seven miles from Arvin. This introduction gave Randall his start in the film industry and began one of the great partnerships in entertainment history.

Back at Hudkins Stables, Randall began working closely with Rogers. The beautiful palomino immediately captivated Randall, and he made sure to stick closely to the horse and the singing cowboy. In Randall's mind, that might not have constituted being Trigger's official trainer yet, even though a part of his job at Hudkins included working with them part time. Not until he went to work exclusively for Rogers and[5] after the singing cowboy purchased Little Trigger and moved him to the Arvin facility would Randall's job title have been "Trigger's" trainer. Randall would manage all the "Triggers" that were used on film and in personal appearances.

Cheryl Rogers-Barnett confirmed that Trigger and all his doubles were trained by Glenn Randall and her dad.[6] Early Roy Rogers publicity maintained that Trigger had been trained by Rogers since the horse was five years of age.[7]

"When I started working with Trigger," said Randall, "I discovered right away that Roy's claims about the horse sure weren't exaggerated. He was smart, full of action, and hungry to learn. I've worked with horses since I was a boy in Nebraska. But from that morning when I started working with Trigger, I knew he was the savviest horse I'd ever seen."[8]

Glenn Randall told Roy Rogers biographer Elise Miller Davis how he wound up touring with the King of the Cowboys who had show dates to fill and was looking for a good trainer: "About a week before he was scheduled to leave for Baltimore, Roy came

Roy Rogers and Little Trigger during a personal appearance with trainer Glenn Randall close behind wearing a black hat. When Corky Randall was shown this photograph, he remarked, "I think this is their first tour together. Glenn was staying close to Roy and Trigger, not knowing how each would react [to the crowd]."

up to my place for a sober-faced talk with me. 'Glenn, I'd like you to go on this trip with me,' he said. 'I'd feel better if you'd handle Trigger on the road.' Roy worried about Trigger all the way across country on that first trip. He wouldn't turn in himself until he saw that the horse had been stabled down properly."[9]

Rogers and Randall did not sign a formal contract; a handshake sealed their association. Rogers knew he needed a dependable and expert trainer to travel with his horse. "At first, it wasn't easy to find the right kind of quarters in every strange city we pulled into," said Randall. "It was on Roy's mind a lot in those days." Eventually they knew the best stables in every city, and Randall booked Trigger's reservations in advance.[10]

Glenn Randall must have been very pleased when Roy Rogers purchased Trigger Jr. The trainer took a great deal of joy in showing the beautiful stud (Joel "Dutch" Dortch collection).

As Roy Rogers' trainer, equine confidant, and advisor, Glenn Randall became the middleman in one of the best horse deals in Hollywood history. Since Rogers didn't buy the original Trigger until late in 1943, Randall could have been training the palomino for as long as two years and would, therefore, have been the person on hand to advise Rogers on the purchase. As Randall claimed later, the $2,500 paid for Trigger was the finest investment Rogers ever made. Considered a fortune in the 1940s, it was nevertheless pretty near a steal. According to one biography, Rogers talked over the matter with Randall and he, too, agreed that the singing cowboy should own Trigger.[11] According to Corky Randall, his father was instrumental in every equine purchase Rogers made while they were working together. Not only did Rogers give Randall control over his horses, the two men also shared their stock. Rogers and Dale Evans did not own the palomino Liberty Horse act—they belonged to Randall.

The Randall Ranch

Glenn Randall eventually was able to move from Bakersfield to Van Nuys, most likely in the mid–1940s. The Outpost on Riverside Drive in Van Nuys was where Randall kept Little Trigger briefly. Since Rogers did not own Trigger outright till 1943, Randall may not have had him on his property until then.

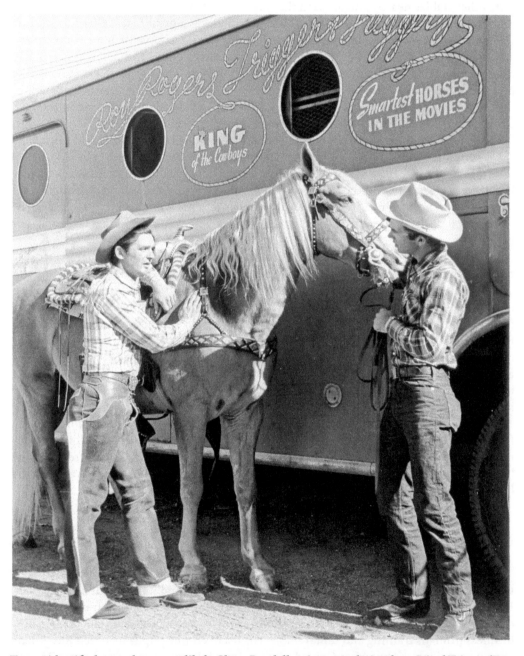

Two unidentified wranglers, most likely Glenn Randall assistants, admire the original Trigger (Roy Dillow collection).

Glenn Randall moved to Longridge Avenue, also in Van Nuys, a mecca for Hollywood working-horse people. According to one of Randall's wranglers, Don "Jug" Reynolds, the place was about an acre and a half, with a small boarding facility of about eight stalls. (Cheryl Rogers-Barnett thought it was between two and three acres.) Though small, Randall had access to the Van Nuys wash, that ran parallel and in-between Longridge and Fulton streets, adjacent to the property and went on for a great distance. There were other stables nearby and all used the wash to exercise horses. According to Rogers-Barnett, who often frequented the stable, "The ranch was a great place. Glenn Sr.'s house was on the east side of Longridge and the stables were a couple of houses north and across the street. The Van Nuys wash was immediately behind the ranch and was like riding on the beach, beautiful with deep sand. In the 1940s when Trigger was still making movies, on off-days Cheryl would ride him into the wash joined by Randall's daughter Dolores and other neighborhood children. When it was decided to cement-in the L.A. River, Glenn Randall and the other horse people had to move. He and his wife, Lynn (aka Minnie), lived further back on the property, behind Corky Randall and his wife."

From there the Randalls moved not far away to Sherman Way in North Hollywood (this was by the old Hudkins Stables, which were where part of Forest Lawn Cemetery is now, very close to the Autry Museum Center) about two or three acres. Glenn Randall made a last move to Pine Street in Newhall. Corky and his wife, Pinky, lived in a house on the front of the property, while Glenn Sr. and his wife, Lynn, lived in a house farther up the canyon.

Glenn Randall bought all of the Hudkins brothers' stock, stages, wagons, etc. He renamed his stable business the Randall Ranch. Cheryl Roger-Barnett claimed, "Glenn owned the biggest collection of horse-drawn vehicles in Hollywood. Glenn Sr. furnished most of the horses for all of the western TV shows. His biggest job came when he furnished over 300 horses for the movie *Paint Your Wagon* (Paramount Pictures, 1969)." Rogers-Barnett remembers the Newhall ranch was about 50 acres and at one point accommodated over 300 horses, mules, and burros. Randall even boarded camels and other more exotic livestock. Like the Fat Jones and Hudkins stables before, Randall kept an inventory of vintage horse-drawn vehicles, including stagecoaches, covered wagons, chariots, buggies, and hundreds of saddles of many different styles.

The Randall Ranch eventually became a focal point for horsemen and horsewomen from all over the world. The Randalls crossed paths with just about every actor and film-maker involved with horses and action back in the glory days of the silver screen. By the late 1980s only 15 commercial stables remained. Development slowly nibbled away at the land replacing it with condominiums and retail stores.

Other Horse Students

Because "Trigger" was highly visible, Glenn Randall, Sr., eventually earned a reputation as one of the finest horse trainers in motion pictures, and many wanted his services. Rogers and Randall worked out an agreement whereby Randall could train horses for other western stars. He supplied mounts to the movie industry, rodeos, and other show business from his training and rental stable. His list of equine pupils included Rex Allen's chocolate stallion, Koko. After Gene Autry's trainer, Johnny Agee, passed away, Randall worked with the last Champion. Randall also trained White Flash for Tex Ritter, many

Glenn Randall with Allan Lane's Blackjack, Rex Allen's Koko and Roy Rogers' Trigger Jr., all trained and boarded at the Randall Ranch in Newhall, California, circa 1960 (Roy Dillow collection).

of John Wayne's horses, and Slim Pickens' Appaloosa, Dear John. Randall and Corky trained horses for such television shows as James Garner's *Maverick* and for television commercials such as the last palomino to play Mr. Ed.

When Glenn Randall purchased horses for his Liberty Horse ensemble, Rex Allen's Koko was part of the string but because of his unique color was never considered for the act. Though not as well known as Randall's other equine charges, Koko "the Miracle Horse of the Movies," could have been trained to the same degree as Little Trigger but it wasn't necessary. Allen's movies had limited budgets and did not often lend themselves to horse tricks that required more shooting time. Like his cowboy master, Koko arrived on the B-western scene as it was winding down and was not showcased like his peers.

Rex Allen wrote about Koko in his autobiography *Arizona Cowboy*: Glenn Randall said, "You know, I've got a chocolate-colored horse with a white mane and tail that I bought in St. Louis. I thought Dale Evans might like him, but he's a stud and a little too much horse for a woman.' I stabled him at Glenn Randall's while he was being trained, and kept him there for several years while I lived in Tarzana. Of course, when I bought my ranch, I kept him out there until he died."

Rocky Roe, who heard Rex Allen at a film fest in Knoxville in 1990 claimed Glenn

Glenn Randall on Soda, originally trained as a cutting and roping horse before the gelding was used by Dale Evans and renamed Buttermilk (Petrine Day Mitchum collection).

Randall, Sr., suggested he not use the stallion until his second movie, *Hills of Oklahoma* (1950) as the horse was not completely trained to work on a movie set.

Rex Allen often lamented that he almost wore Koko out while filming and touring because the stallion was so hard to match with its unique color. Corky Randall maintained the stud was never considered as a mount for Dale Evans, contradicting the story Rex Allen often repeated. "It just wouldn't have looked right. Koko was about 15 hands with a 'bulldog' type build like Little Trigger." Randall went on to describe him as "chunky."

In a conversation with this writer, Corky did not think that Koko was ever considered for Evans, claiming the stallion was too much for her. Rex Allen, Jr., later admitted that his dad made up this story because it sounded good. It's been said that it was Roy Rogers who first showed Koko to Rex Allen at Glenn Randall's stables, and for the Arizona cowboy it was love at first sight.

Rocky Roe also witnessed Dale Evans reading a fan letter during a taping of the *Happy Trails Show* in Knoxville, Tennessee, inquiring about her connection to Koko. Witney and Republic Pictures also balked at using Koko. They felt he would detract from Trigger with his beautiful coat and features, however, Roy Rogers believed Trigger could hold his own aesthetically with any horse.

Eventually Glenn Randall Sr. toured with his own horse acts, leaving Corky to tour with Roy Rogers and Dale Evans. Trigger Jr. did, in fact, appear solo without his famous celebrity owner as such venues at the Western Idaho State Fair, where he was accompanied by Randall. Roy Rogers allowed the use of his "Triggers" on the touring circuit to keep them in tune and as a way for his trainer to make a living when the cowboy star was involved in other projects. "Trigger" even made solo personal appearances at a number of Sears locations while Roy Rogers and Dale Evans were in Houston for the 1952 Houston Fat Stock Show and Rodeo. "Trigger will greet his friends daily." The palomino's $25,000

Glenn Randall, Yakima Canutt, and Charlton Heston talking horses and chariots on the set of *Ben-Hur,* circa 1958.

air-conditioned trailer was also on display. When Rogers gradually stopped touring with "Trigger," Glenn Randall continued to work with other clients.

Along with managing Trigger and his doubles, one of the other high points of Glenn Randall's career was his masterful work training the four whites (Altair, Rigel, Antares, and Aldebaran) that Charlton Heston drove in the chariot race in the mega-movie *Ben-Hur* (MGM, 1959). Randall was in charge of some 40 horses used in the epic. The heart-pounding chariot race sequence still thrills audiences today. It was filmed with limited special effects. Along with the second unit director, the legendary Yakima Canutt, Glenn Randall Sr. produced one the most impressive action sequences ever put on film. In a dramatic contrast to the silent era production of *Ben-Hur*, horses were not injured or killed during filming.

Ironically, the most difficult task Randall faced in *Ben-Hur* was in the more benign sequence when Sheik Ildrim, owner of the Arabian horses, first introduced them to Judah Ben-Hur. After dinner in his tent, Ildrim clapped his hands and a curtain was pulled, revealing four white horses standing free, with no halters or reins. "If I had a song to sing, I would sing you the song of horses," the sheik says before he asks the horses to step inside to greet Ben-Hur. The horses' movements—entering the tent, playfully nuzzling and licking Ben-Hur's hand, and eventually leaving—were controlled with hand signals from Randall, who was kneeling on the floor out of camera range.

Glenn Randall in Roman costume on tour with the *Ben-Hur* horses, circa 1959–1960.

Glenn Randall bought the horses used in *Ben-Hur* after the production ended in Italy, Corky claimed his father bought nine and brought them to America. He would bill them as The Ben-Hur Horses. Randall toured with his son Glenn Jr., and the *Ben-Hur* horses for a few seasons. Corky substituted for his brother briefly driving a chariot when Glenn Jr. was injured.

Personal Appearance Tours

Glenn Randall's career extended beyond television and movies. He earned a living with horses by performing, teaching and boarding. In his later years Randall produced a wild west show at Great America Theme Park in New Jersey. In his 80s he was working for Arabian Nights.

Glenn Randall excelled in the highest levels of dressage, with beautiful extension in all forward and lateral movements. He would canter his horse on stage and complete the most difficult of movements, the canter backwards. The horse would canter in a very high degree of collection then slowly canter down to where he was cantering on the spot. His weight then shifted slightly backwards so the equilibrium was tilted, flowing to the back of the horse. As the animal was so perfectly balanced, it cantered backwards. Randall mastered these and other challenging dressage movements, including extensions in passage, Piaffe, Spanish walk, Spanish trot, and the canter on three legs. The origins of these

Rocky Mountain region rodeo stock contractor Leo J. Cremer (left) with Glenn Randall on Little Trigger. Gene Autry was a partner in the World Championship Rodeo Company, which furnished livestock for major rodeos. In 1954 he acquired Montana's top bucking string from Cremer's estate (Wes Girt collection).

movements go back to war on horseback when the animals were taught to inflict lethal damage. They weren't called "war horses" for nothing.

Buford "Corky" Randall

Born in 1929 in Gering, Nebraska, Buford "Corky" Randall was diagnosed with polio at an early age. Instead of using metal spikes as legs supports—the standard treatment then—his father, Glenn, Sr., insisted the boy exercise. Corky rode thoroughbred colts by age 10 and by high school he worked at Republic Pictures.

Corky Randall grew up helping his dad with Rogers' horses and took over when the King of the Cowboys started his television show. Corky eventually toured with Rogers, caring for Little Trigger and Trigger Jr., just as his dad had. Corky also worked the Roy Rogers Liberty Horses act. The Randalls and the Rogers families borrowed each other's horses. (It's a happy coincidence the double R initials Rogers adopted could also have

Corky Randall circa 1951, at a horse show in top hat and tails, riding Golden Zephyr, aka Trigger Jr., in an English saddle and double reins (Petrine Day Mitchum collection). Insert: Corky Randall in 1979.

applied to the Randall Ranch.) Corky often drove the Rogers children to and from appearances. He knew Roy Rogers and "Trigger" personally on a day-to-day level. Ironically he knew very little about such things as Roy Rogers memorabilia and had only seen a few of the King of the Cowboy's movies. Corky was always busy and didn't see the need to.

As an expert trainer and horseman, Corky Randall could also size up different riders. When asked who was the best horseman of the B-western cowboys, he responded, "Wild Bill Elliot because he could sit a cutting horse." When asked how Roy Rogers became such a great rider beyond natural talent and practice, Corky replied, "He was usually riding stallions."

Corky met his wife, Joan "Pinky," after Glenn Sr. hired her to ride and exercise his stock. They were married in 1951. On tour, they performed a choreographed Fred Astaire and Ginger Rogers ballroom dance on horseback.

Screenwriter Jeanne Rosenberg, co-writer of *The Black Stallion* (with Melissa Mathison),described Corky with, "He had this rough exterior which masked this enormous heart and sense of humor and incredible generosity…. He was very protective of them [horses]. And he had this enormous handlebar mustache. He just looked like a character with those boots and his hat…. He sort of talked with this cowboy drawl."

Corky Randall cues Trigger Jr. during a photograph session for *New York Mirror* magazine (October 1958) while Dale Evans and Roy Rogers pose (Roy Dillow collection).

The high point of Corky Randall's career came in 1978 when director Caroll Ballard hired him and his father as wranglers on *The Black Stallion* (United Artists, 1979), arguably one of the best horse movies ever made. After Glenn, Sr., helped Corky train Cass Ole and actor Kelly Reno, it was Corky who went on location during the actual filming.

Regarding the pivotal film in Corky's career, his brother Glenn Randall, Jr., acknowledged, "I talked Corky into doing *The Black Stallion*. Up until that time, he was basically a boss wrangler. It was a bigger horse involvement (training-wise) than anything he'd ever attempted." Corky always credited that particular film as his launching pad.

The Black Stallion cinematic brilliance belongs as much to the Glenn Sr. and Corky Randall as it does to director Caroll Ballard. Often described as poetry in motion, its soul and magic are due not only to Ballard's mastery as a filmmaker, but most especially to the performance Corky Randall elicited from the four-legged star on camera, a gorgeous Arab stallion named Cass Olé. Corky would go on to cite the black stud as his all-time favorite equine actor and described the animal as almost human. According to Corky, Cass Olé did all of the tricks in the movie and was in most of the sequences.

Animal safety on the set of movie was a top priority for Corky Randall. He worked alongside American Humane's Film and TV Unit. *The Black Stallion* contains some of the most challenging horse scenes ever attempted. Stunt horses were used during the backyard escape and run through town. Corky, who had the authorization, almost shut down the set when a stunt horse nearly drowned in a tank of water during the filming of the ship sinking sequence (the footage was used in the movie).

Corky Randall's credits as livestock coordinator and trainer include such movies as *The Black Stallion Returns* (MGM/United Artists, 1983), *Silverado* (Columbia Pictures, 1985), *Indiana Jones and the Last Crusade* (Lucasfilm/Paramount, 1989), and *Back to the Future III* (Amblin Entertainment/Universal, 1990). Corky traveled the globe, winding up in Mexico as livestock coordinator on *The Mask of Zorro* (Sony Pictures Entertainment, 1998) starring Antonio Banderas. Corky's son, Bruce Wayne Randall served as a wrangler, and brother Glenn Randall Jr. was second unit director and stunt coordinator on the film.

Corky Randall worked on such television shows as *Spin and Marty* (Disney, 1955), *The Fall Guy* (Glen A. Larson, 1981–1986), *Return to Lonesome Dove* (de Passe Entertainment, 1993), and *Walt Disney's Zorro* (Disney, 1957–1958). During the Zorro show Corky worked with Tornado, the black charger actor that Guy Williams rode. Walt Disney, an avid polo player, was known to hang around the set talking to Corky about horses.

American Humane's Film and TV Unit worked alongside Corky to monitor animal safety on the set of numerous films. "Corky always had a deep sense of safety for livestock and he never cut corners, he never took liberties, even though it may have meant we had to work a little bit harder or we had to do a little bit extra," stated Glenn Randall, Jr. A two-time winner of American Humane's Performing Animal Top Star of the Year (PATSY) Award, Corky also received the 1982 Humanitarian Award from what was then the Society for the Prevention of Cruelty to Animals Los Angeles and helped further legislation safeguarding animals.

Reflecting on his life with his brother, Glenn Randall, Jr., stated, "We both were raised by a horse trainer, and we both owed our livelihoods, from the time I was a child, to the performance of horses. The horses always came first. Before the kids got fed, the horses had to be fed. They were the top priority."

Guy Williams' understudy Wayne "Buddy" Van Horn on the set of Walt Disney's *Zorro* in the mid–1950s. Corky Randall trained and handled the masked avenger's mount, Tornado. Note Trigger's tack and the R on the tapadero.

Presumably Glenn, Jr., or Corky handled Trigger or Little Trigger on screen when a scene called for it. Who else was better suited? Whether those horses were being cued on camera or off, no one knew how to signal them. As extras they would have been dressed in regular cowboy outfits (which is what they wore anyway).

"He was more than a brother to me as a child," said Glenn Randall, Jr., "He was almost a father because dad was always gone on location and tours". Corky Randall died in 2009 after a prolonged battle with cancer. He was 80.

Glenn "J.R." Randall Jr.

Glenn Randall, Jr., is a book unto himself, though not linked to Roy Rogers and Trigger to the extent his father and older brother were. He was an accomplished stuntman, stunt coordinator and second-unit director, with a resume as long as your arm including: *Ben-Hur* (MGM, 1959), *Harum Scarum* (MGM, 1965), *Planet of the Apes* (20th Century–

Fox, 1968), *Little Big Man* (Paramount, 1970), *Diamonds Are Forever* (United Artists, 1971), *Blazing Saddles* (Warner Bros., 1974), *The Towering Inferno* (20th Century–Fox, 1974), *The Black Stallion* (United Artists, 1979), *Raiders of the Lost Ark* (Paramount, 1981), *E.T. The Extra-Terrestrial* (Universal, 1982), *Star Wars: Episode VI—Return of the Jedi* (Twentieth Century–Fox, 1983), *The Fugitive* (Warner Bros., 1993).

Glenn Randall, the Gold Standard

While Rogers frequently acknowledged Glenn Randall in interviews, his role was strictly behind the scenes. Randall's part in making Roy Rogers "the King of the Cowboys" and Trigger "the Smartest Horse in the Movies" was enormous, but he never received screen credit in a Roy Rogers movie. Randall did make one brief cameo appearance in *Heldorado* (1946) in a rodeo performance sequence. After Rogers sang "My Saddle Pals and I" with the Sons of the Pioneers, Randall may be seen handing Little Trigger off to Rogers. *Heldorado* is, by the way, a great example of Rogers' live performance act of the time.

Glenn Randall was in his retirement years when western films began to wane in popularity. The old horse trainer sold his ranch and held a public auction to liquidate his holdings. He retired with his wife, Lynn, to a spacious home in the Santa Clarita Valley close to the Randall Ranch site.

Glenn Randall was honored on numerous occasions including the Golden Boot Award, the Rodeo Historical Society's Hat's Off Award, and a spot in the prestigious National Cowboy Hall of Fame in Oklahoma City. He was also honored with a dinner dance and reception at the Los Angeles Equestrian Center in Burbank, California, in April 1986. More than 300 friends and admirers from rodeo and movies attended the gala. Lynn and the children, Glenn Jr., Corky, Pinky, Joan, and Dolores, were present. Dale Evans opened the celebration with a blessing. Former bronc rider Jerry Gatlin acknowledged Randall on behalf of the Hollywood stuntmen for whom he helped train their "falling horses." Roy Rogers thanked and praised Randall for his work with "Trigger."

Randall closed the banquet by saying, "When I go, I visualize myself going off into the sunset driving four white horses to a chariot and leading old Trigger."[12]

Though B-westerns had a broad appeal for this writer and millions like him, horses were not just scenery and ambiance: they were the focal point. Through hard and dangerous work, men like Glenn Sr. and Corky Randall helped create thrilling equine performances and magic on film. They did it humanely with great patience and care. Roy Rogers on Trigger and Alex Ramsey on the Black Stallion were glorious fantasies and the Randalls were crucial in making them possible.

Glenn Randall passed away in 1993. Roy Rogers and Dale Evans were asked to give a eulogy at his funeral. Unfortunately, Dale had suffered a heart attack a few days before and the couple was forced to cancel what surely would have been a heartfelt and well-deserved tribute to a great friend and partner.

12

The Smartest Horse in the Movies

*"Of all the movie horses I've trained, I've always said Trigger was the smartest
and most brilliant. Of all the things you've seen him do on the
silver screen, I give a lot of credit to the boss man who rode him and to the director
who always got the most out of the story point. Trigger was the
'in Horse' of the motion picture business. In his early pictures, he did the
complete picture without the use of doubles. Its hard to express my
thoughts of Trigger ... he was a great star."*—Glenn Randall[1]

Little Trigger was once showcased in a two-page magazine spread titled "Partners and Pals." The palomino was pictured bowing, throwing a kiss, sitting, in a dressage move, and an "end of the trail" pose. Pure public relations, the text painted Roy Rogers as "Trigger's" sole trainer. There is no periodical identification or date, but judging by Rogers' clothes it looks to be around the time of Republic Pictures sponsored a national campaign (along with roadside billboards) promoting him as "King of the Cowboys."

The text reads:

Unchallenged as the "smartest horse in the movies," Trigger, Roy's magnificent equine partner, is a palomino stallion, sporting more than 50 "cue" spots on his shining golden coat. When Roy first purchased Trigger, as a colt, he began training by teaching him the simplest tricks. As the lessons progressed, Roy discovered that Trigger was capable of learning everything in the way of tricks that could be dreamed of. The beautiful steed responded consistently and immediately. It took very little time to teach him anything new. In fact Roy says that he seemed to get the idea from words alone. Now Trigger, who is almost as famous as his master, has more than sixty tricks and is probably the most widely known horse in the world. Trigger is nine years old now and at the height of his ability as an actor. Rarely temperamental, he does become nervous when fans, under the impression that hairs from his tail are lucky, attempt to get the prized trophies.

A 1950s syndicated newspaper cartoon in the same vein as *Ripley's Believe It or Not* by cartoonist Manning Hall outrageously claimed Roy Rogers' educated horse Trigger "understands a vocabulary of over 400 words" and "does some 500 tricks and still learning a new trick-a-day."

As far back as August 1940, *Movie Life* magazine ran a page titled "Tricky Trigger" featuring five charming shots of Roy Rogers and Little Trigger right before *The Carson City Kid* movie was released. *Movie Stars Parade* magazine published a one-page spread in 1942 featuring Little Trigger's talents and the tag line, "He gets glamour close-ups and co-star billing in the movies—meet Roy Rogers' 'Trigger.'" A two-page spread in *Movies* magazine (circa 1942) titled "It's a Cinch!—Trigger's out to teach the younger

Little Trigger rearing at liberty. Glenn Randall signed the photograph for a fan (Roy Dillow collection).

generation a thing or two—if it will listen!" showcased Rogers and Little Trigger showing a colt named Golden Boy how to perform a series of tricks. In 1943 *Movie Life* offered fans a two-page spread titled "Trigger's Tricks" with Rogers and Little Trigger once again in a series of poses. "Partners and Pals" was still another two-page spread (publication unknown) with more of the same. Trigger Jr. was quoted in a one-page spread (magazine unknown, 1950s) titled "Rock 'n Roll," four photos of the palomino and his master demonstrating some fancy steps and a short paragraph ending, "Like Roy says, anyone can learn to Rock 'n Roll. All it takes is good common horse sense." *Polly Pigtails*, a magazine for girls, ran a two-page spread with a number of photos titled "Take It from Trigger" (June 1946).

Glenn Randall was constantly asked questions about the training methods he used on "Trigger." Regrettably he never produced a biography, much less a book on how he trained horses. His knowledge was passed along to his son Corky, and both were reluctant to discuss trade secrets gained over years of hard work and experience. Still, there have been a number of articles written on the Randalls where they discuss some of their training methods (refer to the bibliography).

While the original Trigger was not trained to the degree Little Trigger was, he could do some tricks, such as untying a knot in a rope (Roy Dillow collection).

When Glenn Randall was in his heyday in Hollywood, the term *horse whisperer* was not in use, but it would have applied. Randall knew that in order to train a horse successfully he had to understand its true nature and not impose his training methods forcefully. Watching a great horse trainer is like watching a magician. They work miracles and make it look easy. This is because they speak the language of the horse, through tone of voice, hand gestures, and body language. Horse whisperers, like Monty Roberts, refer to this language as Equus.[2]

Horses are prey animals. Their eyes are on the sides of their heads; they can see almost 350 degrees around, with small blind spots directly in front and in back. Horses can hear a hundred times better than humans and also have a very keen sense of smell. They're constantly looking out for danger and will run at an instant.[3] They're also very herd oriented, seeking safety in numbers. Their strong flight response and social nature has kept the species alive for thousands of years. Trainers work within this context and are especially aware of specific problems they face when engaging horses in front of crowds or in unusual places like movie sets.

During filming a trainer works from a distance, out of camera range and without the use of voice commands. For this level of training it is imperative that the horse have extraordinary confidence in its trainer. Training "Trigger" to accept unusual situations was just as involved and important as training him to perform actual tricks. Roy Rogers had extraordinary demands of "Trigger." Little Trigger went with Rogers on most of his public appearances; often they were indoors—not necessarily in arenas covered in the appropriate turf, but in lobbies or on theatre stages. Little Trigger accompanied Rogers safely and quietly on visits into children's hospital wards and orphanages. The palomino would hold one end of a spinning rope while Rogers and the more able children jumped. Little Trigger was even trained to ride in public elevators. It was because of special circumstances like these that Glenn Randall housebroke Little Trigger. Not an easy thing to do with a horse. It took persistence and patience on Randall's part to teach Little Trigger to relieve himself on command.[4]

The movie-going public is largely unaware of what it takes to use horses in movies and television shows. Time is money, and directors have little tolerance for animals that compromise a production. It's essential that the horses hit their marks and tolerate whatever action a story demands. While an audience sees only a horse carrying a rider, the horse sees and hears camera equipment, boom mikes, reflectors, sound trucks, film crews, and more. Such a setting is stressful for a horse.

Glenn Randall not only had to know the horse-training business, but he had to know how to work within the confines of the picture business. He had to familiarize himself with directors and understand what kind of horse was needed—not just with respect to breed and color, but what would be required. Just as important, he also had to educate film makers as to what a horse could and would not do.

The Movie Star Horse

It would be wrong to refer to the original Trigger as having little or limited training. While he wasn't schooled to the extent Little Trigger was, any cast horse used on a movie set was trained beyond normal limits.

Only a very few horses have the potential to succeed in motion pictures (some esti-

The original Trigger bowing at liberty.

mates are one in five hundred). Some manage a movie or two but eventually falter from boredom and routine. A horse that's consistently focused to perform, as Little Trigger was, is rare.

Celebrity horses had a small staff who looked after their needs: a groom who constantly combed, brushed, and trimmed manes and tails; a veterinarian; and even a make-up person to enhance horse's eyes with mascara for close-up shots. Star horses even required stand-ins for the lengthy lighting and technical preparations required before shooting scenes. Without stand-ins, lead horses could become fidgety by the time cameras were ready to roll. It was essential that a star horse had to be fresh and willing to work when it was brought onto a set.

Training Methods

Glenn Randall generally started training horses to do simple tricks after they were two years of age. When they were four or five, he advanced them to more strenuous tasks. In order to accomplish all he did with "Trigger," Randall trained in his barn every morning including weekends and holidays. A horse is primarily trained through repetition. Once a horse learns the proper response to a cue, it becomes a habit that is rarely forgotten.

Horses are single-minded; they can only focus on one thing at a time. If a horse has no confidence or even fears a trainer, it will not concentrate, much less respond properly to cues. The way to build confidence in a horse (or any animal for that matter) is by understanding the difference between punishment and brutality. "Trigger" respected Randall, but he was not afraid of him.[5]

Roy Rogers with Little Trigger performing a variety of tricks: the end of the trail pose, kissing, sitting, and bowing after a performance well done (Roy Dillow collection).

Randall's horses performed at liberty, a type of training referred to as "managed." Little Trigger was a managed horse. He was taught to respond to voice cues, whip cues, and hand signals.[6]

Ralph McCutcheon, another great trainer at the time, who schooled Dice and Highland Dale/Fury, approached his equine students the same way Randall did, and noted, "There's a big difference between a trick horse and a trained horse. A trick horse memorizes and is largely inflexible. Give him a variation on the five or six tricks he knows and he's lost. With his trainer's help, a trained horse can adapt what he knows to whatever action the story calls for."

Randall disciplined and corrected with a simple reward punishment method: for punishment he would take a whip and sting the subject on the leg like a fly. For a reward, kindness and a soft voice went a long way towards getting horses to perform.[7]

Whip-breaking was the process by which Glenn Randall produced a managed horse.

Little Trigger walking upright as any well-trained circus horse could (Roy Dillow collection).

It sounds worse than it was. It began with the animal at liberty in a small square pen. Randall would tap the horse on the rump with a long whip until it turned and faced him. The horse was tapped again on the same place till it walked up to him. Randall then gently rubbed the whip over the horse's body, even before a petting reward, as a way to reinforce the idea that the whip was an aid and extension of Randall's arm. After such a foundation, a managed horse was taught rudimentary conduct in front of movie cameras, then minor dramatics when cued: stop, pose, look right or left. After such basics it was taught more demanding tricks: to paw on the ground, charge with ears pinned back, whinny, take a bow, rear up, pretend to be in pain or play dead.

It's easy to understand why a managed horse was essential on a movie set. A trainer and director had to be assured that the animal would obey, not misbehave, and not revert to its strong flight instinct and run away. Whip training had to be completely impressed on a movie horse.

Writer Sam Henderson said of Glenn Randall, "People close to him have stated that he always had the horse's confidence. He praised the horse when he did well and scolded him when he miscued. But he only scolded him immediately after a mistake. He knew that if he waited until later to correct the animal, the horse would not realize why he was being disciplined."[8]

"Trigger" as Student

Roy Rogers and "Trigger" would be required to perform on screen and across the country in varied and unusual settings and situations. Trigger, Little Trigger, and Glenn Randall could handle anything a script or show called for. You name it and the palominos and their trainer delivered. With Randall's expertise "Trigger" would secure the tag line "the Smartest Horse in the Movies."

Randall often referred to Little Trigger as an exceptional learner. He pointed out that the horse was especially good at mouth work: untying ropes, retrieving articles, and so on. Randall said that eventually the palomino had a repertoire of well over one hundred tricks, some never before asked of a horse.

"He's the smartest horse I've ever known," Rogers said. "He almost knows when you are talking to him. I have had people ask me if Trigger ever talked to me. That's because he does all his tricks as simply as a trained acrobat."[9]

Inquiries about Trigger actually being able to talk may have come from young and overly enthusiastic fans who were more than ready to play along any fanciful PR. A *Motion Pictures* magazine article (circa 1944) by Dian Manners titled, "TRIGGER Talks About His Boss" is part interview. "We were astonished at Trigger's ability to talk. We hadn't known about that talent and doubted if Republic Pictures or Roy were as yet hep to this nag's jive." The palomino's tone was sarcastic, making jokes at his master's expense.

Trigger Jr., who was accomplished in certain dance routines, could also perform a few tricks (Roy Dillow collection).

Roy Rogers once said that when he wanted Trigger to count or to tell his age, he would turn one foot toward the horse, who would start tapping his hoof. When he had tapped enough, Rogers would pull his toe back, and the horse would stop tapping.

Counting (simple addition and subtraction, as well as counting to twenty) was one of their primary routines and used in more publicity stories than any other trick. Little Trigger could sign his name on a sheet of paper by making an X with a pencil. He could drink milk from a bottle. Not only could he rear when asked, but he could also walk 150 feet on his hind legs. All cues for the tricks were from subtle hand motions by Rogers.

At one point in time "Trigger" was credited with knowing fifty-two tricks. That number eventually grew to around one hundred, according to a *Western Horseman* article from April 1961. The public relations machine wasted no time reporting "Trigger's" tricks, offering every number imaginable.[10]

One might ask whether the original Trigger deserves the recognition he has achieved, considering that he gained his reputation from the skills of other horses. It's worthwhile to reiterate that no one horse could have done all that was asked of the original Trigger. Rogers and Randall weren't going to compromise him through overuse. It would be like expecting Sean Connery to have performed all the stunts in his role as James Bond. Between movies, with all the action that scripts demanded, with all the traveling involved in personal appearances, one single horse would have broken down over time. Even though the original Trigger could perform a few specialties such as rearing and nodding his head on cue, his most powerful assets were his beauty and camera charisma. Most important, he ran full out. Said Rogers, "He was just a flawless horse. He never made a mistake in his life. All those running shots down hills, up hills, sideways and every ways. He never once fell with me, in all those pictures."[11]

One of the attributes that sets cast horses apart from the supporting ones is their ability to calm down quickly after a hard run. The original Trigger was a pro at this. He could slide to a stop and hardly moved out of his tracks even after Rogers dismounted and dropped the reins. Movie horses had to be trained to tolerate hobbles, checking their flight instinct. They had to stand quietly, no matter what was going on around them. In some instances Randall was out of camera range, keeping a horse in place by holding onto its leg with his hand or with a string hobble that wouldn't photograph.

Trigger was anything but shy when cameras were rolling. Not only would the palomino stand steady with his ears up and alert, but given the slightest chance, he would steal the limelight from Roy Rogers by hamming it up for the camera. It's been suggested that the high-frequency hum of the motion picture camera, a sound the human ear cannot pick up, was a cue for Trigger to be on his best behavior. It has even been suggested that the hum would wake him from a sound sleep. Legend has it that Trigger liked to know what was going on at all times. The minute an assistant director yelled, "Quiet on the set!" and noises ceased, the palomino's ears would perk up and he would check to see where Rogers and Randall were.[12]

Trigger the Fearless

The original Trigger had a reputation on movie sets for doing stunts that other horses refused. One of the most legendary was recounted in director William Witney's book *Trigger Remembered*. Witney wrote that in *Far Frontier* (1948), Trigger actually

Glenn Randall and Little Trigger bid farewell to two young fans before boarding a plane.

dodged barrels without hesitation and even jumped one thrown from a fast moving truck by bad guy Roy Barcroft. Witney discussed the same sequence in the 1992 Tys Ockersen documentary *Roy Rogers—King of the Cowboys.*

During the filming of *Sunset in the West* (1950), the script called for a stuntman to jump from a running horse onto a train with lots of steam coming from the wheels. After going through five palomino doubles that balked, director Witney and stuntman Joe Yrigoyen settled on the original Trigger to accomplish the feat.

Joe Yrigoyen said, "Trigger was like a beautiful Mercedes and rode like one as well. It was exhilarating. Being a horseman, he gave me inspiration and much confidence. Trigger would do anything I asked him and would deliver every time. He was the king."[13]

Gelding "Trigger"

Trigger lived around other stallions and geldings. None were used for breeding. They were kept in a bachelor setting, which tended to produce calmer, less stallion-like behavior. One rarely hears about the Roy Rogers palomino remuda living around mares.

Just speaking aesthetically, stallions tend to have a more muscular build, thicker necks and heads. A gelding's crest and/or the arch of its neck are pretty much lost. By

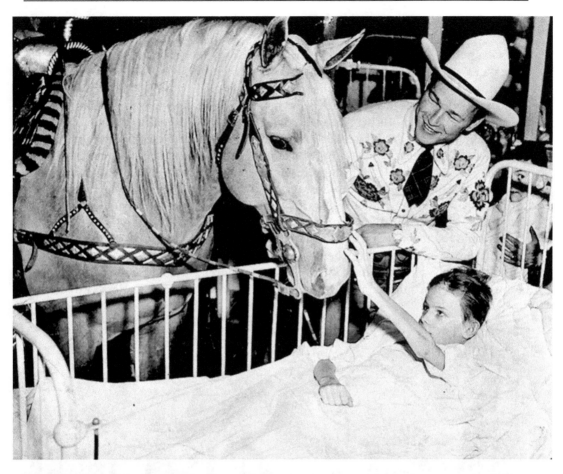

Roy Rogers and Little Trigger visited many a hospital and orphanages while on tour—great publicity but done as a goodwill gesture for less fortunate fans. Here even the cantankerous Little Trigger seems to understand how vulnerable young patients were.

leaving the animal intact, extra testosterone helps growth hormones build up muscling that wouldn't be there otherwise. Ceasing a stud's hormone level, his flowing mane does not continue to grow nor is the tail as long. Not only does gelding alter a horse's physicality but its temperament and intelligence change as well. Any experienced horseman would understand why Roy Rogers never bred or gelded the original Trigger, Little Trigger, or Trigger Jr.

Randall and his horse-trainer peer—Ralph McCutcheon both preferred to train stallions. McCutcheon began with geldings, but in the 1930s he started using studs exclusively as his major stars. In a "Scene Stealers" article by John Donovan (periodical and date unknown), "Geldings have a definite tendency to quit and are not as responsive as a good stud. You have to remember that I don't use any wires or ropes to force my animals into position. I operated strictly through hand and voice controls, using the natural impulses and spirit of the horse. The stud is always more interesting to watch, because he is actually enjoying himself. He knows it's a game and that he'll be rewarded. It's just not possible for an altered horse to show that kind of interest."

Care, Diet, Equipment and Grooming

Given the variety of venues Little Trigger performed in, he had to be well shod. He wore standard iron shoes on the ground and sometimes iron shoes with hobnails between the nail holes for pavement when in a parade. Sometimes a horse's hooves were shod with soft rubber shoes to soften kicks, and his teeth covered in gauze to prevent serious bites if an equine fight was being staged. Many times Little Trigger wore rubber boots to prevent slipping on waxed floors for inside work such as a television studio or hospital. Frank Carrol, a San Fernando Valley blacksmith, shod Trigger every six weeks.

Dr. Charles Reid, a Hollywood veterinarian, checked the health of Rogers' remuda at least three times a year. They were wormed regularly and had their teeth examined periodically. Two grooms and handlers kept Little Trigger in tip-top form. His daily exercise routine was partly walking and partly going at a lope.

At times cotton was stuffed down a horse's ears when gunfire was part of a scene. Cardboard stirrups were used when a horse was expected to fall on its side. If a horse were to roll on a hard standard stirrup and get injured, it would be hard to get it to perform the same stunt again. In the television episode "Phantom Rustlers," Roy Rogers

Roy Rogers and Little Trigger show Golden Boy how the grown-ups perform, *Movies* **magazine, mid–1940s (Roy Dillow collection).**

asked Little Trigger to lie on his side. As the palomino performed the stunt, Rogers moved the stirrup and cover (tapadero) out of the way so the horse wouldn't poke himself in the belly. Dale Evans performed the same stunt with her horse Pal in the pilot for her *Dale Evans Queen of the West* show.

Trigger got a daily rubdown and a highly regulated diet: a flake of the choicest $55-a-ton hay, and specially prepared grain (varied blends of oats, barley, hay, bran, corn, and mineral salt) depending on work and schedule requirements.

For personal appearances both Little Trigger and Trigger Jr. were treated to a neat cross-curry checkerboard pattern over their rumps. All this cosmetic care served Little Trigger well especially during special occasions when he had to look his best: once as an honored guest at President Roosevelt's birthday ball; once at the Paramount studio commissary as the guest of honor during a lunch hosted by his *Son of Paleface* co-star Bob Hope; and even for a special luncheon at the world famous Waldorf Astoria in New York.

Saddles and Other Tack

Roy Rogers started with borrowed tack from Hudkins Stables where Republic leased Trigger. About six different combinations of tack were used before Rogers had his own saddles. The Hudkins brothers used at least three different silver saddles, and one with tapaderos with round spots and sheepskin martingale. Two Hudkins saddles had a yoke martingale. There were three regular saddles: one with the sheep-skin martingale and one with a plain martingale; a few movies were made with just a plain saddle and no martingale. Roy Rogers later owned four high-end quality saddles that were shared among his string of palominos. All were very ornate, referred to as parade or show saddles. The matching bridles and breastplates stayed with each saddle accordingly for the most part. During the television years, Rogers bought plastic saddles for his horses. Collector Roy Dillow described Roy Rogers' saddles as:

Single R tapadero used in movies, television and personal appearances (it's the saddle Rogers sells in *My Pal Trigger* for a bag of grain). First Bohlin saddle Roy Rogers owned. Displayed on Trigger at Christies but sold separately for $386,500. Once used on Buttermilk during a parade in Paradise Valley. Rogers bought this Bohlin silver saddle before he bought Trigger and used it on Little Trigger first in personal appearances.

Double RR tapadero with big round conchos used for a few television show scenes. Also used on the three Triggers basically as a rodeo and parade saddle. Once owned by Buck Jones. Made by Bohlin and ended up on Trigger Jr. in the museum. Sold separately for $242,500 to the same buyer who bought the jeep Nellybelle; they were later displayed at a cowboy film festival in Memphis.

Pointed six-star tapadero came with a small R in a little circle below, used once during a parade on Trigger and rarely after. It was the original movie saddle on Trigger at the museum. It had a few little diamonds and was custom made for Rogers by Bohlin. (Used on Trigger for a while in Apple Valley when Rogers was having repairs done on the Bohlin saddle with RR tapaderos.) Sold for $103,500 at the High Noon Auction in 2010.

The McCabe saddle. No tapaderos, sold for $412,500. Never used on Trigger, but used on Trigger Jr. in the View-Master reel. Used on tour several times, on display in Sears stores and on other events around the country. The McCabe saddle was made in

Roy Rogers with his fabulous McCabe saddle, which was decorated in gold, silver, and rubies. Trigger wore it in a Pasadena Tournament of Roses Parade. Trigger Jr. may be seen wearing it in the Roy Rogers View-Master reel (Larry Roe collection).

1931 by 16 highly specialized craftsmen during the Depression at a cost of $20,000 and was decorated with 136 ounces of gold, 1,400 ounces of silver, and 500 rubies. The maker's mark read: "Gold and silver by John E. McCabe/Leather by J.P. Davis, Hollywood, California." It included a matching martingale and bridle. The final price of $412,500 was more than double the previous price paid for a silver saddle.

Plastic saddles. Two were on a base color of white with red eagles and blue stripes, with the Double R brand on the tapaderos, which were blue with red eagles. Two more were the same as previous except the tapaderos were a blue base color with white Double RR brand and red eagles. A plastic Rose Parade saddle, cream to white in color, had green leaves and yellow roses. Two additional matching saddles were blue, white, and red with no brands, made by All Western Plastics. One dark pink and white saddle was made for Buttermilk.[14]

Trigger appeared in fancy show tack in his first film with Rogers, *Under Western Stars* (1938). In the movies that followed, his tack is changed from production to production for aesthetic reasons or because of upkeep and use. This is normal given the wear and tear saddles go through over time. The original silver saddle was modified throughout Rogers' career. The breast plate changed, and some silver was added to the front of the leg straps that hold the stirrups and the tapaderos, which fit around them. The silver pieces were smaller than those used on the original tapaderos.

Trigger wore a martingale throughout *Under Western Stars* but not in any of the promotional photos shot before, which may indicate he was having a problem during production. He did not use one after.

The *Under Western Stars* saddle rented from Hudkins Stables along with Trigger was also used in the movie *Shut My Big Mouth*, made at Columbia at around the same time.[15]

Trigger was usually filmed in show tack but on occasions when Roy Rogers was playing an out-of-work cowboy or an historical figure like Billy the Kid or Bill Hickok, Trigger was in plain brown leather tack. In *Southward Ho* (1939), Trigger is seen in a military tack. In *My Pal Trigger* (1946), Trigger plays his own father, the Golden Sovereign, and is ridden by Dale Evans in English tack. Finally, in the *Son of Paleface* (Paramount, 1952), Little Trigger may be seen in special custom-made red, white, and blue plastic western tack.

Rogers sported jockey attire and rode a Thoroughbred on an English racing saddle during a steeplechase sequence in *Wall Street Cowboy* (1939). In *Spoilers of the Plains* (1951) Rogers, playing an oil company worker, used a protective suit to stop a pipeline fire. Trigger also wore protective gear.

It's been rumored that Rogers used a saddle sized for a woman. The filming techniques and old camera angles usually made the actors and actresses appear taller than they actually were. Circa 1995 Robert W. Phillips received a letter from one Art Grigg of Huntington Beach, California, with a photo of Roy Rogers and two unidentified people standing in front of a fancy show saddle. Mr. Grigg had read an article by Phillips in *Western Horseman* and noted an error: apparently Phillips referred to a saddle at the Roy Rogers and Dale Evans Museum as made by Edward H. Bohlin. His letter is as follows:

> I believe the ruby studded saddle that you refer to in your article is the one in the enclosed picture, which is the one under plastic cover at the RR museum. If in fact it is, then it is almost certainly not a Bohlin saddle.
>
> The saddle in the picture was made around 1931 by Davis and McGabe of McGabe Silversmiths,

and their names appear on the saddle. It was made for a Mrs. Musik who owned a championship horse named Diamond, which she kept in Palm Springs.

An interesting fact is that the saddle shown in your article was also intended for a woman, being a Bohlin model designated the Miss Dickson. There also were other saddles with the Dickson name. The largest of these was the Dick Dickson, named after the Fox West Coast Director. There was a Dick Dickson Jr. saddle which was a size in between the others mentioned. There also was a Dickson Jr. Special which had a Cheyenne roll cantle. I assume the Miss Dickson model may have been named after the daughter of Dick Dickson.

So Roy being of slight stature compared to some of the cowboys, used a smaller size saddle and in these two cases ones intended for women. Art Grigg.[16]

Rogers said that he got his fancy Bohlin show saddle some time around 1943. Actually it was used for first time in *Heart of the Golden West*, released November 16, 1942. One has to have the uncut version to verify this, because Trigger does not wear it until the last scene. The saddle was not used in the next Roy Rogers feature, *Ridin' Down the Canyon*, which was released December 30 of the same year. In the next movie, *Idaho*, released March 10, 1943, the saddle is used only in one scene. About halfway through the movie, Rogers rides up, dismounts, reads a letter, and talks with actor Harry Shannon. In *King of the Cowboys*, released on April 9 of the following year, the Bohlin saddle is used for almost the entire production and would remain a prominent fixture for the rest of movies Rogers and Trigger made at Republic Pictures. Roy Rogers used a model similar to the Dick Dickson style on Trigger. He paid $50,000 for a ruby-studded Crown Jewel Bohlin saddle in 1950.[17]

Movie People and Television Commercials

After a time Glenn Randall became somewhat disenchanted with the movie business. While he still trained horses for Hollywood productions, eventually it was his son Corky who actually worked horses in front of cameras once a film went into production.

Both Glenn Sr. and Corky Randall gained a reputation in Hollywood for their directness towards movie action directors. They were adamant as to which horse stunts were possible and which weren't. Corky did not mince words when it came to his disgust with movie people. With typical outspokenness he said, "They don't understand livestock, and they'll look at you and say, 'Well, you're a trainer, make him do it.' You get a director that doesn't understand horses, you have to have the power or fortitude to tell him it can't be done." Glenn Sr. said, "Livestock people know you don't make a horse, or any animal, do anything. You coax and you train, but to step right up there and make him do it—you can't."[18] Corky claimed the biggest problem he had with directors was getting them to understand the thinking process of horses. Most directors, accustomed to a number of retakes with human actors, expected the same of equines. A horse is good for a take or two; it's difficult to get them to repeat a trick over and over.

13

Ride 'em, Cowboy

*"A man gets to know a lot about a people watching the way they act
with horses. Roy Rogers isn't a range cowboy, and he had never pretended
to be one. Yet, put to the test, he could put in a day's work with the best.
He has a natural seat on a horse that plenty of Texas line-riders world envy.
Roy got it from riding bareback. He has kept himself in better shape than most men
his age, partly because he has to in order to do the things
he does in movies, but mostly because he has a personal pride
in good health that's more important."*—Glenn Randall[1]

Roy Rogers had great luck and timing, but they would have meant very little if he hadn't had the talent and ambition to seize opportunities that come but once in a lifetime. Replacing Gene Autry laid a challenge before him. Though Rogers already had the right look and singing voice, as much as anything he had to refine his equestrian skills.

B-western movie stars, including singing cowboys who usually made the transition from radio, had to ride horses as part of their job. Good editing and stunt doubles helped, but only up to a point. Cowboy stars on tour were often expected to ride horses in abnormal situations, such as parades or on visits to hospitals and orphanages, often in front of noisy and unpredictable fans. These actors needed to be prepared for awkward situations that only a skilled rider should attempt.

Action cowboys were usually much better horsemen than their singing cowboy counterparts. Roy Rogers was the exception. Beyond his charisma on screen and talents as an entertainer, he was a great rider. While he did not enter into show business from a rodeo background, he rode effortlessly and with great style. His hands were usually soft on Trigger's reins and his body language was flexible and smooth. As a natural rider, all Rogers needed beyond a little refinement were the right horses and a great trainer.

In her autobiography, *Cowboy Princess,* Cheryl Rogers-Barnett wrote, "Dad had never done any serious riding before he got into the movies, but he was a truly gifted athlete who caught onto the basic principles very quickly. Dad worked with great wranglers and stunt men. He was what they called a quick study and it didn't take him long to pick out the horsemen who he thought rode best and then figure out the mechanics of what they were doing that he liked."

It's been rumored that before William Boyd became Hopalong Cassidy he was afraid of horses. Whether that's true, he became a decent rider. While one would not equate him with equestrian skills such as those of Wild Bill Elliott or Dick Jones, Boyd was okay. He was rarely doubled by a stuntman doing fancy riding, quick dismounts or Pony Express

In his prime as a rider, Roy Rogers was so accomplished that he could ask Little Trigger to rear up even while the palomino was not wearing tack. Note how relaxed and confident the King of the Cowboys was (Roy Dillow collection).

mounts. On a subliminal level, his horsemanship was played down. This made sense given his lack of experience and age—Boyd was 40 when he started playing Hopalong Cassidy. (Amazingly, Hopalong Cassidy hardly ever referred to his horse, Topper, by name in his movies. The animal was strictly just beautiful transportation and didn't even receive screen billing.)

A horse trainer teaches not only a horse but its owner as well. Besides rating Little Trigger as one of his finest pupils, Glenn Randall also rated Roy Rogers as a great student. He acknowledged that Rogers was a quick study and often got results that were as good as his own. If the King of the Cowboys had been able to schedule the time necessary to become a horse trainer, there's little doubt he would have been up to the challenge.

Director William Witney was correct when he assessed Rogers' skills on a horse: "Roy was a perfect 10." Rodeo veterans Ken Maynard, Yakima Canutt, and Hoot Gibson may have been better riders, but Roy Rogers was more charismatic in the saddle.

Riding experts say that the best riders begin learning when they're children. A person who starts riding as an adult will never be as natural. Rogers began to ride when he was a kid. He told Thys Ockerson, in the documentary *Roy Rogers King of the Cowboys* (1992), that he learned to ride at about age eight, riding bareback. "Out on location when the sun would be coming up, I used to practice to see how steady I could make my head go, by watching my shadow. You could get the rhythm of the gait between your ankles, your knees, and your hips. Good riding is all a matter of practice."

Tonight Show guest host Burt Reynolds once introduced Roy Rogers by saying, "This man is smooth as silk on a horse." Amen to that. In his prime, Rogers mounted, rode, and dismounted Trigger effortlessly. His skill as a rider and Trigger's aptitude as a highly trained horse were demonstrated spectacularly in a chase sequence in *Robin Hood of the Pecos* (1941). In order to hide from a posse, Rogers removed Trigger's bridle as they galloped towards a herd of loose horses. He next removed the saddle as they came to a stop. The palomino was let loose among the herd and Rogers hid with the tack behind a rock. After the posse passed through, Rogers whistled for Trigger, saddled him, and they made their escape.

Spurs

Roy Rogers didn't use a whip or spurs in a way that would hurt horses, he used them along with leg pressure and voice commands. Both he and Glenn Randall used spurs to cue their mounts. Rogers wore spurs all the time, cookie spurs that are smooth and round, not pointed like most spurs.

Step Mount

Rogers' natural athletic ability enabled him to ride and fight almost on a par with professional stuntmen. Nevertheless, studios are always cautious when it comes to stars doing stunts, and they didn't give Rogers free rein. One of the few stunts they did allow him to do on film was a step mount. It was executed by Rogers running at a stationary horse, jumping on the stirrup with his left foot and letting his momentum carry him onto the saddle as he swung his right leg over, at the same time reaching for the saddle

Roy Rogers demonstrating the step mount on to the original Trigger. The trick was to hit the stirrup dead center and not yank on the bridle and hurt Trigger's mouth (Roy Dillow collection).

horn and reins as Trigger took off. It was so smooth it seemed he did not so much jump as levitate. Other cowboys did the hop, but there was always a hitch somewhere in their motion. Not Roy Rogers. From the time he started towards Trigger until he was in the saddle it was one continuous, fluid poetic movement.[2]

In *On the Old Spanish Trail* (1947) Rogers did a step mount onto Trigger (after his first encounter with adversary Tito "the Gypsy" Guizar) that was smooth and natural, like any experienced cowboy would execute. In *Red River Valley* (1941) Rogers did an easy step mount in front of leading lady Gale Storm. She commented on it and Rogers asked her if she'd like to give it a try. She did, successfully, and rode off on Trigger. At the beginning of *Down Dakota Way* (1949), after a scuffle with a couple of bad guys, Rogers did a running step mount onto Trigger. He did the same thing a little while later in front of a country school house.

Riding Bareback

A rider not using stirrups must have near perfect balance on a horse, especially in the faster gaits. Note such films as like *Troy* (Warner Bros., 2004) and *Alexander* (Warner Bros., 2004) where actors, for historical accuracy, had to ride without stirrups.[3] Brad Pitt

Joe Yrigoyen doubles for Roy Rogers, on the left, in the climax of *Under California Stars* **(1948), Rogers on the right. Both men were rearing Trigger bareback (Roy Dillow collection).**

in Troy and Ian McKellen as Gandalf in *The Lord of the Rings: The Return of the King* (New Line Cinema, 2003) rode bareback but were only shown while their mounts were standing still. Lead players are rarely shown engaging horses bareback at a trot or canter; a couple of exceptions are young Kelly Reno in *The Black Stallion* (1979) and Kevin Costner in *Silverado* (Columbia Pictures, 1985).

After the cinch on Trigger's saddle gave way from a cut, Roy Rogers took a spill during a fox hunting sequence in *Bells of San Angelo* (1947). With a brief inspection of the sabotage, a stuntman (probably Joe Yrigoyen) made a quick mount and sped down the trail. Rogers was seen in the next cut riding Trigger bareback at a full gallop, a stunt seldom executed by other singing cowboy stars. Rogers also rode bareback at full gallop in *Trigger Jr.* (1950) and *South of Caliente* (1951).

Accidents and Riding Mishaps

Sooner or later even the most experienced rider will have a mishap with a horse. Roy Rogers certainly had his share and, in some cases, in front of an audience. Here are some of the most memorable.

Roy Rogers mixing it up with stuntmen in this dangerous sequence from *Spoilers of the Plains*. Insert: director William Witney (Roy Dillow collection).

On one such occasion Rogers had a narrow escape from serious injury while rounding an arena. "Trigger" slipped, throwing Rogers from the saddle. It was the worst of all scenarios—his spur got hooked in the stirrup. "The crowd was furious when Trigger didn't stop running," Glenn Randall said. "They became almost hysterical watching him drag Roy by one leg. But the truth was that Roy's heel accidentally was giving that horse a cue to run. And poor Trigger was just caught between the devil and the deep blue sea. Several wranglers and I ran into the arena and stopped Trigger. Luckily Roy wasn't hurt except for scratches and bruises."[4]

Mike Johnson remembered sitting with Rogers in the kitchen of his sister Cleda's house while he talked about a horse-related accident that almost cost him his eyesight. It seems a "wrangler, or whoever, saddled an imitation Trigger and didn't tighten the cinch strap sufficiently. When Roy went to mount, the saddle came crashing down with him. In consequence he chipped his collarbone and the chip went into his blood stream. The doctor informed him that blood had two directions to flow. One way was to the brain, which would probably have killed him, and the other was to the eye, which is what actually happened. The end result was that Roy lost all peripheral vision in his right eye. Ironically it didn't affect his ability to shoot since the centre portion of his eye sight was unaffected."

Dusty Rogers told this story: "One time when Dad, Dale, and Trigger were in England, Roy and Trigger were performin' their act on a big stage, and the stage collapsed!

Trigger fell down through the stage. Everyone rushed over to get to Trigger and get him out. When they got him out on a solid surface, he scrambled to his feet without bein' hurt; just displayin' a few minor scratches here and there. It could have been a lot worse!"[5]

In the 1992 Tys Ockersen documentary *Roy Rogers—King of the Cowboys,* director William Witney described a dangerous close call for Trigger and Rogers. While filming a running insert with a crew on a camera car, a heavy reflector light that wasn't secured properly rolled off, straight into the path of the cowboy and his horse while they were running alongside at a full gallop. With seconds to react Trigger jumped the reflector and Rogers managed to hang on. Witney was mortified but the duo escaped without a scratch.

Another accident was reported in Frank Rasky's biography *Roy Rogers: King of the Cowboys* (*Evening Express*, Monday, March 8, 1954). Rogers was driving to a movie location in Lone Pine, California. The trailer in which he was hauling "Trigger" broke away from his car and turned over and down a hillside bank. The trailer ended up on its side. "Trigger" was unharmed. Rogers seemed more shaken up than his horse.

In a 1952 article called "A Slice of My Life" (published in the magazine *Who's Who in Western Stars*), Rogers wrote about things that happened in his life that year. According to the article, he and Trigger were rehearsing a scene for the TV show on the set in Mineral City on August 11, 1952. A blustery wind was throwing dust in everyone's face and making the other horses nervous. Rogers tied Trigger behind a portable wall. Rogers said that he hadn't taken twenty steps when a gust of wind blew the wall over on Trigger's back, knocking him to the ground. Naturally, everyone ran to help the horse. Rogers said that Trigger got up shaking his head, something that he would do when he was mad for whatever reason. Rogers ran his hands over Trigger's hide, looking for breaks or cuts. A vet checked the horse, too, and gave him a clean bill of health—though all agreed his disposition had suffered temporarily. That was a small price to pay considering that the wall could have killed or seriously injured Trigger.

As reported by Elise Miller Davis in her book *The Answer Is God* (p. 52), according to Art Rush, towards the end of a Madison Square Garden engagement as Rogers was entering the arena on "Trigger" at a dead gallop, the palomino's foot penetrated the very wet turf, hit concrete, and slipped. Rogers was thrown through the air and slammed into a concrete wall with a thud.

Roy Rogers and Dale Evans hosted the 1966 edition of the Ringling Bros. and Barnum & Bailey Circus. Apparently, the King of the Cowboys was loaned a horse for the occasion. *Reminisce Magazine* (July–August 2001, source Jerry Dean) reported on that occasion with a photo caption reading, "Roy Rogers gives a crowd of 6000 in Greensboro, North Carolina, a scare when he takes a bad fall after being thrown off a white stallion while performing with the Ringling Brothers and Barnum and Bailey Circus. Fortunately, the 55-year-old cowboy singer isn't seriously hurt." Where's Trigger when you need him?

The original Trigger took a fall while he and Roy Rogers were fleeing a mounted gang in the 1939 movie *In Old Caliente*. At approximately 26 minutes the horse and rider tumbled but quickly recovered unhurt. The stunt does not look planned; otherwise another horse and rider would have been used.

Joe Yrigoyen

Joe Yrigoyen (pronounced yer-go-en) was probably Roy Rogers' best known stunt double and often rode Trigger and his look-alikes. With his brother Bill, Joe Yrigoyen started in the movie business performing stunts at Nat Levine's Mascot Pictures, which produced serials in the early sound era. The Yrigoyens stayed with the company after it was incorporated into Republic Pictures and doubled for cowboy and serial stars such as Gene Autry, Wild Bill Elliott, Rex Allen, and for many villains too. Stuntmen performed the more dangerous mounts: drops from a porch roof onto a horse, crupper mounts (over a horse's rump) or Pony Express mounts (while an animal was in full gallop).

Joe Yrigoyen was the human equivalent of Little Trigger. Typical of so many great performers and performances of the time, he was uncredited, and Roy Rogers got all the glory. According to Mike Johnson, as Roy Rogers was very protective of his screen persona, he preferred not to discuss stuntmen. Rogers would talk about Yrigoyen if asked, but he would not instigate the conversation.

Ace action director William Witney said Joe Yrigoyen could do anything and there would never be another like him. Yrigoyen was not only a great rider and on screen fighter, but he was creative; his ideas were often written into a script. He was even good at driving six-horse stagecoach teams as he did in *On The Old Spanish Trail*. Even fellow ace stuntman Dave Sharpe couldn't do certain stunts Joe Yrigoyen performed. Sharpe

Stuntman Joe Yrigoyen mounts Trigger the hard way in a scene from *In Old Amarillo* (1951), directed by William Witney. Note the stuntman's reflection in the window (Roy Dillow collection).

was acrobatic but wasn't as skilled with horses. Witney claimed Yrigoyen could read his mind; all he had to do was holler, "Knock on it!" and that was Yrigoyen's cue to do his thing. He made Rogers look like he could anything on a horse.

Serious students of Roy Rogers' movies can always tell when Joe Yrigoyen was doubling for the King of the Cowboys. Though Yrigoyen was good, he did not sit a horse with the silky smooth manner Rogers had. Yrigoyen was stockier and nearly always had his hat slightly pulled down. Burying his face behind his shoulders in order to hide from the camera was not something Rogers ever did. It looked awkward and was done at the director's request.

Rocky Roe met Joe Yrigoyen in Knoxville, Tennessee, while the stuntman was touring with six Lipizzan stallions. "Joe made us believe no one could do it like Roy Rogers," Roe stated. Yrigoyen spoke well of Roy Rogers and loved Trigger. According to Roe, Yrigoyen admitted how Rogers didn't like how he rode Trigger, claiming he was too rough and even asking director William Witney to keep him off as much as possible. Yrigoyen did not intend to hurt Trigger; Witney demanded action and he was trying to deliver." Republic Pictures, in order to cut costs and follow trends, brought Witney in to move Roy

Joe Yrigoyen riding Trigger double California and making a transfer in *Heart of the Rockies* (1951).

Rogers from being less of a singing cowboy into more of an action cowboy. When Roe met Witney, the director also confirmed to Roe that after a while, he only used Yrigoyen on Monarch and California.

Yrigoyen was very active as Roy Rogers' double from the mid–1940s until the early 1950s. Yrigoyen's stunt highlights for Rogers' films include: a scene in *Roll On, Texas Moon* (1946) where he performs a fancy "Cossack drag mount"—hanging on the side of the horse, while grasping the saddle horn, with the horse at a run. Another was when Rogers and "Trigger" jump a fence in *South of Caliente* (1951) it's actually Yrigoyen on a Trigger double. *In Sunset in the West*, (1950) Yrigoyen makes a transfer from "Trigger" to a locomotive steam engine.

Joe Yrigoyen's film resume is lengthy and includes: *How the West Was Won* (MGM, 1962), *The Wild Bunch* (Warner Bros., 1969), and *Blazing Saddles* (Warner Bros., 1974). Yrigoyen also worked on *Gunsmoke, Zorro, Bonanza*, and *Davy Crockett*. In Yakima Canutt's autobiography, *Stunt Man,* he noted that Yrigoyen doubled for actor Stephen Boyd, driving Messala's chariot team of four black horses in *Ben-Hur (MGM, 1959).*[6]

Yakima Cannutt's staging of the chariot race in *Ben-Hur* (MGM, 1959) still thrills because there were very limited special effects. The industry has gone CGI (computer generated image) crazy now. Smart directors are using live action whenever possible with partial CGI support. Mike Johnson makes sense when he says, "Unlike the old days when real human beings performed these tasks, today everything is done with blue screens and digital effects. End result; no real thrills."

In 1985 Roy Rogers presented Yrigoyen with the prestigious Golden Boot Award awarded to those who have achieved greatness and contributed significantly to Western film and television.

Joe Yrigoyen was born in 1910 in Ventura, California, and died there in 1998.

Crupping

A crupper is a leather strap attached to the back of a saddle or harness that extends to the tail and loops around the dock which is the extension of the horse's spine. (The dock is hidden by the horse's long tail hair). The crupper is used to keep tack from sliding forward. Crupper is often spelled crouper, possibly because the croup on a horse is between its dock and loin, above the point of the hip and basically in the same area a crupper is used.

Glenn Sr. and Corky Randall referred to the correct manner for rearing a horse as crupping. Because the croup on a horse is more or less its hindquarters, when a stunt man hops on a horse from the rear it's referred to as a crupper mount. Glenn Randall simply added an "ing" and applied it to proper rearing. He used the term when discussing a horse that was rearing with its hindquarters directly under its front, practically standing straight up. Circus horses rear that way; it also explains why they can walk on their hind legs for a number of paces. Little Trigger was taught how to rear up and walk forward the same way. The original Trigger reared straight up, as did Rex Allen's Koko. Crupping is the most efficient and effective way to get a horse on its hind legs. It's easier to maintain its upper body weight and the rider. If a pose is at a 45-degree angle, it is harder to maintain. Simply put, it's easier to hold a dictionary at arm's length above your head than in front of it.

Why Roy Rogers allowed a taxidermist to pose Trigger incorrectly with his upper body and head in front rather than upright and over his legs has always been a mystery.

Roy Rogers and Trigger's Signature Rearing Pose

The classic rearing pose was something B-western cowboy stars were often asked to do, and some were better at it than others. A horse rearing up on its hind legs with a cowboy on its back became a symbol for the B-western genre. It's no coincidence that a cowboy on a rearing palomino was used on the poster of director Mel Brooks' satire *Blazing Saddles* (Warner Bros., 1974). Ironically, rearing—which has to look effortless and exuberant—is considered a dangerous habit in horses and is discouraged by horse trainers.

With Roy Rogers and Trigger, the image that comes most often to mind is the rearing pose. During personal appearances and for the closing shot in movies, Rogers often put his golden palomino up on its hind legs, smiled and waved with his free hand. Appropriately, the last shot of Roy Rogers and Trigger in their last film for Republic Pictures, *Pals of the Golden West* (1951), is of them riding off, stopping, turning towards the camera and rearing up. The last scene of the last film Rogers and "Trigger" did together, *Son of Paleface*, also featured the rearing pose.

"Patted twice just under the mane, he would back away. Patted just two inches lower than that, he'd rear up in the pose which became a trademark," noted Duane Valentry.[7]

While Roy Rogers may not have been the first cowboy to strike the rearing pose, he made it his own and is the cowboy most closely associated with it. No other cowboy star did it as often or as well. Roy Rogers and Trigger executed the feat effortlessly, with flair and a grace that was hard to match. No one looked better on a rearing horse; only Clayton Moore and Silver came close.

Consider the Roy Rogers film *The Bells of Rosarita* (1945), with guest appearances by a posse of Republic cowboy stars: Allan "Rocky" Lane, Bob Livingston, Sunset Carson, Wild Bill Elliott, and Don "Red" Barry. During the film's climax at Gabby Hayes' wild west show, they ride together into the big top to take a bow and go into the rearing pose. Rogers appears solo in the center ring on Little Trigger. When he cued the palomino to stand on its hind legs, it was plain to see how much better they executed the stunt. Crupping explains the discrepancy between Little Trigger and the horses ridden by Rogers' Republic cowboy pals. Little Trigger reared up straight and maintained the position long and beautifully. The rest came down as quickly as they reared up: Sunset Carson was not in full control; Don Barry was forced to duck and hold on because Bob Livingston lost control and hit him across the face as they were rearing up; and Rocky Lane had a hold of the saddle horn. Only Wild Bill Elliot made a half-way decent attempt.

To be fair, Rogers' peers didn't execute the rearing pose that often, nor did their mounts. Rearing up is risky and puts extra strain on a horse so why bother if one doesn't have to. Also, not everyone had Glenn Randall in their corner training their horse 24/7. It takes a good a horse person to sit calmly and balanced when a horse is in that pose.

Rogers didn't use the rearing pose in the opening of his television show, perhaps because that's how the *Lone Ranger* show opened. Rogers instead chose to open with a shot of himself on Trigger at a full gallop. However, he used the rearing pose at the close of each show after he'd delivered "The Cowboy's Prayer." For some episodes Rogers wel-

Roy Rogers started using a rearing pose immediately; there are countless photograph examples over three decades. The following all feature the original Trigger. Little Trigger was the only other Rogers horse that did the pose as well and as often. The pose was used on a variety of product boxes, posters, publicity stills, comic and magazine covers, etc. The top left photograph is from Rogers' debut, *Under Western Stars,* with rented Hudkins tack. It was also used on the cover of the Roy Rogers Memorial Service program in 1998. At top right, in a mid-movie career shot, Rogers by then was using his own Bohlin saddle. The photograph at lower left was taken during the television show period. The lower right shot features the plastic tack Rogers preferred later in his career (Roy Dillow collection).

Republic Picture's top cowboys ride together in *The Bells of Rosarita*. From left: Alan "Rocky" Lane, Sunset Carson, Don "Red" Barry, Roy Rogers (on the original Trigger), Wild Bill Elliot, and Bob Livingston (Roy Dillow collection).

comed his fans on Little Trigger, rearing up a couple of times in front of the Double R Bar Ranch sign.

Dale Evans even reared up on Trigger on occasion and did well with time and practice, so that has to count for something. She gets shortchanged with respect to riding. Buttermilk was a handful and she rode him well.

While there are a few photos of Gene Autry on Champion in the rearing pose, Autry opted for the safer end of the trail pose and used it during personal appearances. It emulated the well-known image of an Indian on his pony, the horse's four legs close together and its head hanging low. Autry's horse stepped up with four feet on a small box when doing the stunt. There are a few photos of Rogers and Little Trigger in the end of the trail pose.

Autry also used the bowing pose at the beginning of his television show. Champion bowed on one knee, as could the original Trigger. Little Trigger could not only go down on one knee but could stretch both front legs forward for a bow.

Of the Rogers remuda, only Trigger and Little Trigger performed the rearing pose. Trigger Jr., Monarch, California, Pal, and Buttermilk did not do the stunt. Because Glenn Randall, Sr., rented Monarch and California to other productions, training them to rear on command was not safe. As to why Trigger Jr. never learned, perhaps he wasn't suited. Possibly an aging Roy Rogers wanted to phase out the pose; horsemen get very practical with experience.

As it turned out, the earliest photo of Rogers rearing up was featured in the *Roy Rogers Press Book*, he was riding a rented white horse; the last photo of the King of the Cowboys in his signature pose was taken on the set of *The Fall Guy* television show in 1984, in which he was riding a rented white horse.

Saddle Pals can only imagine the pride and pleasure Rogers took from riding a fine horse like Trigger. Putting the palomino up on its hind legs must have been as great a thrill for Rogers to do as it was for fans to see.

Coda

Two occasions mark the end of Rogers' career as a horseman: a *Fall Guy* television show guest appearance in 1984 and the AMC biography special *Roy Rogers—King of the Cowboys* broadcast in 1992.

The last appearance of the "Trigger" character on television occurred on an episode of *The Fall Guy* television show in 1984. The 73-year-old Roy Rogers rode a look-alike for the occasion and even cued the horse into one last rearing pose.

The closing shot of the *Fall Guy* episode was of Rogers on "Trigger" riding towards the camera and performing his signature rearing pose. The expression on Rogers' face in a still photo of the sequence shows a little apprehension. This was probably due to his advanced age and his unfamiliarity with the "Trigger" double he was riding. Rearing a horse is dangerous, and one may assume Rogers hadn't performed the stunt in a while. Rogers was hanging on to the saddle horn with his right hand, something he never did as a young man. This occasion in all likelihood was the last time Rogers performed his signature rearing pose in public. However, at 73 years of age, he always loved motorcycles and rode them in his spare time. He probably saw them as a vacation from horses.[8]

In the closing scene of *Roy Rogers—King of the Cowboys,* Rogers is shown on foot, leading a bay horse into the desert. Apparently a palomino was not available. Roy Rogers was 81 when the documentary was filmed and it seemed he couldn't or wouldn't ride anymore. In an issue of *Memories* magazine dated 1989 he was quoted as saying, "Every year my bowling ball gets heavier and my horse gets taller." Sadly, there comes a time when every rider realizes his time in the saddle is over—even a rider as great as Roy Rogers.[9]

14

Trigger Collectibles and Memorabilia

*"You name it, he was on it. And Roy Rogers the King of the Cowboys
became the most widely merchandised personality in the entertainment
industry."*—Larry Mahan (*Horse World* television show, circa 1995)

With respect to their personal wealth, Roy Rogers was small potatoes compared to
Gene Autry. Rogers may have ridden the range in style, but Autry owned it. Still Rogers
bested Autry with regard to merchandising. With the help of agent Art Rush, Roy Rogers
licensed hundreds of items featuring his likeness and that of his horse. For that matter,
no other B-western horse was merchandised to the extent Trigger was. Only Autry's
Champion, the Lone Ranger's Silver, and Hopalong Cassidy's Topper came close. One
would be hard pressed to find collectibles related to Rex Allen's Koko or the Durango
Kid's Raider. Horses were true sidekicks in movies, and many fans who collect cowboy
character–related toys and memorabilia are interested only in items having to do with a
hero's horse.

Thanks to the Internet, Trigger items are becoming commonplace, and even rare
ones appear on occasion. The Web, and eBay especially, have blown the lid off collecting
to a large degree because availability affects value. eBay is also a great resource for learning
about collectibles and networking with fellow collectors.

Republic Pictures was shortsighted when it ceded merchandising rights to Roy
Rogers in lieu of a raise. Rogers parlayed that concession into an incalculable gain. Rogers
even used his children to promote certain items. Dusty Rogers was featured in a television
commercial for a Roy Rogers telephone.[1]

The Roy Rogers empire had many characters whose image could be marketed: Dale
Evans, Buttermilk, Bullet, Pat Brady, and his jeep Nellybelle. The majority of items featured Rogers and Trigger, but the palomino had a fair share of solo pieces.

Serious Trigger collectors appreciate the artists and sculptors who took the time to
portray Trigger accurately. Three cases in point: the Breyer plastic Small Champ figure,
the plush toy, and the last Hartland Roy Rogers and Trigger set issued in 2005. All accurately bear one white stocking on the left hind leg, not the four prominent white stockings
that are usually seen (more striking but not a true representation).

The following list of Trigger toys, collectibles, and books, is by no means complete.
Whole books have been dedicated to Roy Rogers memorabilia and collectibles (most are
easily available online). Books and magazine articles related to Trigger are plentiful;
check the bibliography. Ironically, the Roy Rogers and Dale Evans Museum didn't have

Roy Rogers with the large ornate Estes Tarter horse statue, Tennessee Walker in body type, from bottom of base to tip of ears 16.25 tall by 14 inches long. Insert: An 8.5-inch statue with a removable saddle, tapaderos, and wire reins (Roy Dillow collection).

a great collection of manufactured memorabilia and collectibles. Private collectors had them beat by miles.

Fantasy Items

A distinction should be made between genuine vintage Roy Rogers collectibles and those produced for flea markets or antique malls. Some items are newer and made to look like vintage pieces; they are not licensed.[2]

Miscellaneous Toys and Books

Alarm clock: As with wrist and pocket watches that featured Trigger, the Ingraham Clock Company had the license to manufacture the Roy Rogers and Trigger animated alarm clock first around 1951; later, with only minor differences in artwork, the Bradley company assumed production in the mid–1950s. With a desert scene background, this clock came with various colored frames.[3] Trigger's legs moved each second.

Books: Roy Rogers' Trigger to the Rescue, illustrated by John Higgs, (Cozy Corner Book, WP #2038–25, 1950; also back of the "Roy Rogers and Dale Evans Cut-Out Book.") • *Roy Rogers' Trigger and Bullet* in "Wild Horse Roundup" by Elizabeth Beecher and August Lenox, 28 pages (Whitman and Simon & Schuster; produced by Western Printing & Lithographing Company; a Cozy Corner Book, 1953). These books featured either photographs of Trigger or paintings by artists such as Mel Crawford and Joseph Dreany.

Ceramic Trigger Figure: Almost 12 inches tall; available in the 1990s from the Museum. Two versions made from the same mold, one closer to Trigger's darker color and one lighter like Little Trigger in hue, both very fragile.

Coloring books: Trigger was featured in several large-sized coloring books. One of the most prized is from 1946 with a painting of Rogers on the rearing palomino. Other examples include *Roy Rogers' Trigger and Bullet Coloring Book*, 1956, 8.5 × 11 inches (Whitman Publishing Company) • *Roy Rogers' Trigger and Bullet Coloring Book*, authorized edition, drawings by Nat Edison, 6.5 × 7.5 inches (Whitman #1315, 1959) • *Roy Rogers and Dale Evans with Trigger Coloring Book* drawings by Peter Alvardo, 50 pages (© 1951 by Roy Rogers Enterprises, Whitman Publishing Company).

Left: Roy Rogers' Trigger to the Rescue, **Cozy Corner book.** *Right: Roy Rogers' Trigger Coloring Book* **issued by Whitman Publishing Company. Cover painted by Al Andersen.**

Official Roy Rogers and Trigger—with 12 pieces of Separate Equipment; Louis Marx & Co., Inc., 1950s. The 10 × 13 × 4 inch illustrated cardboard box contains a 10-inch tall, hard plastic Trigger with a 7.25-inch tall (to the tip of the raised hand) hard plastic removable Roy Rogers figure, and vinyl accessories.

Cup and bowl: China ware; issued by the Universal Company, ovenproof.

Figures: Some unauthorized figures of Roy Rogers and Trigger have been produced, for example the scarce 1950s Marx Roy Rogers and Trigger figures in box. Contractual agreements between Marx and Roy Rogers Enterprises broke down before the item was issued, consequently this toy can be found with and without Rogers' name on the box.

Some of the more popular Trigger collectibles were produced by the Hartland Plastics Co. There are a couple of different versions of large Roy Rogers and Trigger figures, each approximately 3 × 8.5 × 5 inches. Hartland also produced smaller plastic Triggers that measure 7 × 11.5 inches and these were originally sold with a Roy Rogers figure both in a box and attached to a card. Alvar Bäckstrand and Roger Williams sculpted the models for Hartland Plastics.

Hartland produced a number of versions of Trigger including a Small Champ; a Walking Palomino with a wavy tail; a Walking Palomino with a straight tail; a Semi-rearing Palomino; and a Rearing Palomino. The semi-rearing palomino was reissued with the Roy Rogers figure in 1992–1994 and 2005. There were six different Trigger saddles

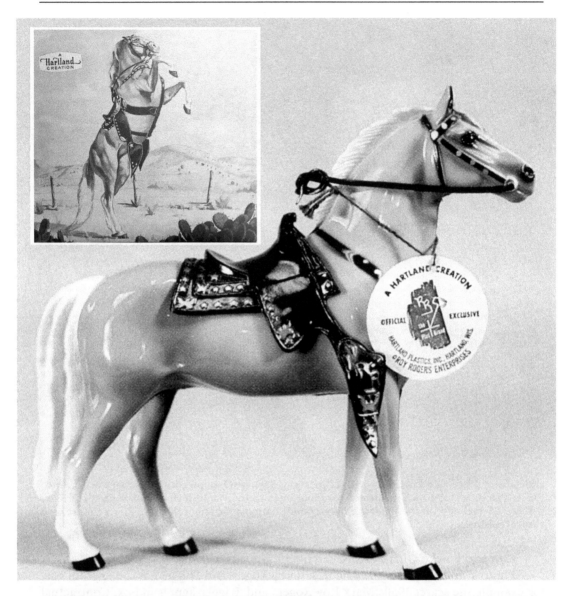

Hartland Trigger figure manufactured by Hartland Plastics complete with saddle, reins, and tag. Box and side flap including the "Trigger Honorary Ownership Card." Insert: The box sported a painted portrait of a rearing, portly Trigger printed in red halftones, 1950s (Roy Dillow collection).

issued between 1950 and 1960. The double RR was used on the blue with silver trim and blue with white trim saddles. There was the plain blue saddle with the RR brushed on, the letters were not raised. The Hartland Trigger had bridles and martingales painted directly on the figures. Any Hartland palomino without a martingale was not a Trigger figure.

A Trigger figure manufactured by Hartland Plastics and sold without Roy Rogers came with a full mane and wavy tail and was complete with saddle, reins, and tag. The box sported a painted portrait of a rearing, overweight Trigger, printed in red halftones only. Description on the box cover: "Roy Rogers' Palomino Horse 'Trigger' with Roy's saddle. All parts removable—hand painted—tough. A Hartland Creation; Hartland Plastics Inc. Hartland, Wisconsin; no 800P. Trigger Smartest Horse In The Movies—Official! Exclusive! Exact!"

Buttermilk was also issued in a number of versions, including a Small Champ and a Cubby walking. The Cubby walking version was reissued with a Dale Evans figure in 1993–1994 and in 2005.

Roy Rogers and Dale Evans appeared in person at a trade show held at the Hotel Pierre in New York City in the mid–1950s to promote their Hartland figures, which were among the most popular. Paul Champion, head of the company, visited Rogers and Evans in California to secure rights for the figures.

Hartland originally shipped its character sets in generic cardboard boxes. After a time, they produced very colorful and creative boxes for most sets. In some cases, such as the solo Trigger figure, they used the same covers for a Black Beauty figure and Silver, changing the top, bottom, and ends to match the character.

A Breyer Trigger figure, based on the Small Champ design, was issued complete with a *Golden Stallion* videotape in 2000.

Hair from Trigger's tail and mane: Supposedly from a lady named Connie Brothers. She and her trained cats once toured with Rogers' show. One of her jobs was to curry "Trigger" before every show. She saved all the loose hair. After she died, her caregiver found a program from Rogers' show among her possessions. Inside was an old 6 × 6 inches cellophane envelope that had mane and tail hair rolled up inside. There is absolutely no way to prove the hair is authentic. It was most likely from a touring "Trigger." As this was a one-time eBay auction, it seems credible.[4]

Trigger hauler and van trailer: Lie Mar Company. Box: 4 × 6.5 × 11 inches. Lithographed toy metal van, metal cab hauler. Patterned after the actual truck and trailer used to transport Rogers' palominos. Accurately produced with "Roy Rogers and Trigger and Trigger Jr." written on sides and a lithographed painting of Rogers on a rearing Trigger. It was made with and without a remote control unit, the one without is more common. The appearance of the caps (tractors) is different on the two versions. The doors open and close, 1957.

Trigger High Stepper: child's stepping stool (the sort designed to be placed in front of a bathroom sink); 1950s.

Hobby horses: **Roy Rogers' Trigger hobby horse**. The N.N. Hill Brass Company, Philadelphia, 39 inches long, 1955–56 • **Roy Rogers' Trigger play horse**. The Stern Toy Company. 20 high with 18.5 inches wheel base. Plush toy with plastic seat and metal wheels, 1958. • **Roy Rogers' Trigger toddler's riding horse** by Suzy Goose. 24 inches high, steel frame with plastic head, seat and wheels, 1950s • **Trigger rocking horse**. Trane-Rite Molding Products, approximately 33 inches long, 1950s • **Roy Rogers' Trigger rocking horse**. N.N. Hill Brass Company. 25 long by 17 inches tall, paper lithography, plastic rein with four bells, 1950s • **Trigger spring horse**. Rich Industries Inc., approximately 39 inches long, 1955.

Horseshoe: Mounted on a solid walnut shield base with a gold-plated inscription.

Inflatable toy: Roy Rogers' Trigger inflatable toy. Ideal Toy Corporation; #5274; rust-colored vinyl, 17 high and 21 inches tall, 1955–1956.

Roy Rogers "Trigger" leather jacket, 1955–56. Wm. Schwartz and Company, imported suede with calfskin yoke. Rogers rearing Trigger on yoke, wool quilt lining. Colors: spice, sand, palomino. Sizes: 2–7, 4–12.

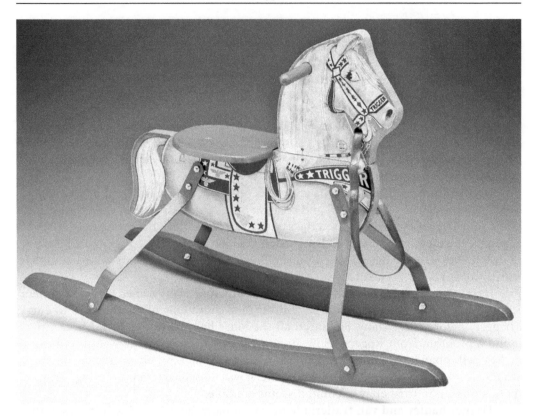

Roy Rogers Trigger rocking horse made by Hill Toys & Bells (N.N. Hill Brass Company). Red painted metal and wood with bell decorated blue plastic rein, 25½ inches long by 18 inches high.

Trigger 10 cent kiddie ride: Model #1, coin-operated ride by Re-Deo-Kiddieland Corporation, 1950s. Roy Roger's Trigger; authentic galloping reproduction, down to Rogers' distinctive saddle and trappings in genuine leather. "Ride Trigger—10 cents." One minute ride, manufactured by Exhibit Supply Company from Chicago, Illinois. Motor driven, with gait regulated by reins. Overall height is 54 inches; height at saddle 45 inches; width 20 inches; weight approximately 360 pounds; golden palomino color. Fiberglass with metal and wood base measuring 48 × 18 × 13 inches. Has sold for as much as $7000 on eBay. Carousel Workshop offers a new version for around $6000.

Life **magazine**: Roy Rogers and "Trigger" on the cover dated July 12, 1943, volume 15, number 2. The cover article runs from page 47 to page 54 and is titled, "King of the Cowboys—Roy Rogers Kisses the Horse, Not the Heroine," by H. Allen Smith.

Little Golden record: Roy Rogers, Dale Evans and chorus sing "A Cowboy Needs a Horse" and "Happy Trails to You."

Photographs where Trigger is prominent are very popular with collectors. Photos are usually 8 × 10 inches, black and white. Some very rare portrait shots exist that feature Trigger solo, eBay is a great way of finding obscure one-of-a-kind candid shots taken by fans at Rogers' personal appearances.[5]

Plush Trigger: Posable with articulated neck, back, legs, and tail; 17 tall by 19 inches long; a newer Breyer item. Unlike many representations of Trigger, the posable plush toy has pretty accurate markings, including the correct single rear left stocking. Trigger plush

Trigger, a 10-cent coin-operated ride by Re-Deo-Kiddieland Corporation (Janey Miller collection).

toys were issued previously by the Stern Toy Company, a 17-inch unlicensed version was issued by Brooklyn Doll and Toy Company in 1982.

Bullet and Trigger Picture Puzzle: Frame Tray Inlay, Whitman Publishing Co., Made in USA, No #2628, approximately 11.5 × 15 inches, copyright 1953, Roy Rogers Enterprises.

Roy Rogers' Trigger pocket knife: Made by the Novelty Knife Co. in the U.S. The knife measures approximately 3.5 inches long. The front of the blade shows Trigger rearing up and also a head view. The back of the knife is black plastic or resin, manufactured circa the 1990s and is not a vintage item. There were vintage Roy Rogers pocket knives featuring Rogers on Trigger, and at least one was manufactured with palomino alone.

Roy Rogers' Trigger animated pull toy: N.N. Hill Company, 1955.

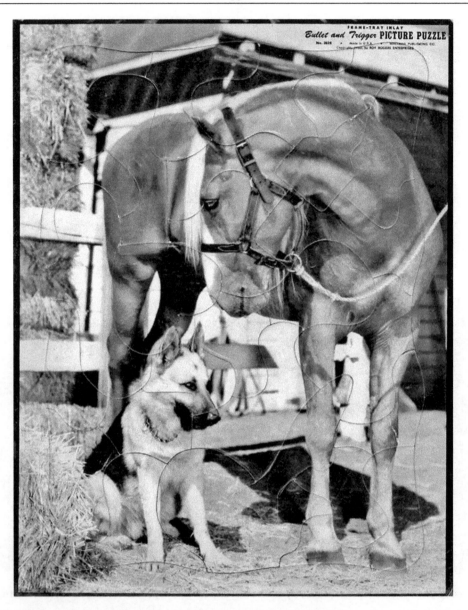

Bullet and Trigger Picture Puzzle. Frame tray inlay, Whitman Publishing Co., made in USA; no. 2628; approx. 11.5 × 15 inches; copyright 1953, Roy Rogers Enterprises.

Roy Rogers Trigger horse trailer and jeep: Ideal Toy Company, plastic, 1950s. Includes: Nellybelle jeep, Pat Brady, Roy Rogers, and Trigger figures. Total length 15 inches.

Roy Rogers/Trigger Tricycle: 24 long by 18 wide by 34.5 inches tall, 1950s. Metal tricycle with hard rubber tires. 11x15 inches die-cut cardboard head of Trigger with a jeweled bridle attached with two bolts to the handlebars. Metal frame with RR in front. Real horse hair tail attached beneath seat, pin-striping added along frame back/sides.

Trigger Inflated Bouncer and Hobby Horse Head: Both items sold at Sears and manufactured by Doughboy Industries Inc., New Richmond, Wisconsin. The rideable bouncer, with a full image of Trigger, 22 tall by 22 inches long. The hobby horse head attaches to a little buckaroo's waist belt.

Trigger manure tray/bowl: Molded from manure taken from Trigger's stall; manufactured by Apple Valley Creations, 9 inches square. According to Roy Rogers on *The Tonight Show*, the manure was collected from his ranch in Apple Valley; however, the original Trigger had died before the King of the Cowboys lived there. Rogers told guest host Burt Reynolds about a fellow in Victorville with a thousand-pound press who could mold a variety of items. He would collect used hay to make ash trays.

Trigger marble: measured .75 inches diameter.

Trigger pin-back button: Color illustrated head portrait issued in 1953 by Post's Grape-Nuts Flakes. A Roy Rogers Museum version was also issued in 2004 with Little Trigger pictured.

Trigger Post Raisin Bran tin: lithograph medal.

Trigger steel lunch box: American Thermos, 6 × 8.5 × 3 inches, circa 1956, no thermos. Featuring a doctored painting of Trigger, or meticulously copied, presumably by illustrator Ed Wexler. He worked for the American Can Company, who produced these boxes in Brooklyn, New York, for the King Seely/American Thermos Company. The actual source painting was done years before by Sam Savitt for *Roy Rogers' Trigger Comics* number 5. In the original version, Trigger is leading a herd of horses escaping a prairie fire. In the Wexler version, Trigger is shown alone on a grassy plain.

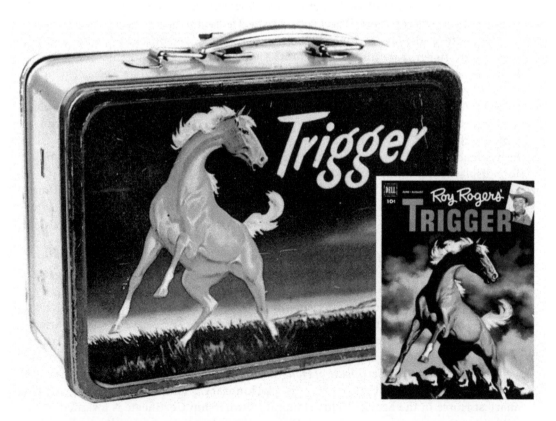

Trigger steel lunch box manufactured by American Thermos. Illustration presumably by Ed Wexler after *Roy Rogers' Trigger Comics* no. 5 painted by Sam Savitt.

Trigger trivet: Black with gold glitter image of Trigger rearing. 5.5 inches diameter. Tag on the back says "Plymptons Genuine Abalone." Originals molded by hand, colored by Nature. Made in California. This item was made later for the museum; it's not a vintage collectible.

Roy Rogers' Trigger Trotter Ride-on Toy: Pogo stick with plastic "Trigger" head, approximately 30 inches tall, Lareo Company, Inc.

Western Horseman Magazine: December 1949 issue with a cover article titled, "Trigger: First Get a Good Horse," by Roy Rogers as told to Aaron Dudley. A *Western Horseman* issue from April 1961 with an article titled "A Horse Named Babe" by Duane Valentry is also very desirable.

Specialty Trigger Items

Some Trigger specialty items were not mass-produced for sale to the general public, and are therefore rare and highly prized by collectors. *The Roy Rogers Press Book* discussed in Chapter 4 would qualify here even though Trigger was not featured in it.

Harland Trigger plaque: Twenty-nine inches in diameter; color on heavy board. Made for promotional display only by Rogden Company, Chicago. A Trigger plaque hanging on a wall behind Paul Champion, the marketing manager of Hartland Plastics, may be seen on page 123 of Gail Fitch's book *Hartland Horsemen* and on page 137 of P. Allan Coyle's *Roy Rogers and Dale Evans Toys & Memorabilia*.

Sears store display: In June 1999 an anonymous buyer purchased a vintage Roy Rogers and Trigger store display was for $3900.00 on eBay. The Indiana seller offering the item guessed it was from the late 1950s, probably manufactured for Sears. The figure of Roy Rogers on Trigger in the signature, rearing pose was made of molded composition material. The base measured 42 inches long, 12 wide and 7 inches high; the whole piece measured 46 inches from floor to the tip of Rogers' fingers; from Trigger's ears to the tip of his tail it measured 41 inches. The Rogers figure was separate. Trigger was screwed to the base and could be removed for shipping. That Sears would manufacture such a unique store display is testimony to Roy Rogers' popularity.

Taxidermy Trigger: The great B-western unique artifacts, like the first Roy Rogers comic book, Champion's bridle with pistol shanks, Lash LaRue's whip, and Clayton Moore's Lone Ranger mask, all take a back seat to Trigger. Even in his present state, he is the ultimate B-western artifact and collectible.

Trigger Certificate of Honorary Ownership: This card is special because of the story behind its creation. According to Duane Valentry, writing in *Western Horseman* magazine, "When Trigger was in his prime, J.B. Ferguson, wealthy Texas oil and cattle man, tried to buy him for his ranch near Houston, offering Rogers $200,000 (see "Trigger Trivia," Chapter 15, for more details). Rogers turned down the offer as he did all others, reportedly saying, 'Trigger belongs to all the boys and girls of America—they made stars of Trigger and me.'" Pleas for ownership were typical of the fan mail Trigger would get. To make such kids happy, *Trigger Certificate of Honorary Ownership* cards were sent out. The cards read, "This is to certify that _____ is an Honorary Shareholder in 'Trigger,' 'The Smartest Horse in the Movies.' This Honorary Ownership Certificate is awarded to the children of America in recognition of their years of devotion and loyalty, and for supporting us in our motion pictures, radio and television shows and personal appearances."

Top: Roy Rogers and Trigger vintage Sears store display. *Bottom:* Trigger Honorary Ownership Card.

These plastic cards measure 3.5 × 2.5 inches. Their white surface is printed in light brown ink including a silhouette of Trigger with the text. The Honorary Ownership certificates were also printed on some Hartland boxes.

Trigger Estes Tarter statues: For serious Trigger collectors the Estes Tarter golden statue is the Holy Grail. One of the most unusual and beautiful items of Trigger memorabilia, the metal statues were expertly crafted in the mid–twentieth century by the well-known sculptor Estes Tarter. True Cast products company in Los Angeles manufactured them in a metal known as spelter (zinc plus lead), and then the mold was brass-plated.

The gold statuettes of Trigger were awarded annually from 1949 until about 1956 to schools across the country. Established in 1949 by Roy Rogers, in cooperation with the National Safety Council, the child safety award program reached 27,000 U.S. schools in 1955. To participate, schoolchildren needed to document their schools' safety program and, most of all, have a clean record for safety throughout the academic year. School safety teachers evaluated finalist entries and awarded first, second, and third place winners. Roy Rogers and Dale Evans made presentations to the winning schools in person. Each received a large golden Trigger statue and complete three-dimensional projection equipment for classroom use. Contributed by Sawyer's View-Master, the equipment included a projector, a screen, polarizing glasses, and educational reels in full color. Best-in-state awards were given the smaller Trigger statues, which were contributed by the Farmers Insurance Group Safety Foundation.[6] The statues were usually displayed in a school's trophy case. When a school was closed down some found their way into the collector's marketplace and periodically on to eBay.

Three different versions of the statue were issued. The first was based on the same mold used for the gold palomino horse clocks popular in the 1940s–50s (the sculptor remains unknown). The bridle, saddle, and horse were formed by one complete mold. Some were inscribed, "Official Roy Rogers' Trigger The Wonder Horse." Some were inscribed on their base, with the name of the school; some versions were produced with a clock.

The second gold-colored Trigger statue was sculpted by Estes Tarter and came with a removable saddle, tapaderos, and wire reins. The name "Trigger" is impressed in the gold-colored base. The artist's name, Estes Tarter, is impressed on the back of the base. The figure stands 8.5 high by 8.5 inches long. (There is a gold metal 6.25 inches tall version with Western tack molded on, red rhinestones, and chain reins. This version is not inscribed.) In 2005, one of these statues in great condition with a bright patina and red saddle blanket sold on eBay for $610. Some come with a red saddle pad, simply a piece of felt cut to fit under the saddle like a real pad would.

Estes Tarter also sculpted a third and the most elaborate version of the Trigger statue. It also came with a removable saddle. Highly detailed and ornate, both the bridle (with chain reins) and breastplate were inset with red stones. The body type of the horse is similar to a Tennessee Walker. This figure stands 16.25 high by 14 inches long and a smaller version measures 13.75 inches tall. The large version also comes without a base.

It is unknown if Estes Tarter was commissioned to sculpt Trigger specifically or if a pre-existing statue was offered to Roy Rogers and company for these National Safety Council awards. It's reasonable to suggest the statue might have been a representation of the original Trigger and paid for by Sears. Rogers may have been involved in its creation especially given the resemblance of the second statue to his actual horse.

The statues were also awarded as prizes in the Roy Rogers Safety Slogan Contests from the 1950s sponsored by Sears & Roebuck. According to announcements, the grand award winner would "appear on the stage with Roy Rogers" to be "presented with a miniature gold-colored statute of his famous horse Trigger—plus—a photograph of the winner sitting in the saddle on Trigger!" At the bottom of entry blanks, it stated that "the decision of the judges—Roy Rogers, Dale Evans and Gabby Hayes—is final." Some versions may have been sold commercially.

Trigger Stuart figure: Not rare like the aforementioned items, but the plastic Trigger figure produced by the Stuart Toy Company qualities as a specialty item for its pure beauty and resemblance to the original Trigger.[7] It was sold separately and also found in the Mineral City set. The Stuart Manufacturing Company was based in Cincinnati, Ohio, and produced plastic play set figures and horses from about 1950 through the late 1960s. Stuart Manufacturing made horses in three different poses: rearing, standing, and running. The Roy Rogers, Dale Evans, Pat Brady, Bullet and Trigger (60mm) figures were originally produced for the 1953 Roy Rogers RR Bar Ranch cereal premium set but were

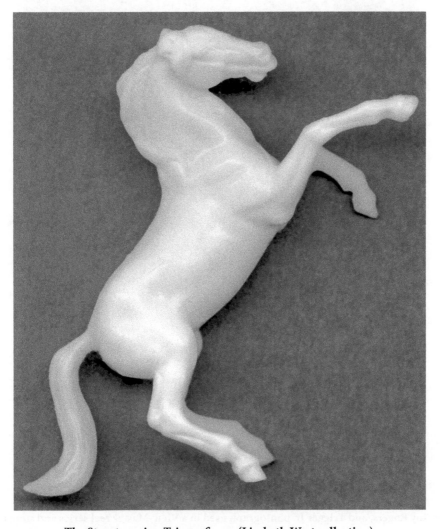

The Stuart rearing Trigger figure (Lisabeth West collection).

never labeled as characters under the Stuart banner. C.F. Block and Associates (Chicago, Illinois) originally created the Roy Rogers character figures and horses; Como Plastics (Columbus, Ohio) did the mold castings.[8]

The most beautiful of the Stuart horses, the 60mm rearing figure, came in reddish-brown (and brownish red), white, cream, off-white, black, tan (palomino), and silver/gray marbled. This mini-masterpiece could take a place in a museum as a great example of equine sculpture. Stuart expert Lizabeth West describes the figure as "considered by many to be the most beautiful of the vintage play set horses. This model is like a miniature sculpture. Its head and neck has a well-defined artistry that reflects nobility of the horse."[9]

View-Master display: In the 1950s stores often had several large View-Master displays that had one or more viewers attached to them so that customers could preview the latest reels. Tru-Vue and View-Master were competitors through the 1940s. Tru-Vue

Trigger, Roy Rogers, and Trigger Jr. photograph used in a View-Master reel series and store display poster.

had years earlier acquired the exclusive rights to show Disney characters in 3D. View-Master saw the potential for Disney sales and bought out Tru-Vue. The selection of photos used are unique to the Roy Rogers reel, including one great portrait shot of Roy Rogers standing between the original Trigger and Trigger Jr. The store display is even more unusual and features the aforementioned photograph. The photo image on the poster measures 13.5 × 16.5 inches.

15

Trigger Trivia

*"Nothing is exciting as a horse. Planes, cars, trains are okay for speed.
But for excitement, there's nothing like a horse."*—John Wayne[1]

Adelphi Hotel: While touring Great Britain in March 1954, Roy Rogers and Dale Evans came down with influenza and ended up secluded in the Adelphi Hotel in Liverpool. Some 4,000 fans crowded Lime Street outside and kept up the chant, "We want Roy Rogers!" A publicity stunt had been planned whereby Rogers and "Trigger" would make a grand entrance from the mezzanine floor to the main lounge. As that opportunity was lost, it was decided to have Little Trigger deliver a bouquet of flowers to Rogers and Evans as they lay in bed. Little Trigger reared up, took a bow or two outside the Adelphi Hotel and entered, becoming the first horse to set a hoof inside. The palomino took more bows from a first floor window as hundreds of fans watched. He also made his mark at the registration desk with a pencil clutched between his teeth, something he'd done before in Glasgow, Edinburgh, and Birmingham. Followed by an entourage of guests, young admirers, and reporters, the palomino finally went into the residents' lounge for a very unique press reception.[2]

Allen, Woody: In Woody Allen's Oscar-winning comedy *Annie Hall* (United Artists, 1977) the comedian delivers a retort to musician Paul Simon, who plays a Hollywood record producer. As Simon shows off his Beverly Hills mansion to Allen and actress Diane Keaton (the title character), he tells them that the previous owners were singer Nelson Eddie and gangster Legs Diamond. The quintessential New Yorker, Allen sarcastically added another celebrity to the list: "Trigger."

During a PBS *American Masters* episode on Woody Allen, a clip was featured with him mentioning Trigger.

"I met Roy Rogers' horse Trigger at a party once and ended up living with him."

"Did you ever meet Roy Rogers?"

"I have no interest in meeting Roy Rogers. I was just interested in Trigger."

"What about the smell?"

"Trigger didn't seem to mind."

American Humane Association: The AHA presented a Trigger with a special award to honor his silver anniversary in show business, circa 1963.

Babe Before Trigger: According to Duane Valentry in an April 1961 issue of *Western Horseman* magazine, a former sulky racer, a black mare named Babe was Leonard Frank Slye's first horse. He was a pre-teen when his father bought her to use pulling a plow

258

Trigger's birthday was often used as a publicity gimmick, especially while on tour, and it didn't matter which "Trigger" was on hand. From left, Bob Nolan, Lloyd Perryman, Tim Spenser, Hugh Farr, Roy Rogers, Pat Brady and Karl Farr sing "Happy Birthday" to Little Trigger (Roy Dillow collection).

when the family moved to a farm near Duck Run, Ohio, along the Scioto River. Len tended to her needs and it was on her that he first learned to ride. Though way past her prime, Len rode her to school and back. He learned to ride well enough to win a race at the Scioto Country Fair in 1919.

Band of Brothers: In the HBO World War II television mini-series *Band of Brothers* (2001), the GIs named their German shepherd mascot Trigger.

Bob Dylan's Theme Time Radio Hour (Sirius XM Radio): In the season 3 episode, circa 2006, "Happiness," Dylan gave a long, enthusiastic introduction about how/when/ why Dale Evans wrote "Happy Trails," then played the song. During another show, "Famous People," Dylan spoke about Roy Rogers finding Trigger and how the horse got its name. Bob Dylan, a serious musicologist, loves vintage western songs. "My favorite horse, the smartest in the movies, was a golden palomino named Golden Cloud. Roy Rogers saw Golden Cloud, fell in love and bought him for $2500. Roy's sidekick Smiley Burnette saw how quick the horse was and said, 'You've got to name him Trigger.'"

Craven, Richard, Award: In 1958 Roy Rogers and Trigger received the Richard Craven Award from the American Humane Society. The award was presented annually for outstanding feats performed by animals before a live audience in theatre, rodeo, or other live entertainment venues (television and film feats were not eligible).

CSI: The last *CSI* show of the 2005 season, titled "Grave Danger," included a scene where agent Sara Sidle (Jorja Fox) walks into the office of Gil Grissom (William Peterson), picks up something framed on his desk and asks, "What's this?" He explains that it's an honorary certificate of ownership for Trigger that children used to get when they wrote to Roy Rogers. He had one as a child and lost it. He found one at the Roy Rogers Museum that used to be in California but is now in Branson, Missouri. Grissom talks for quite some time about Roy Rogers, Trigger, and the recent move. Sara asks, "Roy Rogers the cowboy?" Grissom says that would be "Roy Rogers, King of the Cowboys!" She looks at him funny and says, "You framed it?" The look on his face seems to say, "What's so unusual about that?" She sets the certificate down and they continue with the show. The episode was directed by Roy Rogers fan Quentin Tarantino.

Fan club: There is no evidence of an official Trigger fan club. Having anything but a one-off wouldn't make sense. Roy Rogers' own fan club would have kept its members up to date about any specific Trigger related stories or personal fan mail. Mike Johnson was a member of the British Roy Rogers fan club and still has original magazines which do not mention a separate Trigger club. Trigger did provide a monthly letter in British versions of his comic book!

Fan mail: Despite not having his own fan club Trigger received an enormous amount of mail in the 1950s. Doreen M. Norton, in her 1949 book, *The Palomino Horse*, wrote, "Trigger is a motion picture star in his own right. He gets an average of two hundred fan letters a month, addressed to him!" Responses to fan letters sent to "Trigger" were answered on paper autographed with a hoof print. Said Norton, "When a boy in Liverpool, England, wrote a letter, addressed simply, 'Trigger,' it found its way to Roy Rogers."

Ferguson, J.B.: In the fall of 1952, Roy Rogers had been booked at the Houston Fat Stock Show when he received a telegram from wealthy Texas oilman J.B. Ferguson, who already owned an impressive stable of Thoroughbreds and Quarter Horses. Ferguson offered Rogers $200,000 for Trigger. Ferguson indicated that he wished to buy Trigger as a birthday gift for his son. Rogers had received numerous offers to buy Trigger in past years but never considered them.[3] He ignored the telegram and continued on tour. At the same time, the story broke in the Houston paper. The paper quoted Ferguson as being deadly serious and gave the impression that Rogers, too, was seriously considering the offer. By then the original Trigger was almost nineteen and Trigger Jr. had already been acquired.

When Rogers arrived in Texas, hundreds of children greeted his train. They were all concerned over the possibility that he might sell Trigger. When Rogers reached the Shamrock Hotel where he was staying, there were stacks of telegrams and telephone messages urging him not to consider Ferguson's offer.

The story took on a momentum of its own even after Rogers made it clear Trigger was not for sale at any price. Rumors started circulating that Rogers was in such a financial bind that it was necessary to sell his beloved palomino. Back in California, letters were arriving from kids all over the country who'd broken their piggy banks and sent pennies, nickels, and dimes to the King of the Cowboys hoping to provide the needed financial assistance.

Rogers was finally able to put the issue to rest by calling a giant press conference at the Shamrock Hotel. Ferguson was also on hand. Rogers thanked him for his offer but told him he would not sell Trigger for all the money in Texas. After the crisis passed, secretaries back in California were faced with the task of returning money to thousands of loyal Trigger fans.[4]

It's been rumored that Ferguson loaned Rogers a sorrel to breed with Trigger at his Valley Ranch, the foal going to Ferguson as a consolation. Nevertheless elsewhere in this book, Rogers stated definitively that Trigger never sired a foal.

The Golden Stallion Menu: Pioneertown was built in 1946 as a movie set for western

The **Golden Stallion**

PIONEERTOWN
CALIFORNIA

The Golden Stallion Menu from the Pioneertown restaurant, founded in 1946 by a group of Hollywood investors as a living movie set consisting of 1870s frontier town and named for the Sons of the Pioneers. Trigger was pictured without tack and not identified. The item pictured was autographed by Gene Autry and is from the collection of the author.

films including those of Gene Autry, the Cisco Kid, Annie Oakley, Range Rider, and Buffalo Bill, Jr. Some of the original investors included Roy Rogers, the Sons of the Pioneers (the town was named after them), Bud Abbott, Russell Hayden, and Hollywood gossip columnist Louella Parsons.

Although Dusty Rogers did not recall that his father ever owned a restaurant or diner in Pioneertown and had not seen any paperwork, an eatery called The Golden Stallion existed there and a photo of the original Trigger graced its cover (pictured without tack in profile, rearing, and not identified by name). The item pictured was, ironically, signed by Gene Autry and found on eBay).

Generation gap: As tastes changed in the 1960s, a generation gap emerged between adults and adolescents. In September 1960 during halftime at a Pittsburgh versus Dallas football game in Texas, police arrested 43 youngsters after Roy Rogers, Dale Evans, and Trigger were pelted with ice.

Grauman's Chinese Theatre: The original Trigger was one of a rare few animals that was immortalized at Grauman's Chinese Theatre in Hollywood, California. Trigger and Roy Rogers were honored in 1949. Gene Autry's Champion, Tom Mix's Tony and Lassie were some of the other four-legged stars that had been so honored. Sid Grauman

The regal, original Trigger plants his front hoof in cement at Grauman's Chinese Theatre in Hollywood on April 21, 1949. Dale Evans (standing left) is facing Grauman dignitaries and members of the Riders of the Purple Sage (right). Glenn Randall is kneeling at left with a very proud Roy Rogers (kneeling right center). Eddie Dean, Pat Brady and Hoot Gibson were also in attendance (Roy Dillow collection).

was the host. (Previously, Little Trigger had placed his hoof prints in cement at the Hitching Post Theater in Los Angeles.)

Before celebrities signed their name in a slab of wet cement at Grauman's Chinese Theatre, they did a private rehearsal where certain factors like pressure and technique were explained for the best results. Subsequently the theatre has practice samples in its archives of each celebrity signing.

Jeopardy: Trigger's appearance in the 1938 Warner Bros. color film *The Adventures of Robin Hood* is common knowledge, so much so that it was once a question on the ABC network game show *Jeopardy*. Trigger and company have been subjects on *Jeopardy* a number of times over the years. Some examples are as follows:

> **January 2007**: The category "Hollywood Rides" offered the answer "Nellybelle, Buttermilk, Trigger" to provoke the question, "What was *The Roy Rogers Show*?"
> **January 2008**: A category on characters with gun parts as names noted Trigger.
> **February 2009**: In a category "No Animals Were Injured" contestants were asked to name the animal shown who was reputed to do close to 100 tricks.
> **March 2013**: Roy Rogers and Trigger were featured in a category on horse colors. The answer was, "What color of horse did cowboy star Roy Rogers ride?" The photo used was of Roy Rogers riding the Trigger double Pal.
> **July 2015**: In a "Compound Words" category a question was "Dale Evans' horse was named this, like a dairy drink."

Junk food: According to Cheryl Rogers-Barnett, the original Trigger liked mayonnaise sandwiches and Coca-Cola. She described Trigger as being like a goat when it came to eating habits: he would eat anything. He even shared coffee with Roy Rogers on occasion.

Life **magazine**: According to Mike Johnson, "The *Life* magazine cover [July 12, 1943] was shot in Chatsworth/Iverson's Ranch where most of Roy Rogers' movies were filmed. It's interesting Little Trigger was used for the occasion. Rogers would have known a trick horse would have offered more variety of poses a photographer might request. Like the role Little Trigger played on screen, when there was a show to put on, there he was. It just so happened the rearing pose came out the winner. Ironically the Old Man looked better doing it simply because he was a better-looking horse. It's interesting to see the San Fernando Valley in the background as it looked back then. Now the whole area has been developed and has become, in a sad irony, the porn capital of the world."

Little Trigger Productions: Even though Cheryl Rogers Barnett didn't have a warm relationship with Little Trigger and he was not her favorite, she thought enough of him to name her company "Little Trigger Productions." As the palomino's existence was never on public record even years after it had passed, its name and likeness had not been copyrighted. Rogers-Barnett wisely registered both, finally, in Utah in 2014. The name and a picture of Rogers-Barnett with Little Trigger is her company logo.

The Loved One: Comedian Jonathan Winters' character the Reverend Wilbur Glenworthy, owner of Whispering Glades cemetery and mortuary, mentions Trigger during a phone call in *The Loved One*, a 1965 black-and-white comedy about the funeral business in Los Angeles (MGM, 1951).

> "Yes, madam. Yes, yes.
> He'll be in very good company.
> Rin-Tin-Tin, Lassie, Trigger, Silver.
> They're all here."

The 30 Greatest Horses in the Arts: Trigger, along with the Lone Ranger's Silver and Gene Autry's Champion, made a list titled "The 30 Greatest Horses in the Arts," comprised of steeds immortalized by artists, writers, musicians, and filmmakers, from Black Beauty and Seabiscuit to the screaming stallion in Picasso's *Guernica*. The list was compiled by Marc Lee and published February 10, 2009, in the *London Telegraph*.

Nelson, Willie: Like B.B. King's guitar Lucille, country legend Willie Nelson's old Martin N-20 acoustic is very also well known. It's been signed by some of Nelson's musician friends, and the front is so worn that it has an extra hole next to the actual sound hole. Nelson named the instrument "Trigger Jr." C.F. Martin & Co. issued a 13 × 17 poster (circa 2017) of the well-worn instrument captioned "This Is My Guitar—on naming his model N-20 'Trigger'"

Top: **Roy Rogers with Trigger Jr. in front of their custom-made hauler and trailer (Joel Dutch Dortch collection).** *Bottom:* **Dale Evans admires Roy Rogers rearing on Trigger in front of their custom-made trailer/hauler (Roy Dillow collection).**

Only Fools and Horses: According to Wikipedia, Trigger, a character in a British sitcom titled *Only Fools and Horses*, is named after Roy Rogers' palomino because the actor, Roger Lloyd Pack, looks like a horse.

Pioneer Town Race: In the 1950s, Western character actor Dick Curtis opened a ranch used as a Western movie location and tourist trap. The *American Movie Classics* network has, from time to time, run a short filler on the ranch, called Pioneer Town. The *AMC* short features early color footage of Dale Evans on Trigger in a mini-parade; Roy Rogers and his daughter on Little Trigger; and brief footage of Roy Rogers on Trigger racing a group of ranch hands.

On one occasion a group of local cowboys were at Pioneer Town with their horses. They decided to confront Rogers and the original Trigger and challenged them to a race. Rogers politely told them Trigger was not a racehorse, but a schooled picture horse. Not satisfied, they heckled the King of the Cowboys to the point where their remarks got a little personal and nasty towards Trigger. Rogers could tolerate unkind remarks towards himself but not towards his horse. When he'd had enough, he pulled out a wad of greenbacks, placed them on the ground, covered them with a rock and said, "Cover it and you've got a race for a quarter mile." The cowboys managed to cover Rogers' bet and the race was on. After a quarter mile course was laid out, the cowboys approached the starting line. Roger joined them and sat calmly on Trigger, studying his opponents and their mounts. All were riding Quarter Horses, and Rogers was pretty sure some had run professionally. Without giving much of a thought to backing out, Rogers soon found himself and Trigger in the middle of the pack, surrounded on both sides. He leaned forward and hissed in Trigger's ear as he'd done often in running inserts when he needed a little more speed. Trigger went into third gear, laid his ears back, and jolted forward. Trigger loved competition and wasn't about to lose. After winning, Rogers returned to the finish line and picked up his winnings. With a little grin he looked at his competitors and said, "Thanks fellows. Trigger and I'll oblige anytime."[5]

Reportedly a similar incident occurred on the set of *My Pal Trigger*. Republic had hired professional jockeys for the race scene at the end of the movie, and they, too, wanted to find out if Trigger was as fast as claimed. The outcome was the same as that of the Pioneer Town race.[6]

Bob Nolan of the Sons of the Pioneers remembered the view most cowboys got of Trigger: "a long white tail floating in their faces."

Police horses: In the 1980s Rogers donated horses to the mounted police patrols of Boston, New York City, and Philadelphia. As clever publicity and a goodwill gesture, Rogers even suggested naming each mount "Trigger."

Presley, Elvis: In his youth Elvis Presley was well aware of Roy Rogers. Remember the Nudie Cohn–like red shirt Elvis wore in *Lovin' You* (Paramount Pictures, 1957) while singing "Teddy Bear"? Presley's favorite horse, Rising Sun, could well have been chosen for its palomino color in reference to Trigger.

According to Noel Blanc, who is the son of Warner Bros. cartoon voice artist Mel Blanc (Bugs Bunny, Porky Pig, Daffy Duck, etc.), the King of Rock and Roll sought out the King of the Cowboys in the early 1960s. Elvis was 29, Rogers was 53. (The 2006 interview posted online on the *Roy Rogers Roundup* Facebook page.)

Mel Blanc had a lakefront home on Big Bear Lake in San Bernardino County. Rogers had built a cabin in the area for his family when he owned the Pleasure Point, the oldest continually operated local marina.

While filming *Kissing Cousins* (MGM, 1964) at the sawmill at Cedar Lake, located south of Big Bear, Elvis asked for an introduction to Rogers who was friend of Blanc.

Elvis drove to the Blanc residence and went for a cruise on the lake with Mel and Noel. Before long Roy Rogers' boat, Yellow Jacket, pulled along-side. It seems Roy was Elvis' favorite cowboy and Elvis was Roy's favorite singer. They tied their boats together and drifted on Big Bear Lake visiting for about two hours.[7]

Roosevelt, Eleanor: On his 61st birthday, in 1943, President Franklin D. Roosevelt invited Roy Rogers to the White House for a March of Dimes Ball. The cowboy felt out of place among the other Hollywood celebrities present. Mrs. Roosevelt invited him to the kitchen where they ate hamburgers and talked about one of her favorite subjects: Trigger![8]

16th American Airbourne Squadron: During the World War II, a 16th American Airbourne Squadron bomber was named after Trigger.

Smokey and the Bandit: Burt Reynolds drove a 1980 Pontiac Trans Am named Son of Trigger, powered by the Pontiac 301 Turbo.

Super Password: This game show differed from its predecessor, *Password*, in that each word acted out was one of four clues for a specific person or thing. A broadcast in 1975 offered the clues "Roy Rogers," "museum," "partner," and "stuffed."

The Tail Waggers Club: After covering 50,000 miles in one year on personal appearance tours in the late 1950s, Trigger was admitted to the Tail Waggers Club, a company for illustrious equine travelers. Famous racehorses were also among the members.[9]

Trailer deluxe: In the mid–1950s, when "Trigger" made personal appearances with Roy Rogers at such places as the Cow Palace in San Francisco, stock shows in Ft. Worth, or Madison Square Garden in New York City, he traveled in comfort and safety in a custom-built trailer pulled by a 3.5 ton Burma Road Dodge truck. The vehicle was the result of the practical experience and ideas gathered over years by Rogers while touring. Construction took three months and required ten sets of blueprints before Rogers was satisfied with the design. The truck required high-test gasoline, stored in two 40-gallon fuel tanks. It came with a two-speed axle and was capable of 50 mph on the highway, averaging seven miles to the gallon. Both truck and trailer were equipped with air and hydraulic brakes. As a backup safety measure, there was an extra set of brakes on the tractor. The combined rig sat on 10 wheels with puncture-proof tubes in all tires. The overall weight of the entire outfit was 12 tons; it measured 35 feet in length and was 11 feet high. There was also a separate generator on board for the 110-volt lighting system that supported both DC and AC electric currents for the trailer. Both vehicles were fully insulated. The stalls of the trailer were air-conditioned.

The trailer included air-conditioned living quarters for the driver and trainer or groom. The horse compartment sported three fully padded stalls with feed bins for "Trigger" and his equine company and kennels for Rogers' hunting hounds. Each side of the trailer featured loading ramps and rungs on the outside to tie "Trigger" while he was being groomed and tacked. A tack room accommodated "Trigger's" saddles, bridles, and miscellaneous riding equipment and had bunk beds for the driver and trainer or groom. The modest but stylish living quarters consisted of a stainless steel kitchen complete with refrigerator, butane cooking stove, and a small table for meals. Other creature comforts included indirect lighting, electric heater, hot and cold running water, wardrobe closets, and bedroom.

The trailer interior was paneled throughout in combed mahogany. The floor was of a composition material and fully carpeted. The exterior of the trailer was a streamlined design, finished in blue and cream colors with chrome trim. All the windows were copper screened, and screen doors were included inside of the living quarters.

Trigger burgers: After Roy Rogers licensed his name to a chain of restaurants in the mid–1950s, a sandwich at Roy Rogers Restaurants was named for his horse. A joke, possibly originated in *Cracked* magazine, started circulating about "Trigger burgers" being on the menu.[10]

Trigger statue: When Trigger died in 1965, Rogers contacted Fiber Glass Menagerie of Alpine, Colorado, to make a larger-than-life fiberglass likeness. It was 23.5 feet tall and featured Trigger in the signature rearing pose. It was placed at the front of the Roy Rogers and Dale Evans Museum in Victorville and later moved to the museum's new location in Branson, Missouri. After it closed, the statue was shipped back to California in 2014 and placed at Sunset Hills Memorial Park and Mortuary in Apple Valley (not far from where Roy Rogers and Dale Evans were buried). "I had a chance to keep him from going to auction and I grabbed it," stated local community leader Bob Tinsley, "I just couldn't see letting him go anywhere else."

According to the Victorville *Daily Press* on October 31, 1995, vandals struck at the Roy Rogers and Dale Evans Museum and sprayed graffiti on the pedestal supporting the statue of Trigger. The statue was removed from Sunset Hills due to complaints regarding its anatomically correct genitalia, which is offensive to some park visitors. In March of 2018 the Trigger statue found a final home, complete with a ribbon-cutting ceremony, at the Spirit River Center located on Apple Valley Road, about 8 miles west of Sunset Hills Memorial Park and Mortuary. Besides a makeover and paint job, Trigger was left unaltered according to co-owners Chet Hitt and Bob Tinsley.

Trigger Street and Trigger Place: There are streets in Chatsworth, California, in the San Fernando Valley, named to reflect the fact that Roy Rogers and family had a home and ranch there: Trigger Street, Trigger Place (which probably came later, after the subdividing of lots on Trigger Street), and Dale Court. Trigger Place is not far from Trigger Street, heading in a southwesterly direction on Valley Circle Boulevard, past the Oakwood Cemetery on the right; after Cactus Avenue and Dale Court, the road eventually intersects with Trigger Place. Trigger Street is another right turn.

Trigger Street Productions: Actor Val Kilmer grew up in the San Fernando Valley and lived next to Roy Rogers and Dale Evans.

In a 2004 *Biography* channel interview Kilmer reminisced about how he would knock on their door and ask if Rogers could come out and play. "That was great fun," Kilmer said. Not to mention surreal. "Trigger was stuffed in the recreation room, where you could see him through the curtains."[11](Cheryl Rogers-Barnett claims the mounted Trigger was never at the Chatsworth ranch.) The Kilmer family eventually owned the Roy Rogers ranch in Chatsworth.

Kilmer met Kevin Spacey at Chatsworth High School in the San Fernando Valley. The two friends shared early dreams of becoming famous actors. During a March 2015 episode of *The Charlie Rose Show* on PBS Spacey mentioned Trigger: "When I was growing up in Los Angeles, my best friend and I had a dream of creating a theater at my friend's ranch in Chatsworth that was previously built and owned by Roy Rogers, the American western star. We were going to perform new plays as well as Shakespeare, but more importantly were firmly determined to make a big impression on the world! When Rogers built his ranch the San Fernando Valley was nothing but orange groves so he was able to name the streets himself. There was a Dale Avenue, and a Trigger Street (the street signs, according to neighbors, have been stolen and replaced on a number of occasions). Even though these childhood dreams never came to fruition the memory still lingered, and when in 1997 the time came to name my production company I remembered Trigger Street. The name evoked my early aspirations and that innocent idea of endless creativity and the power to change things—a road that would go on and on. Hence, Trigger Street Productions was born."

Wieghorst, Olaf: Wieghorst was a mounted policeman in New York until 1944, before he became famous for his paintings of western scenes and horses. Rogers appeared at Madison Square Garden in 1937; Wieghorst likely attended a show and either sketched or photographed "Trigger" for reference. That alone suggests the painting is of Little Trigger—it bears more than a passing resemblance to him. The portrait hung in Roy Rogers' home, in the Apple Valley museum, and later in the lobby of the Victorville museum. Over the years the painting increased in value but hung with no fanfare publicly until someone told Rogers how valuable it was. It sold at the Christie's Fine Art Auctions in Arizona at the High Noon auction, January 2002, for $25,300.

Yankee Slugger Mickey Mantle: In May 1957 four New York Yankees, including Billy Martin, Mickey Mantle, Yogi Berra, Hank Bauer and Whitey Ford, were involved in a brawl at the Copacabana nightclub. One of their opponents suffered a concussion and broken jaw. A lawsuit was filed. Mickey Mantel's testimony goes as follows:

Grand juror: "Well, did you see a gentleman lying unconscious on the floor near the Copa entrance?

Mantle: "Yes I did,"

Grand juror: "All right. Do you have an opinion as to how this could have happened?"

Mantle: "I think Roy Rogers rode through the Copa, and Trigger kicked the man in the head"

The grand jury laughed and the case was later thrown out for insufficient evidence.[12]

Len Sly (left) in his teens with his first horse, a former sulky racer mare named Babe. The second person is unknown (Roy Dillow collection).

16

Trigger's Peers

*"Gene and I were both competitors, but we didn't hate one another
because it was just a job as far as I was concerned. I do think
I had the better horse though."*—Roy Rogers[1]

I caught the B-western craze when it was making the transition to television. I did not grow up with the first cowboys who were mostly of the action variety: Tom Mix, Ken Maynard and Buck Jones. I was more affected by the following tier which included singing cowboys. Fans who went through the B-western era in theaters in the 1920s and 1930s would tell you the first horse heroes were up there with Trigger and they were as varied as the colors of their coats.

Tom Mix honored his chestnut partner with a movie titled *Just Tony* (20th Century–Fox, 1922).[2] He and Tony built on the image William S. Hart and his great pinto pony Fritz pioneered before. What Mix added was showmanship with fancy attire and ornate show tack.[3] Gene Autry's Champion also preceded Trigger and set standards. Rogers was not a pathfinder like Mix and Autry were.

Ken Maynard was teamed with a palomino named Tarzan[4] and used him in every western he made between 1923 and 1940 except one. Tarzan, named after writer Edgar Rice Burroughs' jungle hero, received billing as the "wonder horse" and the "white wonder."[5]

A number of horse hero movies aimed at children were made in the 1940s and 1950s. Some were based on books such as *Black Beauty* (20th Century–Fox, 1946) by Anna Sewell; *Florian* (MGM, 1940), an A-budget movie about the Lipizzaner stallions in Austria in the 1880s, based on a 1934 novel by Felix Salton (the author of *Bambi*); *Smoky* (20th Century–Fox, 1946) from Will James' classic novel about a wild black stallion who refused to be tamed; and *Gallant Bess* (MGM, 1946) which took place during World War II.

Most horse hero movies were set in the west, such as *The Wild Stallion* (Monogram, 1952) with Ben Johnson and a few-spot leopard Appaloosa named Top Kick; *Snowfire* (Allied Artists, 1958) which starred the Ralph McCutcheon–trained King Cotton. Television continued the horse hero trend with such stars as Fury and Flicka.[6]

Later the Kirk Douglas contemporary adult western film *Lonely Are the Brave* (Universal Pictures, 1962) was as rare as it was timely, a cowboy out of place in the modern world. The gorgeous sorrel he rode, Whiskey by name, was emblematic of the West the Douglas character loved. When it's killed, Douglas knows his world is over. That's about as close as later western films got to the connection Roy Rogers had with Trigger. Hollywood

Clayton Moore and Silver in a striking rearing pose like the one used to open *The Lone Ranger* television show.

returned to the hero and horse partnership recently; horses have been presented anthropomorphically in small degrees, as in the Antonio Banderas film *The Mark of Zorro* (TriStar Pictures, 1998) and the Viggo Mortensen movie *Hidalgo* (Buena Vista Pictures, 2004). *Spirit: Stallion of the Cimarron* (DreamWorks Animation, 2002), an animated westerndrama, tells its story from the point of view of horses. The principals are highly anthropomorphized, even to the extent of eyebrows and forward facing eyes for a wider range of facial expressions.

It would take an entire book to discuss Trigger's peers. I will acknowledge three: Champion, Silver and Dice.

Champion the Wonder Horse

An important difference between Trigger and Champion was in the way their owners Roy Rogers and Gene Autry related to them publicly. While "Trigger" was played by a number of doubles and stunt horses, Roy Rogers wanted to impress on his fans that the palomino was a single real animal. The one-horse-illusion approach could be attributed

Gene Autry with the original Champion. Like the original Trigger, the dark bay came from Hudkins Bros. Stables (Roy Dillow collection).

to Autry but to a far lesser degree, he took a more businesslike approach to his mounts. Even though he nurtured the movie ideal of the singing cowboy with a wonder horse and knew Champion was important to his success, he still viewed the horse in more practical terms and was more casual towards him. "Champion" and "Trigger" even appeared as solo attractions with their trainers Johnny Agee and Glenn Randall and still drew crowds.

Gene Autry was very candid when he discussed all his Champions. Again, this was in direct contrast to Rogers, who saw Trigger as the horse who broke the mold. Autry's official Web site carries a detailed history of the different "Champions" who served him. They're even listed with individual names to distinguish one from another: Original Champion, Lindy Champion (a working-touring horse and pretty much the Autry version of Little Trigger), Champion Jr., Little Champ, touring Champion, Television Champion, and Champion Three. Noting different "Triggers" beyond Trigger Jr. was unthinkable on the Rogers site. Trigger's most important double was finally acknowledged officially in 2005 when a glossy color photo was offered for sale. Amazingly it was titled "Roy, Dale & Lil' Trigger Standing."

Gene Autry and Roy Rogers were different in another important way regarding their screen mounts. Rogers was in love with one particular palomino, the original Trigger. While Autry no doubt had affection for his equine partners, it seemed his connection never went as deep. Autry did not try to give the impression he was riding the same horse throughout his career; they were not even the same color. His first Champion was a dark chestnut; the second, the one referred to as the "strawberry roan" Champion, was a red chestnut; and the third, used for movies and television, was a sorrel with a flaxen mane and tail.[7] According to author David Rothel, Gene Autry owned a palomino named Pal early in his movie career and planned to use the horse later in his color movies. Roy Rogers and Trigger appeared on the scene before Autry had the opportunity.[8] However, Autry did tour with a palomino trick horse named Robin Hood during some of his live appearances.[9] Can you imagine Rogers riding a chestnut in personal appearances? As real working cowboys use a string of horses in order to avoid riding an animal that was spent, in B-western fantasies a cowboy was limited to one horse. In a sense, Gene Autry, with his casual approach to the horses referred to by one name, was more true to cowboy reality than Roy Rogers.

In *Comin' Round the Mountain* (1936), Champion got top billing, but a solid-colored mustang stallion with a star on his forehead was the equine star of the movie. The mustang, Diablo, not only drove the plot but won the climactic race. Trigger seldom took a subordinate role to another horse in a Roy Rogers movie; exceptions were Trigger Jr. and Frog Milhouse's Ring-eyed Nellie (refer to Chapter 8, "Golden Stallion, Silver Screen").

Gene Autry's shrewd business approach was applied to all aspects of his career. When a particular "Champion" got old, Autry simply replaced the animal and made no secret about it. According to Karla Buhlman, vice president of Gene Autry Entertainment, a radio show from 1946 exists where it was suggested that a contest be held asking whether or not Autry should retire the old Champion and bring on a new one!

Having his wonder horse mounted would never have occurred to Gene Autry. He was not an outdoorsman or hunter, like Rogers. Taxidermy was not something he had a lot of experience with. The story of how Autry reacted to news that Rogers had Trigger mounted has been circulating among fans for years. Allegedly, Autry was somewhat surprised, then amused. Cal Thomas reported in *Jewish World Review,* "Gene Autry once

Gene Autry with Lindy Champion (left; born the day of Charles Lindbergh's historic flight, it was the first horse to make a transcontinental flight from California to New York) and his trick palomino Robin Hood at Flushing Meadows Park in Queens, New York, on the occasion of the 1939 World's Fair. Note the Trylon and Perisphere, the main symbols of the event, in the background.

told me that when his horse, Champion, died, he was asked if he would like him stuffed and placed in his museum. 'How much would it cost?' asked the multimillionaire. When he was told the price, Autry responded, 'Hell, no, bury the SOB!'"[10]

Champion's Fictional Origins

Fictitious stories having to do with the origins of a cowboy's horse were popular and went a long way toward establishing an equine star's celebrity. They were good for business as they added to an animal's value as a marketing and merchandising tool.

Gene Autry and Champion Jr., the "Strawberry Roan," wearing his trademark pistol shanks bit. Autry paid $500 for the stallion that was originally named Boots because of his four white socks.

There are a number of fictional accounts of how Gene Autry acquired Champion told in different media: from radio to movies, recordings, and once on television. An episode on the Gene Autry radio show titled "How Gene Found Champion" may have been the first. Next came Autry's first color movie feature, *Strawberry Roan* (1948), followed by a Mutual Broadcasting System radio serial, *The Adventures of Champion*, which lasted for one season (1949–1950). Then came a *Gene Autry Show* television episode titled "Horse Sense," produced in 1952. A spoken word LP was also released titled "The Story of Champion." "The Story of Little Champ" was also recorded in July 1950 released by Columbia.[11]

When it came to movies having to do with the origins of their mounts, Rogers' was superior to Autry's. By the time Autry got around to filming *Strawberry Roan* his best work was behind him. Autry produced *Strawberry Roan* in 1948 through his own production company. Although it was filmed in color, the streamlined budget showed. Gone were the large crowd scenes and big production numbers of his Republic glory days. Compared to movies like *Back in the Saddle Again* (1941), *Strawberry Roan* is pretty sparse.[12]

The *Strawberry Roan* song was an old standard written by Curly Fletcher and had been covered by dozens of stars including Marty Robbins and Roy Rogers. It's sometimes referred to as America's greatest horse ballad. It didn't seem to matter that the horse in Autry's movie that played the title character was a chestnut and not a strawberry roan.[13]

Gene Autry's version of the *Strawberry Roan* opened with the title character standing in profile while the credits rolled.[14] The story has to do with a boy (played by Dick Jones) who tried to break-in a wild stallion and was injured in the process. In a rage the boy's father, played by *My Pal Trigger* villain Jack Holt, tried to shoot the animal. Autry, Holt's ranch foreman, stopped him and freed the stallion. He realized the horse might be just what the boy needed to restore his crushed spirit. The majority of the film involved Autry's attempts to save the strawberry roan and heal Jones. Holt was angry with Autry throughout most of the movie, a role similar to the one Gabby Hayes played in *My Pal Trigger*.

The Adventures of Champion

Through his film production company, Flying A Productions, Gene Autry managed to do for Champion what Roy Rogers never did for Trigger: give him his own weekly television show. On September 30, 1955, Autry released *The Adventures of Champion* which ran for 26 half-hour episodes until March 1956 (Fridays at 7:30 p.m. on CBS). For a brief time, Champion eclipsed Trigger in popularity.

The Adventures of Champion was set in the Southwest of the 1880s and told the story of 12-year-old Ricky North, played by actor Barry Curtis, and his stallion, Champion. Jim Bannon (the fourth actor to play Red Ryder on film) played Ricky's Uncle Sandy North. *The Adventures of Champion* took place in the same setting found in the comics but with a slightly different family: Uncle Smoky became Uncle Sandy, and Ricky West became Ricky North, the only person that Champion would allow on his back. The television series apparently gave the impression that Uncle Sandy owned the ranch; Autry was seldom (if ever) mentioned.[15]

As previously noted, Gene Autry's horse also got his own radio adventure serial, a

Gene Autry rode two sorrel Champions on television and in later movies as well.

spin-off from Autry's *Melody Ranch* CBS radio network program. *The Adventures of Champion* consisted of 15-minute episodes broadcast on the Mutual Broadcasting System, serialized stories running five installments each from Monday to Friday.

Champion's Unique Six-Gun Bit

The six-gun bit that Champion wore became an Autry trademark and was more unusual than any tack Trigger used. It was not actually made from a real six-shooter, but from a metal toy gun that was cut in half and from which a mold was cast. After a cleaning, the parts were welded to a stainless steel bit connecting both halves. Adjustments were made for the angle of the mouthpiece, and the bridle loop was welded to the end of each half-barrel.

The Champs

In 1957 Gene Autry signed a number of rockabilly Texas musicians to record as The Champs on his fledgling Challenge Records label in Hollywood. In January 1958 the instrumental "Tequila" was released as the B-side of a single. A surprise hit, "Tequila" charted quickly and made it to number one by March of the same year. Daniel Flores, a.k.a. Chuck Rio, a talented saxophonist, keyboardist and singer from Rankin, Texas, wrote it. A touring band was formed to further promote the single after it topped the charts. Seals and Crofts, before they became a popular folk duo, joined the Champs at that point and remained for seven years.

The Autry organization (in the person of spokesman Alex Gordon) would neither confirm nor deny when asked if the Champs were named after Gene Autry's horse. This writer first heard the story on an oldies radio station in Los Angeles.

According to Johnny Bond's book *30 Years on the Road with Gene Autry* (Create-Space, 2016), Autry once recorded for a company called Champion Records.

Silver, a Fiery Horse with the Speed of Light

Although the Lone Ranger appeared mostly on radio, serials, and television, he was of the B-western era and starred in two B-western color movies. More a symbol than an ordinary cowboy, the Lone Ranger was the most fanciful of the B-western heroes. That says a lot. Producers of his television show were more interested in entertainment and family values than realism. Children never questioned what they saw; they accepted and believed. The Lone Ranger was always clean-shaven and his hair always cut; he was immaculate though constantly in the saddle. His costume was clean and pressed even though he slept in it, including his mask! The Lone Ranger was also asexual; unlike Roy Rogers and Gene Autry, who both had romantic involvements with their leading ladies, the Lone Ranger was beyond such nonsense. It was as if he'd taken an oath of celibacy when he donned his mask and vowed to uphold law and order. The Lone Ranger was pure and true. Symbolically it makes sense he would ride a white horse.

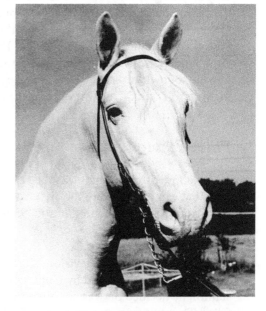

Brace Breemer's own horse, Silver's Pride, was 27 years old at the time this picture was taken. The photograph was sent to Lone Ranger fan Frank E. Swain of Pulaski, Virginia, in 1966 by Brace Breemer's widow, Leta (Dawn Moore collection).

As with Trigger, many horses played Silver over the years in personal appearances, movies, and television. Beautiful though the different white stallions were, it was almost impossible to tell them apart.

Not only was the Lone Ranger iconic in nature, but Silver matched his larger-than-life persona. Silver and Scout, Tonto's trusty paint, were well trained, never tired, and never injured while serving the masked man and his Indian companion. The Lone Ranger and Tonto traveled light. They did not need pack horses loaded with supplies; it never rained or snowed on them.

The Lone Ranger's horse came from a context different from that of Trigger or Champion. Silver first existed as a larger-than-life fictional character on radio and in print. Like his masked master, Silver premiered as a character on the radio as vocal and sound effects.

On January 30 1933, radio station WXYZ began broadcasting the very successful *The Lone Ranger* show. In the first stories it was revealed that the masked man found Silver in Wild Horse Canyon. The horse had been fighting a buffalo bull and was about to be gored to death when the Lone Ranger intervened and saved its life. The masked man and his Indian companion, Tonto, nursed the stallion back to health.

With the transition into children's books, pulps, and comic books it became necessary that the Lone Ranger and Silver characters make personal appearances. The first Silver to appear in public was a rented horse named Hero owned by Carl A. Romig. Hero was used in July 30, 1933, by Brace Beemer who narrated the *Lone Ranger* radio show and appeared as the Ranger at a school field day hosted by the Detroit Department of Recreation at Belle Isle.[16] Beemer eventually did promotions with his own horse Silver's Pride.

In 1938, "Hi Yo Silver" (DeVaughn and Erickson) was a hit song for the one and only Roy Rogers and reached to number 13 on the charts.[17]

The Lone Ranger became so popular on the radio and in print that it was just a matter of time until he appeared on the silver screen in a series of chapter plays. Lee Powell was the first actor to play the Lone Ranger on screen in the 1938 *Lone Ranger* Republic serial. Silver was portrayed by Silver Chief and listed that way on movie posters.[18] For the follow-up serial, *The Lone Ranger Rides Again* (1939), Bob Livingston assumed the title role and Silver was once again played by Silver Chief.[19]

Enter Clayton Moore

No individual animal was the real Silver in the sense there was an original Trigger. Two that came close were the Silvers that actor Clayton Moore used in the Lone Ranger television show, which aired in the 1950s. According to Moore, they were of Morgan and Arabian mix—Morabs.[20]

In 1949, after he was cast as the Lone Ranger, Clayton Moore personally chose the Silver he would ride on television. Silver #1 was hand-picked from stock at a San Fernando Valley horse ranch owned by Hugh Hooker. Moore had an eye for horses, and the white stallion he decided on was an impressive 17-plus-hands tall, referred to on screen as "big fella." The stallion was registered as White Cloud and was about 12 years of age. Silver #1 did not know many tricks but was very impressive when he reared and he stood quietly for anyone due to his gentle nature.[21]

Hi-Yo Silver. According to Clayton Moore, two Silvers were used in the *Lone Ranger* television show and in both feature movies. The first horse, nicknamed Liver Lips, would tongue the copper roller on his bit and consequently his lip would hang down. Moore also noted that the horse had a dark spot on its hindquarters. A second Silver was used when John Hart took over the Lone Ranger role during the 1952–1953 seasons. The only dark spot on the second Silver was on the left ear (provided by Steve Jensen from the Adam Mendoza collection).

In 1945, Silver #2 was born outside Danville, Iowa. He was a stallion from registered Saddlebred stock and was first named Tarzan's White Banner. He eventually reached 15.2 hands at the withers and weighed 1150 pounds fully grown. The name was derived from his sire, Tarzan, coincidentally the same name as Trigger's sire though not the same horse. Virginia Lee Perry, his first owner and trainer, sold Tarzan's White Banner when he was four years to Charles VanDyke of Peoria, Illinois. That same year George Trendle, owner of the Lone Ranger Radio Broadcasting Company, purchased the stallion from VanDyke for the *Lone Ranger* television series and registered him as Hi-Yo Silver.

Trendle's Hi-Yo Silver was in California during the 1952–1953 television seasons and took over the role as the Lone Ranger's mount while John Hart played the *Lone Ranger*, Moore having left temporarily over a contract dispute. During the season when the production company was not filming, Hi-Yo Silver was used for Lone Ranger public appearance tours and promotions. The high-strung stallion had a reputation for being skittish on the set if he heard camera motors running. There were those who had trouble riding him. However, Hart had very nice things to say about his four-legged co-star: "He was half American saddle horse and half Arabian—pure white, with big, dark blue eyes, no pink in them. And very, very smart. He was a stallion, a stud, and they're very nervous and jumpy. Nobody had really used him before, and I picked him out and worked him for about a month before we even started shooting. After fifty-two episodes, I really hated to part company with him."[22]

When Clayton Moore returned to *The Lone Ranger* the following year, he too used Hi-Yo Silver almost exclusively and also took the horse on publicity tours. Glenn Randall trained and stabled Hi-Yo Silver at the Randall Ranch in Newhall, California, during the filming seasons.

For the *Lone Ranger* episodes featuring the character Dan Reid, the Lone Ranger's nephew, a third white horse was rented, this one from the Spahn ranch. Dan Reid's horse was named Victor and, in the story line, was supposedly sired by Hi-Yo Silver.

In 1954 Trendle sold the *Lone Ranger* show rights to Jack Wrather. Hi-Yo Silver and the silver-laden saddle and tack were not included in the $3,000,000 deal Trendle and Wrather negotiated. Trendle wanted an additional $25,000 for the horse and tack. An agreement was reached when Wrather suggested splitting the difference instead. Trendle agreed, and Hi-Yo Silver and all copyrights to the Lone Ranger character were sold to the Wrather Corporation of California.

After the motion picture *The Lone Ranger and the Lost City of Gold* was completed in 1956, Hi-Yo Silver and Scout were put in the care of horse wrangler and stuntman Wayne Burson and his wife Louise at their ranch in California. Wayne Burson had appeared in several westerns in the 1940s and 1950s and had been Hi-Yo Silver's wrangler on the Lone Ranger set. He had also doubled for Tonto in the television series. Along with the Bursons, Clayton Moore and Hi-Yo Silver toured the country performing for audiences till 1962. After that the stallion retired to the Bursons' ranch, where he enjoyed a life of leisure till he died in 1974 at the age of 29.

One of best-known Silvers was a stand-in stunt and chase double named Traveller. His owner, Bill Ward, in full Lone Ranger costume, rode him exclusively during scenes involving chases and jumps. Whenever a scene demanded that the Lone Ranger unseat a fleeing outlaw by leaping from Silver at full gallop, it was almost always Bill Ward performing the stunt from Traveller. Clayton Moore never rode Traveller during the run of the show, as the horse wouldn't let just anybody ride him. After he was retired from film making, Traveller became Tommy Trojan, the University of Southern California Trojan mascot ridden during football games.

Silver #1 was pretty much retired after a brief stand-in appearance for Hi-Yo Silver in the 1956 movie *The Lone Ranger* (Warner Bros.) with Clayton Moore. He was sold to the Ace Hudkins stables and, being fairly old, was used only for close-ups and head shots.

In a 1976 *People* magazine interview, Jay Silverheels, who played Tonto, recalled that

Silver actually was somewhat of a slow-running horse and Scout had to be reined in "lest he leave the masked rider in that traditional cloud of dust."

Although Silver and Scout were basically beautiful transportation on the *Lone Ranger* television show, each had a special scene in the two full-length color feature films. In *The Lone Ranger* (Warner Bros., 1956) Scout actually ran to the Lone Ranger for help when an angry crowd threatened to hang Tonto. In *The Lone Ranger and the Lost City of Gold* (Warner Bros., 1958) Silver found an abandoned infant and later rescued it again. In a short comedy sequence Scout was actually sleeping next to Tonto. Both were sharing a blanket which Scout pulled much the same way Little Trigger did in *Son of Paleface* when he shared a bed with comedian Bob Hope.

Hi-Yo Silver, Away!

Unlike Roy Rogers, who had the foresight and opportunity to own his screen name and likeness, and unlike William Boyd, who bought the film rights to the Hopalong Cassidy character, Clayton Moore did not have the opportunity to own the Lone Ranger

Clayton Moore on the first Silver with Dale Evans on Buttermilk and Roy Rogers on the original Trigger at the Los Angeles Coliseum in the mid–1950s. Silver topped out at 17 hands; Buttermilk, at 15 hands—he looked like a pony in comparison (Dawn Moore collection).

character. Moore was hired to play a role and remained a work-for-hire actor.[23] Nor did Moore own any of the Silvers he rode as the Lone Ranger. The closest he got was to work Silver #1 on the trails around his Tarzana residence.[24]

If equine B-western celebrity is a long-distance race, Silver will win it simply because he's a fictional character. It's conceivable the Lone Ranger might be the subject of a movie or television show in the future in spite of the disappointing 2013 film fiasco starring Armie Hammer and Johnny Depp. If so, Silver, as part of the myth, will be present in his full glory. Fictional characters like Zorro, Robin Hood, and Sherlock Holmes come to life on the screen every now and then in updated versions. Bio-pictures will probably never be made of the lives of Roy Rogers and Gene Autry.

Trigger may have eclipsed Silver as the premiere B-western horse, but the white stallion's catch phrase, "Hi-Yo Silver, away," endures.

Dice: Beauty and Brains

Dice was a flashy black and white overo (pronounced oh-VAIR-oh) owned by Ralph McCutcheon, a man with talents as a trainer on a par with Glenn Randall. The overo paint was descended from horses brought to North America by Spanish conquistadors, and with its dramatic irregular, scattered markings was revered by Native Americans. A horse described as overo generally has a single-color tail. Paints come in three specific coat patterns: overo, tobiano, and tovero.[25] Tonto's horse, Scout, was a tobiano, and the Cisco Kid's mount, Diablo, was an overo. Viewed together, these two paint types are quite different.[26]

Although many well-known stars rode Dice (real name Pair O'Dice) on screen, what he didn't have was a long and permanent career with a cowboy celebrity equal to Roy Rogers. Had Dice been teamed with such a cowboy for the length of his motion picture career, there's no telling what fame he might have achieved. It could be said that Dice was a match for Trigger and Little Trigger together. He had Trigger's striking looks and camera presence combined with Little Trigger's endurance and talent.

Born in Greely, Colorado, Ralph McCutcheon grew up around horses and was active in the rodeo circuit in his youth. McCutcheon's ranch, Rancho Maria, was in Sand Canyon near Santa Clarita (Newhall-Saugus) in northwest Los Angeles. McCutcheon's lifelong dream of a career as a horse trainer was realized when he acquired Dice. Born around 1928, Dice was quick to learn under McCutcheon's direction, and as soon as the animal was ready, they began making appearances at local rodeos. It was at a horse show in Colorado that the head of livestock procurement for MGM Studios noticed him and asked McCutcheon if Dice could be screen-tested for a western film. Dice passed with flying colors and beat out eight other horses for a role in the Richard Dix movie *It Happened in Hollywood*. McCutcheon was hired as trainer and went on to enjoy a successful career in both movies and television.

Dice was a hard horse to forget once you saw him on screen. He earned a reputation among filmmakers as a great performer with a repertoire tailor-made for the movie business. Dice was especially valuable to moviemakers because of his extraordinary ability to track—that is, he was able to follow a predetermined path on cue. This is difficult for horses but very important for a filmmaker who works with pre-positioned cameras in a lighted set. Tracking was a tremendous asset while working under a deadline and, especially, a tight budget. In rehearsals, human actors blocked scenes so they knew when and how to hit certain marks after cameras started rolling. In rehearsals Dice worked at liberty; McCutcheon walked him at the desired speed along a predetermined path. When the director, actors, and crew were ready to film a scene, Dice was turned loose and cued. He did not veer from the original walk-through.

Many well-known stars rode Dice on screen, including Arthur Lake (best known as Dagwood Bumstead in 28 *Blondie* pictures from 1938 through 1950) in *It's a Great Life* (Columbia, 1943) (Petrine Day Mitchum collection).

Ralph McCutcheon's horses Domino and Dice with Gregory Peck during the 1946 Vanguard Films production of *Duel in the Sun* **(Bruce Hickey collection).**

Many Western stars rode Dice. Wild Bill Elliott used Dice when Columbia cast him as the lead in its 15-chapter serial *The Great Adventures of Wild Bill Hickok* (1938). Dice was even cast as an Arabian (true Arabs are not paints) in *Tarzan's Desert Mystery* (RKO Pictures, 1943) with the one and only Johnny Weissmuller. Columbia Pictures hired Dice extensively, which secured McCutcheon the position of head horse trainer and handler for the studio.

Dice was also featured in *Cowboy from Brooklyn*. About 35 minutes into the movie, star Dick Powell arrived at Grand Central Station in the heart of New York City. He serenaded a waiting crowd of fans in the grand ballroom. After he finished, co-stars Pat O'Brien and Ronald Reagan presented him with Dice as a gift. The overo appeared from behind a curtain, fully tacked. He was cued by Ralph McCutcheon to rear up. Powell, whose character was afraid of animals, ran away, leaving Dice standing in a corner.

Dice has often been confused with other overo paints working in Hollywood at the same time. He did not appear with Gene Autry in *Comin' Round the Mountain* (1936) as a renegade Mustang stallion. It has also been reported that Autry rode Dice in *Strawberry Roan* (1948) when in fact the flashy paint was the same animal who would become Duncan Renaldo's mount, Diablo, in *The Cisco Kid* television series. Dice has also been confused with another overo named Domino who was ridden by Charlton Heston in *The Big Country* (United Artists, 1958) and *Diamond Head* (Columbia Pictures, 1963). Rocky Roe claims trainer Ralph McCutcheon also owned Domino, used later to double for Dice as he got older. Domino was featured in *The Texan* (CBS, 1958–1960) television series starring Rory Calhoun.

The high point of Dice's career occurred in 1946 when he was cast as the lead horse with Gregory Peck and Jennifer Jones in director King Vidor's epic Western *Duel in the Sun* (Selznick International, 1946). Ralph McCutcheon was hired as technical advisor and horse supplier. *Duel in the Sun* was produced by none other than David O. Selznick, who saw it as a way of duplicating his success seven years earlier with *Gone with the Wind* (MGM, 1939). *Duel in the Sun* featured an all-star cast including the great Lionel Barrymore, silent film star Lillian Gish, and, as the film's narrator, the legendary Orson Welles. Dice was at his peak, in great company, and up to the challenge of such an important movie.

Based on the novel by Niven Busch, *Duel in the Sun* was a huge moneymaker. As much a supporting character as any human on the set, Dice was featured in key scenes along with the two lead actors. Gregory Peck even referred to the overo by name on screen. The producer saw Dice as such an asset that after *Duel in the Sun* was completed, his contract was extended to participate in a cross-country promotional tour. The studio did not allow Dice to be used in any other motion picture while *Duel in the Sun* was playing the national circuit.

Dice's last film was *Thunderhoof* (Columbia, 1948), the story of a wild stallion. Reportedly McCutcheon had difficulty with Dice during the production as the horse was growing old and showing signs of senility. After *Thunderhoof*, Dice was retired and put out to pasture at the McCutcheon stables in Van Nuys, California. In 1958 when Dice's health started to fade, he was humanely put to sleep. He was 30.

With Dice's career earnings Ralph McCutcheon bought and developed a large stable of horses for movie work. A standout in his herd was Highland Dale, a black stallion from Missouri. The horse came to be called Beaut but would go on to even greater fame as Fury.

Like Dice before him, Beaut combined the beauty and talent of Trigger and Little Trigger. He was never teamed with a particular cowboy star. Instead he was used in a variety of movie roles and would eventually build quite a resume: *Black Beauty* (20th Century–Fox, 1946); *Gypsy Colt* (MGM, 1954); *Johnny Guitar* (Republic, 1954); *Outlaw Stallion* (Columbia, 1954); and was ridden by Elizabeth Taylor in *Giant* (Warner Bros., 1956).

Even with all his appearances in A-list movies, Beaut found his greatest fame in a contemporary western television show titled *Fury*. It ran an astounding 116 episodes from 1955 till 1960.[27] The show was later syndicated under the title *Brave Stallion* from 1960 until 1966.

After Beaut retired from his life as a Hollywood star he remained with Ralph McCutcheon. The ebony stallion eventually developed a breathing disorder. He died in 1972 at age 29.[28]

Highland Dale, aka Beaut, was featured in the weekly *Fury* television show on NBC from 1955 to 1960. Elizabeth Taylor rode the ebony stallion in *Giant* released by Warner Bros. in 1956. Insert: owner and trainer Ralph McCutcheon.

A third equine star in the McCutcheon remuda was a solid-colored palomino named California who starred in *The Palomino* (Columbia Pictures, 1950).

Ralph McCutcheon usually worked uncredited including on such block busters as *Giant* (Warner Bros., 1956) and *Ben-Hur* (MGM, 1959).

Bays in the Background

Beyond fabulous stars like Trigger, there were dozens of horses on movie sets during the heyday of the western. They were the extras, the anonymous beasts of burden that pulled stagecoaches, buckboards, and covered wagons. They were the old reliables who carried supporting players and posses on their backs in hundreds of A- and B-western features. Equine extras came in a variety of colors, but 90 percent of the time, they were bay. These anonymous horses were the ones that villains like Roy Barcroft or Leroy Mason rode. Sidekick Gabby Hayes' regular mount Eddie was a bay. As a rule, only star players or Indians rode more colorful mounts.

The bays in the background were loyal, sturdy and dependable. They ran their hearts out, took many a tumble, endured the sound of gunfire, worked long hours, tolerated heavy-handed novice riders, and a few were injured or worse. Although extra horses were looked upon as atmosphere, like the stars, they had to be well schooled with even-tempered dispositions. According to Anthony Amaral's book *Movie Horses—Their Treatment and Training*, in the 1950s studios were paying $10 a day for the use of a background horse.[29]

"Trigger" got lots of well-deserved attention, but it was the bays in the background that added atmosphere and context.

17

Horse Hero Comic Books

*"If you think all men are equal, you ain't never been on foot
and met a man riding a good horse."*—Anonymous cowboy

In the 1940s and 1950s, before the onslaught of television and video games, the major forms of entertainment for kids were movies, radio, and comic books. The cowboy was king in all three. It was the Golden Age of comics and they sold in the millions. Almost every movie cowboy (along with a few cowgirls) was featured within the pages of comic books published by such companies as Fawcett, Magazine Enterprises (ME), and Dell. When the Saturday matinee was over, youngsters left the movie theater and headed straight for the local drugstore to spend what was left of their allowance on comic books. Coincidentally, they cost the same as a movie, a nickel to ten cents.

Comic books were first seen as throwaway kiddy entertainment. Parents and publishers assumed that after a few readings they would be trashed. However, because the stories and characters were so engaging, children started collecting them, some continuing to do so into adulthood.

Horse Hero Comic Books

Many talented writers and artists were the backbone of the comic book industry and they had to be prolific. An amazing powerhouse of creativity—and all for the cost of one dime!

Dell was one of the biggest publishers of comic books. *Roy Rogers' Trigger, Gene Autry's Champion,* and *The Lone Ranger's Famous Horse Hi-Yo Silver* were among the most popular comic books Dell published in the 1950s.[1]

Although some illustrations and scripts remain uncredited to this day, it has been determined that Gaylord Du Bois (pronounced Du Boyce, like "voice") and, later Paul S. Newman, wrote most of the story lines; Sam Savitt painted striking covers for all three titles; and Tom Gill rendered the great interior art in the Hi-Yo Silver comics.

While Dell dominated horse hero comic books, other companies produced their own titles. Charlton Comics Group published two of note: *Rocky Lane's Black Jack* and *Black Fury. Rocky Lane's Black Jack* started with issue #20; it ran from November 1957 until November 1959, ending with issue #28, and included work by Steve Ditko, who would also work at Marvel and draw the first Spiderman comics. *Black Fury* was published

This masterful Champion head portrait by Moe Gollub was featured on the back cover of *Gene Autry's Champion* #3. Gollub also painted a back cover for issue #2 of *Roy Rogers' Trigger*. Real bargains in the 1950s for a mere ten cents.

from May 1955 until March-April 1966, an impressive 57 issues, more than any other equine title. Steve Ditko also penned one *Black Fury* story. By far the best illustrator associated with *Black Fury* was the late Ernest Huntley Hart, who also went by the pseudonym E.H. Huntley. His dramatic and well-muscled depictions of the ebony stallion are prized by collectors.[2]

Pound for pound, DC and Fawcett artists did more dynamic and accomplished interior work than what was done at Dell, Tom Gill being the exception. While his work did not have the flourish of a Gil Kane, who is best known for his work at DC comics on Green Lantern, it was refined and solid.[3] Kane's DC work in *Hopalong Cassidy* and *All-Star Western Johnny Thunder* comics, especially regarding horses, is noteworthy. At Marvel he produced great horse-related western covers for *Rawhide Kid, Kid Colt Outlaw, Ringo Kid,* and *Night Rider comics.*

Roy Rogers Comics

In 1939 Dell Publishing took over a one-shot comic book series from United Features Syndicate (UFS) called *Single Series* and renamed it *Four-Color Comics*. This was a test market venue; if a title was well received, it would be published on a regular basis under

Gene Autry's Champion comics were published under the Dell imprint by Western Printing between 1951 and 1959. All covers painted masterfully in gouache by Sam Savitt: nos. 5, 9, 11 and 19. Equine photograph references were usually not available to Savitt, when a human figure was involved he would pose and photograph himself.

Sam Savitt, one of America's finest horse painters, rendered stunning gouache illustrations for *Roy Rogers' Trigger* comics. This painting graced the cover of issue #7. Savitt knew horse anatomy so well that he could compose an equine in just about any position. Savitt was not provided with photograph reference when he painted Trigger or Champion and subsequently improvised their markings.

its own title. The first western title Dell published in this line was *Roy Rogers Comics* #38, issued April 1944. It came complete with a western character full-color photo cover (a first), two inside black-and-white (or sepia) full-sized photos, and a color photo back cover. Due to its significance in the history of western comic books, it's considered the daddy of them all and as such has become a highly sought-after piece of Roy Rogers paper memorabilia and a prized comic book collectible.[4]

Dell Comics remains one of the best resources for quality photos of Roy Rogers and Trigger in their prime. They were a great showcase for the ornate cowboy outfits Rogers wore and for which he became famous. Trigger is seen in his spectacular show tack. Little Trigger graced a few covers and was featured in many interior cover shots. Even Trigger Jr. showed up a couple of times on inside cover shots. The original Trigger appeared on the covers of five of the *Four-Color* issues: 117, 124, 144, 153, and 177.

Although many of the photos of Roy Rogers appeared to be candid, most were Republic Studios publicity shots that were not used in any other medium but comic books and, with rare exceptions, only in original issues. Noted photographers such as Republic's Ramon Freulich took some of the photos. Like most vintage western comics, Roy Rogers issues are either difficult to locate in nice condition, or, when they are found, very expensive. *The Official Overstreet Comic Book Price Guide* lists them with a hefty market price when in near-mint condition.

When *Roy Rogers Comics* became a monthly title on its own, "Trigger" occasionally shared a cover with his master. The original Trigger may be seen on issues 7, 9, 13, 15, 19, 21, 23, 27, 30, 36, 41, 43, 51, 92 (*Roy Rogers Comics* became *Roy Rogers and Trigger Comics* with this issue), 97, 102, 105, 106, 112, 118, 125, 128, 129, and 131. Little Trigger is pictured with Rogers on the covers of issues 2, 5, 71, 76, 77, and 100. Issue #86 sported a cover with a very early shot of Little Trigger. Pal was featured on the covers of issues 4, 5, and 9 of *Dale Evans Queen of the Westerns Comics*. The photos were printed so darkly that Pal sometimes looks more chestnut-colored than palomino. Buttermilk was pictured with Evans on a number of later covers.

Roy Rogers Comics were eventually reissued as *Roy Rogers and Trigger Comics* in 1967 under the Gold Key imprint. There were many western titles through the 1970s and beyond; *Roy Rogers Comics* alone ran for 159 issues and was fairly representative of the cowboy genre. The high production values, especially the photographs used, remained consistent throughout the years. In their prime, Roy Rogers comics sold in the millions.

Roy Rogers' Trigger Comics

Writers of books, comics, and radio had always used Trigger as a sounding board for Rogers when he was riding alone. This was a way to move a story forward and to humanize Trigger. Through comic books, writers and artists could embellish and broaden a character's legend further than in movies because any scenario could be realized. Trigger rated his own story in Rogers' *Four-Color Comics*. A regular Trigger solo backup feature began in *Roy Rogers Comics* #20 (August 1949) and continued until #46 (1951). They returned from issues 100 to 131,[5] fifty-eight episodes from 1949 to 1959 according to author Ray White (*King of the Cowboys, Queen of the West*, University of Wisconsin Press, 2005). Most were written by Gaylord Du Bois and illustrated by Albert Micale. Trigger appeared in every Roy Rogers comic book, just as he had in every movie. Not even Dale Evans

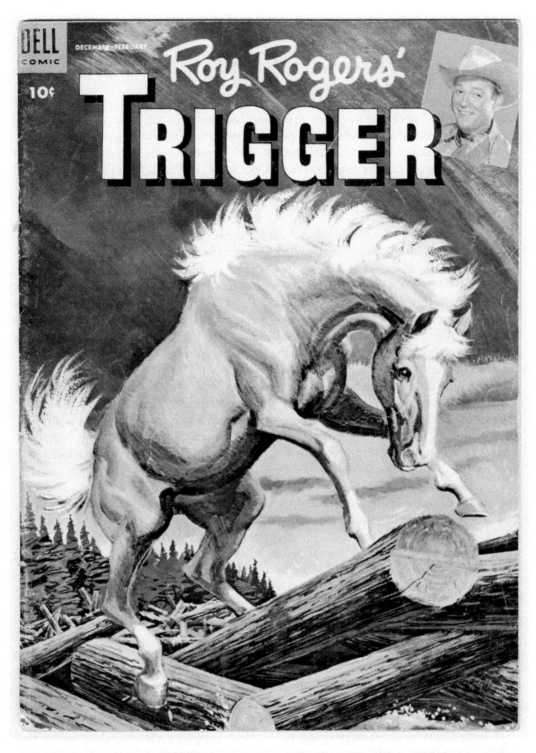

Roy Rogers' Trigger comics #15. Dell horse hero comic covers were done independently from interior stories and did not reflect story lines. Sam Savitt and his editors discussed cover ideas until the best eye-catching concept was agreed upon.

could make the same claim. Ray White noted that the palomino had his own stock phrases: "whee-ump!' "uh huh huh," "eee-ough!" or "ho-ho-ho." Trigger was allotted a story in the initial issue of Dell's *Western Roundup* series in 1952. Trigger also appeared in the King Features Syndicate comic strip *Roy Rogers,* which ran daily from 1949 until 1961 in 186 newspapers across the country.

Giving the palomino his own comic book was a logical move, and he got his own series in Dell's *Four-Color* line. The first appeared in issue #329 (May 1951). The series got its own title for the second issue (November 1951), complete with a photo of the original Trigger gracing the cover. Published on a bi-monthly basis, fifteen more issues of *Roy Rogers' Trigger Comics* appeared from December 1952 until June 1955 (copyrighted by Roy Rogers Enterprises). Taken together, *Roy Rogers' Trigger* accounts for approximately 50 separate Trigger adventures. All the covers included a small photo of Rogers in the upper right-hand corner.

Gaylord Du Bois established a context for horse heroes in comic books by keeping the animal's owner out of the stories lest human overshadow horse. Roy Rogers did not appear in Trigger stories, although his name came up occasionally.

Photos were periodically used to grace interior and back covers. The first Champion comic book featured a photo cover, as had the second Trigger comic. Photos were not used in the Silver comics. The practice of using photos did not last long. Illustrations were almost mandatory with horse hero comics because covers necessitated exciting scenes to draw potential buyers—scenes that would have been almost impossible to recreate with live action and too expensive to photograph.

Not only did the creative talents in the comic book field work anonymously, rarely getting credit for their text or images; they also worked independently from each other.[6] A few of the talents preferred it that way, seeing comics as a vehicle towards a career in illustration or, better yet, as gallery painters. It's interesting to note, with regards to western comics, that writers seemed to stay for the duration of their careers, while artists moved in and out of the field.

According to author and Roy Rogers expert Ray White, "To get around the 'no signing' policy of comic book publishers, artists often placed their names or initials in conspicuous places within a story. Comic book artists placed their names on grave stones, signs on country stores, etc."[7]

John Buscema, who would later make a name for himself at Marvel comics drawing the Silver Surfer and Conan characters, drew nine Trigger stories featured in *Roy Rogers* comics 100–108. Harry Parkhurst, aka Harry Parks, painted the first cover (*Four-Color* #329, May 1951); Rafael DeSoto signed a portrait of Trigger and a palomino colt used on the back cover of the same issue. *Roy Rogers' Trigger* interior stories were illustrated in part by Ray Thayer and Till Goodan.

Robert W. Phillips incorrectly credited western painter and historian Randy Steffens as one of the men who illustrated interior stories for *Roy Rogers' Trigger* comics. During an interview at his home in North Salem, New York, Sam Savitt confirmed that his own younger brother, Al, had illustrated some interior stories in the same issues. Al Savitt kept a list of all the Trigger stories he illustrated.[8]

Both Savitt brothers were living in the New York City vicinity, close to the Dell offices, when these comics were produced. By 1950 Randy Steffens was in his home state of Texas editing a local magazine. He accepted a number of freelance assignments, including many from *Western Horseman* magazine. With all due respect to Robert W. Phillips, there is no evidence to suggest that Steffens worked for Dell. When comparing a hand-written list Al Savitt provided with a list of stories Phillips thought were attributed to Steffens (to my knowledge Phillips never interviewed Steffens), one finds they are practically identical. This confusion is understandable because Al Savitt and Randy Steffens had similar drawing styles, especially with respect to the representation of horses. Phillips noted that Steffens did interior stories in issues 3, 4, 5, 6, 7, 8, 9, 10, 12, 13, 14, 15, and 16. Al Savitt claimed to have illustrated stories in all but two of the same issues, #6 and #15. It's possible Steffens did these but I will differ to Al Savitt for the rest.

Both Randy Steffens and Al Savitt depicted horses with slight features particularly in the head, often dished (concave profile with prominent eyes) like Arabians. But the two depicted humans differently. Steffens' were very generic and very white Anglo-Saxon protestant, while Al Savitt's looked almost Native American.[9]

When *Roy Rogers' Trigger Comics* ended with issue #17, it merged with *Roy Rogers Comics*.[10]

The Creators

GAYLORD DU BOIS

Gaylord Du Bois had a diverse and prolific career in comic books. Around 1938 Gaylord Du Bois met Oskar Lebeck, who was on the editorial staff of Whitman. Through that connection, Du Bois began writing comic book scripts full time. He was the major—perhaps the only—writer on the Roy Rogers' Trigger Comics from 1944 to 1960. He produced approximately 250 separate adventures.[11]

Du Bois' first Trigger story was published in 1946 in *Roy Rogers Comics* and titled "Trigger Trails the Herd." From July to December 1956, Du Bois' Trigger stories appeared in the renamed *Roy Rogers and Trigger Comics*.

A deeply religious man, Du Bois refused assignments having to do with sex, horror, or the occult. His scripts were known for the moral and emotional values they portrayed, which made him partial to his Roy Rogers stories as the King of the Cowboy's Christian ideals where similar to his own.

SAM SAVITT

Dell cover artist Sam Savitt worked apart from writers and interior artists; it wasn't imperative that his paintings relate to the stories inside. Savitt's gouache covers were dramatic, eye-catching, and powerful images that could stop potential buyers in their tracks. Once seen on newsstands and comic book racks, his dynamic covers were hard to pass up.

Sam Savitt's travels provided him with the opportunity to observe, ride, and train horses of all breeds and temperaments. He became accomplished in both English and western riding styles, disciplines that served his paintings well.

Savitt's first significant comic book work came right out of art school when he was hired by Western Printing to paint a series of Dell comic book covers beginning with *Gene Autry's Champion.* At the same time, Dell was premiering *The Lone Ranger's Famous Horse Hi-Yo Silver* and *Roy Roger's Trigger.* By the time he finished working for Western

Printing in 1960, he had produced covers and interior material for Dell's *Four-Color Comics* line and a variety of miscellaneous titles such as *Ben Bowie and his Mountain Men, Red Ryder Ranch Magazine, Indian Chief, The Cisco Kid, Ben-Hur,* and *Zane Grey's Stories of the West.* He painted 15 of the 17 *Roy Rogers' Trigger* covers; 27 of the *Gene Autry's Champion* covers; and all 36 *Hi-Yo Silver* covers. The list of Savitt covers now stands at just over 150.[12] On rare occasions Savitt penciled interior Tex Rainger stories featured in *Pioneer West Romances* comics.

AL SAVITT

Al Savitt was about five years younger than his brother Sam. Beyond his illustrations for Western Printing in *Roy Rogers' Trigger* and *Gene Autry's Champion* comics, records of his professional work are vague. According to Al Savitt's sister-in-law Bette Orkin, during the comic book years he also did interior illustrations for books and magazines. Many were not necessarily horse stories.[13]

In 1956 Al Savitt received the Thomas Alva Edison Foundation National Mass Media Award for artwork in *A Treasury of Dogs* (published by Western Printing) as the best comic book aimed at children over eight years of age.

Interior pen and ink illustration by Al Savitt, Sam Savitt's younger brother, for *Roy Rogers' Trigger* #17 (June–August 1955) for a story titled "Trigger Comes Home."

TILL GOODMAN

Bill Black asserts in his *Golden Age Greats Volume II: Roy Rogers and the Silver Screen Cowboys—An Illustrated History of the Matinee Western,* that Till Goodan (or Goodman as it's also been spelled) illustrated some of the interior Trigger stories.[14]

Trigger Stories

The comic book version of Trigger was given human characteristics and was wise beyond animal norms. Although Gaylord Du Bois also humanized the Lone Ranger's stallion Silver, his stories were never silly or unnecessarily violent. Du Bois' writings were warm and heartfelt and stand as some of the best of the genre.

In the Trigger comic stories, the palomino was in the care of the Hanford family, and many of the stories took place while he was living on their Circle H ranch. While Trigger was established as Roy Rogers's horse, for unknown reasons, Uncle Mike, Aunt Martha, and their ranch foreman, Curly, cared for him. A particular action of Trigger's would draw the attention of the children, prompting one of his caretakers to recount the palomino's deeds of heroism. These stories were told in retrospect almost completely without dialogue balloons, much like the great *Prince Valiant* Sunday comic strips by Hal Foster—more illustrated short stories than comic books.

In other stories Trigger roamed the open range with a pony named Pinto Jack and a band of mares, protecting them from humans and animal predators and the forces of nature. With issue #109, Trigger resided on Rogers' ranch in the care of a young Mexican boy named Chico.

List of Roy Roger's Trigger Comics

Roy Rogers' Trigger (Four-Color Comics #329), May 1951. Cover: Harry Parkhurst, aka Harry Parks. Inside cover: photo of original Trigger at liberty and rearing up. Inside back cover: photo of the original Trigger in full show tack, bowing. Back cover: illustration by Rafael DeSoto (signed) of Trigger and a foal. Story: "Trigger" by Gaylord Du Bois, interior illustrations by Ray Thayer.

Roy Rogers' Trigger #2, September–November 1951. Cover: a heavily doctored photo of Trigger. Back cover: painting of Trigger wading in a stream, by Morris Gollub. Stories: "Trigger and the Drygulcher of Gunsight Notch" by Gaylord Du Bois, illustrated by Morris Gollub; "Trigger Junior Meets the Test" by Gaylord Du Bois, illustrated by A. Moore.

Roy Rogers' Trigger #3, December 1951–February 1952. Cover: Sam Savitt gouache painting. Stories: "Trigger Tackles a Sidewinder" by Gaylord Du Bois, illustrator unknown; "Trigger and the Underground Railway" by Gaylord Du Bois, illustrated by Al Savitt.

Roy Rogers' Trigger #4, March–May 1952. Cover: Sam Savitt gouache painting. Stories: "Trigger Fights for Life" by Gaylord Du Bois, illustrated by Al Savitt; "Weetamah's Bridle," author unknown, illustrator unknown but probably Al Savitt; "Trigger Trails the Lost" by Gaylord Du Bois, possibly illustrated by Moore.

Roy Rogers' Trigger #5, June–August 1952. Cover: Sam Savitt gouache painting. Stories: "Trigger Wins a Warrior's Plume" by Gaylord Du Bois, possibly illustrated by Moore; "Trigger Shares Danger on the Dark Continent" by Gaylord Du Bois, illustrated by Al Savitt.

Roy Rogers' Trigger #6, September–November 1952. Cover: Sam Savitt gouache painting. Stories: "Trigger Beats the Gun" by Gaylord Du Bois, possibly illustrated by Moore; "Trigger Runs the Gantlet" by Gaylord Du Bois, probably illustrated by Al Savitt.

Roy Rogers' Trigger #7, December 1952–February 1953. Cover: Sam Savitt gouache painting. Stories: "Trigger Takes to the Wild" by Gaylord Du Bois, illustrated by Al Savitt; "Trigger Outruns a Robber" by Gaylord Du Bois, illustrated by Al Savitt.

Roy Rogers' Trigger #8, March–May 1953. Cover: Sam Savitt gouache painting. Stories:

"Trigger in Horse Thief Cove" by Gaylord Du Bois, possibly illustrated by Joe Russo; "Trigger and the Red Renegade" by Gaylord Du Bois, illustrated by Al Savitt.

Roy Rogers' Trigger #9, June–August 1953. Cover: Sam Savitt gouache painting. Stories: "Trigger Fights for Two" by Gaylord Du Bois, possibly illustrated by Joe Russo; "Trigger and the River's Secret" by Gaylord Du Bois, illustrated by Al Savitt.

Roy Rogers' Trigger #10, September–November 1953. Cover: Sam Savitt gouache painting. Stories: "Trigger in Killer Cat," author unknown, illustrated by Al Savitt; "Trigger Turns Detective," author unknown, illustrated by Al Savitt.

Roy Rogers' Trigger #11, December 1953–February 1954. Cover: Sam Savitt gouache painting. Stories: "Trigger and the Carnival Killer," author and artist unknown; "Trigger and the Milk Run," author and artist unknown though the artist may very well be Til Goodan, according to the essay "Cowboy Stars and their Comic Books" (*Golden-Age Greats Volume II: Roy Rogers and the Silver Screen Cowboys* by Bill Black).

Roy Rogers' Trigger #12, March–May 1954. Cover: Sam Savitt gouache painting. Stories: "Trigger in Peril Rides the Storm," author unknown, illustrated by Al Savitt; "Trigger in Deep-Water Rustlers," author unknown, illustrated by Al Savitt.

Roy Rogers' Trigger #13, June–August 1954. Cover: Sam Savitt gouache painting. Stories: "Trigger in Timberland Terror," author unknown, illustrated by Al Savitt; "Trigger to the Rescue," author unknown, illustrated by Al Savitt.

Roy Rogers' Trigger #14, September–November 1954. Cover: Sam Savitt gouache painting. Stories: "Trigger in Tide of Peril," author unknown, illustrated by Al Savitt; "Trigger and the Moaning Cave," author unknown, illustrated by Al Savitt.

Roy Rogers' Trigger #15, December 1954–February 1955. Cover: Sam Savitt gouache painting. Stories: "Trigger in Challenge of the Wolf Pack," author unknown, probably illustrated by Al Savitt; "Trigger in Journey of Peril," author unknown, probably illustrated by Al Savitt.

Roy Rogers' Trigger #16, March–May 1955. Cover: Sam Savitt gouache painting. Stories: "Trigger King of the Herd," author unknown, illustrated by Al Savitt; "Trigger and the Morongo Roundup," author unknown, illustrated by Al Savitt.

Roy Rogers' Trigger #17, June–August 1955. Cover: Sam Savitt gouache painting. Stories: "Trigger in Rangeland Rescue," author unknown, illustrated by Al Savitt; "Trigger Comes Home," author unknown, illustrated by Al Savitt.

Hi-Yo Silver Comics

Although Silver's presence was strong in print and on the radio and he was referred to by name at all times, his role on the big and little screens was limited mostly to being beautiful transportation. His spectacular feats were mostly relegated to books and comic books, and it was in the latter that Silver outdistanced Trigger and Champion. The Dell issues collectively are far superior to anything else published in the horse hero genre. They had the highest consistency of craftsmanship, the strongest narrative, and contained the most interesting characters. *The Lone Ranger's Famous Horse Hi-Yo Silver Comics* also had the longest run of the Dell equine titles, 36 issues.[15]

While Paul S. Newman produced a handful of key stories for *The Lone Ranger's Famous Horse Hi-Yo Silver* and his work is considered his best work in the genre, Gaylord Du Bois contributed the lion's share of texts for the series. He was first to translate the

The Lone Ranger's Hi-Yo Silver comics published under the Dell imprint by Western Printing between 1951 and 1960: nos. 27, 16, 20 and 18. Sam Savitt was a fan of Will James and the legendary western painter's influence is obvious in the dynamic gouache cover for issue #16 (upper right).

stories to comics, embellishing and enhancing the bygone western settings, and he greatly refined the cast of characters, endearing them to readers. Gaylord Du Bois wrote *The Lone Ranger* from 1948 until 1962 and *Hi-Yo Silver* from 1952 until 1960.

Illustrator Tom Gill defined the Lone Ranger's world, giving form to Paul S. Newman's and Gaylord Du Bois's words. With his clean, crisp, stylized work, he brought their stories to life—and fans believed. His visual representation of the Lone Ranger also closely mirrored Clayton Moore's on television.

In 1949 Tom Gill was hired to draw the Gene Autry comic strip. Sadly, by the time he was done, the market for the western genre was saturated and Gill's strips were never published. Luckily he took the strips to Oscar Lebeck, an editor at Western Printing. Gill noted, "Roy Rogers indirectly got me started doing westerns when Gene Autry approached me to do a comic strip to compete with Roy. Once my editors at Dell saw it they took me off other subjects I was doing for them and put me forever more doing westerns."[16]

Tom Gill was offered a half-year run on a western strip, *The Lone Ranger*, an association with a character that would last for 20 years, into the 1970s. His straightforward style became synonymous with the character, bringing a powerful visual continuity to the entire series. At one time or another, Gill worked on all the major titles associated with the Lone Ranger character—*The Lone Ranger*, *The Lone Ranger's Famous Horse Hi-Yo Silver* (his pencils began with issue #7 and ran through every issue), and some of the *Tonto* comic book interiors.[17]

Tom Gill taught cartooning and illustration in New York area colleges and institutions for roughly a half-century. He served as a department chair for the School of Visual Arts in 1948, alumni director in 1969, and consulted into the 21st century. He served several terms as vice president of the National Cartoonists Society, winning its Best Story Comic Book Artist award in 1970.

Interior pen and ink illustration by the prolific Tom Gill for *The Lone Ranger's Hi-Yo Silver* #13 (January–March 1955) story titled "Silver and the Dry Water Hole." Gill and his team also produced interior work for *Lone Ranger* comics and *Tonto* comics.

Silver Stories

The Lone Ranger usually narrated Silver comic book stories. In the first comic book tale, "Birth of a Prince," readers met Silver's sire, the wild horse leader, King Sylvan, and his favorite mare, Moussa, Silver's mother. Silver even had a sidekick, the mischievous Black Scamper, a black colt with a white blaze.

An Indian named Keenay was by far the most interesting character in the Silver myth; he added a metaphorical aspect to the stories. The cleverest of the Apache horse hunters, he swore he would catch Silver or die trying. Keenay spoke in grandiose terms during his quest: "O medicine horse! O silver colt! Great is your wisdom and power! But old Keenay will yet be your master!"

Always traveling alone, Keenay tirelessly pursued Silver. The old horse hunter learned to respect the white stallion, for not only would the animal take flight to keep his freedom, but he would also fight if necessary. Keenay was almost a tragic figure with his obsession for the great white stallion he would never possess. Keenay became Silver's shadow from one adventure and narrow escape to another. To the stallion, the old Apache was his enemy trying to end his freedom; to readers, Keenay was a guardian angel rescuing Silver from others who also had designs on him (a kinder Ahab pursuing his white whale, if you will). In the end, after years of failed attempts, Keenay realized Silver would not be his. Political correctness was not in the cards, another would ride the magic horse.

18

Golden Slumbers, Empty Saddle

*"I can't say enough for him. I can't hardly go into the museum
without getting tears in my eyes."*—Roy Rogers[1]

The last motion picture the original Trigger appeared in was *Pals of the Golden West,*
released in December 1951. Since the palomino was not in *Son of Paleface* (Paramount,
1952) or in any of the countless television variety shows Rogers and Evans did into the
1970s, *The Roy Rogers Show* television episodes completed in 1957 are among his last
filmed appearances.[2]

After *The Roy Rogers Show* came to an end, Rogers and Evans appeared from 1958
to 1960 in fourteen NBC variety hours sponsored by Chevrolet called *The Chevy Show.*
It was during one of these broadcasts, according to Roy Dillow, that "Trigger" was officially retired. The "last ride" presentation took place at a rodeo performance with "Trigger" entering on the back of a flatbed truck. Little Trigger doubled for Trigger on this
occasion. Trigger Jr. was present and introduced as the original Trigger's replacement.
Roy Rogers and Dale Evans continued to appear at fairs and such into the 1970s, most
of the time either without horses or with borrowed ones.

The last time the "Trigger" character was portrayed on television was by a look-
alike in a third season episode of *The Fall Guy* (February 1984) titled "King of the Cowboys." One of Rogers' last appearances on a palomino was during the *Randy Travis—
Happy Trails* television special shown on the Nashville Network in October 1990. Trigger
had indeed left the building.

In 1957, after 19 years in show business, the original Trigger was retired at age 23 to
the Rogers' Chatsworth ranch in California. In 1963 Corky Randall moved Trigger, Buttermilk, Little Trigger, and Trigger Jr. to Hidden Valley. On June 27, 1965, Rogers sold
his ranch and moved to Apple Valley. According to Corky, Trigger was not moved with
the rest of the stock because of his age and blindness. It was thought that the stress of
moving to unfamiliar surroundings would be difficult on the aged horse.

One of Trigger's greatest admirers, William Witney, gave a description of Trigger in
the palomino's final years in his booklet *Trigger Remembered.* Witney was directing a television show in the vicinity of the ranch where the palomino was stabled and made a
point to visit him. According to Witney, Trigger's appearance was so altered that he was
not even sure the horse he was looking at was indeed the Old Man. Trigger was shrunken,
his golden coat dull. He was gray around his eyes and ears. Witney didn't know he was
with the right horse until he looked into Trigger's brown eyes.[3]

Opening credits shot from *The Golden Stallion* **(1949), also used as a lobby card (Roy Dillow collection).**

At the end of Roy Rogers' life, Trigger took the form of a grey motorized cart with handlebars. The aged King of the Cowboys used it to get around the huge Victorville museum. Painted in a script font on the side of the diminutive vehicle was the name "Trigger III."

Trigger lived an easy life until the day he took his final breath, July 3, 1965, almost exactly 31 years after he was born.[4]

Roy Rogers recalled one of the saddest phone calls he'd ever received. It was from one of Trigger's caregivers.[5] "I picked up the phone, and before anything was said, I said, 'Old Trigger died, didn't he?' I just had a feeling ... Danny said, 'Just a few minutes ago.' Danny had turned Trigger out after he'd fed him. He was feeding the other horses and he went and got a cup of coffee. Trigger was lying out there in the field but Danny thought he'd just laid down after he played around a little bit, so he went back out to finish feeding the horses. Then he said, 'I went back out there again, and he was just lying there. So I

Above: Roy Rogers with the aged Trigger at his Chatsworth ranch in the early 1960s. Not long after Rogers sold the ranch the palomino was moved to the Randall Ranch, where he spent his final years. *Right:* Roy Rogers embracing the original Trigger while on his Chatsworth ranch, circa 1963 (both photographs, Roy Dillow collection).

thought maybe I'd better check him.' He went out there and 'Phht (Roy's voice cracks) ... he was gone.'"[6]

Trigger's Obituary

A United Press International obituary (dated March 30, 1966) marked Trigger's passing as July 3, 1965. Written by Vernon Scott, the article was published a year later by *The Youngstown Vindicator*, March 31, 1966, and titled, "Roy Rogers Reveals Death Of Old Trigger In July." Overly sentimental, it mentions another Trigger double, Trigger III.

Hollywood (UPI)—Cowboy star Roy Rogers revealed today that his trusty steed, Trigger, died at the age of 33 almost a year ago. Rogers kept the loss to himself for fear fans across the country would go into shock on learning that the gallant equine had chased his last band of outlaws into that great corral in the sky. Trigger may be gone, but odds are he won't be forgotten. The longtime singing cowboy is going to have Trigger stuffed and mounted for his planned museum. "I never rode another horse in a movie," Roy recalled. Trigger Jr. is a decrepit 24 years old and spends his time lolling around fetlock deep in a pasture and getting a little exercise. Roy doesn't ride much anymore and he lacks the great affection for these nags that he had for good old Trigger I. Because Trigger Jr. is really too old to work anymore, Roy rides Trigger III whenever public appearances call for him to be seen in the saddle. Jr. is kept at Roy's Apple Valley, California ranch while III is stabled at another Rogers' spread in Newhall, California and is worked out regularly by Roy's trainer.

Technically speaking Trigger died one day short of his 31st birthday—he was born on July 4. If one wants to split hairs, he was 30 when he died (it's interesting to note Roy Rogers died on July 6, 1998).

Bischoff's Taxidermy

Unable to face burying his close friend Trigger, Roy Rogers decided to have him mounted by Bischoff's Taxidermy and Studio Prop Rental of Burbank, California.[7] An avid outdoorsman, Rogers hunted a variety of animals in North America and Africa. He kept taxidermists busy for years, and having Trigger mounted probably seemed normal. "So I came up with a plan to preserve Trigger for myself and for all the other people who loved him. I thought about the hunting trophies I had collected over the years and I contacted Everett Wilkensen of Bischoff's, the famous taxidermist in Los Angeles, to see what he could do."[8]

Dale Evans and Dusty Rogers protested the plan, arguing for a funeral and a final resting place with a monument at a pet cemetery, but Rogers' mind was set. According to one source, Dale Evans once said, 'All right. But when you go, I'm gonna have YOU stuffed and put on top of Trigger!' Roy said, 'Fine. Just make sure I'm smiling.'[9] (In 2005 the Branson Hollywood Wax Museum gave a Roy Rogers wax figure to Rogers' new museum by to be placed next to Trigger.)

Roy Rogers ordered that Trigger be mounted in a rearing position in full regalia: bridle, saddle, and martingale. He always referred to Trigger as having been "mounted," not "stuffed" and would correct anyone if they used the latter term. An animal whose hide has been filled with sawdust is stuffed. An animal whose hide is stretched over a cast is mounted. After a taxidermist takes an animal's measurements, a Styrofoam mold is made, over which a fiberglass frame is created. The Styrofoam is removed after the fiberglass hardens. Finally, the animal hide is stretched over the fiberglass mold.

Roy Rogers had a very special place in mind for his four-legged co-star. Trigger was placed on display at the Roy Rogers and Dale Evans Museum in Victorville, California, where he stood until he was moved with the museum collection to Branson, Missouri, in 2003.

More than once, Rogers said that he had Trigger mounted because he couldn't bear the thought of putting the horse into the ground. This statement suggests that the horse was preserved in his entirety, which of course is untrue—possibly the most erroneous statement Rogers ever made about Trigger. In actuality, all that was preserved of Trigger was his hide, mane, and tail. Everything else that made up the fabulous animal—his

The original Trigger in his last pose, compliments of Bischoff's Taxidermy.

heart, brain, internal organs, eyes, and so on—were disposed of.[10] What was preserved was ironically a facade, an illusion, if you will.

Animals, like humans, grey as they age. According to Dusty Rogers in his autobiography, "Trigger lived to be 33 years old—more than 100 years in human terms. His golden hair had grayed considerably, and he was gray around his eyes and ears." It's entirely possible the taxidermist "enhanced" the markings on Trigger's face and put some makeup on his near side. One wonders how much cosmetic work was involved in the mounting process, especially since Trigger does not have any of the regal majesty he had when he was alive. The subtlety of his features is missing, along with much of his musculature. He doesn't even have the definition of a carousel horse. His thick mane and forelock, much of what gave Trigger his beauty, had thinned out, devoid of shape and sheen. If the eyes are truly the windows to the soul, the effect of glass substitutes is that of an empty stare. Like all mounted animals, Trigger looks vacuous, without personality. Trigger was truly an old man when he died, and that's what the taxidermist had to work with: an aged horse.[11]

There is little doubt that Roy Rogers loved the original Trigger. There is also little doubt that Rogers' humble beginning had a huge impact, and he was reluctant to part with material things as demonstrated by what was on display at the Victorville museum. However, Rogers would have done his beloved horse and his fans a greater service had he let Trigger remain a beautiful memory, rather than turn him into a generic substitute of past glory. The life-size bronze De L'Esprie sculpted for the plaza of the Autry National Center in Los Angeles is a far better tribute to Gene Autry and his Champion(s) than

Roy Rogers with the original Trigger on his Chatsworth ranch circa 1963. The horse was retired in 1957 and was showing signs of advanced age (Roy Dillow collection).

the mounted morbid remains of poor old Trigger. It's almost too bad the technology did not exist to freeze-dry Trigger. This eliminates most of the procedure used in traditional taxidermy. The results are much closer to the actual look of a particular subject.[12]

In his final form, Trigger requires regular upkeep. An exterminator is called in to make sure bugs and parasites do not damage his hide. His glass eyes are polished with window spray. His coat, mane and tail still require brushing.[13]

Unfortunately Rogers' decision to have Trigger mounted did not sit well with most fans and the poor old horse became the butt of jokes. "More hay, Trigger?" "No thanks, Roy, I'm stuffed!"[14]

As mentioned earlier, Trigger was not the only animal connected to Roy Rogers who ended up at the taxidermist's. Dale Evans may have originally protested Trigger's fate, but her Quarter Horse gelding, Buttermilk, ended up the same way. Penny Edwards remarked, "I started doing Roy's pictures when Dale was having a baby. I rode Buttermilk first. Years later, when I went to the Roy Rogers Museum, I almost fainted. I knew Roy had Trigger stuffed, but I did not realize that Buttermilk was there too; I loved that horse. I used to go out to Glenn Randall Sr.'s ranch and practice on Buttermilk."[15]

One of Rogers' "Bullet" German shepherds was mounted and joined the others on display at the museum. Trigger Jr. also suffered the same fate and ended up on open display mounted and fully tacked. Unfortunately he was positioned in a very unflattering, dancing pose. To make matters worse, his head and neck were placed in such a way that he looks ewe necked—(a neck bowed not arched). It is surprising that an experienced horseman like Rogers allowed such a basic fault in conformation, especially since Trigger Jr. wasn't ewe-necked when he was alive.

Of all Roy Rogers' animals, Little Trigger had the most dignified exit; he was not mounted. Perhaps that was his best reward for contributing so much to Roy Rogers' career. Nevertheless, Joel "Dutch" Dortch, member of the Happy Trails Foundation, stated, "Roy told me he sure regretted not having Little Trigger mounted and placed in the museum as he did Trigger and Trigger Jr."

In 2010 *The Boston Globe* ran an essay by Associated Press writer Sue Manning titled "Trigger's Taxidermist Now Busy with TV Werewolves" In it she wrote,

> —Bischoff's Taxidermy and Animal FX (as it's now called) is one of the largest movie and television animal prop rental warehouses on the West Coast. It was there retired taxidermist Everett Wilkensen preserved Trigger, "the smartest horse in the movies," along with Dale Evans' horse Buttermilk and the couple's German Shepherd Bullet. Bischoff's owner Gary Robbins estimated it cost $10,000 to $12,000 to mount Trigger in 1965. As of 2017 Bischoff's Taxidermy and Animal FX is still in business and it's never been better. They manufacture animal props for movies, television, music videos and commercial advertising campaigns. Wolf and werewolf gore are the company's most requested props these days.

Bischoff's Taxidermy and Animal FX has been referred to as the "House that Trigger Built."

Horseman, Pass By

Appearing on *A&E Biography* toward the end of his life, Roy Rogers remarked, "The sad part about getting up in years, I think, most of all my sidekicks are gone. It's sad. My horse's gone. But it's life." On July 6, 1998, Rogers, too, passed away.

Roy Rogers and Trigger, two sides of the same coin, in mid-career transitioning from movies to television.

Roy Rogers' family intended that he go out with the same flair with which he lived. That was obvious from his funeral, with its honor guard, horse-drawn caisson, and such. However, given all the "Triggers" Rogers used throughout his career, one wonders why there wasn't a palomino look-alike present. As a very important part of Rogers' image, "Trigger" in fancy show saddle should have been part of the funeral procession. Rogers' trademark white hat could have hung off the right side of the saddle horn, one of his colorful neckerchiefs on the other side, and reversed boots in the stirrups like the "missing man" formation during an Air Force funeral. A riderless palomino would have been a memorable and powerful statement.[16]

When it came to his career, Roy Rogers often cited three lucky breaks: Gene Autry going into the army; being able to sneak on to the Republic Pictures lot for an audition after he learned (almost by accident) that the studio was looking for a singing cowboy; and finding Trigger. Rogers said, "Without those three incidents, there wouldn't have been a Roy Rogers."[17] The golden palomino helped make the King of the Cowboys, and, to that degree, Trigger is not only a bittersweet memory of days gone by; he was the best friend Roy Rogers ever had.[18]

This writer was honored to be quoted in *American Cowboy* magazine (November/December 1998) on the occasion of Roy Rogers's passing, "The morning the King of the Cowboys died, Roy's trusty sidekick Gabby Hayes was waiting with Trigger all saddled and ready. Gabby, in his inimitable style, probably shouted, 'Thar's some bad hombres up to no good and we've gotta stop 'em!' Roy mounted up, Trigger reared beautifully on his two hind legs and they were off into that never-ending sunset."

My Pal Trigger

Roy Rogers rose to fame about the same time teenage girls turned Frank Sinatra into a craze. When Elvis Presley first appeared on *The Ed Sullivan Show* in February of 1956, rock and roll was in high gear. Members of Roy Rogers' fan base were becoming teenagers and moving on. In February of 1964, when the Beatles first appeared on *The Ed Sullivan Show,* a cultural paradigm shift occurred and baby boomers were never quite the same. Still, silent waters run deep and childhood heroes have a strong hold. Though Rogers and Trigger had become distant memories for young adults, by the end of the decade a nostalgia boom hit. Michael Lang, the creative force behind the Woodstock music festival in 1969 (four years after Trigger's death), wanted Rogers to sing "Happy Trails" after Jimi Hendrix's headlining appearance. "I had this inner dream I grew up listening to Roy Rogers sing 'Happy Trails' on the radio and I thought, 'What a perfect way to end the show.' He was the only artist who turned us down. He didn't get it at all."[19] Rogers lived another 29 years.

I last visited the Roy Rogers and Dale Evans Museum in the late spring of 1998 when it was still in Victorville. I went fully aware that Roy Rogers was in poor health and would not be around much longer. I wanted to see him one last time.

Fittingly, it was right after I'd left the Trigger display that I heard someone say, "There's Roy!" I looked down a dimly lit hallway and saw a distinctive silhouette—a figure in a familiar flat-topped-styled cowboy hat with the "Denton Pinch" creased crown. Rogers was driving a grey motorized cart in my direction and stopped directly in front of me. A crowd gathered and flash bulbs began going off. Although I was speechless as I stared into his familiar eyes, I managed to extend my hand. The King of the Cowboys' grip was weak.

Roy Rogers was dressed as one would expect: Western dress pants, black boots, a bolo tie, a Western shirt, and a jacket. Between heart attacks, angina, and diabetes, he looked every bit of 86 years. Decades of touring and making movies showed on the old cowboy's face. He was a little slouched over, looked a little heavy, and his thinning hair was grey. Age spots dotted his face, his breathing was irregular, and he was hard of hear-

One of the last known photographs of Roy Rogers and the original Trigger. Rogers was 52 and Trigger was around 30 at the time. Trigger's mane had thinned out. Within a year after this photograph was taken, the great palomino had passed away (Roy Dillow collection).

ing—probably due to all the gunfire he'd been exposed to on movie sets and hunting trips.

A bodyguard accompanied Roy Rogers, obviously there to make sure enthusiastic fans did not overwhelm their hero. In his fragile state, Rogers could not tolerate a strong hug. A woman gently put her arm around him while another told Rogers what joy he'd brought to everyone's lives. Women teared up and grown men became little boys.

As fans continued to take pictures I discreetly asked the bodyguard about Rogers' health. He candidly replied, "He's not going to be around much longer." My mood went from wonder to bittersweet. Seeing my boyhood hero old and frail was difficult. Everyone present could see he was close to the end.

Roy Rogers was a hero and father figure to a generation who grew up on his movies. Still though a common experience, for some of us he was a private obsession. I will always regret that I could not have a long private conversation with him. I had many questions to ask about his horses, but the time for interviewing him had long past. Rogers had only minutes to reciprocate his fans' individually; no one could feel he owed more after a lifetime entertaining them.

Fantasy and illusion were Roy Rogers' art, and the line between that art and reality blurred. He may have started out merely as an entertainer creating a celebrity persona for himself and his horse, but they represented much more.

While B-westerns may have been conceived as cheap entertainment and simple morality plays, they too became more. Roy Rogers' movies were made with sublime innocence and down-to-earth artistry (especially with regards to horsemanship) at a time when their simple values rang straight and true. In these cynical times with antiheroes as the norm, Rogers' glorious black-and-white movies exist in an eternal state of hope as cinematic anachronisms. Devoted fans require no mature plot lines, no revisionist analysis; it's enough that Rogers and Trigger weren't afraid to meet injustice head on and fight it with great style no matter the odds. Optimism was at their core.

It's a common misconception that B-westerns were only popular with children. Not everyone, especially in the '30s, identified with gangsters and wealthy socialites. The migration that took place at that time from the farm to the city was massive and those involved saw themselves much more readily in Gene Autry and Roy Rogers than they did in William Powell. People could identify with cowboys and their fight against crooked

Trigger the way to remember him best: young and vital. In his present mounted state he only bears a faint resemblance to the glorious creature he once was (Roy Dillow collection).

bankers and corrupt businessmen who wanted their land. Dr. Peter Stansfield in his book, *Horse Opera: The Strange History of the 1930s Singing Cowboy* (University of Illinois Press, 2002) "challenges the commonly held view of the singing cowboy as an ephemeral figure of fun and argues instead that he was one of the most important cultural figures to emerge out of the Great Depression ... small-town film goers saw their ambitions, fantasies, and desires embodied in the singing cowboy and their social and political circumstances dramatized in B-westerns."

Loyal fans could never be angry with Roy Rogers for his dogged adherence to his own public relations. We all have too much affection and respect for him as an entertainer and as a man. Rogers had a career plan and knew public relations were vital to his success. Beyond that, he gave his fans a moral code and the promise of better things, not to mention great entertainment and a wonderful fantasy. As a storyteller he created and nurtured two of the best characters of all time. If I had to do it all over, I wouldn't think twice about believing those fantasies again. Rogers may have embellished the truth and no one was lesser for it.

While many continue to take Roy Rogers at face value and believe everything he said, there are those of us who temper our affection and respect with experience. We remain devoted to his legend—Trigger's too—and all the wonderful things the legends stood for. Their public personas were an unspoken agreement between them and their fans. We were playing make-believe together. Trigger belonged to us all. He was our pal too.

19

Golden Sunset, Blue Shadows

*"He's not for sale at any price. I couldn't part with him. But more
important than that, he's not really mine—he belongs to children
everywhere."*—Roy Rogers referring to Trigger[1]

*"The art of writing is the art of discovering
what you believe."*—Gustave Flaubert

Discussing the demise of the Roy Rogers collection and his waning legacy, with Trigger as the focal point, is a bit like crying over spilt milk. The museum closings, the move to Branson, the auctions, the fate of the taxidermied palomino, resonated with fans because of Roy Rogers' and Trigger's iconic statures. Fans held them in such high esteem, they hated seeing their legacy fade.

Hardcore Roy Rogers fans remain divided: those who believed his legacy would stay strong despite the move to and closing of the Branson museum and auction of his collection, versus devotees who were not pleased by what little was done to preserve and insure his legacy even if only while his fan base was still alive.

"Trigger" carried Roy Rogers (and his family by extension) on his back for over two decades (1938–1960). His likeness stood in front of Roy Rogers' museum and was essential to the Roy Rogers brand. The neglect of Rogers' movies was bad enough, but the public auction of Trigger was seen as a betrayal to some, something we believed would never happen. More to the point, Trigger's auction in 2010, was emblematic of the over-all problems Rogers' legacy began to face in the brief 12 years after he passed.

As Trigger's self-appointed and unauthorized biographer, I am compelled to comment on the failure of relevant parties who did not secure key elements of the Roy Rogers legacy. I was never part of the family inner circle, but I have a fan's distance and perspective. I've talked to a number of hardcore Roy Rogers devotees and found a consensus. I've tried to be fair with admittedly very emotional issues.

Individuals whose celebrity lives on after their fan base goes are rare at best. In another two or three decades Roy Rogers' fans may be all but gone. His legacy and core collection may be of even lesser significance. Rogers and Trigger, as popular as they were at their zenith, do not regenerate fans, contemporary audiences are not aware they ever existed. With Elvis Presley new generations continue to show interest and replace fading baby boomers. That being said, Trigger is gone and what remains is a facade, so why make a fuss? Underneath the Roy Rogers brand over decades was honesty, fair play and happy endings. Trigger stood for all that in a way not even his master could. Purity, how-

Trigger at the Van Nuys wash behind the Randall Ranch, like riding on the beach (Roy Dillow collection).

ever ethereal and imagined, is a scarce commodity (especially these days), Trigger was sacred ground. To quote Shakespeare, he was "such stuff as dreams are made on."

Three Museums

THE AUTRY MUSEUM OF THE AMERICAN WEST

Comparisons between the Autry Center and The Roy Rogers and Dale Evans Museum are understandable but ultimately unfair. The former is a world-class corporate-sponsored research center devoted to the American West. The latter was a modest family-run tourist destination celebrating a Hollywood celebrity and his horse.

It was always Gene Autry's wish to build a museum in Los Angeles dedicated the American West. He got things started by donating much of the initial capital. He was able to negotiate a deal with Griffith Park which is situated next to the Los Angeles Zoo.

Gene Autry had corporate backers (such as Wells Fargo) as would anyone aiming to construct a multi-million dollar institution. The Autry Center was established in 1988; in October 2015 it began using the name The Autry Museum of the American West. There are now two physical sites some eight miles apart that attract about 150,000 visitors a year.

As if looking back on his fabulous life and career, Roy Rogers and Trigger (Rocky Roe collection).

THE ROY ROGERS MUSEUM IN APPLE VALLEY

While Roy Rogers acknowledged The Autry Center as a fine place, his own museum was not conceived with such grandiose goals. He did not have nearly the capital nor did he seek corporate backing. His museum was modest, dedicated to his life and celebrity. A bowling alley across the street from the Apple Valley Inn (Rogers had a contract with management to use his name and display museum pieces; he was not an owner) was converted into a museum, circa 1965. It was located in Southern California's high desert, minutes from where Rogers lived and where he planned to be buried.

Rogers' museum was conceived with a twofold purpose: a venue for his fans to see his personal mementos, which he transferred from the trophy room on his Chatsworth ranch, and an office to conduct his business affairs.[2] Roy Rogers saw his mini enterprise as self-sustaining, if it made money all the better. He referred to it as "kind of a Western Disneyland." When Trigger died in 1965, he was kept at the taxidermist's until the museum opened in 1967. At the time Rogers was still actively touring and making television appearances, subsequently he wasn't available to fans at the museum, certainly not like later when he expanded his holdings and relocated to Victorville in 1976.

THE ROY ROGERS AND DALE EVANS MUSEUM IN VICTORVILLE

Constructed on land owned by Rogers just off Interstate 15 in the high-desert city of Victorville, two hours northeast of Los Angeles, the second venue was renamed The Roy Rogers and Dale Evans Museum and included a business office and modest gift shop. In front of its Fort Apache-styled structure, the museum featured a huge statue of Trigger in the classic rearing pose. At the museum's peak of popularity it was estimated some 200,000 visitors attended each year, and most of them went mainly to see the palomino. Dusty Rogers said, "We close at five and stop selling tickets at 4:30. But people come after that and beg to get in for a few minutes. They drove 3,000 miles just to see Trigger. We let them in—and they go away, happy."[3]

Of the six Roy Rogers' siblings only Cheryl and Dusty showed real interest in the museum and capitalized on the Rogers brand name. It was only when they became full-time employees that things changed. Plans were made to move a family museum into the twentieth century thinking that by adding bells and whistles it would somehow develop into something that it was never intended to be. Ultimately it existed so fans could visit and possibly meet their hero because Roy Rogers and Dale Evans often showed up to greet people. When they died that opportunity died with them.

Roy Rogers was not a businessman in the Fortune 500 sense, preferring instead simple pleasures like family and outdoor sports. He never invested in stocks, oil, bonds, etc. Though Rogers made lots of money in the 1950s through merchandising, and other methods, he lost a lot through bad luck and poor investments.

ROY ROGERS' WISHES

Roy Rogers' will (which was made public, as is common for show business people) passed all of the contents of the museum on to Dale Evans; upon her death their six surviving children would inherit. Those contents included the three mounted horses and one dog. Family attorneys/accountants recommended that in order to avoid the punitive

The King of the Cowboys and Queen of the West riding double on the fabulous Trigger (Roy Dillow collection).

death duties following her death, she transfer the animals into a separate charitable trust not subject to death duties. The horses rightly or wrongly were considered the most valuable assets. As it turned out, upon Evans' death, the government audited everything with the exception of the horses and dog, and death duties were duly paid out of the proceeds of the estate's other equities.

For years the official word from the Roy Rogers Museum was that Trigger, particularly, would go to a public institution. Shortly after the King of the Cowboy's death in 1998, *Los Angles Times* reporter Patricia Ward Biederman noted in her essay "Museum May Be at End of the Trail," "Whether or not the museum relocates, (Dusty) Rogers said, the family has already decided where Trigger and the other animals will ultimately go, the Smithsonian or a Los Angeles–area museum devoted to Hollywood history. (Dusty) Rogers said he couldn't face his parents in heaven if he allowed the animals to fall into indifferent hands. 'Trigger and Buttermilk have to go somewhere where they're treasured,'" After Roy Rogers' passing Dale Evans echoed Dusty's comments on her gospel television show, upon her death Trigger was to go to the Smithsonian Institution.[4]

DUSTY'S DREAM

Roy Rogers, Jr. ("Dusty"), wanted to perform and be a star, he was born into show business. Though in his youth Dusty left home and tried a number of careers (disc jockey and construction), show business was always a possibility. Nepotism was a factor and he can't be faulted for taking advantage. Throughout his life Dusty had exposure (sometimes with his siblings) on television specials, commercials, parades, live appearances, comic book covers, etc. He had a supporting role in *Arizona Bushwhackers* (Paramount Pictures, 1968) with Howard Keel and Yvonne De Carlo. He hosted a television variety program *The Roy Rogers, Jr. Show*. During a *Fall Guy* (ABC, 1981–1986) episode he serenaded his father with his composition, "King of the Cowboys." Dusty Rogers had plenty of opportunities to launch a career while he was a young man, certainly more than most Hollywood hopefuls.

The death of Roy Rogers' long time agent Art Rush created a void, and Dusty took over management of his dad's then-limited show business career. That path got Dusty more involved with his father's museum, eventually taking over from his sister Cheryl.

Patricia Ward Biederman noted in her *Los Angeles Times* essay, "Decline in visitors and a tax bill could force the Roy Rogers–Dale Evans collection out of Victorville. Because of its limited appeal—its graying visitors and Victorville's isolation on the edge of the Mojave Desert—the museum is on the brink of relocation, if not extinction."

Biederman went on to state that the curator, 55-year-old Dusty Rogers, announced he might pack up the family memorabilia, including Trigger, and move the museum elsewhere to a proven tourist destination, most likely Branson, Missouri. She wrote:

> The most urgent threat to the museum is a pending tax bill. The facility operates in the black, Rogers said, but it has to worry about rising energy costs and other expenses. And although the museum is nonprofit, its contents were subject to inheritance taxes that came due in the wake of Evans' death. Evans transferred the most precious artifacts—Trigger, Buttermilk, Trigger Jr. and Bullet—into a trust before she died, so the family will not owe anything on Trigger's assessed value of $400,000.
>
> When Roy Rogers was in his final years it very unlikely he gave a thought to moving the Victorville museum to Branson. Is there a public record of him suggesting it? One assumes the same for Dale Evans, she was also retired when her son Roy "Dusty" Rogers Jr. approached her with the idea." Biederman arrived at the same solution many fans did, "It's at this point, and with hindsight, the family should have liquidated the majority of their parents collection and holdings, kept a core collection, and set up a modest venue, perhaps in the Los Angeles area."

At an advanced age, it's very doubtful Dale Evans would have instigated a complex and herculean move halfway across the country, especially at enormous expense.[5] It's also doubtful Dusty Rogers' non-show business siblings were on board at first for such a move. The relocation to Branson was instigated by Dusty. A source close to the museum claimed the majority of the board was convinced to move by him and a Branson Chamber of Commerce representative. Dusty, hoping to save the declining attendance in Victorville, believed a move to the booming Branson might be the answer. Cheryl was out-voted by the other siblings and the move went forward.[6]

Dusty Rogers told the Associated Press. "We have to survive." With their passing the IRS levied a 58 percent tax on the estate, not including a nearly $150,000 property

Little Trigger takes a bow after a performance with Roy Rogers on May 20, 1951, during "I Am an American Day" at the Hollywood Bowl in Los Angeles (Roy Dillow collection).

tax bill. This was why surviving family members considered moving the museum to a more heavily trafficked tourist area, such as Las Vegas or Branson, Missouri. "If the museum doesn't survive here," Rogers said of Victorville, "it will somewhere else."[7]

The Roy Rogers and Dale Evans Museum in Branson

In 2003 Graebel Los Angeles Movers Inc. moved nine truckloads of memorabilia and household goods from Victorville, California, to Branson, Missouri. The new Roy Rogers and Dale Evans Museum was 26,000 square feet and occupied four acres. Neither the building or land was owned by the family. Located at 3950 Green Mountain Drive, the building included a 300-seat theatre home base for Dusty Rogers and his band the High Riders. Dusty's son Dustin was appointed general manager to run the museum, theater, and gift shop with the help of other family members.

The museum displays were arranged on both sides of a horseshoe-shaped walk which resembled an old western town. The centerpiece behind glass was the taxidermied Trigger. A 23.5-foot-tall fiberglass statue of him reared outside the museum. (In April of 2003 a seven-man crew took almost two hours to install it.)

In his mid–50s, Dusty Rogers was set to ride out his career in his own venue until retirement. Many an audience member who attended his shows in Branson found them heartfelt and enjoyed his singing voice and family anecdotes. In theory the move made sense were it not for the fact that a Roy Rogers' Museum had a limited life expectancy given its demographic. Dusty believed a theatre would increase people's interest in the museum, the two attractions would mutually complement each other. For a while he was possibly correct, however the operating budget as big as the one the museum carried would eventually exceed its income. Fifty thousand dollars plus a month requires a lot of people going through the turnstile just to cover expenses. Instead of cutting its losses in California the museum ended up in a situation where it was forced to close and sell its contents to partially finance an enormous debt. This debt included the cost of breaking a lease with new property owners. Dusty Rogers and company had boarded the *Titanic* and were doomed to hit an iceberg. The theatre and museum were expected to last around 15 years, longer if things went well. They closed in six.[8]

Though for a time the move made sense, in an essay titled "The Rise and Fall of Branson" from the *Distributist Review* published in 2016, Kevin O'Brien writes, "Branson, it seems, is in a long decline. The reason is, in part, demographic. In the 1990s, tour busses from all over North America were flocking to Branson, carrying senior citizens who longed for the mixture of musical variety shows, patriotism and corn-pone hillbilly humor—along with all-you-can-eat buffets—that made Branson a huge success. But this generation has largely passed on, and in its place are middle class, middle-aged Americans who don't plan on seeing eight shows in three days, who have no idea who the Lennon Sisters were, and who are certainly leery of the timeshare explosion that drained a good deal of money from Branson visitors in the past."

Postmortem

MOUNTING TRIGGER

Trigger was the most popular attraction at the Roy Rogers and Dale Evans Museum. Fan reaction to him post-taxidermy was either bittersweet or morbid. Beyond Roy Rogers himself, fans or reporters did not tend to describe Trigger in his final state as beautiful. Comparing photos of the palomino in his glory days to him after taxidermy, he looks like two different animals.

Following his death in 1932, the great Australian race horse Phar Lap was mounted by a New York City taxidermist and placed in an airtight controlled case in the Melbourne Museum. This writer would go so far as to say he looks almost life-like. Comanche, the alleged sole survivor of the Battle of the Little Big Horn, was first mounted in 1891 then restored in 2005 and also placed in an airtight controlled case. The key phrase here being "airtight controlled case."

No matter how one felt about Roy Rogers' decision to have Trigger mounted, he should have ensured Trigger's proper care in perpetuity but did not seem to have specified anything in writing. Dale Evans may have thought it was taken care of when she made an outright gift of Trigger to the museum shortly before her death but apparently it was not. They both dropped the ball, leaving their children to follow through.[9]

TRIGGER AND THE SMITHSONIAN

Sources close to Roy Rogers acknowledged his wish that Trigger be donated to the Smithsonian (no mention of the other animals) upon closure of the museum in Victorville. Earlier he apparently politely refused: "Upon hearing of Trigger's death the Smithsonian Institute in Washington, D.C. asked Roy for Trigger's body for their collection of historical Americana. Roy declined, not wanting Trigger's final resting place to be so far away from himself out in California" (www.royrogersworld.com). For years it was assumed that Trigger would indeed end up there, but in reality the Smithsonian never seemed to be a top contender. Even at that, it was understood, or at least implied, that a similar institution would be Trigger's final destination.

Responding to an e-mail inquiry by Jerry Dean, Valeska M. Hilbig, deputy director, Office of Public Affairs, Smithsonian's National Museum of American History wrote: "When the Museum was approached a few months ago about this donation, our curatorial team carefully considered the offer, as is procedure for all such offers. While the museum is interested in the Roy Rogers story and was honored to be considered for this donation, it was determined that this Museum is not in a position to properly care for, store or display a taxidermied animal. However, at the same time, we requested to explore the possibility to collect other, smaller items from the show with less of a conservation challenge. Our curator did not hear back, regretfully. Of course, we remain interested in exploring other options."

In a May 2006 e-mail exchange between Dave Koch, internet administrator for the Roy Rogers and Dale Evans Museum (and Dusty Rogers' son-in-law) and Joel Dutch Dortch, executive director at Happy Trails Children's Foundation, Koch wrote: "During Museum Board of Directors meeting in Apple Valley in 2004 Dusty Rogers was asked about the possibility of the Smithsonian owning Trigger, etc. He denied there was any truth to the rumor. Trigger, Trigger Jr., Buttermilk, their saddles, and Nellybelle are all owned by the Roy Rogers and Dale Evans Museum itself. His stepmother Dale Evans made an outright gift of them to the Museum shortly before her death in December 2000. Dusty Rogers said that if and when the Roy Rogers and Dale Evans Museum ceased to do business, being organized as a charitable organization under the IRS Code section 501(c)(3), the Museum had to distribute their assets (Trigger, etc.) to another non-profit organization like the Buffalo Bill Museum in Cody, Wyoming or the National Cowboy Hall of Fame and Museum. It is not believed that Trigger, etc. will ever end up in the Autry Museum. In the end, Trigger, etc., will never be owned by a collector, fan, or private individual. The Smithsonian has expressed interest in Trigger, and it will be his last stop when we are done. Nellybelle belongs to the Rogers family."

It was a shock when it was revealed in 2010 that Trigger (along with Buttermilk, Trigger Jr., Bullet and Pat Brady's Nellybelle Jeep) would be sold at auctions co-sponsored by Christie's (New York) and High Noon (Arizona). Apparently the Rogers Museum owed over $1.5 million and the highest value assets were the horses and their tack.

As to selling off the rest of the collection, Roy Rogers specified in his original will and trust, that everything was to be sold off upon his death and the proceeds divided between his children. He never thought the museum would continue, that is why he did not endow it! It was only after Dusty started the ill-fated RogersDale project (a theme park dedicated to Americana built using the Victorville museum as its centerpiece and including 20 acres of Roy Rogers owned property) and turned the museum into a

501(c)(3) (a charitable tax free arrangement with the government) that anyone talked about the museum surviving the King of the Cowboys.

CHRISTIE'S AUCTION

The Roy Rogers and Dale Evans Museum collection was offered to the highest bidders at Christie's Fine Art Auctions in New York City on July 14 and 15, 2010. Collectors got to bid on one-of-a-kind items that the King of the Cowboys actually used. The audience included bidders from as far as England, Germany, and Japan. None of the 347 lots went unsold. The total realized was $2.98 million, according to Christie's, which ran the sale with High Noon Americana. NBC's *Today Show* carried a segment on the auction the day before, Trigger's impeding sale was also covered on *NBC Nightly News* and by major print and online services.[10]

Patrick Gottsch, founder and president of RFD-TV won Trigger for $266,500. The palomino's iconic Bohlin saddle went separately to a private buyer for $386,500. Gottsch

Roy Rogers on Trigger and Dale Evans on Golden Empress after the climatic race in the 1946 *My Pal Trigger* (Roy Dillow collection).

claimed he'd heard from thousands of relieved Rogers fans, "I've received so many e-mails of thank you, just wonderful letters, saying 'Thank you for saving Trigger.'" At the conclusion of the Christie's auction the attendees broke into a spontaneous rendition of "Happy Trails."[11]

The auction of Trigger was a bitter pill for many a hardcore fan. This writer recalled how Roy Rogers felt after the climactic race in *My Pal Trigger*, when he lost to Dale Evans on the Golden Empress. She thanked him after for sacrificing the win by holding back and helping her out of a forced pocket by two heavies, not knowing he was promised ownership of Trigger if he'd won. As she shook his hand she said,

"Roy, all I can say is thank you. I know it cost you the race."

He replied, "It cost me a lot more than that."

RFD-TV—Television Like It Used to Be

If Roy Rogers' legacy, material and otherwise, was going to be saved while his core demographic was still alive, help would have to come from outside his family.

The RFD-TV network is headquartered in Omaha with a production studio in Nashville and branch offices in Dallas, Denver and Atlanta. At first company president Patrick Gottsch announced plans to display both Trigger and Bullet in a new downtown Omaha headquarters in 2011. They were displayed across the country in 2017. Trigger was by then displayed in a generic copy of the tack he once used.

Patrick Gottsch said that there would only be one owner of Trigger and that was Roy Rogers; he considered RFD-TV to be just a caretaker. While a nice thing to say and fans no doubt appreciated the sentiment, RFD-TV and Gottsch own the most important and beloved material remains of Roy Rogers' legacy, from now on they will be calling the shots.

Shortly after the Christies auction RFD-TV published its bi-monthly magazine (September/October 2010) with a cover featuring Roy Rogers with his horse and dog along with the blurb, "Welcome to RFD-TV Trigger and Bullet." In the "President's Letter" column, on the inside cover, founder and president Patrick Gottsch offered a statement having to do with the network's plans for its new acquisitions. "Our plans our simple. We are going to do everything possible to honor the original reason that Roy Rogers started a museum with Trigger and Bullet in the first place—to keep the western spirit alive. We plan on bringing Roy Rogers' movies back to rekindle the Saturday morning western starting in November reintroducing a whole new generation to our 'hero.' And, we want the public to come out and see Trigger and Bullet. (Especially the Kids.) Most of all, we want to make Roy Rogers, and his family, proud that RFD-TV has now taken up the reins. Happy Trails."

In the fall of 2010 RFD-TV, as promised, did indeed run vintage Roy Rogers movies on Saturdays, with Dusty Rogers hosting. For children brought up on high-definition letter-boxed computer-generated color cinematic extravaganzas, the task of reintroducing them to a black-and-white-baby-boomer-singing-cowboy-hero was, to say the least, daunting.

The RFD-TV network broadcast thirty-five pre–1949, edited, 54-minute titles of poor quality. Introductory background information, read by Dusty Rogers and his son Dustin, was limited mostly to cast member names (Roy Barcroft who?). No background, history, context, production notes or anecdotes were offered; instead, Dusty and the High Riders performed.

RFD-TV returned Trigger to Bischoff's Taxidermy for repairs in preparation for his Happy Trails tour in 2011, the 100th anniversary of Roy Rogers's birth. RFD-TV toured Trigger and Bullet's remains across the country for display at a number of venues, culminating with a Rose Parade appearance in January of 2012. One hundred golden palominos in ornate parade tack led their float. In 2014 RFD-TV eventually acquired Buttermilk. In 2016 The Texas Cowboy Hall of Fame at Fort Worth was the last stop of the tour for Roy Rogers' loyal companions.[12]

RFD-TV eventually purchased the Imus Ranch located just south of Santa Fe near Ribera, New Mexico, a western resort boasting some 3,000 acres complete with a 14,000-square-foot Hacienda, rodeo arena, greenhouse, etc., open to the public for family-oriented, western-themed vacations. As of March 2019, Trigger, Buttermilk and Bullet were on display in a western town setting.

AFTERMATH

Had Roy Rogers adopted "Dusty economics" and built himself an equivalent personal monument back in the late 1960s when he still had a sizable young fan base, even it would have eventually failed. Instead he wisely chose to build a modest self-contained and financially viable place that could withstand any shifts in the economy or even modest downturns in his own appeal. Personal museums are never cash cows unless you have the stature and lasting interest that the likes of an Elvis Presley or the Beatles have. It's doubtful if even a John Wayne museum would survive very long were it faced with similar Branson operating costs.

Dusty was probably sincere when he claimed he moved to Branson to promote his father's legacy. The mistake Dusty made was in seeing himself as that legacy. Just as there can only ever be one Elvis Presley, there will only ever be one Roy Rogers. Ads for Dusty's morning show in Branson declared "the legacy continues!" He did not understand the kingdom no longer existed, except in the stories and fading memories of an aging fan base. Branson theatre attendance eventually dwindled and Dusty found himself performing to a mostly empty house. It's obvious in retrospect how poor the decision was to relocate to Branson.[13]

Arguably, blame for the ultimate fates of the museum and its collection can be shared, however; Dusty Rogers was in charge, he was executor. Branson was his idea.[14] Things got worse and ended up in a lawsuit between siblings over misappropriation of funds, which ended in more or less a stalemate.[15]

Legacy

I have a great deal of affection and respect for Roy Rogers, what he stood for; what he accomplished from humble beginnings; the adversities he overcame; the difficult decisions he had to make; and the sacrifices he and those around him had to endure. However, coming to terms with any life requires sorting facts from fiction and drawing hard conclusions. Rogers was always seen in idealized terms; humanizing him is a task I tried to do fairly.

Roy Rogers remained essentially a country boy at heart; however, he was at times contradictory. He was not a saint, but putting his human weaknesses aside, he was fundamentally good and chose to live as much as anyone could as the highly idealized and grandiose character he created both on and off screen. Roy Rogers was willing to take risks and had the courage to reinvent himself, a scenario essential to the hero's path. The journey that country boy Leonard Frank Sly took to become Roy Rogers, the King of the Cowboys and idol of millions, was extraordinary.

Roy Rogers and Trigger are two sides of the same coin. He consistently signed his name along with that of his horse. For decades there has been an unspoken agreement in the press not to defile the image of Roy Rogers. Trigger was sacrosanct up until he was mounted and subsequently turned into a punch line.

While I would love to give this book a happy ending like the ones in Roy Rogers' movies, the best I can offer is a bittersweet close. Though Trigger is gone and only a facade remains, it's how his remains are perceived that offends. He was a breathtaking vision in real life, equine perfection on screen. In the end Trigger was denied his dignity by the King of the Cowboys himself; his fate as a lifeless artifact was sealed. For all his talent and good intentions, Roy Rogers was short on business acumen and foresight. The King of the Cowboys, bless him, wasn't perfect. He was flawed and made mistakes in judgment and, from what I've been told by those who knew him, would have been the first to admit them.

In 2007, Holly George Warren published *Public Cowboy No. 1—The Life and Times of Gene Autry*, a detailed history of the singing cowboy's work and a candid portrait of his life. Warren pulled no punches as she discussed Autry's bouts with booze and extramarital affairs. This more colorful side of Autry had been well known among hard core fans for decades and came as no shock. The real surprise was how Gene Autry's family, friends, and business associates supported Warren's work and gave her access to information. The inclusion of the unsavory in Warren's book does not seem to have diminished Autry with his fans, in fact it humanized him. The same applies to Roy Rogers. Is it any worse to know certain truths about Roy Rogers than it is to believe his public relations? It's doubtful Autry lost one serious fan after Warren's book was published. The same could be said for Rogers in similar circumstances. Beyond the trauma and tragedy of Beatle John Lennon's death, Roy Rogers and Gene Autry are the only two celebrities I shed a tear for when they passed.

GENE AUTRY THE CHAMPION

The same month Roy Rogers' collection was auctioned in New York, in contrast, *The Los Angeles Times* published a story on how the Autry Museum of the American West bought a facility in Burbank that would accommodate curatorial offices, laboratories, two research libraries and about 500,000 artworks and artifacts. The Research and Resource Center would enable the Autry museum to maintain all artifacts under pristine, controlled conditions so that the pieces remained safe for current and future scholars. Add this $75-million expansion to Autry's museum, to his restored movies and television shows, and to the preservation of his entire collection of memorabilia, and what you have is a lasting legacy.

Gene Autry is the only B-western star whose name will endure and carry the legacy of the B-western cowboy into the future and he will do so through the museum that bears his name. This great resource will remain viable for learning and entertainment for decades. Some B-western elements may also survive: the fancy Nudie Cohn–styled

clothes; Bohlin-styled tack; the influ-
ence of the stunt work in films; some
of the music ("Don't Fence Me In,"
"Back in the Saddle Again," "Happy
Trails," and "Tumbling Tumble
Weeds"); the "Hi Yo Silver" catch-
phrase; and possibly the image of a Roy
Rogers-type hero on a rearing horse.[16]

Between the modest Roy Rogers
display housed at the Apple Valley
Legacy Museum at the old Apple Valley Inn and the few items on display in
a gallery at the Autry Museum of the
American West, the King of the Cowboys still has a presence, albeit a small
one. The way Roy Rogers and Trigger
will be remembered in the future is
largely in the hands of the Autry staff,
bless them. The Autry Museum of the
American West became the permanent
home to the Roy Rogers and Dale

Gene Autry and Roy Rogers young and in their prime on the Republic lot.

Evans Archive, the largest collection gathered in one place. By 2019 the museum had
organized and cataloged the most of the collection and made it open for research by
appointment. The scope of the collection is breathtaking and contains publications, press
clippings, photographs, slides, promotional materials, correspondence, sheet music,
ephemera, and business records relating to the film, television, and recording careers
primarily from the 1940s until 2000.

RESTORING AND PRESERVING ROY ROGERS' MOVIES

As one of the founding members of the Sons of the Pioneers, Roy Rogers solidified
his place in western and country music history. Purists and historians will treasure the
classic harmonies and vivid western images that their ethereal music evokes for years to
come. Rogers' musical legacy is in pretty good shape. Companies such as Bear Family
Records made their catalog available. Likewise, performances from Rogers' solo career
were reissued (a Broadway show based on the life of Roy Rogers has been in development).

Unfortunately it's the Roy Rogers movies that remain in sad condition. A number
of poor quality copies may be accessed on YouTube, most are cut, some claim to be uncut.
Comparing Hopalong Cassidy and Gene Autry movies to those of Rogers is as depressing
as it is aggravating. There isn't one single outlet where Rogers' films are available fully
restored and in pristine condition (save for archived UCLA copies of *Trigger Jr.*, *Under
Western Stars* and the 2019 restoration of *Sunset in the West* by the Kino Lorber Studio).
His film history (newsreels, miscellaneous television appearances, guest spots), also of
cultural value and heartwarming to watch, are mostly unavailable.

Above everything else, Roy Rogers was a movie star. For all his touring, recording,
television, and personal appearances, his movies represent his finest moments and were

the foundation upon which he built his fabulous career. All the King of the Cowboys stood for is best exemplified by his silver screen persona. Our collective visits to his museums; the memorabilia we collected; the thrills experienced attending Roy Rogers rodeos; hours watching newsreels and television appearances; the wonderful music we listened to; the times spent reading books; were all ancillary to his movies.

Republic Pictures had a lot to do with the destruction of Roy Rogers' movies. Most

Roy Rogers and Trigger, western perfection, in their iconic signature rearing pose. No duo performed the stunt better.

all 35mm prints were transposed to 16mm for the one-hour time slots allowed on television. Republic also did the same to Gene Autry's movies but that didn't stop them from all being remastered. Autry had the foresight to keep full copies all along, buying them up when ever he could. Roy Rogers did not have that kind of vision unfortunately, and neither did his children.[17]

With the declining interest in B-western cowboys such as Roy Rogers, restoration of his films is important. A fair number of "restored" titles will be seen as sufficient should future film scholars choose to examine his film career. According to Mike Johnson, Roy Rogers' movies exist in a Paramount subsidiary company warehouse located in Glendale, California. The films are in proper storage and accompanied for the most part by their 35mm elements.[18]

Diehard fans would be thrilled with clean, uncut, restored, high-quality versions taken from the original 35mm elements, a solid body of work showcasing the cinematic charisma of Roy Rogers and Trigger for posterity.[19] As of this writing Paramount has restored over twenty movies but they are not commercially available.

TWILIGHT ON THE TRAIL

While Roy Rogers and Trigger had great luck and timing, they were about talent, hard work and sleight of hand. For those who think this book only served to debunk a fantasy, its objective was to understand how it came about and is an appreciation of the savvy and elbow grease required. Roy Rogers was blessed with good looks and charisma; his acting was more than appropriate for the B-western genre; he had a wonderful tenor voice; he could yodel better than just about anyone; he was a natural athlete; a gracefully accomplished rider; he was blessed with a multi-talented wife; he founded one of the best western groups of all time; he rode with the best sidekicks; he partnered with an expert horse trainer; his stuntmen were impeccable; and he damn sure rode some fine horses.

In the end Roy Rogers, Dale Evans and Trigger will have a presence thanks to the financial support and good graces of the Autry Museum of the American West, RFD-TV, the Apple Valley Legacy Museum, Paramount Pictures and the Spirit River Center. Thank you. If Trigger's remains can be maintained for another thirty years, that will see his hardcore fans to the end of their days.[20] While bittersweet, it's as happy as the trail is going to get, the family and fans who care for Roy Rogers and Trigger can be grateful.[21]

The Branson museum fiasco, Roy Rogers' tenuous legacy and the sale of his collection may all be seen as different sides of the same coin. The silver lining has to do with how the fantasy of Rogers and Trigger resonate with true fans and no amount of short-sightedness can take it away completely.[22] The King of the Cowboys and the Smartest Horse in the Movies are with us whenever we want, ours to cherish as we remember them best. They come to life every time we watch *My Pal Trigger*. So stay on that beautiful palomino while you can and don't let go. An anonymous Blackfoot warrior once wisely said, "When legends die so do dreams. When dreams die, so does greatness."

20

Trigger Timeline

*"I have six horses now at Sundance, and I'm partial to Palominos.
If you've ever gotten to know a horse, then you know color isn't
a consideration in their temperament, and yet as a kid I used to love
to watch Roy Rogers ride his Palomino, Trigger, off into the sunset.
I dreamed of having a horse like that."*—Robert Redford[1]

1911: Leonard Frank Sly is born in Cincinnati, Ohio. His family eventually moves to California.

1930: Len Slye teams with Tim Spencer and Bob Nolan to form the Pioneer Trio.

1934: A palomino colt with a wide blaze and one white stocking is born in San Diego, California, under the auspices of breeder, Captain Larry Good. • Len Slye helps found the Sons of the Pioneers.

1936: The palomino colt, now a two-year-old stud, is started under saddle.[2]

1937: Owner and ranch manager Roy Cloud of San Ysidro registers his colt as the Golden Cloud, with the Palomino Horse Association. • Although there is no documentation of the sale, it's during this year that the Golden Cloud was probably acquired by Hudkins Stables and is referred to as Pistol. • Little Trigger may have been born in this year, though there is no documentation. • Len Slye leaves the Sons of the Pioneers; Republic Pictures changes his name to Dick Weston and grooms him as its next singing cowboy star.

1938: The Golden Cloud/Pistol is ridden by actresses Priscilla Lane in *Cowboy from Brooklyn* and Olivia De Havilland in *The Adventures of Robin Hood*. • Dick Weston is renamed Roy Rogers for his first starring feature and selects Golden Cloud/Pistol as his on-screen mount. *Under Western Stars* marks the first B-western movie appearance by Roy Rogers and the newly named Trigger. • The first fictional account of how Rogers came to own Trigger is told at the beginning of the film *Come On, Rangers*.

1939: The Golden Cloud/Pistol is ridden by actor Gilbert Roland in the film *Juarez* and by Tyrone Power in *The Rains Came*. • Roy Rogers hires horse trainer Jimmy Griffin.

1940: Roy Rogers acquires Little Trigger to use in personal appearances. • Rogers appears without Trigger in a supporting role to John Wayne in the movie *Dark Command*.

1941: According to writer David Rothel, trainer Glenn Randall claimed to have started working with "Trigger," replacing Jimmy Griffin. • Trigger Jr. (registered name Allen's Gold Zephyr) is born May 11, his owner is Paul K. Fisher of Souderton, Pennsylvania. • Buttermilk is born.

Little Trigger on tour during the war and ready to entertain the troops (Roy Dillow collection).

1942: Roy Rogers and "Trigger" debut at the 17th annual Madison Square Garden Rodeo in October. During the show's run, "Trigger's" birthday is celebrated. • The Golden Cloud/Pistol is ridden by Victor Jory in *Shut My Big Mouth*. • The Golden Cloud/Pistol appears in the Charles Starrett movie *Bad Men of the Hills* as Russell Hayden's horse.

1943: Russell Hayden in *Silver City Raiders* rides Golden Cloud/Pistol. • The original Trigger is purchased by Roy Rogers from the Hudkins Brothers, with a final payment completing the total purchase price of $2,500. The Hudkins Stables bill of sale is dated September 18. This is the first official paperwork noting the horse's name as Trigger. By this time Rogers has made 40 movies with the palomino. • Roy Rogers and Little Trigger appear on the cover of *Life* magazine. • *Hands Across the Border* is released. It's the first movie where Trigger is central to the plot and the second fictional version of how Rogers came to own him. • Trigger gets screen credit and is billed as "the Smartest Horse in the Movies" for the first time, in *Silver Spurs*. • Little Trigger debuts in *Song of Texas*.

Noble "Kid" Chissel, as "Jim the outlaw," poses with Trigger on the set of *Song of Arizona* (1946). Who could blame the supporting actor for posing with his fabulous co-star? (Roy Dillow Collection).

1944: Roy Rogers and Trigger make their debut in *Four-Color Comics* (April). • Roy Rogers and Little Trigger appear in *Hollywood Canteen*. • *Lights of Old Santa Fe* is released, and Trigger drives the plot as part of an on screen package deal with Rogers that's being fought over by two rival rodeos. • Rogers rides "Trigger" on a war bond drive on the Paul Revere trail from Boston to Concord, Massachusetts.

1946: *My Pal Trigger* is released, the definitive fictional account of Trigger's beginnings. • According to *Screen Guide* magazine (October) Trigger is valued at $20,000. • Roy Rogers and the original Trigger appear at a parade in New York City before a Madison Square Garden rodeo.

1947: During a rodeo appearance at Chicago Stadium Roy Rogers (astride "Trigger") proposes to Dale Evans (riding Pal) while waiting to make their arena entrance (this story is disputed by some who believe that Rogers probably proposed over breakfast.) • A Transfer of Ownership for Allen's Gold Zephyr, a.k.a. Trigger Jr., is drawn between John Ewell and seller P.K. Fisher.

1948: *Roy Rogers Comics* makes its first appearance on newsstands in January. Trigger, of course, is part of the cast of characters. • *Under California Stars* is released in Trucolor. The plot centers around the kidnapping of Trigger. • Rogers buys the Hitching Post Theatre in Beverly Hills. He and Little Trigger place their footprints in cement in the courtyard.[3]

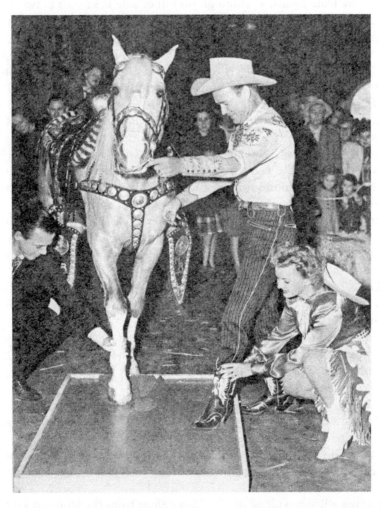

Roy Rogers and Dale Evans assist Little Trigger as he leaves his hoof prints in cement at the Hitching Post Theatre (which showed nothing but westerns) on Hollywood Boulevard in 1948. An entry sign commanded young fans to "Check Your Guns at the Box Office." Kids usually showed up in costume and fired cap pistols during gunfights on screen.

1949: In April 21, Roy Rogers and the original Trigger place their prints in cement at Grauman's Chinese Theatre in Hollywood. Dale Evans, Pat Brady, the Riders of the Purple Sage, Eddie Dean (master of ceremonies), and Hoot Gibson are in attendance.[4] • *The Golden Stallion* is released in Trucolor. • Rogers and Trigger appear on the cover of *Western Horseman* magazine in December. The lead feature is titled, "Trigger: First Get A Good Horse." • In December, King Features begins syndicating the Roy Rogers comic strip featuring Trigger to newspapers all across America. • *The Palomino Horse* by Doreen M. Norton is published. Trigger is referred to as "the best known Palomino in America." • Trigger's canine pal Bullet, a German shepherd, is born.

1950: *Trigger, Jr.*, is released in Trucolor. • *Trigger Tricks*, a weekly television show, is proposed. The series is intended to showcase all of his famous rodeo and personal appearance stunts. Roy Rogers makes his first Network television appearance promoting *Trigger Tricks* on *The Gabby Hayes Show*. • Buttermilk first appears in *Twilight in the Sierras*, ridden by Dale Evans. • Although no bill of sale is known between John Ewell and Roy Rogers, the PHBA provided a certificate of registration dated July 12, 1950 to certify Trigger Jr. was owned by Rogers.

1951: *Pals of the Golden West* is released and marks the last movie appearance by the original Trigger. • *The Roy Rogers Show* premieres, along with a 30-minute special that promos both the television show and the *Son of Paleface* movie, with Bob Hope. • *Roy Rogers' Trigger Comics* makes its debut in the Dell *Four-Color* series (May) and reportedly accounts for earnings of $10,000. • The third *Roy Rogers' Trigger Comics* (December) appears, sporting a cover by renowned equine illustrator Sam Savitt. • Businessman John Fergeson offers Roy Rogers $200,000 for Trigger (*Open Road* magazine 1952). • Roy Rogers pays $50,000 for the ruby-studded Crown Jewel saddle originally created by Edward H. Bohlin, Hollywood's foremost saddle maker and silversmith, for Mrs. H.L. Musick, a millionaire sportswoman from Los Angeles.

1952: In Los Angeles, actress Mabel Smeyne (aka Mable Smaney) files a lawsuit against Roy Rogers Enterprises. She alleges that Rogers and others recklessly failed to control "Trigger" on the movie set of *Son of Paleface*, allowing him to kick her. The jury renders a verdict in favor of Rogers and "Trigger."

1953: Little Trigger is among the guests who surprise Roy Rogers on the television show *This Is Your Life*. • "Trigger" wins a PATSY award (animal equivalent for the Oscar) for his role in *Son of Paleface*.

1955: *Roy Rogers Comics* becomes *Roy Rogers and Trigger Comics* in August. • The last issue of *Roy Rogers' Trigger Comics* (#17) is published. • Two biographies on Roy Rogers are published: *The Answer Is God* by Elise Miller Davis and *Roy Rogers: King of the Cowboys* by Frank Rasky. Both discuss "Trigger."

1957: The last of *The Roy Rogers Show* television episodes are completed. These half-hour black and white programs are the last filmed appearances of the original Trigger. • The original Trigger is retired at age 25 to the Rogers' ranch in Chatsworth, California.

1958: Roy and "Trigger" receive the Richard Craven Award from the American Humane Society. The award is presented annually for outstanding feats performed by animals before a live audience.

1960: During a live broadcast of *The Chevy Show* from the Houston Livestock Show and Rodeo in Texas "Trigger" is officially retired. After the episode Rogers never uses the original Trigger or Little Trigger in public again. According to Roy Dillow, Roy Rogers went so far as to present Trigger Jr. on tour as Trigger; then later in the same show as Trigger Jr.

Roy Rogers, on jockey attire no less, rides a thoroughbred in English tack during a steeplechase sequence in *Wall Street Cowboy* released in 1939 (Roy Dillow collection).

1963: Trigger is moved to Hidden Valley, California. Little Trigger dies this year or next; it is unknown precisely when.

1965: Trigger dies on July 3 at 31. Rogers decides to have him mounted by Bischoff's Taxidermy and Studio Prop Rental in Burbank, California. • Rogers contacts Fiber Glass Menagerie of Alpine, Colorado, to make a larger-than-life fiberglass likeness (23.5 feet tall) of his equine co-star.

1966: Bischoff's Taxidermy completes work on Trigger and he goes on display temporarily in their showroom.

1967: The first Roy Rogers museum is built in Apple Valley. Trigger is put on display. The fiberglass rearing-Trigger statue is placed at the entrance. • *Movie Horses: Their Treatment and Training* by Anthony Amaral is published; it includes a chapter on Trigger.

1969: Trigger Jr. dies at 28.

1972: Buttermilk dies at 31.

1976: The new museum, renamed the Roy Rogers and Dale Evans Museum, is completed in Victorville, California. • The *It's Showtime* movie documentary appears showcasing Trigger and a number of other Hollywood animal celebrities.

1977: The first VHS and Betamax machines become available to the general public. Old movies and television shows featuring Roy Rogers, Trigger and their peers are more accessible than ever. The nostalgia boom that hit in the early 1970s continues to thrive.

1979: *Happy Trails: The Story of Roy Rogers and Dale Evans*, by Roy Rogers with Carlton Stowers, is published; it includes a chapter on Trigger.

1980: *The Great Show Business Animals* by Dave Rothel is published, with a chapter on Trigger.

1984: The "Trigger" character makes a final appearance on television in an episode of *The Fall Guy*. Roy Rogers rides a look-alike, on loan for the occasion.

1987: *The Roy Rogers Book* by David Rothel is published with comments on Trigger by Roy Rogers.

1989: *Trigger Remembered*, a booklet by director William Witney, is published. It mentions Little Trigger publicly for the first time.

Clayton Moore on the first Silver, Dale Evans on Buttermilk and Roy Rogers on the original Trigger, under the bright California sun at the Los Angeles Coliseum in the mid–1950s (Roy Dillow collection).

1990: The last appearance on television of Roy Rogers riding a palomino happens on the *Randy Travis: Happy Trails* television special broadcast on TNN. The horse is never referred to as "Trigger."

1993: Trigger's trainer, Glenn Randall, passes away on May 5. • In October Roy Rogers auctions the last of his horses, allegedly grandsons and granddaughters of Trigger Jr.[5]

1994: November 14 Roy Rogers and Dale Evans perform publicly for the last time during the Sons of the Pioneers 60th Anniversary Concert in Tucson, Arizona. They sing "Happy Trails."

1995: *Roy Rogers* by Robert W. Phillips is published. It's the first serious and detailed study of Trigger and his doubles. Phillips follows up with essays in *The Southwest Horse Trader* ("Trigger—Known Around the World," parts one and two) and *The Western Horse* ("Trigger: the Smartest Horse in the World").

1996: *Oaktree Express* publishes "The Legend of 'Trigger,' the Smartest Horse in the Movies," another serious essay by Robert W. Phillips on Trigger.

1998: Joe Yrigoyen, Roy Rogers' longtime stunt-double and a man who rode the original Trigger and a number of Trigger doubles, dies on January 10. • Roy Rogers, Trigger's owner, partner, and best friend, dies on July 6 in Apple Valley.

1999: B-western cowboys are honored during the Academy Awards show in March. Actor Val Kilmer leads Triggerson, a grandson of Trigger Jr., on stage as a tribute to Roy Rogers, Gene Autry, and their cowboy peers. The Roy Rogers song "Cowboy Heaven" is played over film clips of those who are mentioned in its lyrics.

2000: George Coan's newsletter, *The Old Cowboy Picture Show* (volume 4, number 12), devotes an entire issue to "Trigger," with updated and comprehensive work by Robert W. Phillips and Leo Pando.

2001: Dale Evans dies on February 7. • Estate taxes become a problem between the Roy Rogers and Dale Evans Museum and the IRS. Trigger is valued at $400,000. • The

An enormous crowd estimated at 105,000 saw Roy Rogers and Little Trigger, visible left of the center circle, at the County Sheriff's Annual Rodeo at the Los Angeles Memorial Coliseum in August 1950.

The lucky winner of the "Spend a Day with Roy Rogers" contest, sponsored by Post Cereals in the mid–1950s, greets the one and only original Trigger, every little buckaroo's dream (Roy Dillow collection).

first estate sale is held from March 31 to April 1 at the Roy Rogers and Dale Evans Museum; many Trigger items go on the auction block.

2002: The Roy Rogers and Dale Evans Museum announces that it will close and relocate to Branson, Missouri. • The History Channel program *America's Lost and Found* presents a ten-minute segment on Trigger. • *The Encyclopedia of TV Pets* by Ken Beck and Jim Clark is published. It includes a section on Trigger and mentions Little Trigger.

2003: The grand opening of the new 26,000-square-foot Roy Rogers and Dale Evans Museum and Happy Trails Theater in Branson is set for Memorial Day weekend, May 24, with the original mounted Trigger as the centerpiece. • Trigger places 32nd on an

Animal Planet two-hour cable television show titled *50 Greatest Movie Animals.* • *Cowboy Princess* by Cheryl Rogers-Barnett and Frank Thompson is published. It includes a chapter on Trigger and Little Trigger. • A second all-Trigger issue of *The Old Cowboy Picture Show* newsletter is released in March (volume 7, number 2).

2005: *Hollywood Hoofbeats,* by Petrine Day Mitchum and Audry Pavia, is published. It includes a section on Trigger and an acknowledgment of Little Trigger.

2006: The mounted Trigger is featured in a Santa Monica Press book titled *The Ruby Slippers, Madonna's Bra, and Einstein's Brain: The Locations of America's Pop Culture Artifacts* by Chris Epting.

2007: *An Illustrated History of Trigger* by Leo Pando, with foreword by Corky Randal, is published McFarland. Look-alikes Monarch and California are mentioned for the first time as well as a number of movie solo appearances by the Golden Cloud.

2009: The Roy Rogers and Dale Evans Museum and Happy Trails Theater in Branson closes on December 12. • Corky Randall passes away.

2010: The Roy Rogers and Dale Evans collection, including Trigger, is sold at five different venues including Christie's in New York City and High Noon in Mesa, Arizona. *NBC's Today Show* does a feature on the Christie's auction the day before. RFD-TV, of Omaha, makes the winning bid on Trigger.

2011: RFD-TV returns Trigger to Bischoff's Taxidermy for repairs in preparation for a Happy Trails tour to mark the 100th anniversary of Roy Rogers's birth, which was acknowledged with cover stories on *American Cowboy,* December/January 2012 and *Cowboys & Indians* magazines (December 2011).[6] • A special edition "Legends of the West" issue of *American Cowboy* is released. Trigger tops a list of the greatest horses of the silver screen over Silver, Fritz, Tony, and Tarzan.

2012: In honor of Roy Rogers on the occasion of his 100th birthday, the mounted remains of Trigger and his canine pal Bullet are center-pieces on a spectacular 75-foot-long float titled "Happy Trails" (designed and built by Phoenix Decorating), compliments of the RFD-TV television network, for the Rose Parade in Pasadena on January 2.

2014: RFD-TV acquires the mounted Buttermilk from a private collector in Maine.

2016: The Happy Trails Tour ends at the Stockyards in Fort Worth. Trigger, Bullet and Buttermilk go on display at the Texas Cowboy Hall of Fame.

2018: The large museum statue of Trigger gets a final home at the entrance of the Spirit River Center in Apple Valley.

2019: Trigger, Buttermilk and Bullet go on display at the RFD-TV Ranch south of Santa Fe, New Mexico. • *Trigger: The Lives and Legend of Roy Rogers' Palomino* is published as a revised and expanded second edition by McFarland.

Chapter Notes

Preface

1. Jerry Dean: "I know that my love of the old movie cowboys stems entirely from the love I have for the life I remember having as a child. Roy et al. remind me of that. It was my parents who provided that life as I was growing up, and it is the two of them who I am remembering as I recall Roy and Trigger."

2. From e-mail correspondence circa 1999.

3. Spoken during a 1998 broadcast of *Siskel & Ebert at the Movies* (Buena Vista Entertainment).

4. Some actors—for example, Jack Nicholson—refuse to do public relations for their films. There are a number of reasons for this and they have to do with the creation of characters on screen. The more familiarity an audience has with an actor, the harder it is for that actor to disappear into a character.

5. E-mail dated May 13, 2005.

6. The literal translation of Tír na nÓg (from Irish Gaelic) is "Land of the Young." It is used to refer to the afterlife.

7. "Aye, we all see it, but that doesn't mean it's real necessarily." From the motion picture *Moby Dick* (Warner Bros., 1956).

8. "He Wishes for the Cloths of Heaven" by William Butler Yeats: "But I, being poor, have only my dreams; / I have spread my dreams under your feet; / Tread softly, because you tread on my dreams."

Introduction

1. From *Apocalypse*, 1931.

2. Gary A. Yoggy, ed., *Back in the Saddle: Essays on Western Film and Television Actors* (Jefferson, NC: McFarland, 1998), p. 182.

3. Quoted in David Rothel, *The Great Show Business Animals* (La Jolla, CA: A.S. Barnes, 1980), p. 214.

Chapter 1

1. Dusty Rogers told Thys Ockersen in his documentary *Roy Rogers, King of the Cowboys* that he and his siblings have a duty to carry on his dad's and mother's legacy.

2. On March 30, 1966, a UPI Telephoto/Files report read, "Hollywood: Cowboy star Roy Rogers revealed 3/30 that his trusty steed, Trigger, died at age of 33 almost a year ago. Rogers kept the loss to himself for fear fans across the country would go into shock on learning that the gallant horse had died." Rogers and Trigger were shown in a 1954 file photo that was suggested for use with story by Vernon Scott (Source: Janey Miller).

3. Cheryl Rogers-Barnett maintains a web site at www.cherylrogers.com/.

4. Joe Curreri, "Forget the Girl—Kiss the Horse," *Persimmon Hill*, vol. 13, no. 2, 1990.

5. Vol. 12, no. 3, April 2004.

6. Author Dana Cain also recognized Little Trigger in her book *Film and TV Animal Star Collectables* (Norfolk, VA: Antique Trader, 1998), p. 76: "'Little Trigger' was used as Trigger's stand-in, and frequently traveled to promotional appearances, allowing the 'real' Trigger to relax."

7. "Corky is no do-it-yourself fan. He served a long apprenticeship to his father." Joan Fry, "Training the Black Stallion, Part II," *Horse and Rider,* January 1982.

8. October 24, 2005; February 16, April 8, May 21, and June 24, 2006.

Chapter 2

1. Spoken by reporter Maxwell Scott (Carleton Young) in *The Man Who Shot Liberty Valance* (Paramount, 1962).

2. Roy Rogers and Dale Evans with Jane and Michael Stern, *Happy Trails: Our Life Story* (New York: Simon & Schuster, 1994).

3. *The Roy Rogers Story*, http://petcaretips.net/roy_ _rogers._html.

4. "This tour brought out 168,000 people for a total of $278,000 in Madison Square Garden, New York. The engagement grossed $1.1 million in a little over a month; the Houston Fat Stock Show and Rodeo played to 171,000 spectators and a $468,000 gate in 12 days." Duane Valentry, "A Horse Named Babe," *The Western Horseman,* April 1961, p. 58.

5. Todd McCarthy and Charles Flynn, eds., *Kings of the Bs* (New York: E.P. Dutton, 1975).

6. In *The Roy Rogers Book* by David Rothel (Madison, NC: Empire, 1987), Rogers says just enough about Trigger to imply that one horse did the majority of the work and look-alikes were brought in for minor tasks. "I have always owned four or five extra palomino horses in case anything should happen to Trigger. So in long-distance shots where they weren't identifiable, we would use one of the other horses to give Trigger a break." It

was noted by Sam Henderson in "Leonard Slye: The King of the Cowboys" (*The Western Horse*, December 1989, pp. 40–41) that Rogers had several "Triggers": one to ride in parades, one for rodeo appearances, one to stand in for the more dangerous roles, another for fast-paced action scenes, and the original Trigger for the close-ups.

7. I saw the Roy Rogers Rodeo show at the state fair in Albuquerque in 1957. In retrospect the horse was quite stocky. Now I'm inclined to believe it was Little Trigger. Years later when I lamented to a friend that "Trigger" was a composite of more than one horse, he remarked, "At least he wasn't just two guys in a costume!"

A photograph of Roy Rogers riding the original Trigger during a personal appearance was published in *Happy Trails: A Pictorial Celebration of the Life and Times of Roy Rogers and Dale Evans* by Howard Kazanjian and Chris Enss (Guilford, CT: Globe Pequot, 2005). The photograph was most likely taken in Southern California—judging by the type of hat Rogers was using, sometime around 1946.

8. When individuals were groomed as movie stars by major studios, name and background changes were the first things they underwent.

9. A similar and shorter piece by Trigger, Jr., titled "Rock 'n' Roll" was also published; again, the publisher is unknown.

10. There are no movie cowboys anymore in the tradition of Roy Rogers, Gene Autry, and William S. Hart. What we have today are actors who occasionally appear in westerns, like Kevin Costner, Clint Eastwood, Robert Duvall, and Tommy Lee Jones.

11. The images of a wonder cowboy and horse had been around since the silent era. Al Rogell, who directed action cowboy Fred Thomson's first western films, described his equine star Silver King in a superlative fashion. "He did all of the work … everything in the early pictures—the mouth work, the jumps, the chases, the falls, quick stops—and could untie knots, lift bars, etc. Thomson trained him to do certain things and expected him to perform them." Rogell had to be talking about a horse with trick and stunt doubles. Rogell also made the tall, handsome Fred Thompson out to be an expert with horses. Though Thompson studied for the ministry, it was his screenwriter wife Francis Marian who convinced him he had a future in movies. A skilled athlete, his experience with horses was average at best.

Chapter 3

1. On *The Merv Griffin Show*, filmed at Snuff Garrett's ranch; with guests Gene Autry, Rex Allen, Yakima Canutt. NBC, 1982.

2. *All Politics*, July 6, 1998.

3. Trigger's registration paper was first published in *The Old Cowboy Picture Show* newsletter in 2004, vol. 8, no. 4. It was made available by George Mudryj, a member of the Palomino Horse Association, who obtained it from PHA president Steve Rebuck.

4. Golden Cloud's height is not listed on his PHA registration. Corky Randall said he was 16 hands. The Pedigree Online All Breed Data Base lists him at 15.3 and the Rogers Museum description was 15.2. Both incorrectly listed his birth year as 1932.

5. Georgia Morris and Mark Pollard, *Roy Rogers: King of the Cowboys* (San Francisco: Collins, 1994).

6. There is no biological difference between a warm-blooded or a cold-blooded horse. (All horses are warm-blooded mammals.) Horses descended from the smaller Arabian or Barb are considered warm-blooded. Thoroughbreds are descended from Arabs or Barbs. All other horses are considered cold-blooded, including modern day draft horses descended from the type of large horses ridden by knights of old (Source: The International Museum of the Horse, Kentucky Horse Park, Lexington, KY).

7. Registered Thoroughbred stallions were used to upgrade the remount horses who were generally grade and draft horses.

8. Grace Larson, "Roy Rogers and Gene Autry and Their Tennessee Walkers," *Walking Horse News*, September-October 2000.

9. Jones not only rented horses, he also made money as a rider. Because he weighed over 250 pounds, he once doubled for the equally rotund comedian Fatty Arbuckle.

10. Fat Jones was one of the last of the old-timers who witnessed the birth and rise of the motion picture industry. He passed away in 1963.

11. In the winter of 1916, Will James left Nevada range country to find work in the warmer southern California climate and ended up at the Fat Jones stable. For a time he worked in motion pictures, doubling actors and, in true cowboy fashion, even breaking a few horses. James departed the following spring and went on to write the classic western horse story *Smoky*, which would eventually be turned into a Hollywood film on three different occasions, in 1933, 1946, and 1966.

12. Roy Rogers with Carlton Stowers, *Happy Trails: The Story of Roy Rogers and Dale Evans* (New York: Bantam, 1981), p. 64.

13. In *The Palomino Horse* (Los Angeles: Borden, 1949), author Doreen M. Norton stated that the original Trigger was bought at auction in 1937.

14. Herbert Yates of Consolidated Film Laboratories, Inc., and Trem Carr of Monogram joined their companies to form Republic Pictures, taking over the old Mack Sennett Studios in Studio City.

15. B-westerns generally took from eight days to two weeks to film.

Chapter 4

1. Robert W. Phillips: "The way I have always handled that 'Sly' and 'Slye' situation is the context and situation in which it is being used. If I am referring to hard, biographical name, then to me he is 'Sly.' But if I were mentioning a film credit, then I would have to show 'Slye.' Apparently Roy did some checking into the family history (and his birth record as well as that of his sisters) and learned I was right, for one of the last published interviews he gave, he set the record straight and admitted that he was born Leonard Frank Sly. I often, when using the Sly spelling, attach an asterisk and show in a footnote 'actual birth name, without the "e" added later.' That way folks will not only become educated, they will know that the writer didn't accidentally misspell the name."

2. Robert W. Phillips, *Roy Rogers* (Jefferson, NC: McFarland, 1995), p. 16.

3. Boyd Magers, *Gene Autry Westerns: America's Favorite Cowboy* (Madison, NC: Empire, 2007), p. 104.

4. Magers, *Gene Autry Westerns: America's Favorite Cowboy*, p. 106.

5. Bobby Copeland and Richard B. Smith, *Roy Rogers: A Different View*, 2012.

6. Rogers with Stowers, p. 56.

7. "The Man Who Makes Horses Say Yes," *Western Stars*, July 9, 1950.

8. Dana Cain, *Film and TV Animal Star Collectibles* (Norfolk, VA: Antique Trader, 1998), p. 76.

9. Mark Lasswell, "Remembering Roy Rogers," *TV Guide*, August 1998.

10. Dedicated with gratitude and friendship to Roy Dillow and Larry Rocky Roe.

11. The negative cost was in the region of $65,000, which was exceptionally high for a B-western at that time.

Chapter 5

1. *The Republic Pictures Story*, AMC, 1991.

2. Elise Miller Davis, *The Answer Is God* (New York: McGraw-Hill, 1955), p. 42.

3. First published in *The Old Cowboy Picture Show* newsletter in 2003, vol. 7, no. 2.

4. Rogers' initial salary was $75.00 weekly, and at the end of the contract, his pay had escalated to $1000 weekly. Rogers then signed a term picture arrangement that included a $10,000 bonus and pay of $21,000 plus a $500 clothing allowance for each of 11 films over a two-year period. In February 1950, Republic exercised their option to extend that contract for six more films at $21,667 each. Republic and Roy agreed to another extension for his final two Westerns at $25,000 each (source: Bobby Copeland).

5. Bobby Copeland.

6. Monte Hale, in David Rothel's book *The Singing Cowboys* (San Diego: A.S. Barnes, 1978), said, "They wrote a picture for me called *Don't Fence Me In*. It was to have all of Roy's cast in it: Gabby Hayes, Dale Evans, the Sons of the Pioneers—the whole bunch. This was when they thought Roy was going into the Army. They wrote it for me and gave me the script. I learned every part in it. I studied that script day and night. Then one day they called me up to the front office and told me Roy was not going into the service and that I was not going to make the movie, that Roy wanted to make it. It broke my heart a little bit."

7. Joel Dortch, "Roy Rogers—A Man's Man!" *Shoot!* vol. 22, May–June 2003.

8. Many of the cowboys were ashamed they'd participated in B-westerns. With a few exceptions, most would have rather been stars in A-features and making big bucks with the likes of Errol Flynn, Clark Gable, Jimmy Stewart, et al. The possible exception would be Gene Autry, who didn't have any delusions about his acting abilities and whose business acumen put him right up there with Bing Crosby, Bob Hope and Frank Sinatra. It's not far-fetched to assume even Rogers would have been tempted to move from Republic had some studio like Columbia approached him. Unlike Bob Steele or Don Barry, Rogers never had any acting ambition; he accepted children as his audience.

9. Roy Rogers told this story about *The Front Page* for decades, but he probably meant *Behind the News*, made in 1940 (remade by Republic as *Headline Hunters* in 1955). It's a newsroom story set in a big-city with actor Lloyd Nolan as a cynical reporter with a penchant for sticking his neck out. The description is right, and the star is right, as well as the time period. Once again, we see the lax attitude toward a little thing like facts. Two are wrong here: Rogers got the title of the movie wrong, and despite what he claims to have said to Yates, he did not own Trigger yet.

"'To get me in line, he threatened to take away my upcoming cowboy roles as well, and to put a point on his threat, he said he would replace me with another actor who could ride Trigger in my place.' The horse would make a star of anyone who rode him, he argued. 'Trigger is the one who's earning the paycheck, not you, Rogers,' he said." Roy Rogers and Dale Evans with Jane and Michael Stern, *Happy Trails: Our Life Story* (New York: Simon & Schuster, 1994) p. 106.

10. Jack Mathis, *Republic Confidential: The Players* (Barrington, IL: Jack Mathis Advertising, 1992), p. 2.

11. Rogers and Evans with Stern and Stern.

12. Schedules varied from studio to studio, from production to production, with regard to how much time there was between the completion of a B-western film and its release. Today, the time between completion and release of a film might stretch to a year or more. In contrast, B-westerns were probably more like today's TV shows, with just days of shooting, and only months between the end of filming and broadcasting.

13. Smoke died tragically when he ate some wire that was mistakenly left in with his feed.

14. "One story goes that Pistol was the horse's nickname at this time." Robert W. Phillips, "Trigger: the Smartest Horse in the World," *The Western Horse*, vol. 19, no. 1, issue 1, January 1995. Jay Dee Witney, son of director William Witney, also confirmed Pistol on an online video.

15. "His Palomino registered name was Golden Cloud, but the Golden Cloud name went the way of Leonard Slye. I had already decided to name him Trigger." *Mountain Broadcast and Prairie Recorder*, March 1946.

16. Todd McCarthy and Charles Flynn, eds., *King of the Bs* (New York: E.P. Dutton, 1975).

17. Morris and Pollard.

18. Robert W. Phillips believed that Rogers had acquired two main identical palominos. His hunch was correct, but he did not live long enough to learn about doubles Monarch and California, which belonged to Glenn Randall.

19. A contest to name these fictional colts offered one thousand dollars in cash prizes.

20. According to George Mudryj, member of the Palomino Horse Association, the horse owned by Randy Travis came from Pennsylvania breeder Paul K. Fisher, who sold Rogers Trigger, Jr.

21. Len Simpson, "Trigger Man" *Movie Land*, October 1946.

22. Don Allen, "Trigger and His Doubles," *Pic*, July 1946, p. 65.

23. Allen, p. 66.

24. Mares sometimes injure stallions while they're being bred, and consequently some owners do not want to risk a prized stallion.

25. Sam Henderson, "Leonard Slye: The King of the Cowboys," *The Western Horse*, December 1989, pp. 40–41.

26. Cain, p. 76.

27. In 1955 Post sponsored a "Name the Pony" contest. "Boys! Girls! Give me a name for this pony," Roy said in advertisements. "Names like Beauty, Dandy, and Flash are all good, but you can do better. So get along, buckaroos! Send in your names today!" Each entry had

to be accompanied by a Post Cereal box top. Rogers and Evans with Stern and Stern, p. 141.

28. Rogers and Evans with Stern and Stern, p. 143.

Chapter 6

1. Quoted by Ken Beck and Jim Clark, The Encyclopedia of TV Pets (Nashville: Rutledge Hill, 2002); p. 263.

2. Quote from 1986 appearing in Dan Gagliasso, "Remembering Roy," *Cowboy & Country*, Fall 1998.

3. When administrator@royrogers.com was asked in 2005 about Little Trigger's background the reply was, "Little Trigger could have been purchased from Ray Corrigan, but we don't have any lineage or ownership papers here on that particular horse. Sorry."

4. Little Trigger didn't really require registration papers (they just say an animal is a purebred) as he was not used for breeding. The only papers necessary were current health certificates for traveling from state to state and parts of Europe.

5. Don Allen, "Trigger and His Doubles," *Pic*, July 1946, p. 66.

6. Republic Pictures paid rental on Trigger for movies, but Rogers had to pay rental for the personal appearances before he owned the palomino.

7. Carol R. Johnson, letter to Bobby J. Copeland.

8. (New York: Julian Messner, 1955). Chapters 13 and 15 discuss "Trigger."

9. Bobby J. Copeland, "Early Roy Rogers—Two Versions," *Westerns and Serials*, number 40 (no month posted), 1993.

10. Copeland, "Early Roy Rogers."

11. He also believed Little Trigger might have been acquired from the Fischer Farms in Pennsylvania where Trigger, Jr., was purchased. No evidence has ever surfaced to prove the Fischer connection. Robert W. Phillips, *Roy Rogers* (Jefferson, NC: McFarland, 1995), p. 20.

12. In an article titled "Who Was the Smartest Horse in the Movies?" published in the July 1992 issue of *Classic Images*, Mike Newton claimed that Roy Rogers "found the horse at Corriganville, owned by Ray 'Crash' Corrigan, who was also a Republic cowboy star."

13. Merrill T. McCord, *Brothers of the West* (Bethesda MD: Alhambra, 2003), p. 112.

14. McCord, p. 112.

15. "The event will be celebrated this morning at a party in the Plantation Room of the Hotel Dixie. On hand with Mr. Rogers will be the Sons of the Pioneers, the singing group, who appear with the actor and the horse in Republic westerns. Trigger, Mr. Rogers and the Pioneers opened last night in the rodeo at Madison Square Garden."

16. "He has flown in a plane and traveled by ship, and at one time was given a birthday party at one of New York's most exclusive hotels—a party attended by various other film horses and at which raw carrots were the treat of the evening." From a Roy Rogers comic book special section titled, "Trigger! Smartest Horse in the Movies!" Reprinted in *Roy Rogers Western Classics* (AC Collector Classics number 3, 1990).

17. Reprinted in *Roy Rogers Western Classics* number 3, 1990.

18. Beck and Clark, p. 262.

19. Rogers and Evans with Stern and Stern, p. 149.

20. David Rothel, *The Roy Rogers Book* (Madison, NC: Empire, 1987), p. 66.

21. Bobby J. Copeland, *Silent Hoofbeats: A Salute to the Horses and Riders of the Bygone B-Western Era* (Madison, NC: Empire, 2001), p. 102.

22. Frank Rasky, *Roy Rogers: King of the Cowboys* (New York: Julian Messner, 1955), p. 117.

23. Larry Roe.

24. There are many movie sequences where Trigger and Little Trigger's facial markings may be scrutinized with the frame-by-frame and pause options on most DVD players. Luckily movies like *Son of Pale Face* and *Trigger Jr.*, are both available on DVD. In the latter Trigger's blaze may be seen very closely after he loses a fight with the rogue stallion, the Phantom. When Rogers first notices the palomino has been blinded and when a vet examines him in the following sequence, one may see his blaze clearly on both sides. An even better view is provided after a second fight with the Phantom and Trigger is knocked on the ground. He's wearing protective goggles and a mask but it slips off and the blaze is clear.

25. Larry Roe.

Chapter 7

1. William Roper, Roy Rogers: King of the Cowboys (T.S. Denison, 1971).

2. Dusty Rogers claimed his father was always on the lookout for good palominos and would put them in training with Glenn Randall. Some just didn't take to training or did not have suitable dispositions. These horses were sent to a working cattle ranch in the San Joaquin Valley partially owned by Roy Rogers.

3. TWHBA record #931975 states that Allen's Gold Zephyr was foaled on January 1, 1941. The Palomino Horse Breeders Association record #4055 states that Rogers bought Trigger, Jr., in 1948 (source: Larry Roe).

4. David Rothel, *The Roy Rogers Book* (Madison, NC: Empire, 1987), p. 33.

5. Three of the breeding stallions used by Fisher were offspring of one of Gene Autry's Champions.

6. Ken Beck and Jim Clark, *Encyclopedia of TV Pets* (Nashville: Rutledge Hill, 2002).

7. Johnny D. Boggs, "Val Kilmer—Playing Cowboy," *Cowboy & Country Magazine*, summer 1999.

8. Joel Dutch Dortch.

9. After winning the Triple Crown in 1933 Sir Barton was purchased by the U.S. Remount and was sent to Wyoming Remount Station, where he stayed until his death in 1937.

10. Duane Valentry, "A Horse Named Babe," *Western Horseman*, April 1961.

11. Naomi K. Chesky, "In Search of a Palomino," *The Fence Post*, January 3, 1994.

12. *Cowboy Princess Rides Again* (Nashville, TN: Riverwood, 2015), p. 143.

13. As heard by Larry Roe during a *Happy Trails Theater* taping session at the Cintel studios in the mid to late 1980s for later broadcast on the Nashville Network.

14. Page 32.

Chapter 8

1. Roy Rogers, "Trigger and Me," publisher and date unknown.

2. Experts have said that a well-conditioned horse can run about two miles full out before it's spent. However, an experienced rider can get much more distance

from his mount by alternating gaits. A horse can replenish oxygen in a trot and go on for about 50 miles.

3. *Cowboy from Brooklyn* was released in the United Kingdom as *Romance and Rhythm.* First acknowledged in *The Old Cowboy Picture Show* newsletter, 2004, vol. 8, no. 4.

4. Rocky Roe was the first to discover Trigger in *Shut My Big Mouth.*

5. Released in the United Kingdom as *Wrongly Accused.*

6. It was Rocky Roe and George Coan who first discovered Trigger in *Bad Men of the Hills.*

7. Russ Hayden was Lucky Jenkins in the Hopalong Cassidy movies. He kept the nickname—unlike Windy Hayes, who was not allowed to—but changed the last name. He may have had a better relationship with the powers at Paramount, because they didn't stop him.

8. Rocky Roe was the first to identify Trigger in this lobby card photo, which was published in Bobby J. Copeland's book *Silent Hoofbeats* (Madison, NC: Empire, 2001, page 60). This unique photo was taken with actor Russell Hayden. Oddly, Trigger was identified as Banjo, even though Trigger at one point in *Silver City Raiders* was called Comanche. The lobby card was discovered by saddle pal Derwood Harris.

9. Trigger was first discovered in *Silver City Raiders* by Rocky Roe. The film was screened in 1989 by Harold Smith at a Riders of the Silver Screen club meeting.

10. For *Saddles and Sagebrush* Hayden rode a beautiful chestnut. By the time he starred in *Riders of the Northwest Mounted,* he was riding a sorrel.

11. It's reasonable to suggest that Trigger may have been used in other Columbia movies with Hayden, since Hayden made seven other movies for the studio: *The Royal Mounted* (1941), *West of Tombstone* (1942), *Lawless Plainsmen* (1942), *Down Rio Grande Way* (1942), *Riders of the Northland* (1942), and *Overland to Deadwood* (1942). In *Riders of the Badlands* (1941), Hayden rides two different palominos, neither of them Trigger.

12. William Roper, *Roy Rogers: King of the Cowboys* (Minneapolis: T.S. Denison, 1971).

13. Monarch is also seen in the "Trigger's Doubles" photograph.

14. A cremello is a cream-colored horse with pink skin and blue eyes; the mane and tail are white. A cremello is born a light cream or gold color. Although this color may fade to nearly white in adulthood, a cremello is not a white horse; white horses are born white.

15. The Double R Bar name did not apply until the television series. The ranch gate showed a circle with an RR inside a circle with the word Ranch on the bottom of it. The ranch was referred to, several times, as the Double R Ranch. Rogers apparently hadn't added the Bar yet. He was interested in a clean-cut image, after all (source: Jerry Dean).

16. Coincidentally, in the film, Rogers' ranch was located in Victorville—17 years before he moved there in real life.

17. Mare is akin to bellwether, a castrated ram, usually wearing a bell around its neck, that is used to lead sheep and lambs to the slaughter. Since the bad guys were using this mare to lead a wild horse herd, it would be natural for them to have called her the Bell Mare. What's odd is that Rogers and company referred to her by the same name before they figured out what the bad guys were up to blame the scriptwriters.

18. Rick Lyman, "Whoa, Trigger! Auteur Alert!" *The New York Times,* September 15, 2000.

19. Quentin Tarantino helped sponsor a Saturday Morning Film Club kiddie-matinee double bill which included William Witney's *The Golden Stallion.* In his introduction, Tarantino noted that there was a resemblance between Trigger and Uma Thurman. Louis Black, *Austin Chronicle,* August 24, 2001.

20. William Witney, *In a Door, Into a Fight, Out a Door, Into a Chase* (Jefferson, NC: McFarland, 1996), p. 94.

21. The Hatton phrase is "Hi Ho" as opposed to the Lone Ranger's "Hi Yo."

22. It was actually Trigger who jumped over the barrel, as William Witney said—not some stunt horse.

23. Bullet Von Berge was the AKA registration name of the German shepherd called Bullet. He was later billed as a "wonder dog." (*Happy Trails Forever* website, www.ourchurch.com/view/?pageID=157671.)

24. Early in this exciting sequence two stuntmen make the initial jump from one wagon to the next. The first stuntman makes the leap without a problem. As the second makes the leap, the wagon swerves slightly and he loses his hold, sliding off the wagon and under the rear wheel! As it goes over his chest, the scene is cut.

25. Smiley Burnette's horse was first known as Black-eyed Nellie, then Ring-eyed Nellie and finally just Nellie.

26. Where possible, composers, release dates, labels, and album titles are noted. In a career as long as Roy Rogers,' many songs were recorded more than once and released on different compilations and in a variety of formats, from 78 LPs to CDs.

Chapter 10

1. Lawrence Scanlan, *Wild About Horses: Our Timeless Passion for the Horse* (New York: HarperCollins, 1998).

2. Most likely a money-saving move by Republic.

3. Autry opened his show with a voice-over: "Hello, folks. Say, I've got a swell story I want to tell you today. Champ and I are ready for action."

4. Source: Larry Roe.

5. Roy Rogers and Dale Evans with Jane and Michael Stern, *Happy Trails: Our Life Story* (New York: Simon & Schuster; 1994), p. 164.

6. "Val Kilmer led Triggerson, Trigger Jr.'s grandson, on stage." Johnny D. Boggs, "Val Kilmer—Playing Cowboy," *Cowboy & Country,* Summer 1999.

Chapter 11

1. Roy Rogers' television show stunt double, quoted in Ken Beck and Jim Clark, *The Encyclopedia of TV Pets* (Nashville: Rutledge Hill, 2002), p. 260.

2. Cheryl Rogers-Barnett with Frank Thompson, *Cowboy Princess: Life with My Parents Roy Rogers and Dale Evans* (Boulder, CO: Taylor Trade, 2003).

3. According to Bobby J. Copeland's *Silent Hoofbeats* (Madison, NC: Empire, 2001), p. 54, Johnny Goodwin trained Dick Foran's horse, Smoke (aka Smokey, Smoky), an almost dirty looking palomino. Corky Randall also recalled that Goodwin trained one of the Silvers Clayton Moore used on the *Lone Ranger* television show.

4. Len Simpson, "Trigger Man," *Movie Land,* October 1946, page 70.

5. Davis, p. 42.

6. Beck and Clark.

7. *Movie Fan* magazine article, March 1953. In an article titled "Trigger's Tricks," which appeared in *Movie Life* magazine in 1943, it was claimed, "Most 'high schooled' horses do not learn advanced tricks until they are four or five years old, but Roy started coaching Trigger when he was a year old to kneel, bow, and pick things up."

8. Mario DeMarco, *Gene Autry and Roy Rogers*, vol. 1 (West Boylston, MA: Published by the author, n.d.).

9. Elise Miller Davis, *The Answer Is God* (New York: McGraw-Hill, 1955), p. 42.

10. From an article titled "Roy and Trigger" by Glenn Randall, source unknown. This article was excerpted in DeMarco.

11. Davis, p. 42.

12. *Western Horseman*, vol. 51, no. 9, September 1986.

Chapter 12

1. *Western Clippings*, no. 36, July–August 2000 (Source: Bobby Copeland).

2. On *The Pat Sajak Show*, Sajak interviewed Roy Rogers and made reference to the *Life* magazine issue with Rogers and Little Trigger on the cover. Sajak read a passage that mentioned the palomino's repertoire of tricks. Rogers acknowledged that horses aren't as smart as dogs and noted how they require hand gestures to perform.

3. Known as a flight or fight response—if threatened, a horse's first instinct is to take flight. If it cannot flee, it will defend itself.

4. Allegedly Randall did it by poking the palomino, just when he should want to go, in the ribs right in front of his hind legs. At first he'd be poked repeatedly with the thumb. Little Trigger would flinch every time, but eventually he'd do his business. After some practice he required only a shorter cue.

5. A horse is a reflection of the person who trains and handles it, one only has to look at who's managing it to see the source of the problems. A gentle and confident horse reflects a gentle and confident trainer.

6. "The Randalls' movie horses are what's known as managed horses in that they perform at liberty, without restraint, in response to Randall's voice and whip cues. A seasoned movie horse … is trained to come to the trainer, then go out away from him. He'll circle at a trot or hand gallop, do figure-eights, rear and paw, back, play dead, pin his ears and charge, whinny, and bow." Joan Fry, "Training the Black Stallion—Part I," *Horse and Rider*, December 1981.

7. Roy Rogers: "Unlike so many trainers who rewarded horses with cubes of sugar after they have properly followed their cue, Glenn explained to me that a pat, a kind word, and perhaps an occasional carrot would get the trick done just as well. He would later tell me he was amazed at the quickness with which Trigger learned." Roy Rogers with Carlton Stowers, *Happy Trails: The Story of Roy Rogers and Dale Evans* (New York: Bantam, 1979), page 64.

8. Sam Henderson, "Leonard Slye: The King of the Cowboys," *The Western Horse*, December 1989, pp. 40–41.

9. Duane Valentry, "A Horse Named Babe," *The Western Horseman*, April 1961, p. 56.

10. Ken Maynard's palomino, Tarzan, was most likely as smart as "Trigger." Tarzan was often showcased in his master's films; he was even the centerpiece of the movie *Come on Tarzan* (KBS/World Wide Studios, 1932). Although the assumption has never been substantiated, most experts agree that when one saw Tarzan or Tom Mix's horse, Tony, performing a special trick on film, it was really them, and not a double.

11. Rogers was quoted in *Horseworld*, a television show aired around 1995. He said the same in print: "During all those hard rides for pictures and television, he never fell once. We had to do more retakes for human actors than for Trigger" (*Persimmon Hill*, vol. 13, no. 2, 1970). And again: "How that boy loved to run! All I had to do was shift my weight forward and he was off like a streak of lightning. Sit deep in the saddle and he'd shutter right down like the best roping horse there ever was." Roy Rogers and Dale Evans with Jane and Michael Stern, *Happy Trails: Our Life Story* (New York: Simon & Schuster, 1994).

12. There are trainers who maintain that some horses eventually become camera-wise. When they detect the red light on a camera, they know a scene is being shot and it's time to focus. When the light shuts off and the camera stops, they relax.

13. *Western Clippings*, number 22, March-April 1998.

14. Bernard Thon started making leather saddles in an apprentice program sponsored by the VA in Lusk, Wyoming, after World War II. Leather and saddletrees were scarce when the U.S. government appropriated beef and leather for the war effort. After the war, T.C. "Tommy" Nielson, owner of the saddle shop, made a deal for the Lusk facility. He and Thon set up plastic riding tack business. "Although the saddles were built on regular rawhide-covered trees, the ground seat was made of and shaped with leather, while the seat, fenders and 3-inch stirrup straps were made of quarter-inch plastic. Also of plastic were the fork covers, jockeys and horn coverings made from eighth-inch plastic. Padded seats were sewn and glued in place. All straps and decorations were welded in place with a hot iron. Unlike leather, which is soaked in water and cured for shaping, the plastic had to be heated or warmed in an oven and glued to the saddle while still hot." Roy Rogers ordered two cream-colored plastic saddles trimmed in blue and red, one for himself and another for Dale Evans. Trigger and Buttermilk were not pleased; the saddles were cold and stiff in inclement weather, and hot and sweaty when the temperature rose (Anna Koch, "Synthetic Saddlery," *Star-Tribune*, September 26, 2005).

15. Source: Larry Roe.

16. The Grigg letter was not dated. I received it in August of 1996. Mr. Grigg has since moved to Wilcox, Arizona.

17. Research compiled by Roy Dillow and Larry Roe.

18. Joan Fry.

Chapter 13

1. From an article titled "Roy and Trigger" by Glenn Randall excerpted in *Gene Autry and Roy Rogers: Kings of the Movie Cowboys*, vol. 1, by Mario DeMarco (published by the author; no date).

2. Clayton Moore explained in his autobiography, "In a running-start mount, you run, leap towards the horse, put your foot in the stirrup, and mount—you do the whole thing on the run." Clayton Moore with Frank Thompson, *I Was That Masked Man* (Boulder, CO: Taylor Trade, 1996).

3. Most experts agree that stirrups were invented

in China around 322. They were not used in Europe till the eighth century.

4. Davis, p. 52.

5. "Triggers, Buttermilk, Bullet and Nellybelle," *Happy Trails Forever* website, www.ourchurch.com/_view/_ _?_page_ID=_157671.

6. Yakima Canutt with Oliver Drake, *Stunt Man* (New York: Walker, 1979).

7. Duane Valentry, "A Horse Named Babe," *The Western Horseman*, April 1961, p. 57.

8. "As much as people believed Roy enjoyed riding horses, it wasn't known publicly until the early 1970s that his true love was motorcycles." Sam Henderson, "Leonard Slye: The King of the Cowboys," *The Western Horse*, December 1989, pp. 40–41.

9. Larry Roe met screen legend Ben Johnson March 31, 1989 at a film festival in Knoxville, Tennessee. When Johnson, a professional cowboy and expert horseman, was asked to name a half dozen movie cowboys who he thought rode really well, the first he mentioned was Roy Rogers. He was also quick to say that Rogers usually rode stallions.

Chapter 14

1. On a *Tonight Show* appearance with guest host Burt Reynolds, Rogers said that at one time he had as many as 400 items out and he was second only to Disney in merchandising.

2. They are sold by people producing fakes for the antique market.

3. The same clock was sold in Canada with a background mountain scene and sometimes shows up on eBay.

4. According to collector Jerry Dean.

5. On January 21, 2006, a professional 4 × 5 inch photo negative dated June 20, 1947, of Roy Rogers and Little Trigger closed on eBay for $713.75. Item number: 62442_62841.

6. *Double R Bar Ranch News*, November/December 1955.

7. Were I to play out a *Citizen Kane* scenario and pick a toy that is my own Rosebud, the last words on my lips would be "Silver." This is a reference to the white Stuart rearing horse I got as a child. It came with a red cowboy figure, a black saddle and bridle. My grandmother bought the set at Woolworth's when I was about five or six. Because the figure came with a fringed shirt, I named him Bill after Guy Madison, who played Wild Bill Hickok on television. I called the horse Silver after the Lone Ranger's horse simply because it was white.

8. Lizabeth West, "Unraveling the Stuart Mystery," *Plastic Figures & Play Set Collector*, number 68, October 2000.

9. Lizabeth West narrowed the designer of the premium/Stuart rearing horse down to two possibilities: C.F. Block and Associates with Kirk Melzer, or Melzer with the assistance of an ad agency Block brought in to help (he couldn't remember which agency). West was unable to locate Kirk Melzer; however, Block said that they used a photo of a rearing horse and strived for accuracy and that the project was a group effort. West also offers the following speculation: Perhaps Melzer did the drawing, as he worked on other projects for Block as well. Possibly Block hired an ad agency to polish the idea or provide input regarding the design, then come up with the advertising.

Chapter 15

1. Joe Curreri, "Forget the Girl—Kiss the Horse," *Persimmon Hill*, vol. 13, no. 2, 1970.

2. Frank Rasky, *Roy Rogers: King of the Cowboys* (New York: Julian Messner, 1955).

3. In 1942 a wealthy Baltimore sportsman offered Rogers $15,000 for "Trigger." *Junior Rodeo Fans*, May 1943.

4. Roy Rogers with Carlton Stowers, *Happy Trails: The Story of Roy Rogers and Dale Evans* (New York: Bantam, 1981), p. 151.

5. Roy "leaned forward and hissed in Trigger's ear. He always used this in the running inserts when he needed a little more speed. The big stallion laid his ears back and jolted forward, nearly putting Roy behind in the saddle." William Witney, *Trigger Remembered* (Toney, AL: Earl Blair Enterprises, 1989), p. 65.

6. Both stories are told by Witney in *Trigger Remembered*.

7. During the Western Film Festival in Memphis in the mid-'70s Mike Johnson met Felton Jarvis, one of Elvis Presley's last record producers. Felton claimed Elvis' favorite cowboy was Wild Bill Elliot because he wore his guns backward. There are childhood photos of Elvis decked out in a cowboy outfit wearing his guns exactly the same way.

8. Rasky.

9. Rasky.

10. The East Coast Roy Rogers fast food restaurants numbered 800 in their heyday in the late 1980s. At one time the company names Roy Rogers and McDonald's were used interchangeably on the East Coast to signify fast food. Some Roy Rogers restaurants still exist. CKE Restaurants bought and converted most.

11. Johnny D. Boggs, "Val Kilmer—Playing Cowboy," *Cowboy & Country Magazine*, Summer 1999.

12. Tony Castro, *Mickey Mantle: America's Prodigal Son* (Lincoln, NE: Potomac, 2008).

Chapter 16

1. December 1992 article by Eric Mink in *Knoxville News-Sentinel*—picked up from the *St. Louis Dispatch*.

2. *Horse Illustrated*, vol. 9, no. 6, June 1985.

3. Tom Mix's wonder horse, Tony, was put to sleep at age 39, two years after his master was killed in a car wreck. Mix died October 12, 1940, and Tony died October 10, 1942.—Bobby Copeland.

4. "Maynard's drinking kept him permanently surly. Maynard would also, to the horror of the cast and crew, take out his frustrations by beating his palomino horses. One of his more violent sessions was recorded by the sound engineers and played back for [Nat] Levine. How could this man, this cowboy hero who supposedly loves horses and Tarzan above all, whip his horses mercilessly, the animals screaming in torment? The answer, of course, was very simple. Hollywood had made Ken Maynard a movie hero. Those who were horrified were horrified because they were believing the illusion they themselves were responsible for creating." From Jon Tuska, *The Vanishing Legion: A History of Mascot Pictures 1927–1935* (Jefferson, NC: McFarland, 1999), p. 136.

One day in a fit of temper, he ran one of Tarzan's doubles at a tree with his spurs dug deep into the horse's flanks. As the horse tried to shy away from the tree, Maynard stepped off the horse, jerking the reins with him, thereby pulling the horse's head into the tree with a sickening thud that knocked the poor animal to the ground." From William Witney, *In a Door, Into a Fight, Out a Door, Into a Chase* (Jefferson, NC: McFarland, 1996), p. 32.

5. Raymond E. White, "B-western Horses," *Western Horseman*, vol. 66, no. 6, June 2001.

6. *Fury* had 116 episodes that ran 1955–1960; *My Friend Flicka,* 39 episodes on CBS from September 1955 until June 1956.

7. People use the terms chestnut and sorrel for horses that are red in color. There are those who refer to the redder versions as sorrel; some refer to the redder versions as chestnut. Horses with flaxen manes and tails are generally called sorrel by some people, but not by all. There are even some who consider sorrel a term only for horses who are ridden in a western saddle and use the term chestnut for horses ridden in English tack. To complicate matters more, some breed registries use only one term, either chestnut or sorrel; some use both.

8. David Rothel, *The Gene Autry Book* (Madison, NC: Empire, 1988), p. 87.

9. Whitman Publishing produced a children's book titled *Gene Autry and the Golden Stallion,* something Autry may have even approved of.

10. Cal Thomas, "My Lunch with Roy Rogers," *Jewish World Review,* July 8, 1998.

11. A Little Golden Record 78 based on the 1950s television show *Champion The Wonder Horse* was released as a 78 RPM 6-inch yellow vinyl disk. The Little Golden Record was numbered 226 and included two songs: "Champion the Wonder Horse" and "Bridle and Saddle." The tunes were sung by Mike Stewart and the Sandpipers, accompanied by Mitch Miller and His Orchestra.

12. *The Strawberry Roan* was almost derivative. In point of fact two other *Strawberry Roan* films were made before Autry's—one in the United Kingdom by the British Film Corporation in 1945 and one in 1933 by none other than Autry's old pal Ken Maynard. It was released by Universal and filmed around Lone Pine, California. This version went a long way towards popularizing singing cowboys.

13. Roan is a coat color that comes from a mix of white hairs with a base coat of another color. It gives the horse a lightened appearance, while the mane, tail and head remain the original color. A red base, or chestnut, plus roan produces a strawberry roan. Since roan can occur combined with any color, the appearance of roan horses varies greatly. Roan horses are born roan and stay the same color throughout their lives. Autry's "Champion" in this instance had no white hairs in his coat; he was a solid chestnut.

14. Roy Rogers' film *The Golden Stallion* would open the same way a year later.

15. Episode titles include "Calhoun Rides Again," "Renegade Stallion," "Mystery Mountain," "Lost River," "A Bugle for Ricky," "Canyon of Wanted Men," "Medicine Man Mystery," "King of the Rodeo," "Hangman's Noose," "Outlaw's Secret," "Stone Heart," "Badmen of the Valley," "Return of Red Cloud," "Saddle Tramp," "Diehards," "Rails West," "Andrew and the Deadly Double," "Salted Ground," "Deerhunters," "Cross-road Trail," "Brand of Lawless" and "Real Unfriendly Ghost."

16. The *Lone Ranger* radio show lasted until September 1954, a staggering 2,596 episodes.

17. The color feature *The Lone Ranger and the Lost City of Gold* (Warner Bros., 1958) opened with a theme song titled, "Hi-Yo Silver." This newer version was writ-

ten by Lenny Adelson and Les Baxter and encapsulated the Lone Ranger legend.

18. In this first serial, Tonto, played by Victor Daniels (aka Chief Thunder Cloud), rode a horse named White Feller (White Fellah), not Scout.

19. Silver Chief was the white horse actor Thomas Mitchell rode as Scarlett O'Hara's father in *Gone with the Wind* (MGM, 1939).

20. Wranglers and owners described Silver #1 as a Tennessee walking horse and Silver #2 as equal parts Arabian and Saddlebred.

21. Apparently Moore was introduced to Hugh Hooker by Bill Ward, his stand-in and stunt double as well as one of the *Lone Ranger* television show's wranglers (1949 through 1954). In an interview with author Ken Beck, Ward acknowledged that he bought White Cloud from Hooker, who was starting a Hollywood rental facility, Studio Stables, shortly after the series began.

22. *Persimmon Hill*, vol. 13, no. 2, 1970.

23. Clayton Moore's dedication to the Lone Ranger character was misunderstood by some fans; many assumed he did not relinquish the character even in his private life. In a July 2006 letter Moore's daughter Dawn wrote, "While dad embraced the character, he absolutely was 'Clay' at home—not the Lone Ranger. Over the years, there have been suggestions that he became a little wacky thinking he was this fictional character. He didn't. He indeed loved the character, but I would say that 'obsessed' might be a little misleading."

24. Moore actually owned a buckskin horse named Buck.

25. "Each paint horse has a particular combination of white and any color of the equine spectrum: black, bay, brown, chestnut, dun, grullo, sorrel, palomino, buckskin, gray or roan. Markings can be any shape or size, and located virtually anywhere on the paint's body."—American Paint Horse Association Web site, http://www.apha._com/breed/index.html.

26. With the tobiano type the spots are generally "regular and distinct as ovals or round patterns that extend down over the neck and chest, giving the appearance of a shield." In overo types "the white is irregular, and is rather scattered or splashy."

27. Some claim there were well over 150 episodes.

28. Corky Randall recounted one humorous anecdote concerning his dad, Glenn Sr., and Ralph McCutcheon. One night the two old cowboys had been out for a drink. They had a dog with them. On the way home they were stopped by a policeman after he noticed their car was moving a little too slowly. They were pulled over, and as the officer walked towards their vehicle the dog stuck its head out the window. McCutcheon proclaimed to the policeman, "the dog was driving."

29. B-westerns generally cost around $90,000 to make. Rogers' more elaborate productions topped the $100,000 mark.

Chapter 17

1. Dell produced two equine titles in conjunction with popular television shows, *Fury* and *My Friend Flicka.*

2. Little is known about him. He had a long career at Timely during the 1940s as a funny-animal artist and worked at Charlton from about 1959 to 1962. He worked on and off for Stan Lee at Marvel Comics through the 1950s, mostly as a writer, and even came back in the early 1960s during the Silver Age superhero revival. In-

formation on illustrator Ernest Huntley Hart is from Michael Ambrose, editor of *Charlton Spotlight*.

3. Both Hopalong Cassidy and his horse, Topper, got an artistic boost when Gil Kane took over the artwork of the *Hopalong Cassidy* comics produced by DC in the 1950s. Kane started with issue 118, and Cassidy and Topper were never the same.

4. Before *Roy Rogers Comics* became a monthly title, 13 issues were published as part of Dell's *Four-Color* line.

5. To note the change, issue 100 featured a cover shot of Rogers on Little Trigger with three small gouache portraits of a palomino, each painted by Sam Savitt.

6. Much to my amazement, during my first interview with cover artist Sam Savitt in 1995, he did not know Tom Gill had done the interior work on *The Lone Ranger's Famous Horse Hi-Yo Silver* or that Paul S. Newman and Gaylord Du Bois had written the stories. When Gill and Newman contacted me a few years later on separate occasions, they did not known Savitt was the cover artist. As a kid, reading and collecting these comics in the 1950s, I never dreamed I would one day identify these men to each other!

7. Ray White, "Quick Draw: The Comics of Roy Rogers, Dale Evans and Trigger," conference paper ca. 1990. Robert W. Phillips claimed that many of the artist's signatures are not visible to the naked eye and were buried in the artwork on some covers and interior splash pages. He accidentally discovered this while studying pages with a magnifying glass.

8. His work may also be found in three issues of *Gene Autry's Champion Comics*. In no. 7, August–October 1952, "Champion and the Ghosts of Red Dog" and "Champion in Waterfall Hide-out"; in no. 10, May–July 1953, "The Sure Real Deal" and "The Fugitive Bank Robber"; and in no. 12, November–January 1954, "Champion Roundup Trouble" and "Champion Proves His Point."

9. It would be thrilling to say Steffens, with his impressive resume, contributed to the Trigger comics. After all, he was an authority on the dress, tack, weaponry, and equipment horsemen used worldwide. He specialized in the American West and spent a lifetime documenting it. Steffens illustrated and wrote a regular column for *Western Horseman* magazine that was eventually collected into a series of books: *Hints for Horsemen*, *Horseman's Scrapbook* and *Handy Hints*. Steffens even worked as a stuntman on *The Adventures of the Cisco Kid* show on television, often doubling for star Duncan Renaldo.

10. Apparently Mr. Ed wasn't the only palomino who could speak. According to Mike Johnson, Trigger wrote a monthly column in the UK edition of *Roy Rogers' TRIGGER comic*. World Distributors (Manchester) Limited., 6 pence (about 10c). Publication date is around 1953. "Guess you must have heard that Roy and I have been mighty busy lately on account of we were giving a rodeo in New York. It has given me very great pleasure to be able to answer your many requests and star in another issue of *TRIGGER COMICS*, and sometimes I figure that I'd like to take you all for a ride on my back, but I guess that's impossible, as I'd finish up like an old swaybacked mule, so in the meantime I think the next best thing is to let you get on with reading *TRIGGER COMICS* No. 2. Hasta la vista, Amigos! Trigger".

11. In excess of 8 percent of his total literary output, rivaled only by his greatest achievement in comics, a 20-year run on *Tarzan Comics*.

12. After seeing an article in *Equus* magazine #150 in 1990, titled "The Mustangs of the West," with paintings by Sam Savitt, I suspected that he might have painted the covers for *Roy Rogers' Trigger*, *Gene Autry's Champion* and *The Lone Ranger's Famous Horse Hi-Yo Silver*. I wrote Savitt in care of *Equus* asking about the Dell covers. A few weeks later a letter of confirmation arrived. Bette Orkin, his wife, had kept records of his work. When I met them in 1995, I'd already accounted for more than double the Savitt covers on her list. Savitt was eventually able to confirm even more for a variety of Dell titles that Robert W. Phillips and I discovered in the following years. Sam Savitt viewed his covers for Western/Dell as merely a means to an end, paying bills, etc. He never made an effort to regain possession. He eventually wised up after his wife built a successful cottage industry from his gallery art and prints. By the time Savitt returned to Western Printing to retrieve his originals they were long gone. Of his 150 plus covers, he only saved three. This writer has only seen another dozen original Dell covers via various online sources. In the 1950s when Sam Savitt was working for Western Printing, illustrators were not allowed to sign. It was a way for companies to maintain reproduction rights. My research (eventually published as a cover article on Savitt in the fourth issue of *Illustration* magazine, 2002) was referenced in an affidavit drawn up by his lawyer and cousin Joseph J. Savitz to claim authorship of the work. The affidavit was notarized in the Commonwealth of Pennsylvania, County of Luzerne. It consists of seventeen claims including the following:

"The undersigned, Sam Savitt of North Salem, Westchester County, New York, being duly sworn according to law deposes and says that: 6. In 1950, he was doing comic book covers for Roy Rogers' horse, Trigger, Gene Autry's horse, Champion, and the Lone Ranger Hi-Yo Silver horse. 7. He did the above cover book pictures for approximately 5 years from 1950 to 1955, painting approximately 140 covers for Western Printing and Publishing Company, which he believes subsequently became Dell Publishing Company. 13. That a collector of comic book covers, namely Leo Pando of N. Richland Hills, Texas has apprised the deponent of Pando's collection of comic book covers and has asked the deponent to authenticate the same, having listed many works of the deponent after extensive research accomplished by Mr. Pando.

"The undersigned hereby states that the above facts are true and correct to the best of his knowledge, information and belief. (signed) Sam Savitt. Sworn to and subscribed before me, a notary public, this 20th day of September 1995. [Signed] Roberta S. Trimble, Notary Public—Wilkes-Barre, Luzern County."

13. Books with Al Savitt's illustrations include: *History in Harness: The Story of Horses* by Mildred Boyd (Criterion, 1965); *Heroic Horses and Their Riders* by Kate Klimo (Platt & Munk, 1974); and *What Goes On in Horses' Heads* by Eric Hatch (Putnam, 1970). Orkin confirmed that on occasion, Sam helped Al finish illustration jobs when deadlines were tight.

14. Robert W. Phillips attributed some interior Trigger stories to A. Moore and some remained unknown. Tim Lasiuta also theorizes that A. Moore may be a ghost name like Manyhands.

15. Many American comics were published in other countries, such as Australia, by a British company called World Distribution, Ltd. It is likely that Western Printing sold reproduction rights in other markets like France, Spain, Ireland, Scotland, and Mexico. The Dell Western Printing line was no exception. Interior stories

were mixed with other covers to create unique foreign issues, which also carried their own issue numbers. World Distribution comics are different from their American counterparts, especially when it comes to production values: the covers are flat, washed out, with little gloss due to the low-grade cover stock and newsprint pages.

16. Phone conversation with the author.

17. Jose Delbo finished *The Lone Ranger* series at Gold Key when the Tom Gill reprints ended (Source: Tim Lasiuta).

Chapter 18

1. Dan Gagliasso, "Remembering Roy," *Cowboy & Country*, fall 1998.

2. The last broadcast episode of *The Roy Rogers Show* was titled "Johnny Rover" (June 9, 1957). Four were produced but not aired at the time: "Fishing for Finger Prints," "Phantom Rustlers," "Doc Steven's Traveling Store," and "Born Fugitive."

3. *Roy Rogers: King of the Cowboys*, documentary by Thys Ockersen, Holland, 1992.

4. Wrote Beverly Olsen of Thousand Oaks, Ca.: "Roy Rogers' golden palomino died suddenly on July 3, 1965. He had been active and very alert for an old boy of 34 years. Trigger was being cared for here on Hidden Valley Ranch, formerly Rogers' Frontier Ranch. A special vehicle and trailer was being built to transport him in comfort to Rogers' new ranch in Apple Valley, Ca." Beverly Olsen, "Trigger Dies" (Letter to the Editor), *Western Horseman*, 1965.

5. The year 1965 was a hard one for Roy Rogers. Not only did he lose his beloved Trigger, but his son Sandy died while in the service and stationed in Frankfurt, Germany.

6. Rebekah Ferran Witter, *Living with Horse Power!* (North Pomfret, VT: Trafalgar Square, 1998).

7. Bischoff's Taxidermy and Studio Prop Rental has been in business since 1922. They were located at 54 East Magnolia Blvd., Burbank, California 91502.

8. Roy Rogers and Dale Evans with Jane and Michael Stern, *Happy Trails: Our Life Story* (New York: Simon & Schuster; 1994). "Too many people loved him, I just couldn't bury him," Roy Rogers said to Thys Ockerson in the documentary *Roy Rogers: King of the Cowboys*, 1992.

9. Stan Freberg on radio's *The Stan Freberg Show*, 1998.

10. According to the Internet Movie Database (http://_www.imdb.com/name/nm1022326/bio), after an investigation revealed that Trigger's meat had been sold to several small eateries in the Southwest (contrary to the Prevention of Food Adulteration Act of 1954), butcher John L. Jones was sentenced to five years in prison. Even if one had access to local newspapers and police records, proving the meat in question came from Bischoff's Taxidermy of California and was the actual remains of the original Trigger would be extremely difficult after 40 years.

11. "The horses, remarkably enough, look exactly like huge toys; there's little or no sense that they were ever real animals." Comments on Trigger and company from Michael Barrier, "What's New," Archives: October 2004; http://www.michaelbarrier.com.

12. "Taxidermy," episode of *Modern Marvels*, broadcast on the History Channel in 2005.

13. Rogers and Evans with Stern and Stern.

14. Joel Achenbach, "Achenblog: Daily Humor and Observations," *The Washington Post*, December 9, 2005.

15. *Wrangler's Roost* newsletter; source: Bobby Copeland.

16. A Silver look-alike was present at Clayton Moore's memorial service complete with his saddle on loan by the Wrather Corporation.

17. As heard by Larry Roe during a *Happy Trails Theater* taping session at the Cintel studios in the mid to late 1980s for later broadcast on the Nashville Network (TNN).

18. "But if there's a heaven for horses, that's where Trigger is." Roy Rogers quoted by Joe Curreri in "Forget the Girl—Kiss the Horse," *Persimmon Hill*, vol. 13, no. 2, 1970.

19. Source: www.contactmusic.com/.

Chapter 19

1. Roy Rogers, "Trigger and Me," publication and date unknown.

2. Rogers' secretary at the time, Bernice Sinard, ran the museum; Frances "Francy" Williams (later Rogers' secretary) oversaw the box office; his sisters Cleda and Kathleen were in charge of the gift shop.

3. *Roadside America* Web site, www.roadsideamerica.com/pet/trigger.html.

4. It was alleged that the only reason Dale Evans donated the horses to the museum was that Roy Dusty Rogers, Jr., promised her they would never be sold but would be donated to another museum. Unfortunately that was never put in writing. No contract or agreement was ever made public between her, Dusty, or any other member of the family with the Smithsonian or any other museum.

5. According to reliable sources approximately $500,000.

6. At that critical point, had the Rogers' siblings decided to downsize and run on a shoestring budget using volunteers, then the core Roy Rogers collection (including Trigger) might have survived, at least while their fan base was around. A smaller version of the museum may well have worked had it remained in Victorville. After all, that was where Rogers and Evans were buried and where many tangible memories remain in the form of the Happy Trails Highway, Roy Rogers Drive, etc.

7. Stephen M. Silverman, "Unhappy Trails for Roy Rogers Estate," *People*, July 2001.

8. Had Dusty and his siblings owned the land and buildings as their father had in Victorville, then an expensive financial loss might have been significantly mitigated. With no corporate sponsors to speak of, it's amazing the museum's accountants didn't set off the alarm much earlier.

9. Like many (including Dale Evans and Dusty Rogers), I was mortified when I heard Roy Rogers had Trigger mounted with his hide and mane fitted over a mold. In degrees I've gotten used to him but am still uneasy. Were it left up to me I would remove Trigger's hide, mane and tail from the mold then destroy it, then bury the palomino's last physical remains in an appropriate box in close proximity to Roy Rogers. Trigger, in his present state, is not the glorious persona he was in his prime.

10. The Roy Rogers and Dale Evans estate was dispersed over five auctions: Christie's in New York on July of 2010; High Noon in Mesa, Arizona, in January of

2010; a second High Noon auction in Mesa, Arizona, in 2002; Burley Auction Gallery April of 2011; and Brian LeBel's Old West Show and Auction in Denver, Colorado, in June of 2010.

11. Trigger topped out just slightly higher than his estimated price. The saddles went through the roof, each for close to double pre-auction estimates. A mounted animal is viewed as a trophy or a novelty. In western circles, a Bohlin saddle, especially a famous one, is like owning a Stradivarius violin. Trigger, Trigger Jr., Buttermilk and Bullet were originally tax-exempt by virtue of the separate trust set up by Dale Evans before she passed away. After the children, in theory, became beneficiaries from the sale of the animals then, like everything else, they became taxable items. Roy Dusty Rogers, Jr., may have been the executor of the trust, but that did not eliminate or excuse all six remaining beneficiaries from tax liabilities.

12. An animal that's been preserved by a taxidermist must be kept in a cool, dry, environment, away from excessive light. Dust, moths and human skin oil will damage a hide and discolor fur and hair. A hide should not be touched any more than possible. There is a limit on how many times a hide can be glued and dyed. Comanche, the sole surviving U.S. cavalry mount of the Battle of the Little Big Horn, resides in an airtight humidity-controlled glass case at the University of Kansas in Lawrence. That's the only way to truly preserve a mounted hide.

13. While there's nothing wrong with an individual's career dreams, they're a problem when fueled by group resources. One party is in effect supplementing their own dreams at the expense of others and, in this case, another individual's hard won legacy. In 2018 Dusty Rogers joined the most recent version of the Sons of the Pioneers.

14. Had Cheryl been in charge it's probable a core Roy Rogers collection would have remained under one roof with Trigger as the centerpiece. Had the museum stayed in Victorville, the family could have sold off the unused surrounding land, which would have settled any outstanding tax liabilities and still left money towards an operating budget. Either way the museum was on owned land and the payroll budget trimmed, then that together with its 501 status should have guaranteed that the place would at least have broken even. It's also possible that they could have moved (at least the key items) to the old part of town and opened a smaller venue.

15. Cheryl Rogers Barnett sued Roy Dusty Rogers, Jr., for misappropriation of funds. As executer of the trust, that in and of itself required him to provide a better explanation than simply blaming the economy. Having eroded a sizable inheritance in a few short years was essentially what Cheryl was suing over, since bad management on its own was not a crime. Dusty would have had to have personally benefited at the expense of his siblings in order for a justified suit. In the end Dusty was not found negligent—whether or not there was intent does not make one guilty. The beneficiaries were all equal in the eyes of the IRS to ensure that payments were made. The beneficiaries could not claim ignorance of what Dusty did. The kids all had a fiduciary responsibility to know what was going on, especially the ones who were board members of the museum. (Barnett vs. Rogers: https://caselaw.findlaw.com/mo-court-of-appeals/1631945.html).

16. Gene Autry's name will historically outlast his peers for a variety of reasons, "Rudolph, the Red-Nosed Reindeer" and "Here Comes Santa Claus" not the least

of them. Then there's "Here Comes Peter Cottontail" during Easter.

17. According to Roy Dillow, Roy Rogers received copies of each movie but they were never maintained and eventually misplaced. The same holds true with the television show episodes. Rogers sold the rights before they went into syndication and never got a dime after that, the only exception being what he received from Nestle's ads.

18. All of the post-1949 titles are available unedited and uncut, as are quite a few of the pre-1949 titles. Where an uncut print is lost, the 54-minute version and its elements are safe. The only unknown factor is the Trucolor elements, a two-strip color process. Some will be fine, but others may be unstable and the color may have turned.

19. Regrets: Why were Art Rush's business papers concerning Rogers' destroyed without recognizing their value? Will a photo of Golden Cloud on the set of *Gone with the Wind* ever show up? Why didn't anyone write a comprehensive book on Glenn Randall, Sr., and sons?

20. Because Trigger's remains are not in an airtight box, they will continue to deteriorate. It's doubtful they will undergo an expensive restoration process once they are no longer presentable.

21. A top-of-the-line core collection is now a pipe dream: Trigger and Bohlin saddle, Rogers' Gilmore gun rig, a classic Nudie outfit, a Stetson with a denton pinch, a *This Is Your Life* leather bound script, the OM-45 Deluxe Martin Guitar, vintage movie posters, an Estes Tartar horse statue, etc., are scattered into the four winds.

22. This chapter was adapted from material first featured in three issues of *The Old Cowboy Picture Show* newsletter and *The Old Cowboy Picture Show Revised* book published in 2009 and 2010 respectively.

Chapter 20

1. Jill Rappaport and Wendy Wilkinson, *People We Know, Horses They Love* (Emmaus, PA: Rodale, 2004).

2. Inferred. Horse trainers agree that a horse is not started under saddle before two years of age.

3. "The Life of Dale Evans and Roy Rogers," *Movie Life Yearbook* (Bilabra, 1946).

4. The audio of this event may be found on *The Roy Rogers Collection (1937–1990)*, released by Rhino Records in 1999.

5. According to Joel Dutch Dortch, board member of the Happy Trails Foundation.

6. This author was quoted in the article by editorial director Dana Joseph. "Although Rogers' main mount appeared in every single film and all the TV episodes, there were two other Triggers that helped carry the load. Little Trigger mastered many tricks and Trigger, Jr., performed many of the dance routines. Both traveled with Rogers on the road. 'In Roy's view and to the public eye, it was like all three horses were one,' says Leo Pando, author of *An Illustrated History of Trigger* (Jefferson, NC: McFarland, 2007). 'Whatever horse he was riding, whatever horse he was on—that was Trigger. Although neither Trigger, Jr., nor Little Trigger was sired by the original Trigger, Rogers worked closely with horse trainer Glenn Randall to train all three. One result of Trigger's fame,' Pando says, 'was that Randall became Hollywood's go-to guy when it came to horses,' earning accolades for his involvement in many films like *Ben-Hur* (1959) and *The Black Stallion* (1979)."

Bibliography

Information pertaining to Trigger came from a variety of sources. In their autobiographies, Roy Rogers, Dale Evans, and their son Dusty all mentioned Trigger in general public relations terms; daughter Cheryl Rogers-Barnett went into more detail and has been willing to augment what she learned.

In his *Roy Rogers: A Biography, Radio History, Television Career Chronicle, Discography, Filmography, Comicography, Merchandising and Advertising History, Collectibles Description, Bibliography and Index* (1995), Robert W. Phillips devoted an entire chapter to Trigger, discussing and analyzing him as never before.

Finally, there is the loving tribute *Trigger Remembered* by William Witney, who directed Roy Rogers' films from 1946 to 1951. Witney got to know the animal very well and his book is loaded with interesting anecdotes and reminiscences.

Text on Trigger generated by the national media (newspapers, magazine articles, books, etc.) was by and large cut from a public relations template. Exceptions are two articles by Robert W. Phillips: "The Legend of 'Trigger': The Smartest Horse in the Movies" (*Oaktree Express,* vol. 3, no. 2, 1996), and the two-part article "Trigger—Known Around the World" (*The Southwest Horse Trader,* January 1995 and February-March 1995).

As the man who trained Trigger from 1941 till the mid–1950s, Glenn Randall was the primary source, and fortunately he gave interviews into the 1980s.

Books

Adams, Les, and Buck Rainey. *Shoot-Em-Ups: The Complete Reference Guide to Westerns of the Sound Era.* Waynesville, NC: World of Yesterday, 1986.

Adams, Richard. *Traveller.* New York: Dell, 1988.

Adler, Larry. *Famous Horses of America.* New York: David McKay, 1979.

Allen, Rex, as told to Paula Simpson. *The Arizona Cowboy: "My Life—Sunrise to Sunset."* Scottsdale, AZ: RexGarRus, 1989.

Amaral, Anthony. *Movie Horses: Their Treatment and Training.* Indianapolis: Bobbs-Merrill, 1967.

Autry, Gene, with Mickey Herskowitz. *Back in the Saddle Again.* Garden City, NY: Doubleday, 1978.

Beck, Ken, and Jim Clark. *The Encyclopedia of TV Pets.* Nashville: Rutledge Hill, 2002.

Black, Bill. *Golden-Age Greats Volume II: Roy Rogers and the Silver Screen Cowboys: An Illustrated History of the Matinee Western.* Longwood, FL: AC Comics, 1997.

Bond, Johnny, and Packy Smith. *30 Years on the Road with Gene Autry.* Riverwood, 2007.

Burt, Don. *Horses and Other Heroes: Reflections of a Life with Horses.* Guilford, CT: Lyons, 2002.

Cain, Dana. *Film and TV Animal Star Collectibles.* Norfolk, VA: Antique Trader, 1998.

Canutt, Yakima, with Oliver Drake. *Stunt Man.* New York: Walker, 1979.

Carman, Bob, and Dan Scapperotti. *Roy Rogers, King of the Cowboys: A Film Guide.* Robert C. Carman, 1979.

Copeland, Bobby J. *Silent Hoofbeats: A Salute to the Horses and Riders of the Bygone B-Western Era.* Foreword by William "Buck" Rainey. Madison, NC: Empire, 2001.

Copeland, Bobby, and Richard B. Smith. *Roy Rogers: A Different View.* Madison, NC: Empire, 2012.

Coyle, P. Allan. *Roy Rogers and Dale Evans Toys & Memorabilia: Identification & Values.* Paducah, KY: Collector Books, 2000.

Cunningham, Eugene. *Triggernometry: Gallery of Gunfighters.* Caldwell, OH: Caxton, 1956.

Davis, Elise Miller. *The Answer Is God: The Inspiring Personal Story of Dale Evans and Roy Rogers and the Miracle That Changed Their Lives.* New York: McGraw-Hill, 1955.

DeMarco, Mario. *Gene Autry and Roy Rogers: Kings of the Movie Cowboys.* Vol. 1. West Boylston, MA: Published by the author, n.d.

_____. *Horse Bits from the B-Western Movies and Television.* West Boylston, MA: published by the author, 1995.

_____. *The Lone Rangers of the Silver Screen and Television.* West Boylston, MA: Published by the author, n.d.

Enss, Chris, and Howard Kazanjian. *The Cowboy and the Señorita: A Biography of Roy Rogers and Dale Evans.* Foreword by Roy Dusty Rogers, Jr. Guilford, CT: Globe Pequot, 2004.

_____. *Happy Trails: A Pictorial Celebration of the Life and Times of Roy Rogers and Dale Evans.* Guilford, CT: Globe Pequot, 2005.

Epting, Chris. *The Ruby Slippers, Madonna's Bra, and Einstein's Brain: The Locations of America's Pop Culture Artifacts.* Santa Monica, CA: Santa Monica, 2006.

Fitch, Gail. *Hartland Horsemen: With Price Guide.* Altglen, PA: Schiffer, 1999.

Fox, Charles Phillips. *A Pictorial History of Performing Horses.* Preface by Roy Rogers. New York: Bramhall House, 1960.

George-Warren, Holly. *Public Cowboy No. 1: The Life and Times of Gene Autry*. New York: Oxford University Press, 2007.

Green, Ben K. *The Color of Horses*. Flagstaff: Northland, 1983.

Hake, Ted. *Hake's Guide to Cowboy Character Collectables: An Illustrated Price Guide Covering 50 Years of Movie & TV Cowboy Heroes*. New York: Wallace-Homestead, 1994.

_____. *Hake's Price Guide to Character Toy Premiums*. York, PA: Gemstone, 1996.

Hake, Theodore L., and Robert D. Cauler. *Six-Gun Heroes: A Price Guide to Movie Cowboy Collectibles*. New York: Wallace-Homestead,1976.

Hamilton, Denise. "Dwindling of Stables Alarms Equestrians," *Los Angeles Times*, 1986.

Heide, Robert, and John Gilman. *Box Office Buckaroos: The Cowboy Hero from the Wild West Show to the Silver Screen*. New York: Abbeville, 1982.

Hintz, H. F. *Horses in the Movies*. Cranbury, NJ: A. S. Barnes, 1979.

Holland, Dave. *From Out of the Past: The Pictorial History of the Lone Ranger*. Granada Hills, CA: Holland House, 1989.

Horn, Maurice. *Comics of the American West*. North Hackensack, NJ: Stoeger, 1977.

Horwitz, James. *They Went Thataway: From Tom Mix to Tonto, the Cowboy Movies and the Men Who Made Them. Where Are They Now?* New York: Ballantine, 1976.

Kazanjian, Howard, and Chris Enss. *Happy Trails: A Pictorial Celebration of the Life and Times of Roy Rogers and Dale Evans*. Guilford, CT: Globe Pequot, 2005.

Lenius, Ron. *The Ultimate Roy Rogers Collection: Identification and Price Guide*. Iola, WI: Krause, 2001.

Lindenberger, Jan, with Dana Cain. *501 Collectible Horses: A Handbook and Price Guide*. Altglen, PA: Schiffer, 1995.

Magers, Boyd. *Gene Autry Westerns: America's Favorite Cowboy*. Madison, NC: Empire, 2007.

Martin, Carolyn. *Metal Horse Figurines*. 2004.

Mathis, Jack. *Republic Confidential: The Players*. Chicago: Jack Mathis Advertising, 1992.

McCarthy, Todd, and Charles Flynn, eds. *King of the Bs: Working Within the Hollywood System*. New York: Dutton, 1975.

McCord, Merrill T. *Brothers of the West*. Bethesda, MD: Alhambra, 2003.

Mitchum, Petrine Day, with Audry Pavia. *Hollywood Hoofbeats: Trails Blazed Across the Silver Screen*. Irvine, CA: BowTie, 2005.

Moore, Clayton, with Frank Thompson. *I Was That Masked Man*. Boulder: Taylor Trade, 1996.

Morris, Georgia, and Mark Pollard. *Roy Rogers: King of the Cowboys*. San Francisco: Collins, 1994. 1998.

Moyer, Donn J. *Don "Brown Jug" Reynolds: The Last Little Beaver of the Movies*. Tacoma, WA: Wild West, 2006.

Norton, Doreen M. *The Palomino Horse*. Los Angeles: Borden, 1949.

Overstreet, Robert M. *The Overstreet Comic Book Price Guide*. 34th ed. York, PA: Gemstone, 2004.

Pando, Leo, and George Coan. *The Old Cowboy Picture Show Revised*. Laurinburg, NC: Old Cowboy Picture Show Publishing, Jack Coan Publisher, 2010.

Petty, Kate. *Horse Heroes: True Stories of Amazing Horses*. New York: Dorling Kindersley, 1999.

Phillips, Robert W. *Roy Rogers: A Biography, Radio History, Television Career Chronicle, Discography, Filmography, Comicography, Merchandising and Advertising History, Collectibles Description, Bibliography and Index*. Jefferson, NC: McFarland, 1995.

Rappaport, Jill, and Wendy Wilkinson. *People We Know, Horses They Love*. Emmaus, PA: Rodale, 2004.

Rasky, Frank. *Roy Rogers: King of the Cowboys*. New York: Julian Messner, 1955.

Rogers, Roy, and Dale Evans, with Jane and Michael Stern. *Happy Trails: Our Life Story*. New York: Simon & Schuster, 1994.

Rogers, Roy, with Carlton Stowers. *Happy Trails: The Story of Roy Rogers and Dale Evans*. New York: Bantam, 1981.

Rogers, Roy Dusty, Jr., with Karen Ann Wojahn. *Growing Up with Roy and Dale*. Ventura, CA: Regal, 1986.

Rogers-Barnett, Cheryl, and Frank Thompson. *Cowboy Princess: Life with My Parents Roy Rogers and Dale Evans*. Boulder: Taylor Trade, 2003.

_____. *Cowboy Princess Rides Again*. Nashville: Riverwood, 2015.

Roper, William L. *Roy Rogers: King of the Cowboys*. Denison, 1971.

Rothel, David. *The Gene Autry Book*. Rev. ed. Madison, NC: Empire, 1988.

_____. *The Great Show Business Animals*. La Jolla, CA: A.S. Barnes, 1980.

_____. *The Roy Rogers Book*. Madison, NC: Empire, 1987.

_____. *The Singing Cowboys*. San Diego: A.S. Barnes, 1978.

_____. *Who Was That Masked Man? The Story of the Lone Ranger*. San Diego: A.S. Barnes, 1976.

Scanlan, Lawrence. *Wild About Horses*. New York: HarperCollins, 1998.

Seggerman, Sheri, and Mary Tiegrenn. *1001 Reasons to Love Horses*. New York: Stewart, Tabori and Chang, 2005.

Spitz, Bob. *The Beatles: The Biography*. Boston: Little, Brown, 2005.

Stanfield, Peter. *Horse Opera—The Strange History of the 1930s Singing Cowboys*. Champaign: University of Illinois Press, 2002.

Stern, Jane, and Michael Stern with Roy Rogers and Dale Evans. *Happy Trails: Our Life Story*. New York: Simon & Schuster, 1994

Sullivan, George, and Sullivan, Tim. *Stunt People*. New York: Beaufort, 1983.

White, Raymond E. *King of the Cowboys and Queen of the West: Roy Rogers and Dale Evans, A Career Biography*. Madison: University of Wisconsin Press/ Popular Press, 2005.

Whitlock, Vivian H. "Buttermilk and Trigger." *Western Horseman*, September 1960.

Witney, William. *Trigger Remembered*. Foreword by Alan G. Barbour. Toney, AL: Earl Blair Enterprises, 1989.

Witter, Rebekah Ferran. *Living with Horse Power!* North Pomfret, VT: Trafalgar Square, 1998.

Yoggy, Gary A. *Back in the Saddle: Essays on Western Film and Television Actors*. Jefferson, NC: McFarland, 1998.

Periodicals

Allen, Don, with photos by Bob Wallace. "Trigger and His Doubles." *Pic*, July 1946, p. 65.

"Allen's Golden Zephyr." *Palomino Horses*, July 1944.

Big Reel, March 1997.

Bird, Allen. "A Horse Fit for a King." *Horseman*, May 1978.

"Bob Hope a Cowboy? Trigger Had a Horse Laugh." *New York Herald Tribune Magazine*, June 1, 1952.

Boggs, Johnny D. "Val Kilmer—Playing Cowboy." *Cowboy & Country Magazine*, Summer 1999.

Chesky, Naomi K. "In Search of a Palomino." *Fence Post*, January 1994.

Curreri, Joe. "Forget the Girl—Kiss the Horse." *Persimmon Hill*, Vol. 13, no. 2, 1970.

Curreri, Joseph. "Movie Horses Who Make Their Marks." *Horse Illustrated*, Vol. 9, no. 6, June, 1985.

The Daily Press [Victorville, California], October 31, 1995, p. A4.

Donovan, John. "The Scene Stealers!" Publication and date unknown.

Fry, Joan. "Training the Black Stallion, Part I." *Horse and Rider*, December 1981.

———. "Training the Black Stallion, Part II." *Horse and Rider*, January 1982.

Gagliasso, Dan. "Remembering Roy." *Cowboy & Country* magazine, Fall 1998.

Goodman, Mark. "The Singing Cowboy." *Esquire*, December 1975.

Henderson, Sam. "Leonard Slye: The King of the Cowboys." *The Western Horse*, December 1989.

———. "The Singing Cowboys of Yesterday." *The Western Horse*, Vol. 8, no. 1, issue 30, Spring 1989.

Lasiuta, Tim. "A Tribute to Tom Gill." *Illustration*, Vol. 3, no. 10, June 2004.

Lyman, Rick. "Whoa, Trigger! Auteur Alert!" *The New York Times*, September 15, 2000.

"The Man Who Makes Horses Say Yes." *Western Stars*, July 9, 1950.

Manns, William. "A Saddle Fit for a King." *American Cowboy*, March/April 2002.

McCall, Elizabeth Kaye. "Remembering Corky: The End of an Era." Publication and date unknown.

Newton, Mike. "Who Was the Smartest Horse in the Movies?" *Classic Images*, July 1992.

Norris, Monty. "For Movie Trainer Randall, the Horseplay's the Thing." *Friends*, December 1982.

O'Brien, Kevin. "The Rise and Fall of Branson." *The Distributist Review*, January 12, 2016, http://distributist review.com.

Ol' Waddy. "Trailer Deluxe." *The Western Horse*, October 1959.

Olsen, Beverly. "Trigger Dies." (Letter to the Editor.) *Western Horseman*, 1965.

"100th Anniversary of Roy Rogers." *Cowboys and Indians*, December 2011.

Pando, Leo. "Letters to the Editor." *Oaktree Express*, September 1996.

———. "Oh So" (Letters to the Editor), *The Comic Buyer's Guide*, #1499, January 26, 2001.

———. "Sam Savitt: Horse Painter from a Golden Age." *Oaktree Express*, Vol. 3, no. 3, 1996.

———. "Sam Savitt: Painter, Author, Teacher and Horseman." *Illustration*, Vol. 1, no. 4, August 2002.

Robert W. Phillips. "Champion—Gene Autry's Equine Star and Related Collectibles." *Antique Trader*, August 1994.

———. "Collecting Western Comics." *Antique Trader*, August 1994.

———. "Horses Are Heroes, Too!" Publication and date unknown.

———. "The Roy Rogers Show—Happy Trails and Western Tales." *Television Chronicles*, no. 5, April 1996.

———. "Trigger: the Smartest Horse in the Movies." *The Western Horse*, Vol. 19, no. 1, issue 1, January 1995.

Randall, Glenn. "Roy and Trigger: I'll Match Roy Against Any Texas Line-rider!" *Western Stars*, October 12, 1949.

Rebuck, Steven. "Paul K. Fisher." *Palomino Horses*, March 1991.

Rogers, Roy. "A Slice of my Life." *Who's Who in Western Stars*, vol. 1, no. 2, 1952. Includes 10 solo shots of Little Trigger in a variety of trick poses.

———. "Trigger and Me." Publication and date unknown.

———, as told to Aaron Dudley. "Trigger: First Get a Good Horse." *Western Horseman*, vol. 14, no. 12, December 1949.

———, as told to Adrienne Ames. "How I Trained Trigger." *Motion Picture*, February 1944, pp. 55 and 86.

Rogers-Barnett, Cheryl. "Roy Rogers and Trigger: An Affectionate Remembrance." *Cowboys & Indians*, vol. 12, no. 3, April 2004.

Ross, Carol Ann. "Honoring Glenn Randall, Hollywood Horse Trainer." *Western Horseman*, Vol. 51, no. 9, September 1986.

"Roy Rogers: Trigger Man." *Movie Land*, October 1946.

Saunders, David. "The Art of Rafael M. DeSoto." *Illustration*, Vol. 3, no. 10, June 2004.

Schooley, Jennifer L. "Flashback: The Horses of Zorro." *Western Horseman*, March 2002.

Shiflet, Robert. "Lifetime Memberships Presented to Roy Rogers and Dale Evans in Oklahoma Ceremony." *Palomino Horses*, January 1976.

Sifaki, Carl. "Trigger, Roy Rogers' Boss." *Movie Fan*, March 1953.

Silverman, Stephen M. "Unhappy Trails for Roy Rogers Estate." *People*, July 2001.

Simpson, Len. "Trigger Man." Publication and date unknown.

Smith, H. Allen. "King of the Cowboys: Roy Rogers Kisses the Horse, Not the Heroine." *Life*, Vol. 15, no. 2, July 12, 1943.

Smith, Lewis. "Steel: The Horse the Stars Rode." *Horse Illustrated*, Vol. 9, no. 6, June, 1985.

Spangenberger, Phil. "He Spoke Horse." *Cowboy Magazine*, Summer 1992.

Strassberg, Stephen. "That Horse, Trigger." *Pageant*, February, 1947, pp. 68 and 69.

Sullivan, John Jeremiah. "Horseman, Pass By—the Glory, Grief, and the Race for the Triple Crown." *Harpers*, October 2002.

Thomas, Cal. "My Lunch with Roy Rogers." *Jewish World Reviews*, July 8, 1998.

Trigger. "My Life with Roy." *Movie Thrills*, July 1950.

"Trigger." *Palomino Horses*, June 1991.

Trigger, Jr. "Rock 'n' Roll." Publication and date unknown.

"Trigger's Tricks." *Movie Life*, 1943, p. 44.

Valentry, Duane. "A Horse Named Babe." *Western Horseman*, April 1961.

West, Lizabeth. "Unraveling the Stuart Mystery." *Plastic Figures & Playset Collector*, no. 68, October 2000.

White, Ray. "Quick Draw: The Comics of Roy Rogers, Dale Evans and Trigger" Paper presented at a conference of the American Popular Culture Association, ca. 1990.

White, Raymond E. "B-western Horses." *Western Horseman*, Vol. 66, no. 6, June 2001.

"Win a Wee Trigger!" *Movie Star Parade*, November 1947.

Ziemann, Irvin H. "Gaylord Du Bois—King of the Comic Writers." *The Comic Buyer's Guide*, November 1989.

Zimmer, Steve. "The Art of the Horseman." *Western Horseman*, Vol. 70, no. 1, January 2005.

Newsletters

The Old Cowboy Picture Show. Miscellaneous articles from vol. 2, no. 1 (August 1998) through vol. 8, no. 6 (December 2004). Miscellaneous articles published in 2009.

Western Clippings, no. 22, March/April 1998.

Western Clippings, no. 36, July/August 2000.

Western Clippings, no. 123, January/February 2015. "Roy and Trigger" by Leo Pando.

Western Clippings, no. 133, September/October 2016. "Roy Rogers Before Trigger," by Leo Pando.

Web Pages

a-drifting-cowboy.blogspot.com. "Oklahoma Kid" Jerry England (Warner Bros., 1939) (Hudkins Stable bill).

Clayton Moore, The Lone Ranger. www.members.tripod.com/~ClaytonMoore/index.html. Host Steve Jensen has done a masterful job chronicling Lone Ranger history and keeps up to date with current news.

The Grand Comic Book Data Base. www.comics.org/. Details and history of comic books. Membership is required and well worth it.

Hamilton East Public Library website. David Heighway, historian. "Noblesville and Hollywood: Trigger."

Horse Fame. http://horsefame.tripod.com/. More of a chat room than a history site per se, and a great way to meet fans who love movie horses.

The Official Web Site of Gene Autry, America's Favorite Singing Cowboy. www.geneautry.com/. This site is friendly, nice to look at, and full of great information.

The Old Corral. http://www.b-westerns.com/. The best site on the web for B-westerns. Host Chuck Anderson is well networked and updates regularly.

Palomino Horse Association Home Page. www.palominohorseassoc.com/. Registry founded in 1936 for palomino horses and ponies in all breeds. Includes history and membership information.

Palomino Horse Breeders Heritage Foundation. http://www.palominohba.com/. Formed in 1941 to collect, record, preserve the purity of blood, and improve the breeding of palomino horses.

Those Elusive Stuarts. http://www.vintagestuart7.com/. Toy collectors owe webmaster and Stuart figures expert Liz West a debt for publishing the history behind these beautiful figures on this fabulous site.

A Note About DVDs

Researching Trigger was often complicated by poor quality photographs. Pictures were out of focus, cropped, or doctored to create an eye-appealing effect. Lighting conditions and camera angles also caused problems. An animal may be posed in a way that makes its markings hard to determine. When lighting was diffuse or contrast was high, subtleties were difficult to determine.

Film presents a still greater challenge. The freeze-frame option on VCRs usually offered images that were blurred or out of focus. DVDs were better for freezing individual film frames but could not account for motion blur. Even nature got in the way. A horse with a thick forelock obscured the top part of its blaze.

Still, one appreciates the power of DVD players to move frame by frame and freeze an image. This power was a great aid for studying the markings from one Trigger to another. Case in point: the musical number "Singin' Down the Road" from the 1945 movie *Bells of Rosarita*. The original Trigger was used for his good looks, and Little Trigger was used for his dancing ability. With a DVD player, it's clear that Trigger and Little Trigger were switched in and out of the sequence to create the illusion of one horse.

While some airbrush-doctored photos of the original Trigger exist, to my knowledge, palominos were not touched up on film sets or personal appearances, although it was a possibility.

Index

Numbers in **bold italics** indicate pages with illustrations

A&E Biography: Roy Rogers 191
A-western 16–17
Academy Awards 118, 189, 337
accidents 231–233
The Adventure of Champion 182, 275–276
The Adventures of Robin Hood (movie) 44, 53, 68, 96, 131–133
Agee, Johnny (Champion's trainer) 200, 272
Aherne, Brian *134*
All Western Plastic Saddle Company 225
Allen, Don 86
Allen, Rex 126, 162, 200–203
Allen, Rex, Jr. 174
Allen, Woody 258
Allen's Golden Zephyr (aka Golden Zephyr, aka Trigger Jr.) 1, 28, 115–116, 118, *206*
Amaral, Anthony 287
American Humane Society 55, 258, 259
America's Lost and Found 191
The Answer Is God 71, 76, 233
anthropomorphism 16, 172
Apac (Trigger's dam) 45–47
Apple Valley 89, 109, 302, 317
Apple Valley Inn 116–118, 317
The Apple Valley Legacy Museum 329
Arabian Horse World 108
Arizona Cowboy 201
Arness, James 17
Ascolese, Lucile (first wife) 20
auctions 322–324
Autry, Gene 38, 57, *77*, 179–180, 182, 237, 242, *271*–277, 285, 326–*327*; lawsuit 77; strike 59
The Autry Museum of the American West (Autry Cen-

ter) 48, 315–316, 326–327, 329

B-western(s) 6–7, 8, 9–10, 16–18, 34, 312–313
Babe (horse) 66, 258–259, 268
Badmen of the Hills *139*–140
Ballard, Carrol 208
Bamboo-Harvester 89
Banjo (aka Trigger) 345*ch8n*8
Barcroft, Roy 83–84, 145–147, 151, 161, 287
Bareback (riding) 158, 230–231
Barker, O.C. 115
Barker's Moonbeam (Trigger Jr./Golden Zephyr's dam) 114–115
Barry, Don "Red" 237
Bays in the background 286–287
Beaut (aka Fury) 285–*286*
Belle Mare (horse) 112, 153–154, 345*ch9n*17
Bells of Rosarita 237, 239
Ben-Hur (movie) 26, *204*–205, 236, 286
Berke, William A. 139, 140
Berkeley, Busby 158
The Big Show 149
Bills, Dick 5
Billy the Kid Returns 159
"Birth of a Prince" 301
Biscoff's Taxidermy 305–308, 325
Black Beauty 269
Black-Eyed Nellie/Ring-Eyed Nellie *71*, 126, 164, 346*ch9n*25
Black Fury (comic) 288–289
Black Jack (horse) 162, *201*
The Black Stallion (movie) 207–208
The Bob Hope Chevy Hour 187

Bob Dylan's Theme Time Radio Hour 259
Bohlin, Edward H. (Bohlin saddle) 225–226
bowing pose *215*, *216*, 239
Boyd, William 227, 228, 281; *see also* Cassidy, Hopalong
Brady, Pat 162
Branson 320–321
Branson, Dr. Floyd 48
Breemer, Brace 277, 278
Breyer 249
Brim, Johnny 26, 179
Brothers, Connie 247
Brown, Joe E. 138
Buffalo Bill 32
Buhlman, Karla 272
Bullet Von Berge (dog) 180–181, 184–*185*, 308, 325
Burnette, Smiley "Frog Milhouse" 67, *71*, 76, 82–83
Buscema, John 294
Buttermilk (horse; aka Soda) 126–*127*, *181*, *202*, *281*, 325

Cactus (horse) *65*
Caliente Race Track 47, 50
California (horse) 120–124, 182–183, 236, 239
Campbell, Glenn 5
Canutt, Yakima 147–148, *203*, 229, *235*, 236
cardboard stirrups 222
Carman, Bob 181–182
Carmichael, Hoagie 126
Carrol, Frank (blacksmith) 222
Carson, Sunset 65, 237
Carter, Wilf 137
Cass Olé (aka the Black Stallion) 208
Cassidy, Hopalong 75; *see also* Boyd, William

cast horse 18, 53, 219
Champion 147, 182, 200, 269, 271–277
Champion Jr. *274*
Champion Records 277
Champion the Wonder Horse 271–274
Champion's unique six-gun bit 276–277
The Champs 277
Chandler, Lane 159
The Charge of the Light Brigade 54–55
Charlton Comics Group 288
Chatsworth 191, 302, *304*, *307*
The Chatsworth Historical Society *88*–89
"Chestnut Mare" (song) 11
The Chevy Show 187, 302
Christie's Auction 323–324
Circle H Ranch 279
Cisco Kid 285
The Cisco Kid (television show) 285
Clinton, Bill 42
Cloud, Roy F., Jr. (Trigger's first owner) 42–*44*, 45, 49–50, 53, 193
Coan, George 337
Cohn, Nudie 265, 326
Coleman, Scott 137
Color in Horses (book) 18
color of horses 86–87, 106, 345*ch8n*14; 348*ch16n*7, 348*ch16n*13, 348*ch16n*25, 348*ch16n*26; *see also* cremello; overo; paint/pinto; palomino; roan; sorrel; tobiano
coloring books 244
"Colts by Trigger" 86
Comanche (aka Trigger) 140, *141*, 142
Come On Rangers 83, 146, 159
Comin' Round the Mountain 272
Cooley, Spade 121–122
Copeland, Bobby J. 12, 59, 77, 83
Corrigan, Ray "Crash" 93–97, 162
Cossack drag mount 236
Cowboy from Brooklyn 53, 133, 284
Cowboy Magazine 36, 93
Cowboy Princess 23, 71–72, 101, 120, 227
Cowboy Princess Rides Again 120
Cowboys and Indians magazine 25
Cowboys of the Saturday Matinee 191
"The Cowboy's Prayer" 237

Coyle, P. Allen 352
Craven, Richard (award) 259
Cremello 345*ch9n*14
Crosby, Bing *49*, 50, 57
Crosby, Bob 50
crupper mount 236
crupping 236–237
CSI 259–260
Curtis, Barry 275
Curtis, Dick 265
Curtiz, Michael 55

Dale Evans, Queen of the West (show) 182–183
Dale Evans, Queen of Westerns (comics) 292
dapples (dappling) 19, *112*, 158
The David Letterman Show 4, 32–34, 68
Davis, Betty 134
Davis, Elise Miller 196, 233
DC Comics 389
Dean, Eddie 174
Dean, Jerry 11, 322
De Havilland, Olivia 44, 131–*132*, 137, 168–*169*
Dell Comics (Publishing Company) 288–295
DeSoto, Rafael 294, 297
Devine, Andy 151
Diablo (horse) 285
Dice (horse) 282–285
Dick Dickson saddle 226
Dillow, Roy ix, 36, 61, 62, 147, 177, 223
Dinah/Dina (mule) 126, 159
The Dinah Shore Show *188*
Disney, Walt 168, 208
Ditko, Steve 289
Dix, Richard 282
Django Unchained 156
Domino (horse) *284*–285
"Don't Fence Me In" (song) 166
Dortch, Joel "Dutch" 71–72, 78, 93, 308, 322
Double R Bar Ranch 179, 345*ch9n*15
Douglas, Kirk 269
Du Bois, Gaylord 292, 294, 295, 296, 297—300
Dudley, Aaron 28
Duel in the Sun *284*–285
DVD 10, 47

Eason, Breezy 54–55
Easter (colt) 22, 86–*87*
eBay 242
Ebert, Roger 10
Eddie (horse) 126, 287
Edwards, Cliff "Ukulele Ike" 139
Edwards, Penny 126
Edwards, Ralph 188

Electric Horseman 171
Elliott, Wild Bill 207, 227, 237, 284
The Encyclopedia of TV Pets 106, 126
"end of the trail" pose *216*, 239
English, John 158
"Enter the Lone Ranger" 6
Esquire 101
Eureka Cafe 179
Evans, Dale 82, *119*–120, 126–127, 182–183
Ewell, John 114–115

Fagan, Edna 88–89
Fagan, James 88–89
The Fall Guy 189–*190*, 239, *240*–241, 302
Fantasy (film) 10
Far Frontier 158, 219–220
Farr, Hugh 57
Farr, Karl Max 57
Fat Jones Stable 51
Fawcett (publishing) 289
Ferguson, John B. 86, 252, 260
Fisher, Paul K. 114–*117*
Fisher's Gray Maud (Trigger Jr./Golden Zephyr's dam) 114–115
Fitch, Gail 252
Flash Photos magazine 168, *170*–171
Flicka 269
Florian 269
Flynn, Errol 55, 131–*132*
Foran, Dick 57, 81, 133, 173–174
Four-Color Comics 289–290, 294
"Four-legged Friend" 173
Freulich, Ramon 292
Fritz (horse) 17, 192
Front Page 80, 343*ch5n*9
Frontier Pony Express 159
Frontier Productions 179
Fury (horse; aka Highland Dale) 269, 285–*286*
Fury (television show) 285–*286*

The Gabby Hayes Show 184
Gable, Clark 137
Gallant Bess 269
Garcia, Jerry 39
Garrett, Snuff 189
Gay Ranchero 129
Gene Autry (television show) 275
Gene Autry's Champion comics *290*
Gibson, Hoot 229
Gill, Tom 288, 289, 300

Gold Key 292
Golden Boot Award 210, 236
Golden Cloud 18, 45–46, 48–49, 53–56, 82, 84; 131–142 (solo roles)
Golden Cloud/Pistol 62, **63**, 66–**67**, 81, 131–140
Golden Empress (horse) 146–147, 148, **323**–324
Golden Hours (colt) 86, 146, 149
Golden Saddles, Silver Spurs: The History of Movie Westerns 192
Golden Sovereign (horse) **145**, 146–148
Golden Stallion (movie) 28, 84, 152–157
"Golden Stallion" (song) 174
Golden Stallion menu 260–262
Gollub, Morris 289, 297
Gone with the Wind (movie) 136–137
Good, Captain Larry (Golden Cloud breeder) 42, 45
Goodan, Till 298, 296
Goodwin, Johnny 193
Gordon, Alex 277
Gottsch, Patrick 324–235
grade stallion 48, 87, 92–93
grade horse 48
Grauman's Chinese Theatre 30, 36, **262**–263
The Great Train Robbery (movie) 15
Green, Dr. Ben K. 18
Griffin, Jimmy (Trigger's first trainer) 95, 96, 99, 193, 195, 196
Grigg, Art 225–226
ground rules 18–20
Growing Up with Roy and Dale 21–22
Gunsmoke (television show) 17
Gypsy Colt 285

Hale, Monte 162, 166
Hands Across the Border 80, 143–**144**
"Happy Trails" (song) 173, 179
Happy Trails Ranch 118
Happy Trails Theatre 156–158
Hart, Ernest Huntley (aka Huntley, E.H.) 289
Hart, John 280
Hart, William S. 17
Hartland Plastics 245–247
Harvester (horse) 88–89
Harvester-Trigger **88**–89, 118
Hatton, Raymond 83, 159
Hayden, Russell 81, 139, 140–**141**, 143

Hayes, George "Gabby" 74, **145**–147
"He Spoke Horse" 93
Hearts of the Golden West 129
Heldorado 160
Henderson, Sam 71, 87
Henry, Buzzy **12**, 159
Heston, Charlton **203**–204, 285
"Hi Yo Silver" (catch phrase/yell) 327
Hi Yo Silver (comic) 298–301
Hi Yo Silver (horse) 53, **279**–280
"Hi Yo Silver" (song) 173, 278
Hidalgo (movie) 271
Hidden Valley (ranch) 109, 124, 145, 302
Highland Dale (aka Fury) 285–**286**
Hit Parade of 1947 167
Hitching Post Theatre 262–263, **333**
Hollywood Canteen 99, 166, 173
The Hollywood Palace 188
The Hollywood Reporter 59, 69
Holt, Jack 146–147, 275
Home in Oklahoma 121
Hopalong Cassidy *see* Boyd, William
Hope, Bob 25, 101–102, **163**, 164, **186**–187, 281
"A Horse Named Babe" 252
Horse Opera: The Strange Case of the 1930s Singing Cowboy 312–313
horse operas 17
horse primer 19
horses 13–14
Horseworld (television show) 60, 87, 189
"How I Trained Trigger" 96, 97, 101
Hudkins, Ace 51, **52**, 53, 57, 71–72, 83
Hudkins, Art 28, 51, 55 196
Hudkins, Clyde 51, **52**, 53, 57, 69, 72, 196
Hudkins, Ode 51
Hudkins brothers 18, 54, 196
Hudkins Bros. Stables 50–52, 53, 54, 60, 62, 72, 81, 82, 193, 196, 200; log book 54

An Illustrated History of Trigger 4–5
Imus Ranch 325
In Old Caliente 268
Into the West (movie) 11
Iowa State Fair 101
It's Showtime 168

Jamboree 168
James, Will 51, 269

Jeopardy 263
John, Elton 174
The John Davidson Show 189
Johnson, Ben 51, 269
Johnson, Carol 93–94
Johnson, Mike ix, 17, 25, 89, 99, 102, 232, 234, 236, 260
Jones, Bill 26
Jones, Buck 65, 223
Jones, Clarence "Fat" 51, 53, 131
Jones, Dick 227
Jory, Victor **138**, 144
Juarez (movie) **134**–135

K Circle B Show 5
Kane, Gil 289
Kane, Joseph (Joe) 83
Keenay 301
Kennedy, Fred **52**
The Kid from Gower Gulch 122, 167–168
Kill Bill 2 155–156
Kilmer, Val 118, 189, 267–268
King Cotton (horse) 269
"King of the Cowboys" (campaign) 82
King of the Cowboys (movie) 82
King of the Cowboys (tag line) 82, 211
King of the Cowboys and Queen of the West (comic) 292
King Sylvan (Silver's sire) 301
Kinstler, Everett Raymond 35
KOB-TV 5
Koch, Dave 93, 322
Koko (horse) 126, 162, 200, **201**, 202, 203

Lady (horse) 82, 86, 146–147, 149, 153–154
Lake, Arthur 283
The Land of Eternal Youth 11–12
Lane, Allan "Rocky" 162, 237
Lane, Priscilla 133
The Late, Late Show with Tom Snyder 189
Liberty Horse Act 104,126
Life magazine 11, 248, 263
Lights of Old Santa Fe 65, **150**–151
Lindy Champion (horse) 38
Lippizaner stallions 96
Little Trigger 1, 25, 29, 148, 154, 182; accident 5; age 95; bill of sale 95; birth **92**–93, 95–96, 97–**98**; blaze 105–**107**, 344ch6n24; breed **92**–93; bulldog-type quarter horse 95; color 105–108; contradictions 93; cost 96; dapples 108; death 92–93, 96, 108–**110**,

308; description 95, 97, 106–
108; doubles 35, 36, 93; grade
stallion 48 92; hands/height
95, 346*ch*12*n*4; house broken
214, 346*ch*12*n*4; knee and leg
problems *109*; lawsuit 101;
markings 105–108; misbehavior 99–102; movie debut *98–
99*; mystery 111; name 93;
not mounted *110*; official
documents 92–93; papers 92–
93; personality 99–102; purchase 93, 99; registration
92–93, 99; secret 23–24, 35–
36; stallion *100*; stockings
106, 108; temperament 99–
103; toupee 91; touring 91,
102–*103*; tricks 102, 211–*213*,
216, *217*; weight 106
Livingston, Bob 65, 97, 237,
278
Loco (horse) 106
Lone Pine *16*, 68
The Lone Ranger 277–282, 300
The Lone Ranger (comic book)
300
The Lone Ranger (comic strip)
300
The Lone Ranger (radio show)
278
The Lone Ranger (serial) 278
The Lone Ranger (television
show) 237, 280–281
*The Lone Ranger and the Lost
City of Gold* 280–281
The Lone Ranger Rides Again
65
The Lone Ranger's Hi Yo Silver
comics 298–301
Lonely Are The Brave 269–270
The Los Angeles Coliseum *33,
337*
Los Angeles Equestrian Center
210
Lovett, Lyle 174–175
Lydecker brothers 149

Mackintosh and TJ 118
Madison Square Garden 36, 38,
157
Magic (film) 10
Mahan, Larry 60, 87
Marx (toys) 245
Mathis, Jack 77
Max (aka Bullet) 184–185
Maynard, Ken 229, 269
Maynard, Kermit 162
McCabe saddle 223–225
McCutcheon, Ralph 51, 216,
221, 269, 282–*286*
McDonald, Frank 158
Mefferd, Pat 47, 52
Melody Time 167
Mendoza, Adam 279

merchandising 242
The Merv Griffin Show 42, 189
Milhouse, Frog *see* Burnette,
Smiley
Mineral City 179
Mini the Mare 148–150
Miss Glory (horse) 162
Mr. Ed (horse) 89, 201
Modern Marvels 191
Monarch (horse) 120–124, 147,
151, 164, 236, 239
Moore, Clayton 75, 237, *270*,
278–282
Motion Picture 96
Moussa (Silver's dam) 301
*Movie Horses—Their Treatment
and Training* 287
movie star horse 214–215
Muybridge, Edward 14–15
My Brush with History 35
"My Life with Roy" 41
My Pal Trigger (movie) 17, 84,
86, 89, 120–121, 144–150
mystery (in film) 10

"Name Trigger's colt" contests
88
National Cowboy Hall of Fame
210
National Safe Council 82, 254
Nellybelle 93, 180–181, 223
Nelson, Willie (guitar) 264
Newman, Paul S. 298–300
"No Trick Horses for Me" 17
Nolan, Bob 57, 145, 146–147,
165
North of the Great Divide 121

Occident (Stanford horse) 15
Ockersen, Thys 191–192, 220,
229, 233
The Old Barn Dance 57
The Old Corral (movie) 57
The Old Cowboy Picture Show
(newsletter) ix, 356
The Old Man (aka Trigger)
83
"Ole Faithful" 147
On the Old Spanish Trail 230
Out California Way 166
Overo 282, 348*ch*16*n*26

paint/pinto 348*ch*16*n*25; *see
also* overo; tobiano
Pal (Paramount horse) 143,
292
Pal/Pal O' Mine (horse) 47, 90,
119–120, 160–161, 182–*183*,
223, 239, 292
Palomino 18, 19, 87–88, 108,
147, 149
The Palomino Horse (book) 36
Palomino Horse (magazine) 32

Palomino Horse Association
and Stud Registry (PHASR)
18, 45–47, 84
Palomino Horse Breeders Asso-
ciation (PHBA) 48, 84, 115–
116, 118
Palomino horse breeding busi-
ness 86
"Palomino Pal of Mine" (song)
173–174
Pals of the Golden West 122,
124, 302
Parkhurst, Harry 294, 297
The Pat Sajak Show 189
Patsy Award 208
Peck, Gregory *284*–285
Pecos Bill (Disney cartoon)
133–134, 167
The Pedigree Online All Breed
Data Base 47
The Perry Como Show 115, 187
Phantom (horse) 157–158
The Phil Donahue Show 189
Phillips, Robert W. ix, 8–9, 11,
18, 20, 38, 44, 49–50, 59, 60,
78, 95–96, 98, 122, 193, 225,
294, 342*ch*4*n*1
Pic (magazine) 105, 112–*113*
Pioneer Town Race 265
Pistol (aka Trigger) 18, 60, 68
plastic saddles 225–226
police horses 265
Porter, Cole 166
Porter, Edwin S. 15
Powell, Dick 133
Powell, Lee 278
Power, Tyrone *135–136*
Presley, Elvis 265–266
Professor of Triggernometry ix,
111
public relations (PR) 30–34, 39,
114, 313

Raider (horse) 139–140
Rainbow Over Texas 125, 160–
161
The Rains Came *135–136*
Randall, Corky 1, 5, 26–28, 38,
55–56, 88, 91, 99, 106, 108,
120, 154, 179, 195, *206–209*,
226, 302
Randall, Glenn, Jr. 19, 208–210
Randall, Glenn, Sr. 10,19, 21, 26,
28–29, 30, 35–36, 38, 39, 41,
55–56, 72, 91, 93, 98, 124,
126–127, 160, 186, *195, 201,
202–204*, 211, 213–214, 215–
217, 226, 237, 280,
346*ch*12*n*6–7
Randall Ranch 25–26, 43, 193,
199–200, 280
Randy Travis—Happy Trails
189
Rasky, Frank 94–95, 233

Reid, Dr. Charles (veterinarian) 222

Renaldo, Duncan **144**, 285

Republic Confidenial—The Players 80

Republic Pictures 77

The Republic Pictures Story 191

Reynolds, Don "Jug" 102

Reynolds, Fess 102, 122

Reynolds, Joe 120

Reynolds, Mary 120

RFD-TV 323, 324–325, 329

Ringling Brothers and Barnum and Bailey Circus 233

Ritter, Tex 189, 200

Roan 348*ch*16*n*13

Robin Hood (horse) 272–**273**

Robin Hood of the Pecos 229

Robinson, Orval 48, 120

Rocky Lane's Black Jack 288

Roe, Rocky ix, 36, 42–43, 65, 81, 98, 120–122, 125, 167, 182, 201, 203, 235–236, 285, 345*ch*8*n*6, 345*ch*8*n*8

Rogers, Dustin 320, 324

Rogers, Roy: archive 327; contract negotiations 78–79; contradictory statements 40–41; discussing Little Trigger 38; draft status/military 78–**79**; fictional biography 78–**79**; funeral 309–310; image 38, 69; "King of the Cowboys" campaign 82; legacy 314, 325–326, 329; proposes to Dale Evans 90; public persona 35, 234; riding mishaps 231–233; salary 343*ch*5*n*4; spurs 229; storyteller 38, 313; term players contract 74, 78; truth 32–33, 38–39, 313

Rogers, Roy, Jr., "Dusty" 21–23, 25, 72, 80, 174, 233, 242, 319–320, 321, 322, 324, 325

Rogers-Barnett, Cheryl 2, 21–25, 55, 71–72, 74, 84, 89, 91, 99, 101, 104, 118, 120, 124, 193, 196, 200, 227

The Rogers Family Presents: TV Collection, Pilots & Rarities 119

Rolland, Gilbert **134**–135

Roper, Willian 114

Rothel, David 44, 76, 115, 181, 195, 272

Rough Riders Roundup 159

Roy Rogers (Phillips book) ix, 78, 118

Roy Rogers and Dale Evans Museum (Branson) 320–321, 329

Roy Rogers and Dale Evans Museum (Victorville) 317

The Roy Rogers and Dale Evans Show (television) 187–188

Roy Rogers and Dale Evans Toys & Memorabilia, Identification & Values 252

Roy Rogers and Trigger Comics 292

Roy Rogers and Trigger Sears store display 252–**253**

The Roy Rogers Book 181

The *Roy Rogers Chevy Show* 126

Roy Rogers Comics 289–292

Roy Rogers: King of the Cowboys (AMC biography) 191,241

Roy Rogers: King of the Cowboys (documentary) 191, 229, 233

Roy Rogers: King of the Cowboys (Morris and Pollard book) 46

Roy Rogers: King of the Cowboys (Rasky book) 94–95, 233

Roy Rogers: King of the Cowboys (Roper book) 114

Roy Rogers: King of the Cowboys—A Film Guide 181–182

Roy Rogers Liberty Horse Act **125**–126

Roy Rogers Museum (Apple Valley) 317

Roy Rogers press book 60–62, 64, 66, 239

The Roy Rogers Rodeo 187

The Roy Rogers Show 26, 126–127, 186

Roy Rogers' Trigger (coloring book) 244

Roy Rogers' Trigger and Bullet Coloring Book 244

Roy Rogers' Trigger comics 292–298

Roy Rogers' Trigger to the Rescue **244**

Run Trigger Run (horse) 118

Running-W 54–55

Rush, Art (agent/manager) 9, 25, 72, **75**, 78, 82, 233, 242

Rymill, Walt 47, 120

Saddles 223–226

San Ysidro Stock Farm 43, 45, 50, 53

Savitt, Al 294–295, **296**, 297–298

Savitt, Sam 251, **290**, **291**, **293**, 295–296, 297–298, **299**, 348*ch*17*n*12

Scapperotti, Dan 182

Scout (horse) 278, 281

Serafix (horse) 108

Sewell, Anna 269

Sherwood, Buddy 126, 179

Shut My Big Mouth 138

Siegel, Sol 57, **59**

Silver (horse) 237, **270**, 277, **279**, 280, **281**

Silver #1 (horse) 278, 280

Silver #2 (horse) 279, 280

Silver B (horse) 65

Silver Bandit 121

Silver Chief (horse) 65, 278

Silver City Raiders 81, 140–**141**

Silver Spurs 82

Silver's Pride (horse) **277**–278

Simpson, Len 86

Singing Cowboys (book) 44

The Singing Cowboys Ride Again 189

Sir Barton (horse) 47, 120

16th American Airbourne Squadron 266

Sly(e), Leonard Frank(lin) 9, 19–20, 41, 57–59, 66, 342*ch*4*n*1

"Smartest Horse in the Movies" 82, 91

Smeyne, Mabel 161

Smithsonian's National Museum of American 332–333

Smoke (horse) 81

Smoky 269

Snowfire 269

So What Factor 7–8

Soda (aka Buttermilk) 126, **202**

Son of Paleface 101–102, 105, **163**–164, 186

Song of Texas 82, 98–99, 100

Sons of the Pioneers 30, 57, **58**

Sorrel 19, 348*ch*16*n*7

South of Caliente 236

Spacy, Kevin 267–268

specialty Trigger items 252

Spencer, Tim 57, 173, 193

Spirit River Center 329

Spirit: Stallion of the Cimarron (movie) 271

Stanford, Leland 14

Starrett, Charles 57, 76, 134, **139**

Steel (horse) 131

Steel Dust (palomino AQHA stallion) 48

Steffens, Randy 294–295, 349*ch*17*n*9

step-mount 229–**230**, 346*ch*13*n*2

Stewart, Peggy **52**

The Strawberry Roan (movie) 147, 274–275

"The Strawberry Roan" (song) 275

Stuart Trigger figure 255–**256**, 347*ch*14*n*9

Stunt Man 236

Sunset in the West 236

Super Password 266

Susanna Pass 162

Tail Waggers Club 266
Tapaderos 90, 182, 209, 223, 224–225
Tarantino, Quentin 155–156, 260
Target (horse) 53
Tarter, Estes *243*, 254–255
Tarzan (Golden Cloud's sire) 45–47
Tarzan (Ken Maynard's horse) 269
Tarzan's Desert Mystery 284
taxidermy 252, 272, 305–308
Temple Boy (Pal's sire) 120
Tennessee Walking Horse Breeders Association (TWHBA) 48, 88, 106, *114*, 118
"That Horse Trigger" 97–98
"That Palomino Pal of Mine" (song) 173–174
This Is Your Life 188
Three Mesquiteers 96–97
Thurmon, Uma 155–156
Tir na nOg 11–12
Tobiano 282, 348*ch16n26*
Tonto 278
Tony (horse) 17, 269
Top Kick (horse) 269
Topper (horse) 229
Tournament of Roses Parade 189
track/tracking 282–283
The Trail of Robin Hood 162
trailer 247, *264*, 266–267
trailer deluxe 266–267
Traveller (book) 35
Travis, Randy 86, 189, 302
"Tricky Trigger" 211
Triggaro (horse) 118
Trigger "Barrymore of horses" 53; beautiful transportation 164–*165*; bill of sale 72–*73*, *75*, 84; billing 81–82, 128; birthday 45–*46*, 259; blaze 45–*46*, 344*ch6n24*; bloodlines 45–48; branding 3; breeder 42–*46*; breeding 25, 29, *45*–46, *87*; cameo appearances 166–168, 191–192; care and equipment 222–223; color 45–47, 86–*87*, 105–108, 147, 149; collateral damage 54–56; colts *22–23*, 29, 89; conformation 46–47; contract 74, 76, 198; contradictions 10; corporate logo 11, 12, 35; credits 82–82; death 21, 46, *303*, *304*, 341*ch1n2*, 350*ch18n4*; description 45, *46*; diet 222; display 103–104; documentary appearances 191–192; doubles 29, 35–36, 39, 93, 105, 112, *124*–125;

English tack 147; eye color 68, 106, 302; fall 233; fan club/mail 260; fantasy 9, 10; the fearless 219–220; as fictional character 28; final breath *303*; final years 302–*304*; gelding 220–221; hands/height *44*, 47, 106; honorary registry 48; image 35; jokes 267, 268; junk food 263; last ride 302; last screen appearances 302; at liberty 19, *31*, *129*, *153*; look-a-likes 342*ch2n6*; magazine model 168–171; magic 10; marketing tool *12*; markings 45–46, 105–108; martingale *16*, 223, 225; mounting 321; movie persona 128–*129*; movie reviews 171–*172*; movies about 143–156; mystery 10; name 18, 20, 76, 82–84, 95; New York 36–*37*; obituary *304*–305; offspring *23*, 84–86; postmortem 321; public relations 18, 21; purchase 28, 69–*71*, 74–*75*, 81; racing 47; receipt for purchase of 73; registration papers 45–*46*, 48; retired 186, 302; Rose Parade 325; screen billing 81; as shield *129*; shot *129*, 162; signature pose 35, *65*, 237–240; sire *22–23*; solo roles 131–*142*; songs 128, *172*–173; special scenes 159–164; specialty items 252–257; stallion 84; statue 267; stifle 106; stock footage *142*–143; stockings 45–*46*, 106, 242; as student 218–219; symbolism *12*, 13; tack *90*, 223–226; tag lines 81–82; taxidermy 305–*309*; television appearances 186–191; temperament 1, 84, *87*–88; toupee 91; touring 35–36, 91; trademark 237; training 212–214, *215*–217; traveling 36, 91; truth *31*, 32; ultimate B-Western collectible 252; value 72; weight 106
"Trigger and His Doubles" 105, 112–*113*
Trigger burgers 267
Trigger Certificate of Honorary Ownership 252–254, 259–260
"Trigger, First, Get a Good Horse" 28–29, 252
"Trigger Has Been Stolen" 175
"Trigger Hasn't Got a Purty Figure" 151, 173
Trigger Jr. (Junior) 1, 108, 112–118, *114* (registration papers); 182, 239, 308; descendants 88; registration papers *114*

Trigger Jr. (movie) 156–158
Trigger lunch box *251*
"Trigger Man" 89, 149
Trigger Remembered 36, 41, 47, 83, 96, 102, n120, n158, 219, n302
Trigger statue 267
Trigger Street and Trigger Place 267
Trigger Street Productions 267–268
Trigger 10 cent coin-operated ride **249**
"Trigger! The Smartest Horse in the Movies!" 82
Trigger III (cart) 303
Triggers-on (horse) 118
"Trigger's Tricks" 213
Trigger's Tricks (show) 180, 183–184
Trucolor 151, 157
"Tumbling Tumble Weeds" 166
Turner Movie Classics channel (TMC) 133
Twilight in the Sierras 162

Under California Stars 78
Under Western Stars 36, 44, 46, 55, 59–62, *63–64*, 65, 68, 69, 71, 77, 83–84, 151–*152*
Utah **165**

Van Horn, Wayne "Buddy" **209**
Van Nuys Wash *46*, 200, **315**
Variety 59, 182
veterinarian (Dr. Charles Reid) 222
Victorville 310, 317
Victorville Tribune 152
View Master *256*–257

Walt Disney studios 133–134
Walt Disney's Zorro 208–*209*
Ward, Bill 280
Warren, Holly George 326
Washington Cowboy 59
Wayne, John 78
Webb, Jimmy 174
The Weekly Reader 78
Weissmuller, Johnny 284
Welcome to Sherwood Forrest 131
West, Lizabeth *255*–256
Western Clippings 356
The Western Horse 88,
Western Horseman 28, 72, 252
Westerns Channel 17
Weston, Dick (aka Len Slye) 57–60, 66, 77–78
Wexler, Ed 251
When Cowboys Were King 192
White, Raymond 30, 72, 292, 294

White Flash (horse) 200
Whitey (stud) 87
"Whoa, Trigger! Auteur Alert!" 345*ch*8*n*17
Widow Maker (Disney horse) 134, 167
Wieghorst, Olaf 268
Wild Horse Rodeo 59
The Wild Stallion 269

Wilkins, Arline (second wife) 26
Williams, Guy 208–209
Willing, Foy *154*, 174, *262*
Win a Wee Trigger 85
Witney, William 36, 41, 44, 47, 69, 83, 96, 102, 152, 156, 158, 163, 191–192, 193, 219–220, 229, *232*, 234–235, 302

wonder horse 81–82, 111
Woodstock festival 301

Yates, Herb 36, 74, 76–78, 80, 179, 184
Yrigoyen, Joe 121, 157, 158, 162, 163, 220, *231*, *234*–236

Lightning Source UK Ltd.
Milton Keynes UK
UKHW050718231022
410914UK00019B/350